VENTURE CAPITAL INVESTMENT AND GOVERNMENT INCENTIVES

This book explores the best ways for governments to design venture capital investment incentives.

Venture capital is a multi-billion-dollar industry and a major driver of innovation and national growth. Investment in startup companies by venture capital funds helps finance new inventions and create wealth, economic growth, and jobs. However, because venture capital investment is highly risky and sensitive to market downturns, many governments around the world use special legal and tax incentives to help encourage this form of investment. Since the introduction of the first venture capital incentive in the USA in 1958, scores of venture capital incentives have come and gone. These incentives have experienced varied success, with some failing entirely.

Filling a gap in an important area, this book employs a legal and regulatory approach to examine venture capital policy from a global perspective. It uses an analytical framework to evaluate the design, implementation, and success of incentives, and looks at over 60 examples from 25 countries around the world.

The book is aimed at researchers and policy makers in law, finance and economics, as well as practitioners and investors in the venture capital space. The book introduces the legal aspects of venture capital investment and presents a list of leading practice guidelines and recommendations to help policy makers design effective, efficient, and appropriate venture capital incentives.

Hart Studies in Commercial and Financial Law: Volume 14

Hart Studies in Commercial and Financial Law

Series Editors: John Linarelli and Teresa Rodríguez de las Heras Ballell

This series offers a venue for publishing works on commercial law as well as on the regulation of banking and finance and the law on insolvency and bankruptcy. It publishes works on the law on secured credit, the regulatory and transactional aspects of banking and finance, the transactional and regulatory institutions for financial markets, legal and policy aspects associated with access to commercial and consumer credit, new generation subjects having to do with the institutional architecture associated with innovation and the digital economy including works on blockchain technology, work on the relationship of law to economic growth, the harmonisation or unification of commercial law, transnational commercial law, and the global financial order. The series promotes interdisciplinary work. It publishes research on the law using the methods of empirical legal studies, behavioural economics, political economy, normative welfare economics, law and society inquiry, socio-legal studies, political theory, and historical methods. Its coverage includes international and comparative investigations of areas of law within its remit.

Volume 1: The Financialisation of the Citizen: Social and Financial Inclusion through European Private Law
Guido Comparato

Volume 2: MiFID II and Private Law: Enforcing EU Conduct of Business Rules
Federico Della Negra

Volume 3: Reforming Corporate Retail Investor Protection: Regulating to Avert Mis-Selling
Diane Bugeja

Volume 4: The Future of Commercial Law: Ways Forward for Change and Reform
Edited by Orkun Akseli and John Linarelli

Volume 5: The Cape Town Convention: A Documentary History
Anton Didenko

Volume 6: Regulating the Crypto Economy: Business Transformations and Financialisation
Iris H-Y Chiu

Volume 7: The Future of High-Cost Credit: Rethinking Payday Lending
Jodi Gardner

Volume 8: The Enforcement of EU Financial Law
Edited by Jan Crijns, Matthias Haentjens and Rijnhard Haentjens

Volume 9: International Bank Crisis Management: A Transatlantic Perspective
Marco Bodellini

Volume 10: Creditor Priority in European Bank Insolvency Law: Financial Stability and the Hierarchy of Claims
Sjur Swensen Ellingsæter

Volume 11: Chinese and Global Financial Integration through Stock Connect: A Legal Analysis
Flora Huang

Volume 12: The Governance of Macroprudential Policy: How to Build Regulatory Legitimacy Through a Social Justice Approach
Tracy C Maguze

Volume 13: A Socio-Legal Theory of Money for the Digital Commercial Society: A New Analytical Framework to Understand Cryptoassets
Israel Cedillo Lazcano

Volume 14: Venture Capital Investment and Government Incentives: Law, Regulation and Policy Design
Tamara Wilkinson

Venture Capital Investment and Government Incentives

Law, Regulation and Policy Design

Tamara Wilkinson

•HART•
OXFORD • LONDON • NEW YORK • NEW DELHI • SYDNEY

HART PUBLISHING

Bloomsbury Publishing Plc

Kemp House, Chawley Park, Cumnor Hill, Oxford, OX2 9PH, UK

1385 Broadway, New York, NY 10018, USA

Bloomsbury Publishing Ireland Limited, 29 Earlsfort Terrace, Dublin 2, D02 AY28, Ireland

HART PUBLISHING, the Hart/Stag logo, BLOOMSBURY and the Diana logo are trademarks of Bloomsbury Publishing Plc

First published in Great Britain 2024

First published in hardback, 2024

Paperback edition, 2026

A catalogue record for this book is available from the British Library.

A catalogue record for this book is available from the Library of Congress.

Library of Congress Control Number: 2024937650

ISBN: PB: 978-1-50997-635-5
ePDF: 978-1-50997-637-9
ePub: 978-1-50997-638-6

Typeset by Compuscript Ltd, Shannon
Printed and bound in Great Britain

For product safety related questions contact productsafety@bloomsbury.com

To find out more about our authors and books visit www.hartpublishing.co.uk. Here you will find extracts, author information, details of forthcoming events and the option to sign up for our newsletters.

ACKNOWLEDGEMENTS

This book has been many years in the making, and over that time I have benefited immensely from the helpful and collegiate advice of a number of colleagues and respected academics. In particular, I would like to gratefully acknowledge the support of my doctoral supervisors, Professor Stephen Barkoczy and Professor Bryan Horrigan, whose assistance and expertise have been invaluable. My thesis examiners, Professor Colin Mason and Associate Professor Sofia Johan, also provided me with many useful suggestions that improved my work, as did my two anonymous reviewers (thank you, kind strangers!). Finally, this book would not be before you today without the generous guidance of Professor Marilyn Pittard, Professor Melissa Castan, Professor Andrew Mitchell, Professor Richard Fox, Dr Paul Burgess, Dr Jessica Mant and Liam Elphick.

As always, my deepest thanks and gratitude go to my beloved family: Sue, David, Georgia (and Luna). Making you proud is my greatest achievement.

CONTENTS

LIST OF TABLES AND FIGURES

TABLE OF LEGISLATION

1

Setting the Scene

1.1. Introduction

Venture capital is a niche and often poorly understood asset class that has the capacity to finance the development of life-changing discoveries, create wealth and catalyse global economies.[1] Through its role in funding innovative startup companies that may not otherwise be able to access sufficient capital, venture capital investment helps promote innovation and entrepreneurship, generate new industries, encourage business formation, produce jobs and stimulate competitiveness, exports, sales and economic development (including regional development).[2] For these reasons, venture capital is considered an 'integral part of a healthily functioning economy'[3] even though it represents less than 0.05 per cent as a proportion of GDP in many countries around the world.[4] Furthermore, the positive social and economic outcomes produced by venture capital investment are widely recognised by governments as being worthy of encouragement,[5] and provide a clear rationale for the use of government policy to stimulate this kind of investment.[6] It is

[1] See Stephen Barkoczy, Tamara Wilkinson, Ann L Monotti and Mark Davison, *Innovation and Venture Capital Law and Policy* (Federation Press, 2016) 27–28, 42–43; Stefan Lilischkis, 'Policies in Support of High-Growth Innovative SMEs' (European Commission, June 2011) INNO-Grips Policy Brief No 2, Version 1.5, 39.

[2] See Barkoczy et al (n 1) 26, 28; Rebecca Harding, 'Plugging the Knowledge Gap: An International Comparison of the Role for Policy in the Venture Capital Market' (2002) 4(1) *Venture Capital* 59, 59; Josh Lerner and Brian Watson, 'The Public Venture Capital Challenge: The Australian Case' (2008) 10(1) *Venture Capital* 1, 3, 5, 7; European Commission, 'Effectiveness of Tax Incentives for Venture Capital and Business Angels to Foster the Investment of SMEs and Start-ups: Final Report' (Taxation and Customs Union, 2017) Working Paper No 68, 42; Constantin Christofidis and Olivier Debande, 'Financing Innovative Firms Through Venture Capital' (European Investment Bank, February 2001) 40–44.

[3] Small Business Service (UK) and Almeida Capital, 'A Mapping Study of Venture Capital Provision to SMEs in England' (October 2005) 9.

[4] OECD, 'Entrepreneurship at a Glance 2017' (2017) 124. Israel and the USA are the two major exceptions, as they house the world's leading venture capital economies.

[5] Christian Keuschnigg and Søren Bo Nielsen, 'Tax Policy, Venture Capital, and Entrepreneurship' (2002) 87(1) *Journal of Public Economics* 175, 198; Rebecca Harding, 'Venture Capital and the Regions: Not Always the Most Appropriate Funding Mechanism' (2000) 7(1) *New Economy* 49, 49; Marco Da Rin, Giovanna Nicodano and Alessandro Sembenelli, 'Public Policy and the Creation of Active Venture Capital Markets' (2006) 90(8) *Journal of Public Economics* 1699, 1700.

[6] Ann Leamon, Maria Susana Garcia-Robles and Josh Lerner, 'Best Practices in Creating a Venture Capital Ecosystem' (Multilateral Investment Fund of Inter-American Development Bank, December 2012) 29.

little wonder, then, that governments around the world are interested in increasing venture capital investment,[7] particularly as it can be quite a scarce resource.[8] Since the first formal venture capital programme was introduced in the USA in 1958,[9] government initiatives aimed at supporting and stimulating venture capital investment have proliferated, and government-supported capital represents a large proportion of total venture capital investment.[10] In fact, it has been suggested that all the current successful venture capital markets around the world have benefited from sustained government intervention, and may not have reached the same level of success in the absence of this support (although this is difficult to conclusively prove).[11]

However, not all government venture capital initiatives have been successful; this area of policy has a history of mixed results and, sometimes, outright failure.[12] There are well-recognised and significant challenges associated with designing successful government venture capital programmes,[13] and governments around the world have 'squandered many billions of dollars on ill-conceived efforts to stimulate venture capital'.[14] In some cases, they have even damaged their venture capital industries.[15] These misfires are often the result of poor policy design.[16]

While there has been a surfeit of research undertaken on venture capital investment as a finance instrument,[17] less focus has been placed on researching and

[7] James A Brander, Qianqian Du and Thomas Hellmann, 'The Effects of Government-Sponsored Venture Capital: International Evidence' (2015) 19 *Review of Finance* 571, 572; Gordon Murray, Marc Cowling, Weixi Liu and Olga Kalinowska-Beszczynska, 'Government Co-Financed "Hybrid" Venture Capital Programmes: Generalizing Developed Economy Experience and its Relevance to Emerging Nations' (Kauffman International Research and Policy Roundtable, 11–12 March 2012) 2.

[8] Barkoczy et al (n 1) 29.

[9] See Gil Avnimelech, Martin Kenney and Morris Teubal, 'Building Venture Capital Industries: Understanding the US and Israeli Experiences' (Berkeley Roundtable on the International Economy, March 2004) Working Paper No 160, 22.

[10] Federico Munari and Laura Toschi, 'Assessing the Impact of Public Venture Capital Programmes in the United Kingdom: Do Regional Characteristics Matter?' (2015) 30(2) *Journal of Business Venturing* 205, 213; European Commission, 'Effectiveness of Tax Incentives' (n 2) 37.

[11] Josh Lerner, *Boulevard of Broken Dreams: Why Public Efforts to Boost Entrepreneurship and Venture Capital Have Failed – and What to Do About It* (Princeton University Press, 2009) 5; Leamon et al (n 6) 13, 16; United Nations Economic Commission for Europe, *Financing Innovative Development: Comparative Review of the Experiences of UNECE Countries in Early Stage Financing* (United Nations Publications, 2007) 41, 51.

[12] See Avnimelech et al, 'Building Venture Capital Industries' (n 9) 3, 14–15; Lerner, *Boulevard of Broken Dreams* (n 11) 7.

[13] Douglas Cumming, 'Government Policy Towards Entrepreneurial Finance: Innovation Investment Funds' (2007) 22(2) *Journal of Business Venturing* 193, 198; Barkoczy et al (n 1) 32.

[14] Lerner and Watson (n 2) 10.

[15] ibid; Margaret O'Shea and Candice Stevens, 'Governments as Venture Capitalists' (1998) 213 *OECD Observer* 26, 26.

[16] Avnimelech et al, 'Building Venture Capital Industries' (n 9) 3; Lerner, *Boulevard of Broken Dreams* (n 11) 5.

[17] See Leslie A Jeng and Philippe C Wells, 'The Determinants of Venture Capital Funding: Evidence Across Countries' (2000) 6(3) *Journal of Corporate Finance* 241; William L Megginson, 'Toward a Global Model of Venture Capital?' (2004) 16(1) *Journal of Applied Corporate Finance* 89; Miona Milosevic and Jacqueline Fendt, 'Venture Capital and Its French Exception: Explaining Performance through Human Capital, Policy and Institutional Failures' (2016) 43(5) *Science and Public Policy* 660; Christofidis and

understanding the effects of government policy on venture capital investment.[18] There are clear gaps in research and knowledge around why some policies fail while others obtain more encouraging results.[19] Recognising these gaps, this book builds upon key policy-centred research on government intervention in the venture capital sector to consider how governments can better use incentives to encourage and increase venture capital investment.[20] It does this by breaking incentive policy design down into its composite processes, analysing each of these processes in detail using real-world examples to identify what works (and what does not), and finally delivering a set of leading practice guidelines that should enhance policymakers' capacity to design effective, efficient and appropriate incentives, while avoiding some of the foreseeable mistakes that have impacted prior policy efforts in this space.

In order to understand how and why governments intervene in the venture capital sector, it is worth briefly introducing the salient features of venture capital investment. Thus, this chapter begins by exploring the typical characteristics of venture capital investors, investments and investees, the economic and social benefits provided by venture capital, and some of the reasons why venture capital does tend to be so scarce (see [1.2]). The chapter then sets out the book's methodology, including the parameters around which incentives and examples are considered, how incentives are analysed and which evaluation criteria have been selected to define leading practice (see [1.3]), before outlining the subsequent chapters of the book (see [1.4]).

1.2. Characteristics of Venture Capital

There is no broadly accepted definition of venture capital investment,[21] which is a small and unique asset class.[22] The generally accepted view is that venture capital investment is taken to involve the purchase by investors of newly issued shares (whether directly or through an intermediary) in small, unlisted companies with high growth potential (often referred to as 'startups') that are commercialising innovative ideas or products, with the aim of actively nurturing and growing these companies to achieve a high investment return over the medium to long term.[23] Startups, which are early stage, innovative companies that are generally

Debande (n 2); Jennifer Payne, 'Private Equity and Its Regulation in Europe' (2011) 12(4) *European Business Organization Law Review* 559; Andrew Metrick and Ayako Yasuda, *Venture Capital and the Finance of Innovation*, 2nd edn (Wiley, 2001).

[18] Policy in this sense can be taken to mean a course of action taken by a government to achieve particular aims, as well as the regulations and/or laws required to implement this course of action.

[19] Gil Avnimelech, Alessandro Rosiello and Morris Teubal, 'Evolutionary Interpretation of Venture Capital Policy in Israel, Germany, UK and Scotland' (2010) 37(2) *Science and Public Policy* 101, 103.

[20] See Barkoczy et al (n 1) 32.

[21] OECD, 'Entrepreneurship at a Glance 2017' (n 4) 124.

[22] See Leamon et al (n 6) 24.

[23] See Barkoczy et al (n 1) 26–27.

run by their founding entrepreneurs, should be contrasted with the much broader category of 'small and medium enterprises' (SMEs). Although the two terms are commonly used interchangeably, only a small percentage of SMEs actually constitute innovative high-growth startup companies of the kind in which venture capitalists invest.[24]

1.2.1. Venture Capital Investors

There are two broad kinds of venture capital investors: those who invest their own money directly in startup companies (often referred to as 'angel' investors); and those who invest through 'venture capital funds' (known as 'passive investors').[25] Venture capital funds are managed by 'fund managers', who are responsible for investing the capital contributed by passive investors in startup companies.[26] The blanket term 'venture capitalist' or 'venture capital investor' is used in the literature to broadly refer to all three groups – angel investors, passive investors and fund managers. The term venture capitalist is used in this way in the following chapters, and the specific terms are also used where it is necessary to differentiate between the groups. The government incentives discussed in this book are all specifically targeted at one or more of these kinds of investors (see [4.2]), who have different processes and motivations for making their investments. Their characteristics are considered briefly below.

Angel Investors

Angel investors are generally high net worth individuals with substantial valuable business and entrepreneurial experience.[27] They tend to invest in areas or industries with which they are personally familiar.[28] Angels' primary motivation for investing is to attain profits when they exit their investments, although they may also have more altruistic motivations, such as giving back to the business community.[29] Angels are individuals with limited financial and human capital, so they tend to make smaller investments than venture capital funds (which pool capital contributions from a number of investors), and tend to also invest earlier

[24] See European Commission, 'Effectiveness of Tax Incentives' (n 2) 41–42; Barkoczy et al (n 1) 3–4.
[25] See Barkoczy et al (n 1) 26–27.
[26] ibid.
[27] United Nations Economic Commission for Europe (n 11) 10; Stephen Barkoczy and Tamara Wilkinson, *Incentivising Angels: A Comparative Framework of Tax Incentives for Start-Up Investors* (Springer, 2019) 22.
[28] Barkoczy et al (n 1) 51.
[29] ibid 50; John R Hendon, Joseph R Bell, Brittany Blair and Don K Martin, 'State-Funded Angel Investor Tax Credits: Implementation and Perceived Effectiveness in a Sample of States Within the United States' (2012) 1(1) *Journal of Entrepreneurship and Public Policy* 50, 51.

in a startup company's development.[30] Because of this, angel investors play a vital role in the innovation ecosystem as they help to produce 'deal flow' for venture capital funds to subsequently invest in.[31] The investments made by angels and venture capital funds are therefore complementary and sometimes overlap.[32]

Venture Capital Funds and Fund Managers

As mentioned above, venture capital fund managers are financial intermediaries who operate in a symbiotic relationship with passive investors. Fund managers generally comprise a team of experienced individuals who work together to manage and invest the capital contributed to their fund by passive investors.[33] The main activities of fund managers include selecting and vetting an appropriate portfolio of early-stage investments, supervising and developing these investments, and eventually negotiating exits.[34] Like angel investors, fund managers and passive investors hope to make positive returns when their venture capital fund exits investments in startups.[35] The passive investors who contribute to venture capital funds often include institutional investors such as pension funds, banks, endowments, insurance companies and foundations, as well as family offices and wealthy individuals.[36]

Venture capital funds have special remuneration structures that help align the interests of fund managers and passive investors (who do not take part in investment decisions or fund management).[37] As compensation for their work in selecting and managing investments, fund managers receive periodic 'management fees', which are commonly set at around 2 per cent per annum of the fund's 'committed capital'.[38] In order to encourage positive exits, fund managers are often also eligible to receive special bonus 'carried interest payments' (of around 20 per cent of realised profits) when they exit investments profitably.[39] As a way

[30] Colin M Mason and Richard T Harrison, 'Improving Access to Early Stage Venture Capital in Regional Economies: A New Approach to Investment Readiness' (2004) 19(2) *Local Economy* 159, 160; Barkoczy et al (n 1) 50–51.

[31] United Nations Economic Commission for Europe (n 11) 29–30. Because angels are private individuals who can be quite secretive, it can be difficult to quantify the size and impact of angel markets: Barkoczy and Wilkinson (n 27) 22.

[32] Hans Landström and Colin Mason, 'Venture Capital Research: The Road Ahead' in Hans Landström and Colin Mason (eds), *Handbook of Research on Venture Capital, vol 2: A Globalizing Industry* (Edward Elgar, 2012) 283, 285; Maria Pinelli and Uschi Schreiber, 'Funding the Future: Access to Finance for Entrepreneurs in the G20' (White Paper, Ernst & Young, 2013) 16.

[33] See Barkoczy and Wilkinson (n 27) 22–23; Barkoczy et al (n 1) 52.

[34] See Barkoczy et al (n 1) 53, 66.

[35] ibid 66.

[36] Jeng and Wells (n 17) 253; Mason and Harrison (n 30) 160.

[37] Ronald J Gilson, 'Engineering a Venture Capital Market: Lessons from the American Experience' (2003) 55 *Stanford Law Review* 1067, 1089.

[38] See Christofidis and Debande (n 2) 10.

[39] ibid; United Nations Economic Commission for Europe (n 11) 22.

to demonstrate their confidence in a fund's prospects and attract passive investors, fund managers may also sometimes invest modest amounts of their own capital in the fund they manage. This creates 'buy-in' for the fund manager and further helps aligns the interests of fund managers with those of the passive investors (see [4.2.2.4]).[40]

Venture capital is often described as a 'patient' and 'long-term' form of investment because investments in startups can take a long time to mature.[41] It is common for investments to be held by a fund for around three to seven years, and for investors not to see a return until divestment occurs.[42] As such, venture capital funds, which can take a range of different structures, including companies, trusts and limited partnerships (the most common form used today),[43] usually have a lifetime of around 10 years (see further [4.2.2.2]).[44]

1.2.2. Benefits of Venture Capital

Venture capital is seen to play a positive economic and social role, which is primarily attributed to the well-recognised links between venture capital finance and increased innovation.[45] Innovation involves the development of 'a new or improved product or process (or combination thereof)' that differs significantly from previous products or processes.[46] The benefits of innovation are myriad: for instance, innovation within companies has been observed to increase the chance of business growth and profitability.[47] On the larger scale, innovation plays a role in increasing national competitiveness and living standards, creating wealth, and preparing countries and people for the future.[48] For these reasons, increasing national innovation is a key policy focus for many governments, who strive to create thriving national 'innovation systems'.[49] Encouraging venture capital investment is an important way that governments around the world attempt to do this, because through funding startup companies, venture capital funds innovation.

[40] Payne (n 17) 562; Gilson (n 37) 1071.

[41] United Nations Economic Commission for Europe (n 11) 10, 20.

[42] Stephen Barkoczy and Peter Edmundson, 'Australasian and South East Asian Venture Capital Tax Expenditure Programs (2009) 37(1) *Intertax* 56, 58; Australian Investment Council, 'Investment', www.aic.co/AIC/Investment/How-does-venture-capital-work.aspx.

[43] See Barkoczy et al (n 1) 257.

[44] Christofidis and Debande (n 2) 10; United Nations Economic Commission for Europe (n 11) 22.

[45] Samuel Kortum and Josh Lerner, 'Assessing the Contribution of Venture Capital to Innovation' (2000) 31(4) *The RAND Journal of Economics* 674, 691–92; Milosevic and Fendt (n 17) 660; Lerner and Watson (n 2) 6.

[46] OECD, *OSLO Manual 2018: Guidelines for Collecting, Reporting and Using Data on Innovation*, 4th edn (OECD, 2018) 60.

[47] OECD, *Supporting Investment in Knowledge Capital, Growth and Innovation* (OECD, 2013) 17.

[48] Barkoczy et al (n 1) 21; OECD, 'Innovation and Growth: Rationale for an Innovation Strategy' (2007) 6; Lerner, *Boulevard of Broken Dreams* (n 11) 43–45.

[49] OECD, *Innovation and Growth* (n 48) 3; Barkoczy et al (n 1) 21–22.

Entrepreneurial startup companies are a vital component of any innovation system, because while both large and small companies have the capacity to be innovative, there is evidence that startups provide a significantly higher level of innovation outputs than larger companies.[50] In addition, when startups are successful, they have the capacity to produce a range of benefits, including increased profits, wealth and productivity,[51] job creation,[52] industry disruption, and derivative and spin-off businesses.[53] Startups are also a 'major force in commercializing cutting-edge science',[54] and it has been observed that individuals who have been employed by an entrepreneurial startup company are more likely than others to start their own companies in future, even if the original company fails.[55]

There are several reasons that venture capital investment is particularly vital for, and well suited to the needs of, startups.[56] First, startups generally do not have the resources to finance their own innovative activities (like larger companies do),[57] and they are often starved of financial and human development capital due to their small size and early stage of development.[58] Without injections of external capital, many startups therefore fail.[59] However, it can be very difficult for startups to access debt funding, because they tend to have little or no collateral, no track record, no positive income stream and an extremely high risk of failure,[60] making them an unattractive prospect for lenders.[61] Even if they are able to access debt funding, startups may have serious issues with servicing interest repayments because of their fluctuating (or non-existent) cash flows.[62] Venture capital investors have far higher risk appetites than most debt investors, and are

[50] Hendon et al (n 29) 50.

[51] Massimo G Colombo, Douglas J Cumming and Silvio Vismara, 'Governmental Venture Capital for Innovative Young Firms' (2016) 41(1) *Journal of Technology Transfer* 10, 11; Brander et al (n 7) 572.

[52] Ryan Decker, John Haltiwanger, Ron Jarmin and Javier Miranda, 'The Role of Entrepreneurship in US Job Creation and Economic Dynamism' (2014) 28(3) *Journal of Economic Perspectives* 3, 3–4; Philipp Ständer, 'Public Policies to Promote Venture Capital: How to Get National and EU Measures in Sync' (Policy Paper, 31 August 2017) 3; Lilischkis (n 1) 7–8; European Commission, 'Effectiveness of Tax Incentives' (n 2) 41.

[53] Barkoczy et al (n 1) 4.

[54] Gilson (n 37) 1068.

[55] Elyse Cherry et al, 'No Exit: The Challenge of Realizing Return on Community Development Venture Capital Investments' (Report to The Ford Foundation, 5 October 2000).

[56] United Nations Economic Commission for Europe (n 11) 6; Ständer (n 52) 3; Mason and Harrison (n 30) 160; Da Rin, Nicodano and Sembenelli (n 5) 1699.

[57] Barkoczy et al (n 1) 5.

[58] Fabio Bertoni and Tereza Tykvová, 'Does Governmental Venture Capital Spur Invention and Innovation? Evidence from Young European Biotech Companies' (2015) 44(4) *Research Policy* 925, 926; Karen Wilson, 'Policy Lessons from Financing Young Innovative Firms' (OECD, June 2015) OECD Science, Technology and Industry Policy Papers No 24, 19; Pinelli and Schreiber (n 32) 5, 9.

[59] Barkoczy et al (n 1) 30. See also Pinelli and Schreiber (n 32) i.

[60] Barkoczy et al (n 1) 59; Karen E Wilson and Filipe Silva, 'Policies for Seed and Early Stage Finance: Findings from the 2012 OECD Financing Questionnaire' (OECD, October 2013) OECD Science, Technology and Industry Policy Papers No 9, 7; Mason and Harrison (n 30) 160; European Commission, 'Effectiveness of Tax Incentives' (n 2) 42; Ständer (n 52) 3.

[61] United Nations Economic Commission for Europe (n 11) 5; Hendon et al (n 29) 51.

[62] See OECD, 'Government Venture Capital for Technology-Based Firms' (1997) OCDE/GD(97) 201, 8.

willing to take on risky startup investments in return for equity. Equity investments give startups the development capital they need without the burden of interest repayments, while also allowing venture capital investors a share in any future success the startups may experience.

Second, because venture capital investors hold a financial and reputational stake in the success of their startup investees, they are motivated to help these startups succeed.[63] One of the ways they do this is by contributing vitally important human capital through a range of 'value-adding' activities, which include:[64]

- coaching and advising inexperienced entrepreneurs;
- restructuring investee businesses by improving management teams and compensation plans;
- assisting in the development of business and marketing plans;
- helping prepare for an exit event, such as an initial public offering (IPO); and
- providing access to networks to facilitate recruitment, sales and follow-on investment.[65]

These activities are particularly valuable to startups because while entrepreneurs usually have a great deal of specialised knowledge about their particular area of expertise, they often lack the necessary commercial experience or skills to effectively grow and run a business.[66] Research has demonstrated that active venture capitalist investors who provide value-adding activities to their investees are likely to contribute to increased startup survival and success rates,[67] making the provision of these services 'the most important activity' of venture capital funds.[68]

Third, venture capital investors have developed a range of risk-mitigation strategies that allow them to make risky startup investments that many other investors would avoid. These strategies include careful screening and selection of investees (a process known as 'due diligence'),[69] investing in a portfolio of companies in

[63] Megginson (n 17) 90, 100; Rafael Repullo and Javier Suarez, 'Venture Capital Finance: A Security Design Approach' (2004) 8(1) *Review of Finance* 75; United Nations Economic Commission for Europe (n 11) 6.

[64] European Commission, 'Effectiveness of Tax Incentives' (n 2) 43.

[65] Barkoczy et al (n 1) 27; Mason and Harrison (n 30) 160; Bertoni and Tykvová (n 58) 926–97; Lisa Callagher, Peter Smith and Saskia Ruscoe, 'Government Roles in Venture Capital Development: A Review of Current Literature' (2015) 4(3) *Journal of Entrepreneurship and Public Policy* 367, 368–69.

[66] Keuschnigg and Nielsen (n 5) 175, 176; Barkoczy et al (n 1) 27, 59–60.

[67] Keuschnigg and Nielsen (n 5) 198; Laura Botazzi, Marco Da Rin and Thomas Hellmann, 'Who Are the Active Investors? Evidence from Venture Capital' (2008) 89(3) *Journal of Financial Economics* 488, 511; Paul A Gompers and Josh Lerner, 'Venture Capital and the Creation of Public Companies: Do Venture Capitalists Really Bring More Than Money?' (1997) 1(1) *The Journal of Private Equity* 15, 30.

[68] Milosevic and Fendt (n 17) 665. See also United Nations Economic Commission for Europe (n 11) 15.

[69] Massimo Colombo, Fabio Bertoni and Terttu Luukkonen, 'Venture Capital: Policy Lessons from the VICO Project' (European Commission, 2011) 9; European Commission, 'Effectiveness of Tax Incentives' (n 2) 36, 43.

order to spread risk,[70] syndicating investments with other investors,[71] providing investment in stages as companies meet milestones,[72] and actively monitoring and controlling investees (for instance by taking a seat on an investee company's board of directors).[73] These behaviours allow investors to guide and monitor the operation and growth of their investees, and help control the information and agency risks present in these transactions (see further [2.2.1]).[74] Although these behaviours can be challenging for entrepreneurs to accept, particularly where they lead to a reduction of control for the entrepreneurs, they are usually ultimately beneficial for the development of investee companies.[75]

There is a widespread belief that 'venture capital is instrumental in bringing innovations to market at a rapid pace'[76] and is an 'important driver' of startup success.[77] Evidence suggests that companies that receive venture capital finance are likely to be more productive,[78] more innovative (evidenced by higher patenting rates)[79] and more efficient in a number of ways (including increased sales, higher production costs and higher salaries and wages for employees)[80] than other companies. Research undertaken as part of the VICO project (which analysed the impact of venture capital funding on European startups using data collected between 1994 and 2004) found that venture capital investment has an 'unequivocally positive' impact on the productivity and growth of firms, especially when investments are made at the early 'seed' stage.[81] Likewise, research undertaken in the USA on companies that went public between 1974 and 2015 found that the 42 per cent of these companies that received venture capital investment (around 556 companies) accounted for 63 per cent of market capitalisation and 85 per cent of research and development (R&D) spending by all

[70] Wilson (n 58) 9.

[71] Douglas Cumming and Sofia Johan, 'Pre-Seed Government Venture Capital Funds' (2009) 7(1) *Journal of International Entrepreneurship* 26, 33.

[72] Gilson (n 37) 1073; United Nations Economic Commission for Europe (n 11) 16.

[73] Jeng and Wells (n 17) 247; Yan Alperovych, Georges Hübner and Fabrice Lobet, 'How Does Governmental Versus Private Venture Capital Backing Affect a Firm's Efficiency? Evidence from Belgium' (2015) 30(4) *Journal of Business Venturing* 508, 510; United Nations Economic Commission for Europe (n 11) 6; Josh Lerner, 'Innovation, Entrepreneurship and Financial Market Cycles' (OECD, March 2010) OECD Science, Technology and Industry Working Paper No 2010/3, 17.

[74] Alperovych et al (n 73) 510.

[75] Dirk De Clercq and Sophie Manigart, 'The Venture Capital Post-Investment Phase: Opening the Black Box of Involvement' in Hans Landström (ed), *Handbook of Research on Venture Capital* (Edward Elgar, 2007) 193, 200.

[76] Jeng and Wells (n 17) 242.

[77] Alperovych et al (n 73) 508. See also Mason and Harrison (n 30) 161.

[78] Research undertaken in Belgium between 1998 and 2007: Alperovych et al (n 73) 508–09.

[79] Research undertaken in the USA on manufacturing industries using data collected between 1965 and 1992: Kortum and Lerner (n 45) 691.

[80] Research undertaken in the USA, analysing the impact of venture capital on firms in the manufacturing sector using data collected between 1972 and 2000: Thomas J Chemmanur, Karthik Krishnan and Debarshi K Nandy, 'How Does Venture Capital Financing Improve Efficiency in Private Firms? A Look Beneath the Surface' (2011) 24(12) *The Review of Financial Studies* 4037, 4040, 4042.

[81] Colombo et al, 'Governmental Venture Capital' (n 69) 10–11.

the public companies.[82] This demonstrates that venture capital-backed companies appear to be more successful and disproportionately more likely to undertake high levels of R&D compared to other public companies. At the end of 2022, the seven largest publicly traded companies (by market capitalisation) in the USA were all venture capital-backed companies: Apple (USD 2.2 trillion), Microsoft (USD 1.9 trillion), Alphabet (USD 1.2 trillion), Amazon (USD 856.9 billion), NVIDIA (USD 612.2 billion), Tesla (USD 389 billion) and Meta (USD 315.6 billion).[83] It was noted in 2015 that the rise of Apple, Google and Microsoft alone generated 'hundreds of thousands of high-skilled jobs, billions of dollars for investors, trillions of dollars of benefit for the United States economy, and immeasurable positive spillovers'.[84] Furthermore, it was reported in 2019 that 42 per cent of FDA-approved drugs in the USA between 2009 and 2018 originated from venture capital-backed deals.[85]

Venture capital, through its role in financing innovation, has the capacity to promote startup success, create significant impacts on national and global economies, and contribute to the dissemination of welfare-enhancing innovations. However, as will be seen from the discussion below, venture capital investment is not always easy for companies to access, which is one of the reasons that governments around the world intervene in the venture capital sector. The following discussion outlines some of the factors that lead to venture capital being underprovided by the market.

1.2.3. Scarcity of Venture Capital

Venture capital tends to be a scarce resource. One reason for this scarcity is that, as discussed above, venture capital is an extremely risky asset class. Not only are startup companies at a very high risk of failure, but they also grow slowly, meaning venture capital investments must often be held for many years. During a long investment term, markets and economic conditions can change drastically, impacting eventual returns. Furthermore, because venture capital investments involve taking equity in private, very young companies, investments are also highly illiquid and difficult to exit.[86] Ultimately, because venture capital investments are made at such an early stage in startup development, there is a high probability that most investees will never reach the point of commercial success,[87] and venture

[82] Will Gornall and Ilya A Strebulaev, 'The Economic Impact of Venture Capital: Evidence from Public Companies' (Stanford University Graduate School of Business, 2015) Research Paper 3362, 5.

[83] National Venture Capital Association, *2023 Yearbook* (National Venture Capital Association, 2023) 11.

[84] Gornall and Strebulaev (n 82) 2.

[85] Silicon Valley Bank, 'Trends in Healthcare Investments and Exits 2019: Mid-Year Report' (2019) 29.

[86] United Nations Economic Commission for Europe (n 11) 11; European Commission, 'Effectiveness of Tax Incentives' (n 2) 36.

[87] See Barkoczy et al (n 1) 54–55; Milosevic and Fendt (n 17) 662; Pinelli and Schreiber (n 32) 10; European Commission, 'Effectiveness of Tax Incentives' (n 2) 37.

capital investors will not see a return on their investments. For instance, research from the USA on over 2000 companies that received venture capital funding between 2004 and 2010 indicated that up to three-quarters of investments failed to return even the amount invested in them to investors.[88]

Venture capital as an asset class is also extremely sensitive to economic changes, and has what is described as a 'cyclical' nature, meaning that it has periods of increased and decreased activity.[89] It also suffers from 'information lags' that make it quite slow to respond to changing investment environments, exacerbating the effects of the cycle.[90] During the 'hot' period of a cycle (sometimes referred to as a 'boom'), investors tend to take on more risky investments due to an abundance of capital.[91] In contrast, when the market is experiencing the 'cold' period of a cycle (a 'bust'), exit opportunities may be diminished, and investors may struggle to raise capital.[92] Investment returns often suffer, and investors may migrate to later-stage (less risky) assets and avoid financing new ventures.[93] Evidence of venture capital's cyclicality and sensitivity to shocks can be seen in investment patterns over the past few decades.[94] Financial crises ('black swan events')[95] such as the 2001 dot-com bust and the 2008 global financial crisis have triggered busts that severely impacted venture capital investment levels for many years.[96] For instance, the OECD noted in 2012 that venture capital investment levels were still well below pre-crisis levels following the 2008 global financial crisis.[97] Following the COVID-19 pandemic and subsequent geopolitical uncertainty, the venture capital sector has again suffered, with US venture capital funds in 2023 reportedly suffering their most difficult exit conditions in a decade.[98] In the case of nascent venture capital markets, severe shocks can even

[88] Deborah Gage, 'The Venture Capital Secret: 3 Out of 4 Start-Ups Fail' *Wall Street Journal* (20 September 2012) www.wsj.com/articles/SB10000872396390443720204578004980476429190.

[89] See Barkoczy et al (n 1) 29; Ramana Nanda and Matthew Rhodes-Kropf, 'Investment Cycles and Startup Innovation' (2013) 110(2) *Journal of Financial Economics* 403, 416; Lerner, 'Innovation, Entrepreneurship and Financial Market Cycles' (n 73) 32.

[90] See Lerner, 'Innovation, Entrepreneurship and Financial Market Cycles' (n 73) 25–26.

[91] Nanda and Rhodes-Kropf (n 89) 416. See also Lerner, 'Innovation, Entrepreneurship and Financial Market Cycles' (n 73) 32–33.

[92] See European Commission, 'Effectiveness of Tax Incentives' (n 2) 32.

[93] See Lerner, 'Innovation, Entrepreneurship and Financial Market Cycles' (n 73) 26; Barkoczy et al (n 1) 29; Wilson and Silva (n 36) 7; Pinelli and Schreiber (n 32) 14; OECD, *OECD Science, Technology and Industry Scoreboard 2013: Innovation for Growth* (OECD, 2013) 200.

[94] See Lerner, 'Innovation, Entrepreneurship and Financial Market Cycles' (n 73) 7–8, 32; Jeng and Wells (n 17) 284–85.

[95] See Nassim Nicholas Taleb, *The Black Swan: The Impact of the Highly Improbable*, 2nd edn (Random House, 2010) xxii.

[96] See OECD, *Science, Technology and Industry Outlook 2012* (OECD, 2012) 14; Lilischkis (n 1) 40.

[97] OECD, *Science, Technology and Industry Outlook 2012* (n 96) 14.

[98] See Hannah Zhang, 'VC Exit Value Sags to Lowest Level Since the GFC' *Institutional Investor* (6 July 2023) www.institutionalinvestor.com/article/2bvxcyfqesuymrafaja4g/portfolio/vc-exit-value-sags-to-lowest-level-since-the-gfc; Michael Thrasher, 'Another Sign That Venture Capital Is Slowly Improving' *Institutional Investor* (24 January 2024) www.institutionalinvestor.com/article/2crbj8sww9uo9fypyrpj4/portfolio/another-sign-that-venture-capital-is-slowly-improving.

'truncate the development of the industry'.[99] There is, therefore, a rationale for government support to help the venture capital sector weather and rebound from shocks,[100] or even to act as a contra-cyclical stabilising tool to help mitigate the boom–bust cycle.[101]

Another reason for the scarcity of venture capital is the phenomenon known as 'investment drift'. Investment drift occurs where investors or funds that originally focused on making early-stage startup investments shift towards making less-risky, later-stage investments.[102] While risk is one reason that investment drift can occur, it can also be triggered by the desire to make more economical investments. Because the transaction costs of an investment tend to remain relatively constant depending on whether the investment is large or small (see [2.2.2]),[103] investors may choose to make a smaller number of larger investments in order to minimise transactions costs. As markets mature and fund sizes become larger, investment drift may be more likely to occur. Likewise, in times of economic turmoil and downturns in the venture capital market, investors may choose to mitigate their risks by shifting their investments away from the earlier stages. Investment drift can therefore contribute to the general lack of funding for startups, which is known as an 'equity gap' or, more colloquially, as the 'valley of death'.

Many governments and policymakers around the world are concerned about addressing equity gaps[104] because startups caught in an equity gap struggle to raise the capital they need to finance their development.[105] For example, Poland's national capital fund (Krajowy Fundusz Kapitałowy) was established in 2005 specifically to fill the equity gap in the Polish SME market, which was reportedly the result of demand for capital at the early stage of company development exceeding the financial resources offered by private investors, and the fact that small projects have relatively high preparation and monitoring costs.[106] Likewise, the UK's Enterprise Capital Funds programme is aimed at increasing the availability of growth capital to SMEs affected by the equity gap, which is said to arise where businesses with viable investment propositions are unable to attract investment

[99] Avnimelech et al, 'Building Venture Capital Industries' (n 9) 9.

[100] Colombo et al, 'Governmental Venture Capital' (n 69) 20, 22; Joern Block, Geertjan De Vries and Philipp Sandner, 'Venture Capital and the Financial Crisis: An Empirical Study Across Industries and Countries' in Douglas Cumming (ed), *The Oxford Handbook of Venture Capital* (Oxford University Press, 2012) 37.

[101] See Gilles Duruflé, 'Government Involvement in the Venture Capital Industry: International Comparisons' (CVCA, May 2010) 15; United Nations Economic Commission for Europe (n 11) 92; Lerner, 'Innovation, Entrepreneurship and Financial Market Cycles' (n 73) 35.

[102] Christofidis and Debande (n 2) 47; Mason and Harrison (n 30) 161–62.

[103] See Christofidis and Debande (n 2) 47; Mason and Harrison (n 30) 161–62.

[104] Wilson (n 58) 6; Mason and Harrison (n 30) 161–62.

[105] OECD, *Financing SMEs and Entrepreneurs 2019: An OECD Scoreboard* (OECD, 2019) 84. See also Science and Technology Committee (UK), *Bridging the Valley of Death: Improving the Commercialisation of Research* (Report No 8 of Session 2012–13, 4 March 2013) 8.

[106] See PFR Ventures, 'National Capital Fund', pfrventures.pl/en/kfk.html.

from informal investors or venture capitalists.[107] The US government has also commented on the equity gap, noting in 2011 that for high-growth companies, the gap is particularly acute for companies seeking between USD 1 million and USD 4 million.[108] Only six per cent of all venture capital was reportedly deployed at this stage in the four years leading up to 2011.[109] Although it may be too soon to tell, due to the information lags mentioned above, it is possible that the economic conditions precipitated by COVID-19 may worsen equity gaps in many jurisdictions.

Concerns about equity gaps have existed since at least the 1930s.[110] In reality, these gaps differ between countries and markets,[111] as well as between different business sectors, stages of development and startup locations.[112] Nevertheless, it is well accepted that younger companies at the earlier stages of development are more likely to experience an equity gap, especially those seeking capital for the first time, those that are focused on technology development and those that are located regionally.[113] In order to address equity gaps and the resulting scarcity of venture capital, governments around the world have introduced a variety of 'venture capital incentives' – policy interventions designed to positively motivate and encourage increased venture capital investment. Government venture capital incentives are complex and nuanced policy measures that take a range of different forms and, not coincidentally, form the primary research subject of this book.

1.3. Research Methodology

This book considers how governments can better use incentives to encourage and increase venture capital investment – a question that 'continues to challenge policymakers around the world'.[114] The way the book approaches this task is by looking empirically at the venture capital incentives that are and have been in operation around the world, categorising them by type (to facilitate comparison), identifying the ways in which they operate and are administered, and, based on economic, doctrinal and comparative principles, drawing out lessons

[107] British Business Bank, 'Enterprise Capital Funds: Guidance for Prospective Managers' (November 2014) 3; see also British Business Bank, 'The Enterprise Capital Fund Programme' (September 2019) www.british-business-bank.co.uk/wp-content/uploads/2019/09/ECF_Brochure_Version2_Sep2019_FINAL.pdf.

[108] 'Startup America' (*The White House: President Barack Obama*, 2011) obamawhitehouse.archives.gov/economy/business/startup-america/commitments.

[109] ibid.

[110] Jonathan J Bean, *Big Government and Affirmative Action: The Scandalous History of the Small Business Administration* (University Press of Kentucky, 2001) 17.

[111] European Commission, 'Effectiveness of Tax Incentives' (n 2) 45.

[112] British Business Bank, 'Enterprise Capital Funds' (n 107) 4.

[113] Colin M Mason, 'Public Policy Support for the Informal Venture Capital Market in Europe: A Critical Review' (2009) 27(5) *International Small Business Journal* 536, 536; European Commission, 'Effectiveness of Tax Incentives' (n 2) 46.

[114] Barkoczy et al (n 1) 32. See also Callagher, Smith and Ruscoe (n 65) 369.

for improvement. These lessons are set out in the final chapter as a set of leading practice guidelines to help policymakers design appropriate, effective and efficient incentives.[115] This methodology draws on previous policy-based research on government venture capital incentives, including a number of policy-based reports,[116] working papers,[117] articles[118] and books[119] that explore incentive policy design and evaluation in countries around the world. Each of the steps in the methodology is elaborated on below.

Importantly, the comparative exercise undertaken in this book does not involve comparison between countries or jurisdictions. Differences in countries' venture capital markets, political and legal systems and overall stage of development would make this process extremely difficult and ultimately unhelpful, as it would be comparing apples with oranges. Instead, this book compares different incentives on the micro-level. As will be discussed below, incentives are broken down into composite stages, and comparisons of their features are made on this basis. This allows important information about the design and operation of incentives to be collated, which is more useful from a policy design perspective than a broad comparison of headline issues. The first step of this process involves identifying the kinds of incentives that constitute government venture capital incentives.

1.3.1. Identifying the Incentives Included in this Analysis

In order to ground the discussion of incentive selection, it is useful to first explain some key terminology. First, 'incentives', in the investment context, are defined as 'measurable economic advantages' that governments provide to specific entities 'with the goal of steering investment into favored sectors or regions or of influencing the character of such investments'.[120] Implicit in the concept of an

[115] The term 'leading' practice is used in this book rather than 'best' practice to account for the fact that, based on ever-evolving knowledge and research, the understanding of what is 'best' is continuously changing.

[116] See, eg United Nations Economic Commission for Europe (n 11); Colombo et al, 'Governmental Venture Capital' (n 69); Pinelli and Schreiber (n 32); Duruflé (n 101); Cromwell Schmisseur, 'Information and Observations on State Venture Capital Programs: Report for the US Department of the Treasury and Interested Parties in the State Small Business Credit Initiative (SSBCI)' (Cromwell Schmisseur, February 2013).

[117] See, eg European Commission, 'Effectiveness of Tax Incentives' (n 2); Leamon et al (n 6); Wilson (n 58); Christofidis and Debande (n 2); Wilson and Silva (n 36); Murray et al (n 7); Ständer (n 52); Albert Bravo-Biosca, 'Access to Finance for Innovation: Rationales and Risks of Public Intervention' (The Innovation Policy Platform, 2014).

[118] See, eg Gilson (n 37); Mason (n 113); Douglas Cumming, 'Misinforming the Public about Public Policy Towards Venture Capital' (2011) 13(1) *Venture Capital* 99.

[119] See, eg Barkoczy et al (n 1); Stephen Barkoczy and Daniel Sandler, *Government Venture Capital Incentives: A Multi-Jurisdiction Comparative Analysis* (Australian Tax Research Foundation, 2007); Douglas Cumming and Sofia Johan, 'Government Intervention in the Venture Capital Market' in Stefano Caselli, Guido Corbetta and Veronica Vecchi (eds), *Public Private Partnerships for Infrastructure and Business Development* (Palgrave MacMillan, 2015) 237.

[120] Sebastian James, 'Tax and Non-Tax Incentives and Investments: Evidence and Policy Implications' (Investment Climate Advisory Services of the World Bank Group, September 2013) 1.

investment incentive is the idea that the advantages provided by the incentive are contingent on new investment taking place.[121] Investment incentives are designed to positively motivate changes to investment-related behaviour – ie they are a carrot, rather than a stick.[122] Incentives are often delivered through a 'scheme' or 'programme', which includes the rules and requirements governing the incentive's delivery and operation. In some cases, a scheme or programme might even deliver a range of different incentives. The aim that an incentive, scheme or programme is designed to achieve is referred to as a 'policy aim' (see [2.5]). This book is concerned with incentives that are designed specifically to encourage venture capital investment.

Second, investment incentives for venture capital commonly fall into two broad categories, based on how they are delivered. Incentives that are delivered through direct government outlays are known as 'financial incentives', or, more commonly, 'direct incentives'. Incentives that are delivered indirectly through the tax system are known as 'tax incentives'. There is a third kind of incentive, known as a 'non-financial' incentive, which does not provide an economic benefit, but rather provides some kind of ancillary benefit. A good example of a non-financial incentive in this context is a 'visa incentive', which grants recipients an immigration visa in return for their investments (see further [3.2.6]). Non-financial incentives do not fit completely comfortably within the definition of an incentive mentioned above and are therefore not always considered in analyses of incentives, but they are nevertheless included here as they represent a valid way for governments to directly encourage increased investment.

Third, incentives are classified in this book according to whether they are 'investment-related incentives' (ie they provide their benefits in relation to initial investments), 'profit-related incentives' (ie they provide their benefits in relation to profitable exits) or 'loss-related incentives' (ie they provide their benefits in relation to loss-making exits). This classification builds on the more common 'front-end incentive' and 'back-end incentive' terminology used to classify incentives, but is more nuanced because it takes into account the fact that profit- and loss-related back-end incentives are actually very different in operation and effect. It also takes into account the fact that some incentives are neither front-end nor back-end incentives, but instead apply while an investment is held. By grouping incentives according primarily to the timing of their benefits, incentives that are delivered in different ways but aimed at the same purpose can be analysed in the same way, which is appropriate given that they are similar in most respects.[123] The classification of incentives and the specific kinds of incentive that

[121] Barry Bracewell-Milnes and JCL Huiskamp, *Investment Incentives: A Comparative Analysis of the Systems in the EEC, the USA and Sweden* (Kluwer, 1977) 20.

[122] See Deborah A Stone, *Policy Paradox and Political Reason* (HarperCollins, 1988) 212–13; Barkoczy and Edmundson (n 42) 57; John Braithwaite, 'Rewards and Regulation' (2002) 29(1) *Journal of Law and Society* 12, 12–14.

[123] See Stanley S Surrey, *Pathways to Tax Reform: The Concept of Tax Expenditures* (Harvard University Press, 1973) 6; John Lester, 'Managing Tax Expenditures and Government Program Spending: Proposals for Reform' (2012) 35(5) *The School of Public Policy Publications* 1; Mark Burton and Kerrie Sadiq,

fall into each group are discussed in detail in chapter three, and are also set out in Table 1.

Fourth, the parties who directly receive the benefits of incentives are broadly referred to as 'recipients'. Recipients might be angel investors, venture capital fund managers or passive investors in venture capital funds, depending on how the incentive is targeted (see chapter four). The entities (usually companies) that benefit from the investments made under incentives are referred to as 'investees'. Broadly, all of the entities involved in incentives are referred to as incentive 'participants'. Finally, the entities in charge of implementing and delivering incentives are referred to as 'regulators' (see chapter five).

In order to illustrate the kinds of incentives that fall under the heading of venture capital incentives, Table 1 sets out the different kinds of incentives that are used to encourage venture capital investment, the recipients to whom they may be directed and their general incentive effects.[124] The information shown in the table is explained in more detail in chapter three.

Table 1 Kinds of incentives used to encourage venture capital investment

Incentive	**Delivery method**	**Potential recipients**	**General incentive effect**
		Investment-related incentives	
Tax credits (see [3.2.1])	Tax	Angels and passive investors	Lower the cost of investment by providing a tax credit to reduce tax liability
Tax deductions (see [3.2.2])	Tax	Angels and passive investors	Lower the cost of investment by providing a tax deduction to reduce taxable income
Grants (see [3.2.3])	Direct	Angels and passive investors	Lower the cost of investment by providing a cash grant to put towards investment, or help supplement operating costs (leaving more capital to invest)
Equity co-investment (see [3.2.4])	Direct	Angels, passive investors and fund managers	Use government capital to supplement private investments; help fund managers gain experience by allowing them to manage government capital

(continued)

Tax Expenditure Management: A Critical Assessment (Cambridge University Press, 2013) 20; Christopher Howard, 'Testing the Tools Approach: Tax Expenditures Versus Direct Expenditures' (1995) 55(5) *Public Administration Review* 439, 440.

[124] The classification of different kinds of incentive forms set out in Table 1 is adapted from Barkoczy et al (n 1) 123–31 and European Commission, 'Effectiveness of Tax Incentives' (n 2) 69.

Table 1 ***(Continued)***

Incentive	Delivery method	Potential recipients	General incentive effect
Loans (see [3.2.5])	Direct	Angels, passive investors and fund managers	Use government debt capital to supplement private investments; help fund managers gain experience by allowing them to manage government capital
Visa incentives (see [3.2.6])	Non-financial	Angels and passive investors	Provide immigration visas where individuals make specified venture capital investments
Profit-related incentives			
Tax exemptions (see [3.3.1])	Tax	Angels, passive investors and fund managers	Increase the returns made on profitable investments by eliminating exit taxes; exempt fund manager compensation from tax
Reduced tax rates (see [3.3.2])	Tax	Angels, passive investors and fund managers	Increase the returns made on profitable investments by reducing exit taxes; reduce the tax payable on fund manager compensation
Exit grants (see [3.3.3])	Direct	Angels and passive investors	Increase the returns made on profitable investments by providing a reimbursement to reduce the burden of exit taxes
Re-investment relief (see [3.3.4])	Tax	Angels and passive investors	Increase the returns made on profitable investments by eliminating, reducing or delaying exit taxes when profits are reinvested
Preferential returns (see [3.3.5])	Direct	Angels and passive investors	Increase the returns made by private investors on a co-investment by providing them with preferential returns (eg a larger portion of profits)
Loss-related incentives			
Tax-based loss relief (see [3.4.1])	Tax	Angels and passive investors	Provide more favourable tax treatment of investment losses than the baseline tax system, to help compensate for losses
Investment guarantees (see [3.4.2])	Direct	Angels and passive investors	Subsidise the cost of investment losses by providing reimbursement for a certain proportion of losses

Interventions that are not Considered in this Book

It is worth briefly explaining three kinds of government intervention that are not considered in this book and the reasons they are excluded. First, this book does not examine 'demand-side' incentives, which aim to stimulate demand for venture capital from entrepreneurs and startups.[125] The incentives listed in Table 1 are all 'supply-side' incentives, as they generally aim to increase the supply of venture capital investment in the market. Demand-side incentives involve different mechanisms, policy aims and targets than supply-side incentives (ie they are not aimed specifically at increasing venture capital investment, even though they may indirectly have this effect) so are not appropriate to include in an analysis of venture capital incentives. The role of demand-side incentives increasing deal flow for venture capital investment is nevertheless briefly discussed at [2.4.1].

Second, this book does not consider the various kinds of investment incentives that aim to encourage other kinds of investment (such as broader private equity, debt financing or foreign direct investment) unless they also have a specific focus on venture capital. While these incentives may incidentally encourage some investments that could be classed as venture capital, they are not specifically designed to do this, so are again not appropriate to include in this analysis.

Third, this book does not consider direct government investment in startups (where the government plays the role of venture capitalist). This kind of intervention is not an incentive according to the definition set out above because it does not aim to steer private investment into venture capital or otherwise change the behaviour of private investors (except perhaps incidentally). Furthermore, direct government investment has the capacity to negatively affect market dynamics by displacing private sector investment.[126] Governments generally lack the specialised skills and compensation incentives of private investors that help them select and nurture high-quality investees,[127] and international research indicates that government venture capital is a 'poor substitute' for private sector investments.[128] For instance, government investment is seen to produce fewer social benefits,[129] poorer growth in investee sales and poorer IPO performance than private venture capital.[130] Given the growing recognition of these issues,

[125] Demand-side incentives may include measures such as grants, prizes or loans for entrepreneurs and startups, business assistance and education services, incubator and accelerator programmes, research and development tax incentives, and employee share scheme tax incentives. See further Barkoczy et al (n 1).

[126] See Colombo et al, 'Governmental Venture Capital' (n 51) 12; James A Brander, Edward J Egan and Thomas F Hellmann, 'Government Sponsored Versus Private Venture Capital: Canadian Evidence' (National Bureau of Economic Research, May 2008) Working Paper No 14029, 41–43.

[127] See Douglas J Cumming, Luca Grilli and Samuele Murtinu, 'Governmental and Independent Venture Capital Investments in Europe: A Firm-Level Performance Analysis' (2017) 42 *Journal of Corporate Finance* 439, 441; Gilson (n 37) 1070, 1100–01; Leamon et al (n 6) 16; Mason (n 113) 538.

[128] Bertoni and Tykvová (n 58) 933.

[129] Cumming, 'Government Policy' (n 13) 198.

[130] Alperovych et al (n 73) 508, 510–11.

many governments have moved away from making direct venture capital investments and towards the provision of incentives to the private sector, such as those discussed in this book.[131]

Excluding the three kinds of government intervention set out above allows the analysis in this book to compare like with like. Overarching observations and recommendations about the design and delivery of the incentives included in this book can therefore be made because they all share the same broad underlying aim (encouraging and increasing venture capital investment) and basic mechanism (providing benefits to encourage changes in investment behaviour).

Selection of Examples

As will be seen in the following chapters, this book draws heavily on examples of past and current venture capital incentives. In selecting examples, the first step was to identify where incentives are in operation around the world and what forms they take (as there is no comprehensive and/or current list of global venture capital incentives). This task was principally achieved through: undertaking targeted and methodical internet searches;[132] investigating and cross-referencing incentives mentioned in the relevant literature;[133] and examining country-specific tax and investment summaries produced by PwC and Thomson Reuters.[134] Primary documents produced by governments (eg legislation, programme guidelines, policy and explanatory statements, public announcements, programme reports, publicly released data and internal evaluations) were the most useful resources for ensuring the currency and accuracy of incentive details, although they were not always available. The information provided on current incentives in this book is up to date as of January 2024.

[131] Avnimelech et al, 'Evolutionary Interpretation of Venture Capital Policy' (n 19) 102; United Nations Economic Commission for Europe (n 11) 83–84; Duruflé (n 101) 15–16; Wilson and Silva (n 36) 28.

[132] Searches were primarily undertaken using Google and Google Scholar. The search terms used in the first instance were 'government' AND 'venture capital' AND [country or jurisdiction name]. Where further searching was necessary, the search term 'tax' was substituted for 'government'. Once a particular programme or incentive was identified by name, searches were undertaken using that name in quotes, using Google Translate where necessary.

[133] See, eg EBAN and BOFIDI, 'Compendium of Fiscal Incentives: Tax Outlook in Europe – Business Angels Perspective' (2017); United Nations Economic Commission for Europe (n 11); European Commission, 'Effectiveness of Tax Incentives' (n 2); Duruflé (n 101); OECD, *Business Innovation Policies: Selected Country Comparisons* (OECD, 2011).

[134] See PwC, 'Worldwide Tax Summaries' (2021) taxsummaries.pwc.com/; Alexandrine Armstrong-Cerfontaine, Larry Jordan Rowe, Daniel S Kim and James Bowden, 'Private Equity and Venture Capital Global Guide' (*Thomson Reuters Practical Law*, 2021) uk.practicallaw.thomsonreuters.com/Browse/Home/International/PrivateEquityandVentureCapitalGlobalGuide?transitionType=Default&contextData=(sc.Default)&firstPage=true.

The task of identifying current incentives was fraught with difficulty for several reasons, including the following (many of which have also been identified as problems in other evaluations of government venture capital incentives):[135]

- Incentives are announced, introduced, amended, renamed and discontinued on a frequent basis. Information on current incentives (even that contained in official government documents) is often out of date and cannot necessarily be relied on. Information on incentives that are discontinued is generally removed from public access, making it difficult to gather resources on historical incentives.
- Many governments do not provide information on their incentives.[136] Where incentives are implemented via legislation, their operative provisions can be hard to locate when legislation is not made available online. Furthermore, it can be difficult to identify a single reliable source of accurate information where legislation and regulatory guidance differ, which happens frequently.
- The precise details of incentives are often glossed over or misunderstood by commentators, even in robust academic analyses. Relying on secondary sources without being able to officially verify the details of incentives is therefore problematic. For example, the European Commission has produced an excellent and thorough report on tax incentives for venture capital investment that provides a range of useful policy guidelines and other information. However, the report is not immune to error. At various places, for example, it incorrectly states that Australia's Venture Capital Limited Partnership programme allows tax relief in relation to income (dividends and interest) received in relation to venture capital investment and that it does not provide relief in relation to capital gains tax on investment returns, neither of which is correct.[137] These errors illustrate the dangers of relying on secondary sources to understand how incentives operate.

With these issues in mind, the selection of examples for this book has been restricted to those which have primary documents or multiple detailed and reliable secondary sources available explaining their operation. Incentives that have been previously evaluated (which, as will be explained in chapter six, is a small number) provide the most fruitful examples, as meaningful comments can then be made about their operation and 'success'.

As a result of these constraints, some countries are represented more than others in the selection of examples. For example, countries such as Australia, the UK and the USA are active in their promotion of venture capital, and have a large number of previous and current incentives from which to draw examples. These

[135] See, eg European Commission, 'Effectiveness of Tax Incentives' (n 2) 26–28.
[136] See ibid 201.
[137] ibid 104, 118. Note that the sister programme to the Venture Capital Limited Partnership programme, the Early Stage Venture Capital Limited Partnership programme, does allow an exemption for income received by investors.

countries also provide copious public information on their incentives and have been more proactive than many others in evaluating their incentives. Countries such as France, Ireland, Germany, Belgium, Malaysia and Singapore are also active supporters of venture capital and, even though they do not use English as their national language (or their only national language), they make clear, accessible information on their schemes available. In contrast, while countries such as Japan and China, as well as many South and Central American and Eastern European countries, do support venture capital through the use of incentives, they do not always make reliable information on these incentives publicly available, making their incentives much harder to profile. This, in itself, is a problematic design feature of incentives, as it has the potential to impede use and uptake of these incentives by investors (particularly foreign investors) (see [5.2.1]).

Table 2 details the 61 incentives and/or incentive programmes used as examples in this book. This list is not an exhaustive list of all the government venture capital incentives in existence, merely a snapshot of incentives that provide or have provided a unique, interesting, innovative or commendable approach to incentivising venture capital investment, and that fall within the parameters discussed above.

Table 2 Incentives/programmes considered in this book

Jurisdiction	Incentive/programme name	Incentive(s) provided
Australia	Biomedical Translation Fund programme (2016–present)	Co-investment, preferential returns
	Business Innovation and Investment (Provisional) visa (subclass 188) (unknown–present)	Visa incentive
	Early stage investor tax incentive (2016–present)	Tax credits, tax exemptions
	Early Stage Venture Capital Limited Partnership programme (2007–present)	Tax credits, tax exemptions, tax reductions
	Innovation Investment Fund programme (1998–2014)	Co-investment, preferential returns
	Management and Investment Companies programme (1983–91)	Tax deductions
	Pooled Development Funds programme (1992–2007)	Tax exemptions, tax reductions, recoupment of exit taxes
	Pre-Seed Fund programme (2001)	Co-investment, preferential returns
	Venture Capital Limited Partnership programme (2002–present)	Tax exemptions, tax reductions

(continued)

Table 2 ***(Continued)***

Jurisdiction	**Incentive/programme name**	**Incentive(s) provided**
Austria	Finanzierungsgarantie-Gesellschaft Capital Guarantees (1990s)	Guarantees
Belgium	Tax Shelter Start-Up – Petites Entreprises Débutantes (2015–present)	Tax credits
Canada	British Columbia's Venture Capital Program (1985–present)	Tax credits
	Labour-Sponsored Venture Capital Corporation tax credit (1982–present)	Tax credits
	Québec's Business Investment Company tax incentive (1980s–2003)	Tax deductions
	Venture Capital Catalyst Initiative (2018–present)	Co-investment
Chile	Fondo Etapas Tempranas Tecnológicas (Early Stage Tech Fund) (2012–present)	Loans
China	Tax incentive for corporate venture capital enterprises (2018–2027)	Tax deductions
	Venture Capital Guiding Funds (2008–unknown)	Co-investment
Denmark	Vaekstfonden's business angel programme (2019–23)	Loans
	Export and Investment Fund (EIFO) business angel programme (2023–present)	Loans
Europe	Capital Risque pour les Enterprises d'Amorçage programme (1998–unknown)	Loans
	European Angels Fund (2012–present)	Co-investment
	European Seed Capital Fund scheme (1988–95)	Loans
	Joint European Resources for Micro to Medium Enterprises programme (2007–approx 2014)	Co-investment
France	Investissement Garantie (unknown–2021)	Guarantees
	Garantie de Fonds Propres Relance (2021–24)	Guarantees
	Reinvestment regime (dates unknown)	Reinvestment relief

(continued)

Table 2 ***(Continued)***

Jurisdiction	Incentive/programme name	Incentive(s) provided
Finland	Finnish Industry Investment (Tesi) (1995–present)	Co-investment
Germany	Deutsche Wagnisfinanzierungs-Gesellschaft (1975–84)	Co-investment, guarantees
	INVEST grant for venture capital (2012–present)	Grants (investment and exit)
Hong Kong SAR	Innovation and Technology Venture Fund (2017–present)	Co-investment
Ireland	Employment and Investment Incentive (2011–present)	Tax credit
	Special tax treatment of venture capital fund managers (2008–present)	Reduced tax rate
Israel	Yozma programme (1993–98)	Co-investment, preferential returns
Italy	Tax incentives for investment in innovative startups and SMEs (2012–present)	Tax credits, tax deductions
Japan	Enjeru Zei'sei (Angel Tax Law) (unknown)	Tax deductions, loss relief
Luxembourg	Reserved Alternative Investment Funds regime (2016–present)	Tax exemptions
	Société d'investissement en capital à risque regime (2004–present)	Tax exemptions
Malaysia	Tax exemptions for fund managers (2018–26)	Tax exemptions
	Tax incentives for venture capital investors (2009–26)	Tax deductions, tax exemptions
Malta	Seed Investment Scheme (2016–present)	Tax credits
New Zealand	New Zealand Growth Capital Partners (NZGCP) Aspire Fund (2006–present)	Co-investment
	New Zealand Growth Capital Partners (NZGCP) Elevate Fund (2019–present)	Co-investment
	New Zealand Venture Investment Fund (2002–18)	Co-investment
Norway	Venture Capital Loan Program (2006–unknown)	Loans
Poland	National Capital Fund (Krajowy Fundusz Kapitałowy – KFK) (2005–19)	Grants, co-investment, preferential returns

(continued)

Table 2 ***(Continued)***

Jurisdiction	Incentive/programme name	Incentive(s) provided
Singapore	Angel Investor Tax Deduction Scheme (2010–20)	Tax deductions
	Enterprise Investment incentive (2004–09)	Tax deductions, tax-based loss relief
	Section 13G incentive and Fund Management Incentive (1993–2025)	Tax exemptions and reductions
The Netherlands	Garantieregeling Particuliere Participatiemaatschappijen (PPM) (1981–95)	Guarantees
Turkey	Business Angels Law (2012–present)	Tax deductions
UK	Early Growth Funds (2004–16)	Co-investment
	Enterprise Capital Funds programme (2006–present)	Loans
	Enterprise Investment Scheme (1994–2035)	Tax credits, tax exemptions, reinvestment relief, tax-based loss relief
	Regional Venture Capital Funds (2002–08)	Co-investment
	Scottish Venture Fund programme (2006–present)	Co-investment
	Seed Enterprise Investment Scheme (2012–present)	Tax credits, tax exemptions, reinvestment relief, tax-based loss relief
	Venture Capital Trusts scheme (1995–2035)	Tax credits, tax exemptions
USA	Hawai'i High Technology Business Investment Tax Credit (1999–2010)	Tax credits
	Small Business Investment Companies programme (1958–present)	Loans
	Specialized Small Business Investment Companies programme (1969–95)	Co-investment, loans, reinvestment relief
	Vermont angel tax incentive (2006–08)	Tax credits

1.3.2. Identifying the Stages of Policy Development and Implementation

This book analyses incentives using a 'staged' approach, meaning that it looks at incentives according to the various steps or stages contained in their development, design and implementation. A staged approach allows incentive processes to be broken down into a series of smaller parts, so that they can be more easily conceptualised, described and understood.[138] This approach is consistent with the approach generally used to analyse public programmes, regulations and policies,[139] and has been used in relation to previous analyses of venture capital incentives.[140]

There are five broad 'stages' relevant to government venture capital incentives, which are as follows:[141]

1. conceiving and introducing new incentives (discussed in chapter two);
2. selecting incentive form (discussed in chapter three);
3. targeting incentives towards the appropriate recipients, investments and investees (discussed in chapter four);
4. implementing, administering and monitoring incentives (discussed in chapter five); and
5. evaluating and measuring the success of incentives (discussed in chapter six).

Each of these stages involves a number of design considerations that can have significant impacts on the success of venture capital incentives. Chapters two to six in this book are dedicated to examining each stage in detail, with the key takeaways presented in chapter seven. In reality, the stages are more circular than linear. As will be discussed in chapter six, the results of an incentive's evaluation at stage 5 might well lead governments to revisit stages 2, 3 and 4 to refine their incentives and improve their operation so that they are more appropriate, effective and efficient – terms that are explained further below.

1.3.3. Identifying Evaluation Criteria

In order to identify instances of leading practice in government venture capital incentives, it is necessary to have a working definition of what is meant by the term 'leading practice'. In the context of this book, a leading practice is taken to represent a practice that is an appropriate, effective and efficient way to achieve

[138] See Eric L Windholz, *Governing Through Regulation: Public Policy, Regulation and the Law* (Routledge, 2018) 83.

[139] See, eg Peter H Rossi, Mark W Lipsey and Howard E Freeman, *Evaluation: A Systematic Approach*, 7th edn (Sage Publications, 2004) 40; Jean-Michel Josselin and Benoît Le Maux, *Statistical Tools for Program Evaluation: Methods and Applications to Economic Policy, Public Health, and Education* (Springer, 2017) 2; Windholz (n 138) 83–85.

[140] See, eg OECD, 'Government Venture Capital for Technology-Based Firms' (n 62) 20–21; Barkoczy and Sandler (n 119) 37–38; European Commission, 'Effectiveness of Tax Incentives' (n 2) 174.

[141] These stages are broadly consistent with those used in other analyses of government venture capital incentives, set out in the footnote above. See also International Monetary Fund, Organisation for Economic Co-operation and Development, United Nations and World Bank, 'Options for Low Income Countries' Effective and Efficient Use of Tax Incentives for Investment' (Report to the G-20 Development Working Group, October 2015) 19–20.

a strategic objective.[142] The principles of appropriateness, effectiveness and efficiency (explored below) are commonly used to determine leading practice in different kinds of evaluation, such as programme,[143] tax expenditure[144] and regulatory evaluation.[145] It is important to understand that these principles (and any leading practices identified) are contextual and may have path-dependencies; a leading practice is not a 'silver bullet',[146] but instead represents the best identified way of achieving a particular aim in a particular situation.

Appropriateness is often the first evaluation criterion to be considered in analysing an incentive, as it looks at whether the incentive is 'fit for purpose'. Analysing the appropriateness of an incentive may involve asking whether the incentive is necessary for and capable of achieving a relevant policy aim (and whether this aim is itself appropriate).[147] Appropriateness is a relative concept; for instance, whether a particular incentive is seen as appropriate or not might depend on the maturity of the venture capital market in which it operates (see [3.2]). An incentive's equity or fairness may also impact whether it is seen as appropriate or not.[148] For example, incentives that provide different benefits to similar recipients or that exclude deserving recipients for unjustifiable reasons are inequitable and are likely to be considered inappropriate in that sense.[149] When assessing the appropriateness of an incentive, it may also be worth considering whether the incentive is implemented in a consistent and transparent way that complies with the rule law. In this book, chapter two focuses on assessing incentive appropriateness at the introductory stage. Part of this involves considering whether there are other, potentially more appropriate, effective or efficient, alternatives to achieving the same policy aim.[150] Chapter six looks at appropriateness at the evaluation stage by considering when it will be appropriate to continue the provision of an existing incentive.

[142] See OECD, 'Government Venture Capital for Technology-Based Firms' (n 62) 20.

[143] Josselin and Le Maux (n 139) 1–2; European Commission, *Evaluating EU Activities: A Practical Guide for the Commission Service* (European Communities, 2004) 75; Lester (n 123) 16.

[144] See Neil Brooks, 'The Logic, Policy and Politics of Tax Law' in Tim Edgar, Daniel Sandler and Arthur Cockfield (eds), *Materials on Canadian Income Tax*, 14th edn (Carswell, 2010) 1, 75; OECD, *Tax Expenditures in OECD Countries* (OECD, 2010) 108; Howard (n 123) 440; Hana Polackova Brixi, Christian MA Valenduc and Zhicheng Li Swift (eds), *Tax Expenditures – Shedding Light on Government Spending Through the Tax System: Lessons from Developed and Transition Economies* (World Bank, 2004) 19, 230–31.

[145] See Cary Coglianese, 'Measuring Regulatory Performance: Evaluating the Impact of Regulation and Regulatory Policy' (OECD, August 2012) Expert Paper No 1, 18; Productivity Commission, 'Identifying and Evaluating Regulation Reforms' (Productivity Commission Research Report, December 2011) 10, 13; OECD, 'Recommendation of the Council on Regulatory Policy and Governance' (Policy Statement, 2012) 46; John Braithwaite, 'Regulation' in Kenneth Wiltshire (ed), *Governance and Economic Efficiency* (Committee for Economic Development of Australia, 1994) 163, 163; Windholz (n 138) 108–09.

[146] See Leamon et al (n 6) 13.

[147] Brooks (n 144) 75.

[148] See broadly Coglianese (n 145) 18.

[149] It should be noted, in relation to equity, that incentives are inequitable by design because they give special benefits to certain parties. Nevertheless, incentives should aim to be equitable within themselves as a matter of principle.

[150] See Brixi et al (n 144) 19; Brooks (n 144) 75.

The criteria of effectiveness and efficiency become relevant once an incentive commences operation. Analysing an incentive's effectiveness involves asking whether it is fulfilling or achieving its intended purpose (ie its policy aim), and how well it is doing so.[151] An incentive's form, targeting and implementation all have the capacity to significantly impact its effectiveness. For instance, an incentive that employs a form that does not encourage the intended kind of investment behaviour will not be effective; likewise, an incentive that is targeted at recipients or investees that do not align with the incentive's policy aim will also not be effective. Effectiveness is therefore a necessary (although not sufficient) condition for an incentive to be considered 'successful'. Chapter six looks at some of the practical ways that an incentive's effectiveness can be evaluated.

Efficiency is the second necessary condition for a successful incentive.[152] Efficiency looks at the extent to which an incentive achieves its policy aims in a way that maximises benefits and minimises costs (see [2.6 and [6.3.5]).[153] Analysing an incentive's efficiency involves asking whether its design represents the 'best' way to achieve its outcomes; for example, could the incentive's form, targeting or implementation be improved to produce better outcomes, or to produce the same outcomes at a lower cost? Issues that have the capacity to affect an incentive's efficiency include certainty around the incentive's rules, the generosity of an incentive's benefits and the extent to which an incentive is open to abuse or misuse (see chapter five). Where an incentive's costs are greater than the benefits it produces, it is unlikely to be efficient. An incentive that produces the desired results at a very high cost therefore may not be seen as successful.

It is helpful to clarify some further nuances around the meaning of the term 'success' as used above. First, there are no universal benchmarks for measuring success across different incentives because each incentive may have slightly different policy aims and may operate in a different context. This generally makes it unhelpful to compare the success or outcomes of different incentives (not least because the methodology for data collection and interpretation also tends to differ between countries and institutions).[154] Second, there are practical problems associated with determining incentive success, including that policy aims may not be explicitly set out, data on cost or outcomes may be unavailable or unreliable, evaluations undertaken at different points in time demonstrate very different outcomes and causation can be extremely difficult to establish.[155] These problems are discussed in detail in chapter six. Third, few incentives will be considered wholly successful, with most having some elements that work well and

[151] International Monetary Fund et al (n 141) 11; Productivity Commission (n 145) 10.

[152] The interplay between effectiveness and efficiency is such that effectiveness is essentially a precondition for efficiency (ie an ineffective incentive cannot be described as efficient) and an incentive will only be seen as successful if both principles are sufficiently met (ie an incentive that is effective at meeting its policy aims is unlikely to be seen as successful if it is wildly inefficient).

[153] See Stone (n 122) 49; International Monetary Fund et al (n 141) 16; European Commission, *Evaluating EU Activities* (n 143) 106.

[154] See European Commission, 'Effectiveness of Tax Incentives' (n 2) 26.

[155] See Brander et al (n 7) 572; European Commission, 'Effectiveness of Tax Incentives' (n 2) 27.

some that do not. This book therefore does not attempt the (likely impossible) task of comparing or ranking the relative success of difference incentives. Instead, it focuses on identifying the things that particular incentives do well or poorly in order to provide guidelines for governments looking to improve their own policy initiatives.

This book is not the first work to consider the development of leading practice guidelines for government venture capital incentives, although it is the first to consider both tax-based and direct incentives together with a legal, regulatory and programmatic (ie staged) approach. Other works have also looked at various aspects of leading practice, and this book engages with the principles, recommendations and guidelines presented in this research in the following chapters.[156]

1.4. The Structure of this Book

This chapter has introduced the concepts of venture capital and venture capital incentives, and has explained the research methodology used to analyse venture capital incentives in this book. The remaining chapters of this book, which broadly correspond to the five stages of policy development set out above at [1.3.2], are as follows:

- **Chapter two: Introducing New Incentives.** This chapter sets out a four-step process that governments should follow when introducing a new venture capital incentive. First, governments should clearly identify the market need that the incentive is intended to address; second, they should ensure that appropriate supportive policies for the emergence of venture capital are in place; third, they should develop specific and appropriate policy aims for the incentive; and fourth, they should ensure that the incentive's benefits are likely to outweigh its costs. Following these steps gives a new incentive the best chance of being successful.
- **Chapter three: Incentive Form.** This chapter focuses on the different forms that venture capital incentives can take (set out in Table 1 above) and the implications of form on incentive appropriateness, effectiveness and efficiency. The chapter separates incentives based on whether they are investment-related, profit-related or loss-related incentives, and looks holistically at tax incentives, direct incentives and non-financial incentives.

[156] See, eg OECD, 'Government Venture Capital for Technology-Based Firms' (n 62) 13, 15, 20–21; United Nations Economic Commission for Europe (n 11) 91–98 (venture capital policy recommendations); Lerner, *Boulevard of Broken Dreams* (n 11) (venture capital policy recommendations); Colombo et al, 'Governmental Venture Capital' (n 69) 24–25 (venture capital policy recommendations); Murray et al (n 53) 22 (venture capital policy guidelines); Leamon et al (n 6) 58–60 (best practices guidelines for creating a venture capital ecosystem); Hendon et al (n 29) 57–58 (criteria for angel tax incentives in the USA); Cromwell Schmisseur (n 116) 5–6 (principles for well-designed venture capital programmes); Barkoczy et al (n 1) (venture capital policy recommendations); European Commission, 'Effectiveness of Tax Incentives' (n 2) 175–84 (good practice guidelines for tax incentives).

- **Chapter four: Targeting.** This chapter explores the issues surrounding the targeting of incentives, with particular reference to the targeting of investors, investment activities and investees. An incentive's targeting plays an important role in assuring its appropriateness, effectiveness and efficiency. However, while tighter targeting may help achieve these principles, targeting that is too rigid can also have detrimental effects. This chapter breaks down a range of specific targeting criteria in detail to explain their effects.
- **Chapter five: Implementation, Administration and Monitoring.** This chapter examines how venture capital incentives are regulated, as regulatory processes have important ramifications on incentive effectiveness, efficiency and equity. Issues considered in this chapter include incentive time frames, cost and value, the characteristics an ideal regulator should have, how they should exercise their decision-making power and how the accessibility and integrity of incentives can be improved.
- **Chapter six: Evaluation and Measuring Success.** This chapter deals with the evaluation of venture capital incentives. As discussed above at [1.3.3], measuring the success of incentives is difficult for a range of reasons, and there are many issues governments should be cognisant of in designing or outsourcing their evaluations. The chapter sets out a proposed broad methodology for evaluating government venture capital incentives and considers the benefits that come from robust and transparent evaluations.
- **Chapter seven: Leading Practice Guidelines for Government Venture Capital Incentives.** The final chapter of this book sets out a range of specific guidelines for policymakers to help direct the appropriate, effective and efficient design and implementation of venture capital incentives. These guidelines are based on the research and observations made in the preceding chapters. The chapter concludes with some proposed directions for future research and final thoughts on venture capital incentive policy.

2

Introducing New Incentives

2.1. Introduction

Chapter one introduced the concept of venture capital investment, the role it plays in stimulating and funding innovation, and the important social and economic spill-over benefits that this kind of investment can produce. This chapter builds on that discussion to examine in more detail the reasons why governments introduce venture capital incentives, and to outline a proposed set of steps for introducing new incentives in an appropriate way.

The first part of the chapter sets out some important contextual and background features of venture capital that explain why this kind of investment tends to be under-provided by the market. Specifically, it looks at some intrinsic features of venture capital that lead to so-called 'market failures' and examines how the production of 'positive externalities' can also lead to underinvestment in this asset class (see [2.2]). The chapter then turns to a discussion of how governments can go about the process of introducing new incentives to address this underinvestment in a logical and justified way. This book proposes that governments follow a four-step process when introducing new incentives, comprising the following steps:

1. Identify a market need for increased venture capital investment that can be addressed by a government venture capital incentive (see [2.3]). If no such need can be identified, an incentive should not be introduced.
2. Create an environment conducive to venture capital investment by introducing supportive policies (see [2.4]).
3. Formulate an appropriate policy aim for the proposed incentive, with reference to the objectives the incentive is intended to achieve (ie addressing market need) (see [2.5]).
4. Evaluate the expected benefits and costs of the proposed incentive. If the projected costs outweigh the projected benefits, the incentive should not be introduced (see [2.6]).

Following these steps will ideally help governments introduce appropriate and effective venture capital incentives. Each of these steps is elaborated on in detail in the following parts of this chapter.

2.2. Reasons for Underinvestment in Venture Capital

As was established in chapter one, venture capital is a scarce resource that, for a variety of reasons, is often under-provided by the market. This under-provision is an example of 'market failure':[1] an insufficient supply of venture capital investment to meet demand from startups. Market failure can lead to equity gaps,[2] which in turn lead to the failure of innovative startups. Unfortunately, most venture capital markets suffer from 'serious and persistent market failures' that have the capacity to prevent an efficient allocation of resources and limit the supply of finance from the private sector.[3] These failures are often seen as an intrinsic part of financing innovation that cannot be completely avoided,[4] and it has been observed that as a result, underperforming venture capital markets struggle to self-correct.[5] The under-provision of venture capital by the market therefore provides a justification for government intervention in the venture capital sector: venture capital markets needs government support to thrive because otherwise they will likely experience market failure;[6] and venture capital investment gives rise to a range of useful and good social benefits (known as positive externalities) that make it worthy of this government support.[7] By increasing venture capital investment, venture capital incentives can push markets closer to equilibrium and consequently 'increase entrepreneurial innovation'.[8]

[1] A market failure, broadly speaking, refers to a situation where there is a disequilibrium between the supply and demand of goods: see RS Khemani and DM Shapiro, 'Glossary of Industrial Organisation Economics and Competition Law' (OECD, 1993) 55–56.

[2] Colin M Mason, 'Public Policy Support for the Informal Venture Capital Market in Europe: A Critical Review' (2009) 27(5) *International Small Business Journal* 536, 536; European Commission, 'Effectiveness of Tax Incentives for Venture Capital and Business Angels to Foster the Investment of SMEs and Start-ups: Final Report' (Taxation and Customs Union, 2017) Working Paper No 68, 46–47; Karen Wilson, 'Policy Lessons from Financing Young Innovative Firms' (OECD, June 2015) OECD Science, Technology and Industry Policy Papers No 24, 12.

[3] Mason (n 2) 538.

[4] Mark Dodgson, Alan Hughes, John Foster and Stan Metcalfe, 'Systems Thinking, Market Failure, and the Development of Innovation Policy: The Case of Australia' (2011) 40(9) *Research Policy* 1145, 1146.

[5] See Mason (n 2) 538.

[6] See Philipp Ständer, 'Public Policies to Promote Venture Capital: How to Get National and EU Measures in Sync' (Jacques Delors Institut, 31 August 2017) 3, 10; European Commission, 'Effectiveness of Tax Incentives' (n 2) 41, 46; Wilson (n 2) 12; James A Brander, Edward J Egan and Thomas F Hellmann, 'Government Sponsored Versus Private Venture Capital: Canadian Evidence' (National Bureau of Economic Research, May 2008) Working Paper No 14029, 3–4; What Works Centre for Local Economic Growth, 'Access to Finance' (November 2014) Evidence Review No 4, 7; Albert Bravo-Biosca, 'Access to Finance for Innovation: Rationales and Risks of Public Intervention' (The Innovation Policy Platform, 2014) 11.

[7] Federico Munari and Laura Toschi, 'Assessing the Impact of Public Venture Capital Programmes in the United Kingdom: Do Regional Characteristics Matter?' (2015) 30(2) *Journal of Business Venturing* 205, 207; Bravo-Biosca (n 6) 5;James A Brander, Qianqian Du and Thomas Hellmann, 'The Effects of Government-Sponsored Venture Capital: International Evidence' (2015) 19 *Review of Finance* 571, 577.

[8] Brander et al, 'Government Sponsored Versus Private Venture Capital' (n 6) 5; Gil Avnimelech, Alessandro Rosiello and Morris Teubal, 'Evolutionary Interpretation of Venture Capital Policy in

Venture capital incentives can therefore help galvanise the development of a market that would not otherwise develop on its own.[9]

Before introducing new incentives to increase venture capital investment, however, it is useful for governments to understand the reasons for which venture capital tends to be under-provided by the market. By diagnosing the problem and recognising its causes, governments can design incentives that work to address these causes. The following discussion therefore sets out three of the main factors that underlie the under-provision of venture capital investment: information problems, fixed transaction costs and positive externalities.

2.2.1. Information Problems

There are two kinds of information problems that contribute to making venture capital a risky (and unattractive) asset class.[10] First, information 'deficiencies' (ie a lack of information) arise due to the high level of uncertainty involved in investing in early-stage startups.[11] As discussed in chapter one, startups generally lack track records, have incomplete or under-skilled management teams and operate in new and/or unfamiliar markets, which makes it difficult for investors to distinguish between good and bad investment prospects[12] and can lead to adverse selection.[13] Because investors do not know which investments are likely to succeed, they need to put more effort into selecting investments, for instance by undertaking extensive due diligence, investing in a portfolio of different opportunities to spread risk and specialising in particular areas that they are familiar with. This extra effort leads to an increase in investment costs.

Second, information 'asymmetries' occur when one party to a transaction has more information than the other. For instance, entrepreneurs generally have more information about their company, behaviour and commitment to a project than

Israel, Germany, UK and Scotland' (2010) 37(2) *Science and Public Policy* 101, 103. See also European Commission, 'Effectiveness of Tax Incentives' (n 2) 42.

[9] Bravo-Biosca (n 6) 12. See also OECD, *SMEs in Libya's Reconstruction: Preparing for a Post-Conflict Economy* (OECD, 2016) 95.

[10] Brander et al, 'Government Sponsored Versus Private Venture Capital' (n 6) 4, 11; Mason (n 2) 537; European Commission, 'Effectiveness of Tax Incentives' (n 2) 10; Wilson (n 2) 12.

[11] Ronald J Gilson, 'Engineering a Venture Capital Market: Lessons from the American Experience' (2003) 55 *Stanford Law Review* 1067, 1076–77; European Commission, 'Effectiveness of Tax Incentives' (n 2) 36; Karen E Wilson and Filipe Silva, 'Policies for Seed and Early Stage Finance: Findings from the 2012 OECD Financing Questionnaire' (OECD, October 2013) OECD Science, Technology and Industry Policy Papers No 9, 13.

[12] What Works Centre for Local Economic Growth (n 6) 7. See also Josh Lerner and Brian Watson, 'The Public Venture Capital Challenge: The Australian Case' (2008) 10(1) *Venture Capital* 1, 3; United Nations Economic Commission for Europe, *Financing Innovative Development: Comparative Review of the Experiences of UNECE Countries in Early Stage Financing* (United Nations Publications, 2007) 5; Gilson (n 11) 1077.

[13] See Mason (n 2) 537; Josh Lerner, 'Innovation, Entrepreneurship and Financial Market Cycles' (OECD, March 2010) OECD Science, Technology and Industry Working Paper No 2010/3, 19–20.

investors do, leaving the investors at a disadvantage.[14] Once an investment has been made, the entrepreneur might shirk their duties, engage in risky behaviour or reveal information that is detrimental to the success of the investment, all of which can put the investment at risk. This is broadly known an as 'agency problem' or a 'moral hazard' issue.[15] Venture capital investors employ a range of risk-mitigating strategies aimed at reducing information asymmetries and protecting against moral hazard, including undertaking careful due diligence on potential investees, monitoring entrepreneurs closely to ensure their continued good behaviour (sometimes by taking a seat on investee boards) and implementing a range of control rights.[16] However, these behaviours also increase investment costs.[17] Information problems, adverse selection and moral hazard therefore contribute to market failure and the under-provision of venture capital investment by making investment more costly, leaving less capital available to invest in startups.

2.2.2. Fixed Transaction Costs

The investment costs referred to in the discussion above are similar for all venture capital investments – in other words, they are 'fixed'. What this means is that small investments do not cost investors less to make than large investments. In fact, investing in smaller, younger companies may even impose higher costs due to increased information problems and higher risks of failure and long-term illiquidity.[18]

Fixed transaction costs contribute to market failure and funding gaps for early-stage companies because they mean that small investments are less efficient and

[14] See Michele Cincera and Julien Ravet, 'Financing Constraints and R&D Investments of Large Corporations in Europe and the US' (2010) 37(6) *Science and Public Policy* 455, 456; Lerner, 'Innovation, Entrepreneurship and Financial Market Cycles' (n 13) 19–20; Bravo-Biosca (n 6) 4; Dirk De Clercq and Sophie Manigart, 'The Venture Capital Post-Investment Phase: Opening the Black Box of Involvement' in Hans Landström (ed), *Handbook of Research on Venture Capital* (Edward Elgar, 2007) 193, 196.

[15] See Gavin C Reid, 'The Application of Principal-Agent Methods to Investor–Investee Relations in the UK Venture Capital Industry' (1999) 1(4) *Venture Capital* 285; Harry J Sapienza and Anil K Gupta, 'Impact of Agency Risks and Task Uncertainty on Venture Capitalist–CEO Interaction' (1994) 37(6) *Academy of Management Journal* 1618; Kathleen M Eisenhardt, 'Agency Theory: An Assessment and Review' (1989) 14(1) *Academy of Management Review* 57, 60–63; Mason (n 2) 537.

[16] See Jennifer Payne, 'Private Equity and Its Regulation in Europe' (2011) 12(4) *European Business Organization Law Review* 559, 567–68, 571; Lerner and Watson (n 12) 3–4; Stephen Barkoczy, Tamara Wilkinson, Ann L Monotti and Mark Davison, *Innovation and Venture Capital Law and Policy* (Federation Press, 2016) 57; Josh Lerner, 'When Bureaucrats Meet Entrepreneurs: The Design of Effective "Public Venture Capital" Programmes' (2002) 112(477) *Economic Journal* F73, F76; Mason (n 2) 537; Bravo-Biosca (n 6) 4; De Clercq and Manigart (n 14) 195–97. Investors also engage in other risk-mitigating behaviours, such as staging finance to ensure the continued good behaviour and performance of entrepreneurs: see Gilson (n 11) 1078–82.

[17] De Clercq and Manigart (n 14) 197–98; OECD, 'Business Innovation Policies: Selected Country Comparisons' (2011).

[18] See Lerner, 'When Bureaucrats Meet Entrepreneurs' (n 16) F76; Rebecca Harding, 'Venture Capital and the Regions: Not Always the Most Appropriate Funding Mechanism' (2000) 7(1) *New Economy* 49, 50; Douglas Cumming and Sofia Johan, 'Pre-Seed Government Venture Capital Funds' (2009) 7(1) *Journal of International Entrepreneurship* 26, 32.

economical than large investments.[19] Because of fixed transaction costs, investors incur higher costs when they make a large number of small investments than when they make a small number of large investments.[20] As a result, investment in small companies is generally seen as unappealing, and many investors (particularly large venture capital funds) therefore gravitate towards later-stage investments as a way of mitigating their risks and lowering their investment costs (investment drift).[21] Investment drift provides justification for the introduction of incentives to encourage investment in early-stage companies.

2.2.3. Positive Externalities

It is well accepted that venture capital investment gives rise to a number of important spill-over benefits (known in economic terms as 'positive production externalities'),[22] including increases in innovation, employment and economic growth (see [1.2.2]).[23] These positive externalities are disproportionately significant considering the small size of most startups and the venture capital sector itself. Positive externalities can accrue from venture capital investment even where investee startups are not ultimately successful,[24] and they benefit society at large (rather than just investors and startups). In this sense, venture capital investment exhibits some characteristics of a 'public good'.[25] Because venture capital's social rates of return often exceed its private rates of return,[26] venture capital investment can produce a net benefit that makes it a socially desirable form of investment. This provides a normative justification for government support of the venture capital industry.[27]

[19] OECD, 'Business Innovation Policies' (n 17) 50.

[20] See Mason (n 2) 537; Rebecca Harding, 'Plugging the Knowledge Gap: An International Comparison of the Role for Policy in the Venture Capital Market' (2002) 4(1) *Venture Capital* 59, 60.

[21] OECD, 'Business Innovation Policies' (n 17) 50; Bravo-Biosca (n 6) 5, 11; Constantin Christofidis and Olivier Debande, 'Financing Innovative Firms Through Venture Capital' (European Investment Bank, February 2001) 47.

[22] See broadly Neil Brooks, 'The Logic, Policy and Politics of Tax Law' in Tim Edgar, Daniel Sandler and Arthur Cockfield (eds), *Materials on Canadian Income Tax*, 14th edn (Carswell, 2010) 1, 55; Lerner and Watson (n 12) 8.

[23] Ständer (n 6) 10; Ann Leamon, Maria Susana Garcia-Robles and Josh Lerner, 'Best Practices in Creating a Venture Capital Ecosystem' (Multilateral Investment Fund of Inter-American Development Bank, December 2012) 29; Wilson (n 2) 12–13; European Commission, 'Effectiveness of Tax Incentives' (n 2) 43; Munari and Toschi (n 7) 207.

[24] OECD, 'Business Innovation Policies' (n 17) 52.

[25] See Cincera and Ravet (n 14) 456; Brander et al, 'Government Sponsored Versus Private Venture Capital' (n 6) 5; Richard E Just, Darrell L Hueth and Andrew Schmitz, *The Welfare Economics of Public Policy: A Practical Approach to Project and Policy Evaluation* (Edward Elgar, 2004) 557.

[26] Bravo-Biosca (n 6) 5; OECD, 'Government Venture Capital for Technology-Based Firms' (1997) OCDE/GD(97)201, 6; Douglas Cumming, 'Government Policy Towards Entrepreneurial Finance: Innovation Investment Funds' (2007) 22(2) *Journal of Business Venturing* 193, 197.

[27] Ständer (n 6) 3; Leamon et al (n 23) 26, 29; What Works Centre for Local Economic Growth (n 6) 8; Lerner and Watson (n 12) 8–9; Cumming and Johan, 'Pre-Seed Government Venture Capital Funds' (n 18) 32; Brander et al, 'Government Sponsored Versus Private Venture Capital' (n 6) 5.

Although it seems counterintuitive, the existence of positive externalities produced by venture capital investment can actually lead to or exacerbate its under-provision.[28] This is because, to a certain extent, the benefits produced by venture capital investment are 'non-excludable'. This means that the investment benefits cannot be completely captured by the investors; instead, some 'leak out' into the broader economy.[29] For instance, once an innovation reaches the marketplace, it can be copied for a significantly reduced cost[30] and diffused widely. This non-excludability can be mitigated through the use of intellectual property protections, but not avoided completely. To give a simplified example of why non-excludability might deter investment: where an investor has the choice between an investment that could produce a relatively certain profit and one that has a much higher risk of failure but is likely to benefit society in various ways, many investors will choose the former investment. This is because investors generally do not take the potential social benefits of an investment into account when deciding whether or not to invest (particularly if these benefits are not matched by the potential for strong financial returns).[31] In other words, many people in society want someone to invest in venture capital because of its useful benefits, but they do not necessarily want to be the ones to put their money at risk for the public good. This second part of the positive externalities argument provides another justification for government intervention in the venture capital sector.[32]

2.3. Identifying Market Need

The discussion above has highlighted some of the key reasons why venture capital investment tends to be under-provided by the market, prompting governments to intervene. However, the fact that market failures exist does not mean that venture capital investment levels are deficient in every jurisdiction at all times. For instance, the European Union recognised the existence of 'market gaps for some types of investments at certain stages' in 2014 but did not 'see evidence of a general risk capital market failure'[33] (although whether this is still the case following the economic turmoil caused by COVID-19 remains to be seen). The uncertainty

[28] Bravo-Biosca (n 6) 5; Douglas Cumming and Sofia Johan, 'Government Venture Capital Research: Fake Science and Bad Public Policy' (2019) 21(1) *Venture Capital* 121, 125.

[29] See OECD, 'Business Innovation Policies' (n 17) 52; Lerner, 'Innovation, Entrepreneurship and Financial Market Cycles' (n 13) 13; Cumming, 'Government Policy' (n 26) 197; United Nations Economic Commission for Europe (n 12) 5; Brander et al, 'Government Sponsored Versus Private Venture Capital' (n 6) 5.

[30] Bronwyn H Hall, 'The Financing of Research and Development' (2002) 18(1) *Oxford Review of Economic Policy* 35, 35–36.

[31] What Works Centre for Local Economic Growth (n 6) 8; European Commission, 'Effectiveness of Tax Incentives' (n 2) 38.

[32] See Bravo-Biosca (n 6) 5; Gilson (n 11) 1094.

[33] Wilson (n 2) 20.

around whether market failure or a need for increased investment exists in a particular jurisdiction and whether it impacts the venture capital market overall or only exists in relation to specific regions, industries or subsets of startups is something that governments should interrogate before proposing a new incentive. While there may be commonly held perceptions that particular markets are experiencing failure, these failures may not always be 'empirically significant'.[34]

Ideally, proposed incentives should be designed to respond to evidence of a genuine market need for increased investment (ie there should be sufficient demand from startups to meet an increased supply of investment), rather than being introduced based on governmental opinion or political desire.[35] It is important that policymakers do not 'become enthralled with their own vision and fail to listen to the market's messages'.[36] Unfortunately, governments sometimes neglect to perform the task of identifying market need[37] (or do so poorly). The European Commission was criticised in this regard in a 2019 review of its venture capital policies, which found that 'the Commission increased its support to the venture capital market' without fully assessing market need or absorption capacity.[38] Although the Commission carried out 'ex ante evaluations and impact assessments and analysed market needs by looking at supply and demand', the review found that it had not made a comprehensive quantification of the funding gap (primarily due to a lack of data, which is a problem that is likely to be experienced by all governments implementing venture capital incentives).[39] It was ultimately not clear from the Commission's assessments whether the low levels of venture capital investment as a proportion of GDP in most European Union Member States were due mainly to a lack of supply of venture capital or to a lack of demand for venture capital.[40] The review criticised several aspects of the Commission's behaviour in relation to needs assessment, including: failing to assess market needs and quantify funding gaps before implementing or increasing interventions; failing to explain the reasoning behind estimates of the funding gap; and only undertaking an assessment of market need following a

[34] OECD, 'Business Innovation Policies' (n 17) 53. See also Harding, 'Plugging the Knowledge Gap' (n 20) 70; Hans Landström and Colin Mason, 'Venture Capital Research: The Road Ahead' in Hans Landström and Colin Mason (eds), *Handbook of Research on Venture Capital, vol 2: A Globalizing Industry* (Edward Elgar, 2012) 283, 287.

[35] See Gordon Murray, Marc Cowling, Weixi Liu and Olga Kalinowska-Beszczynska, 'Government Co-Financed "Hybrid" Venture Capital Programmes: Generalizing Developed Economy Experience and its Relevance to Emerging Nations' (Kauffman International Research and Policy Roundtable, 11–12 March 2012) 3.

[36] Leamon et al (n 23) 42. It has been noted that government policies 'have been most effective when they acknowledge the status of their existing markets and take steps appropriate to their individual situations': PricewaterhouseCoopers, 'Innovation: Government's Many Roles in Fostering Innovation' (January 2010) 5.

[37] OECD, 'Business Innovation Policies' (n 17) 53.

[38] European Court of Auditors, 'Centrally Managed EU Interventions for Venture Capital: In Need of More Direction' (2019) Special Report No 17, 4, 18.

[39] ibid.

[40] ibid.

legislative proposal and indicative budget being put forward (rather than establishing need first).[41]

Something that is important to recognise when considering whether there is a market need for increased venture capital investment in a particular jurisdiction is that venture capital markets in different countries and regions not only develop at different paces, but also have quite varied structures, which means that they can look very different. For instance, the USA has a large number of venture capital funds, supported and predicated on the country's active primary and secondary stock markets (see [2.4.2] below). While the USA served as the blueprint for many of Europe's venture capital markets in the 1980s, European countries such as France and Germany had financial systems that were primarily bank-based (rather than stock-market based).[42] Unlike the venture capital market in the USA, which was primarily financed by pension funds, the majority of venture capital in France and Germany in the 1990s reportedly came from banks.[43] Because banks have higher liquidity needs than pension funds and also tend to be more conservative investors, they are less likely to invest in early-stage, high-risk companies like startups.[44] This has led to the venture capital markets in these countries having a very different character to that of the USA. In light of this, it is clear that comparisons between different jurisdictions should therefore not be made for the purpose of identifying market need.

Given the difficulties set out above, finding empirical evidence of a market need sufficient to justify the introduction of an incentive is by no means an easy task (as evidenced by the example of the European Commission). The 'massive uncertainties intrinsic to innovation activities' are acknowledged to make it 'difficult, if not actually impossible', to precisely determine the optimal level of venture capital funding for a market.[45] Furthermore, 'strong data limitations exist due to the very nature of venture capital financing' as investees are generally reluctant to release private information, and market data can be difficult to use for future projections due to the small size of the venture capital market.[46] In the absence of reliable and sufficient quantitative data, surveys and qualitative analyses can sometimes be the only option available to identify and assess funding gaps.[47] Stakeholders that governments may survey include startups (those that have been

[41] ibid 19.

[42] Leslie A Jeng and Philippe C Wells, 'The Determinants of Venture Capital Funding: Evidence Across Countries' (2000) 6(3) *Journal of Corporate Finance* 241, 248; Bernard S Black and Ronald J Gilson, 'Venture Capital and the Structure of Capital Markets: Banks Versus Stock Markets' (1998) 47(3) *Journal of Financial Economics* 243, 244.

[43] Miona Milosevic and Jacqueline Fendt, 'Venture Capital and Its French Exception: Explaining Performance through Human Capital, Policy and Institutional Failures' (2016) 43(5) *Science and Public Policy* 660, 663; Black and Gilson (n 42) 248.

[44] Milosevic and Fendt (n 43) 662. It has been noted that bank-based systems in Europe 'are viewed as less capable of financing innovation and of facilitating path-breaking innovations than the market-driven systems in the USA and the UK': Alexander Popov and Peter Roosenboom, 'Venture Capital and Patented Innovation: Evidence from Europe' (2012) 27(71) *Economic Policy* 447, 449.

[45] Bravo-Biosca (n 6) 3.

[46] European Court of Auditors (n 38) Replies of the Commission 11.

[47] ibid 4.

funded and those that have not), investors (angels, venture capital fund managers and passive investors) and service providers (such as incubators and accelerators, business advisors, intellectual property lawyers, universities and research institutes). The aim of surveying these parties is to try and identify whether quality startups have sufficient access to venture capital; however, it should be kept in mind that all respondents are likely to be subject to bias (ie self-interest) and will probably hold differing opinions about the existence and causes of market failures. Nevertheless, by communicating and engaging with stakeholders as part of their evidence gathering and subsequent policy formation, governments can gain a clearer picture of where problems exist and how they can be addressed.[48] The more 'strong and consistent evidence' that governments can gather about market failures, the contexts in which they occur and their potential solutions, the better chance they have of designing appropriate interventions and achieving their policy objectives and desired outcomes.[49]

Where governments introduce incentives without adequate market need for increased venture capital, the consequences can be detrimental beyond the waste of public resources. Venture capital investors need a sufficient amount of 'deal flow' in order to be able to select high-quality investees from the pool of opportunities. Where the amount of capital in a market exceeds the demand for investment from startups, there is an 'oversupply' of capital that will most likely lead to insufficient deal flow. Oversupply can lead to 'non-absorption' of capital, and may force investors to invest in low-quality opportunities that would otherwise have exited the market through failure.[50] Increased competition for investments caused by oversupply may also lead to investment overvaluation (which, in turn, can trigger harmful market corrections) and a preference for larger deals (which can exacerbate funding gaps for early-stage companies).[51] When investments made in an oversupply situation are exited, returns are likely to be lower than expected due to poor quality and overvaluation, and investors may suffer reputational damage that makes subsequent fundraising difficult.[52] Oversupply of venture capital therefore has the capacity to damage the long-term development of the market and drive away private investors.[53] Many of these negative effects occurred

[48] Leamon et al (n 23) 42; Barry Bracewell-Milnes and JCL Huiskamp, *Investment Incentives: A Comparative Analysis of the Systems in the EEC, the USA and Sweden* (Kluwer, 1977) 10; OECD, 'Government Venture Capital for Technology-Based Firms' (n 26) 11.

[49] Eric L Windholz, *Governing Through Regulation: Public Policy, Regulation and the Law* (Routledge, 2018) 91.

[50] Bravo-Biosca (n 6) 14; European Court of Auditors (n 38) 20. See also Christofidis and Debande (n 21) 47.

[51] Harding, 'Plugging the Knowledge Gap' (n 20) 64–65; László Kállay and Erika Jáki, 'The Impact of State Intervention on the Hungarian Venture Capital Market' (2020) 33(1) *Economic Research-Ekonomska Istrazivanja* 1130, 1143; Christofidis and Debande (n 21) 47.

[52] See OECD, 'Government Venture Capital for Technology-Based Firms' (n 26) 13; Bravo-Biosca (n 6) 9; Avnimelech et al, 'Evolutionary Interpretation of Venture Capital Policy' (n 8) 110; European Court of Auditors (n 38) 20.

[53] Bravo-Biosca (n 6) 14–15; OECD, 'Government Venture Capital for Technology-Based Firms' (n 26) 13. See also Margaret O'Shea and Candice Stevens, 'Governments as Venture Capitalists'

in the Hungarian venture capital market following the introduction in 2010 of co-investment funds established under the Joint European Resources for Micro to Medium Enterprises (JEREMIE) programme (implemented by the European Commission and the European Investment Bank).[54] JEREMIE's introduction in Hungary led to an 'unprecedented' number of investments, and JEREMIE funds became dominant in the market, leading to a temporary oversupply of capital.[55] While the first JEREMIE funds had access to good deal flow, subsequent funds (which were introduced within a short time frame) struggled to find promising opportunities that met the programme's eligibility requirements, as demand had not had sufficient opportunity to replenish.[56] Reports indicate that returns from the JEREMIE funds have not been strong, that the quality of portfolios decreased over the years and that the public capital contributed through the funds largely replaced private capital (see [2.6] below).[57]

In order to avoid the problems caused by an oversupply of capital, governments should recognise the importance of demand when implementing their venture capital incentives.[58] If there is little demand for venture capital investment, then there will be no market need for an incentive. In this situation, governments may instead consider introducing one of the many demand-side measures available (some of which are briefly discussed below at [2.4.1]).[59]

2.4. Supportive Policies for Venture Capital

Successful venture capital markets are, unsurprisingly, more likely to emerge where supportive policies create an environment 'that is conducive to entrepreneurship

(1998) 213 *OECD Observer* 26, 29; European Commission, 'Effectiveness of Tax Incentives' (n 2) 46; Productivity Commission, 'Identifying and Evaluating Regulation Reforms' (Research Report, December 2011) 9; OECD, 'Business Innovation Policies' (n 17) 16–17; Douglas Cumming and Dan Li, 'Public Policy, Entrepreneurship, and Venture Capital in the United States' (2013) 23 *Journal of Corporate Finance* 345, 346.

[54] European Investment Fund, 'JEREMIE – Joint European Resources for Micro to Medium Enterprises' (2024) www.eif.org/what_we_do/resources/jeremie/index.htm?lang=-en. See also Kester Eddy, 'EU-Funded Venture Capital Model Proves to Be Double-Edged Sword' *Financial Times* (2 October 2014) www.ft.com/content/bb6aeea6-374a-11e4-b45c-00144feabdc0.

[55] Patrícia Becsky-Nagy, 'The Special Aspects of Venture Capital's Value Creating Mechanisms in Hungary' (2016) 12(3) *Journal of Entrepreneurship, Management and Innovation* 31, 31, 43, 45.

[56] ibid 45–47.

[57] Kállay and Jáki (n 51) 1143. The cumulative losses of the collective Hungarian JEREMIE funds' portfolio were reportedly over HUF 50 billion by the end of 2017 (which represents 70% of the capital invested by the funds): at 1142.

[58] See Gilles Duruflé, 'Government Involvement in the Venture Capital Industry: International Comparisons' (CVCA, May 2010) 19; Wilson (n 2) 13; OECD, 'Government Venture Capital for Technology-Based Firms' (n 26) 13; Bravo-Biosca (n 6) 9.

[59] See Avnimelech et al, 'Evolutionary Interpretation of Venture Capital Policy' (n 8) 102;Marco Da Rin, Giovanna Nicodano and Alessandro Sembenelli, 'Public Policy and the Creation of Active Venture Capital Markets' (2006) 90(8) *Journal of Public Economics* 1699, 1720.

and venture capital investment'.[60] Likewise, venture capital incentives 'are more likely to have their intended effects on innovation' if they are supported by a well-functioning market.[61] Ensuring that supportive policies for venture capital emergence are in place in a jurisdiction is therefore an appropriate step to take before introducing a new venture capital incentive. While governments may be tempted to skip this step in order to reap the quick political benefits of announcing a new incentive,[62] doing so risks the failure of the incentive and a waste of public capital.[63]

At a high level, the literature shows that business and investment benefit from predictable and enforceable legal/regulatory frameworks governing financial transactions, contracts and property rights,[64] labour mobility,[65] a culture that supports and rewards innovative activities and risk-taking,[66] a stable banking system[67] and a stable political and economic environment.[68] There is also a range of more specific policies tailored to venture capital investment that governments

[60] See Leamon et al (n 23) 35. See also European Commission, 'Effectiveness of Tax Incentives' (n 2) 3, 49; Landström and Mason (n 34) 287; Lisa Callagher, Peter Smith and Saskia Ruscoe, 'Government Roles in Venture Capital Development: A Review of Current Literature' (2015) 4(3) *Journal of Entrepreneurship and Public Policy* 367, 368; United Nations Economic Commission for Europe (n 12) 78; Gil Avnimelech, Martin Kenney and Morris Teubal, 'Building Venture Capital Industries: Understanding the US and Israeli Experiences' (Berkeley Roundtable on the International Economy, March 2004) Working Paper No 160, 11, 45; Duanjie Chen, 'The Framework for Assessing Tax Incentives: A Cost–Benefit Analysis Approach' (Workshop on Tax Incentives and Base Protection, United Nations, 23–24 April 2015) 6; Duruflé (n 58) 4; Avnimelech et al, 'Evolutionary Interpretation of Venture Capital Policy' (n 8) 111; Wilson (n 2) 23–24.

[61] PricewaterhouseCoopers (n 36) 3, 5. See also Stefano Bonini and Senem Alkan, 'The Political and Legal Determinants of Venture Capital Investments Around the World' (2012) 39(4) *Small Business Economics* 997, 1013.

[62] See Sebastian James, 'Tax and Non-Tax Incentives and Investments: Evidence and Policy Implications' (Investment Climate Advisory Services of the World Bank Group, September 2013) 35.

[63] See Milosevic and Fendt (n 43) 675. See also Avnimelech et al, 'Building Venture Capital Industries' (n 60) 15; PricewaterhouseCoopers (n 36) 3, 5; Leamon et al (n 23) 14; Massimo Colombo, Fabio Bertoni and Terttu Luukkonen, 'Venture Capital: Policy Lessons from the VICO Project' (European Commission, 2011) 24; Murray et al (n 35) 23.

[64] Callagher et al (n 60) 383; PricewaterhouseCoopers (n 36) 16; Syed Adil Hussain, 'Growing the Malaysian Venture Capital and Private Equity Industry' (2010) 1(4) *Islam and Civilisational Renewal* 629, 642–43; Robert D Hisrich, Saŝa Petković, Veland Ramadani and Léo-Paul Dana, 'Venture Capital Funds in Transition Countries: Insights from Bosnia and Herzegovina and Macedonia' (2016) 23(2) *Journal of Small Business and Enterprise Development* 296, 309–10; Jing Zhang and Poh-Kam Wong, 'Networks vs Market Methods in High-Tech Venture Fundraising: The Impact of Institutional Environment' (2008) 20(5) *Entrepreneurship and Regional Development* 409, 412; United Nations Economic Commission for Europe (n 12) 25; Krista Tuomi and Lopo De Castro Neto, 'Innovation and Venture Capital Policy in Brazil and South Africa' (2013) 8(2) *Journal of Technology Management and Innovation* 35, 37; Colombo et al (n 63) 19; Deborah A Stone, *Policy Paradox and Political Reason* (HarperCollins, 1988) 53–54.

[65] Leamon et al (n 23) 14, 39; Douglas Cumming, 'Public Policy and the Creation of Active Venture Capital Markets' (2011) 13(1) *Venture Capital* 75, 91; European Commission, 'Effectiveness of Tax Incentives' (n 2) 39.

[66] Colombo et al (n 63) 19; PricewaterhouseCoopers (n 36) 3.

[67] PricewaterhouseCoopers (n 36) 3.

[68] Bonini and Alkan (n 61) 998–99. See also Ashley C Brown, Jon Stern, Bernard Tenenbaum and Defne Gencer, *Handbook for Evaluating Infrastructure Regulatory Systems* (World Bank, 2006) 147–48.

can implement, set out below. These policies are grouped according to whether they encourage demand for venture capital or facilitate the supply of venture capital.

2.4.1. Encouraging Demand for Venture Capital

A country's innovation environment comprises many moving parts; for a thriving venture capital market to emerge, the most important of these parts are experienced investors with capital to invest (supply) and a strong pipeline of promising investment opportunities, known as deal flow (demand).[69] Interestingly, it has been recognised that the relationship between venture capital and deal flow is symbiotic, in that increasing the number of viable startups in a market may encourage increased venture capital investment, and increasing the amount of venture capital investment in a market can also help increase the number of start-ups looking for investment.[70] Conversely, a lack of deal flow can act as a barrier to the growth of the venture capital sector.[71] For this reason, introducing a venture capital investment incentive, such as those discussed in this book, can actually be harmful where a jurisdiction lacks adequate deal flow, because it may encourage over-investment in low-quality investees, leading to poor returns. It has been suggested that this may be the situation in countries including the United Arab Emirates, Saudi Arabia and Egypt, as these countries 'are yet to develop an adequate flow of promising and investible start-ups' and the necessary pre-conditions for venture capital emergence are still 'under development' in these regions.[72]

Governments can encourage demand for venture capital in a variety of ways by making it easier and more attractive for entrepreneurs to start their own companies. First, governments can reduce the administrative and bureaucratic barriers to setting up new businesses (such as high registration costs or complicated processes).[73] Second, governments can de-stigmatise business failure and provide quick and affordable bankruptcy/insolvency processes to help entrepreneurs 'start again' without being unduly penalised for their failures. This can help to encourage the creation of high-risk companies and increase competition and productivity;[74]

[69] See Hussain (n 64) 640; Avnimelech et al, 'Evolutionary Interpretation of Venture Capital Policy' (n 8) 106; Gilson (n 11) 1069.

[70] See Avnimelech et al, 'Evolutionary Interpretation of Venture Capital Policy' (n 8) 110; Fabio Bertoni and Tereza Tykvová, 'Does Governmental Venture Capital Spur Invention and Innovation? Evidence from Young European Biotech Companies' (2015) 44(4) *Research Policy* 925, 925; Lerner, 'Innovation, Entrepreneurship and Financial Market Cycles' (n 13) 35. See also Colombo et al (n 63) 18.

[71] See United Nations Economic Commission for Europe (n 12) 27; Avnimelech et al, 'Building Venture Capital Industries' (n 60) 7.

[72] Imam Seoudi and Salma Mahmoud, 'Public Policy for Venture Capital: A Comparative Study of Emirates, Saudi Arabia and Egypt' (2016) 7(1) *Review of Business and Finance Studies* 19, 36.

[73] Wilson (n 2) 19; Stefan Lilischkis, 'Policies in Support of High-Growth Innovative SMEs' (European Commission, June 2011) INNO-Grips Policy Brief No 2, 7.

[74] See Wilson (n 2) 19; World Bank, *World Development Report 2005: A Better Investment Climate for Everyone* (Oxford University Press, 2004) 104; Leamon et al (n 23) 14; Colombo et al (n 63) 24; European Commission, 'Effectiveness of Tax Incentives' (n 2) 49; Cumming, 'Public Policy' (n 65) 81.

research indicates that 'liberal bankruptcy laws stimulate entrepreneurialism and increase the demand for venture capital'.[75] Third, governments can implement a strong securitisation and intellectual property protection regime (such as accessible patenting and copyright procedures) in order to both increase the excludability of new innovations and create collateral for entrepreneurs so that they can better access funding.[76] These demand-facilitation measures, although they may seem far removed from venture capital, can actually have a marked impact on investment culture and practices.[77] For instance, the US Chamber of Commerce has reported a correlation between intellectual property protection and access to venture capital, noting that economies with 'robust' intellectual property protection (above the median level) are, on average, 45 per cent more likely to attract venture capital and private equity funds.[78]

Governments can also provide direct incentives to encourage demand for venture capital (known as demand-side incentives). These might include: grants to help entrepreneurs start new businesses or develop their innovations; tax incentives for research, development and commercialisation activities that help fund these activities; patent box regimes that reward companies that make money from their patents; business assistance programmes to help entrepreneurs with the process of running a business; incubators and accelerators to help small companies scale up quickly; and clustering initiatives to help create concentrations of innovative businesses in local areas.[79] Governments may also support the demand side by funding university research, which can lead to the production of spin-out companies and help disseminate innovation.[80] Finally, governments can provide pitch training for entrepreneurs and educate small businesses on the benefits and risks of venture capital investment, as was done under Brazil's INOVAR programme (see below).[81]

2.4.2. Facilitating Supply of Venture Capital

The incentives that form the subject of this book are concerned with directly stimulating venture capital investment by providing tangible benefits to investors.

[75] John Armour and Douglas Cumming, 'The Legislative Road to Silicon Valley' (2006) 58(4) *Oxford Economic Papers* 596, 631.

[76] Christofidis and Debande (n 21) 46; Colombo et al (n 63) 19; OECD, 'Government Venture Capital for Technology-Based Firms' (n 26) 5.

[77] In contrast, issues such as corruption, administrative obstacles and a lack of consistent protection for intellectual property have been highlighted as barriers to venture capital investment and startup growth in countries such as Macedonia: see Hisrich et al (n 64) 309–10. See also Seoudi and Mahmoud (n 72) in relation to the United Arab Emirates, Saudi Arabia and Egypt.

[78] Global Intellectual Property Center, United States Chamber of Commerce, *The Roots of Innovation: US Chamber International IP Index*, 5th edn (February 2017) 10.

[79] See United Nations Economic Commission for Europe (n 12) 86–87.

[80] PricewaterhouseCoopers (n 36) 20; Leamon et al (n 23) 39.

[81] United Nations Economic Commission for Europe (n 12) 87.

However, there is also a range of indirect ways that governments can support a supply of venture capital to emerge. These include: making it easier for startup companies to raise capital; allowing the use of convertible and hybrid securities; allowing venture capitalists to structure their funds as flow-through limited partnerships; allowing investment by institutional investors; providing certainty in relation to the taxation of venture capital investments; creating a positive culture around venture capital investment; and facilitating exit options. Some of the ways that governments can achieve these ends are discussed below.

Making it Easier for Start-ups to Raise Capital

Corporate disclosure rules generally aim to protect investors by mandating the disclosure of certain information by companies when they raise capital either publicly or privately. This can be problematic for startup companies for two reasons: first, startup companies are intensely private about their activities (due to their innovative nature) and generally do not want to make the details publicly available; second, startup companies are generally financially constrained and may not have the resources to comply with heavy disclosure obligations. Therefore, where governments tailor their corporate disclosure regimes to carve out lighter disclosure rules for startups, this is likely to facilitate capital raising (including venture capital).[82]

An example of a country that has created a carve out for startups is Australia. Australia's corporate disclosure regime generally requires public companies to provide expensive and thorough disclosure documents when they issue securities, and generally prohibits proprietary companies (eg startups) from doing anything that would require disclosure, such as issuing shares to an investor.[83] However, the regime carves out a range of exceptions for startups and other proprietary companies that allow them to: issue securities to their employees or existing shareholders with a disclosure document; issue shares pursuant to a crowd-sourced funding offer with a crowd-sourced funding offer document (which carries reduced disclosure requirements when compared with a prospectus); and issue securities without a disclosure document in a range of scenarios, such as when the offer is a 'small scale personal offer' or when the investor is a 'sophisticated', experienced or 'professional' investor.[84] The latter scenarios cover most, if not all, angel and venture capital investments, which facilitates proprietary companies' ability to raise capital without needing to prepare costly disclosure documents that would reveal their confidential information. Australia's corporate disclosure regime also includes a special provision for certain startups that implement employee share schemes, which protects their disclosure documents from being made publicly

[82] See Jeng and Wells (n 42) 256.
[83] Corporations Act 2001 (Australia), ss 113(3), 704, 706–708A, 727.
[84] ibid ss 113(3), 708.

available (as they ordinarily would be).[85] This helps protect the confidentiality of startups while still requiring adequate disclosure to be made to employee investors.

In a similar vein, a country's laws around how control rights and cash flow are managed in companies that receive venture capital investment can impact the ease (or desirability) of receiving venture capital investment.[86] The field of 'startup corporate law' has not yet received a great deal of attention as a method for facilitating the provision of venture capital, although, as will be discussed below, the extent to which governments allow the use of non-traditional forms of securities has been acknowledged to affect venture capital funding.[87]

Allowing the Use of Convertible and Hybrid Securities

Governments can facilitate venture capital investment by allowing the use of convertible securities such as convertible preferred shares, convertible notes and SAFE (Simple Agreement for Future Equity) notes. Investors commonly use these hybrid securities to help mitigate the risks of venture capital investment (because they generally combine elements of debt and equity with some upsides of each), among other things. However, governments may be reluctant to allow the use of these securities because they are complex and often not well understood by either investee company owners or inexperienced investors.[88] In disallowing the use of these securities, governments therefore promote investee and investor protection, but perhaps at the expense of facilitating venture capital investment. The following discussion briefly outlines the key features of each kind of security.

Convertible preferred shares generally grant preferred shareholders the right to be paid dividends before ordinary shareholders and give them priority over ordinary shareholders if the investee company is liquidated.[89] This gives preferred shareholders more security over their investment if the investment fails. If it looks like the investment will be successful, preferred shareholders can often choose to convert their preferred shares to a predetermined number of ordinary shares, which grant them voting rights and the chance to fully share in the investment upside. Convertible preferred shares effectively separate cash flow (investment) from investee company control, which is attractive for venture capital investors, who generally want control rights over their investees (although not the only method they have for achieving this purpose).[90] Therefore, convertible preferred

[85] See ibid s 1274.

[86] See Alvaro Pereira, 'Designing Startup Corporate Law: A Minimum Viable Product' (2022) 42 *Review of Banking and Finance Law* 367; Paolo Giudici and Peter Agstner, 'Startups and Company Law: The Competitive Pressure of Delaware on Italy (and Europe?)' (2019) 20 *European Business Organization Law Review* 597.

[87] See Pereira (n 86).

[88] See United Nations Economic Commission for Europe (n 12) 96; Leamon et al (n 23) 38.

[89] Ronald J Gilson and David M Schizer, 'Understanding Venture Capital Structure: A Tax Explanation for Convertible Preferred Stock' (2003) 116 *Harvard Law Review* 874, 882–85.

[90] ibid 885–86.

shares go some way to addressing investor risk caused by information asymmetry and help align the interests of investors and entrepreneurs, making them popular for use in venture capital investments (particularly in the USA).[91]

Convertible notes are debt interests. They involve an investor making an investment in a company that, at a certain date, will need to be either repaid as a loan with interest or converted into preferred equity (usually at a discount).[92] Again, this combines the upsides of debt and equity. Convertible notes can be a useful way to make venture capital investments because they do not require a company to have a robust valuation (which many early-stage startups do not) and are simpler and generally cheaper to implement than investments made through the purchase of convertible preferred shares.[93] However, the fact that a loan may have to be repaid at some stage puts pressure on investee companies (even though this does not generally happen), and the interest component is likewise burdensome.[94] In response to these issues, SAFE notes were developed.

SAFE notes are a relatively recent innovation, introduced in 2013 specifically as a simple way for startups to structure their capital raising deals.[95] SAFE notes are effectively 'deferred equity agreements' that allow an investor to convert a capital investment into preferred equity at a future date (usually when a fundraising round occurs), sometimes with a 'valuation cap' and sometimes at a 'discount rate' (much like a call option without an exercise price).[96] The valuation cap and discount rate offer investors an advantage for their early investments. If the trigger event never occurs, the conversion will never happen, but the initial investment is not repayable.[97] SAFE notes are particularly useful at the earliest stages of investment because they are simple and easy to implement and, like convertible notes, do not require a company to have a solid valuation.[98] Unlike convertible notes, however, SAFE notes do not incur debt or accumulate interest, and are therefore more attractive to startups.[99] Unlike a normal equity investment, SAFE notes do not require startups to give up equity at the investment date. SAFE notes,

[91] See Sridhar Arcot, 'Participating Convertible Preferred Stock in Venture Capital Exits' (2014) 29(1) *Journal of Business Venturing* 72, 74, 84; United Nations Economic Commission for Europe (n 12) 96; Yaron Leitner, 'Convertible Securities and Venture Capital Finance' (2009) Q3 *Business Review (Federal Reserve Bank of Philadelphia)* 18, 27; Scott Ollivierre, 'The Influence of Taxation on Capital Structure in Venture Capital Investments in Canada and the United States' (2010) 68(1) *University of Toronto Faculty of Law Review* 9, 14; Gilson and Schizer (n 89) 875; Douglas Cumming and Sofia A Johan, *Venture Capital and Private Equity Contracting: An International Perspective*, 2nd edn (Elsevier, 2014) 319.

[92] See John F Coyle and Joseph M Green, 'The SAFE, the KISS, and the Note: A Survey of Startup Seed Financing Contracts' (2018) 103 *Minnesota Law Review* 42, 45.

[93] ibid 44.

[94] ibid 46.

[95] ibid 42.

[96] ibid 42. See also Jason Atkins, 'SAFE Notes: A Simple Way to Raise Funds for Startups' (*Cake Equity*, August 2023) www.cakeequity.com/guides/safe-notes#:~:text=SAFE%20note%2C%20also%20known%20as,into%20equity%20in%20the%20future.

[97] Atkins (n 96).

[98] ibid.

[99] Coyle and Green (n 92) 46; ibid.

at this stage, are still most frequently used in the USA venture capital market, but are becoming more prevalent in other countries.

Allowing the Use of Flow-Through Limited Partnerships

Limited partnerships are the internationally favoured vehicle for venture capital funds, and countries that allow their use are therefore more attractive investment destinations.[100] Limited partnerships are 'hybrid' vehicles that generally combine limited liability for passive investors with the flexibility and reduced regulation common to ordinary partnerships. In many jurisdictions, they are taxed like ordinary partnerships, meaning that they receive 'flow-through' taxation (ie they are not taxed as separate legal entities in the same way that companies are).[101] This is particularly beneficial for investors that have a high propensity for making investment losses (like venture capital investors) because partnership losses can be taxed in the hands of the partners and used to reduce their assessable income.[102] Furthermore, limited partnerships generally have closed-end lifespans, which is desirable from a passive investor's perspective because it provides a concrete 'end date' for the return of their capital. However, the consistent use of limited partnerships around the world is not universal and has some way to go.[103] For instance, Australia allows the use of limited partnerships, but generally does not provide these vehicles with flow-through taxation unless they are registered as highly regulated venture capital funds under its Venture Capital Limited Partnership or Early Stage Venture Capital Limited Partnership programmes.[104]

Allowing Investment by Institutional Investors

Governments can increase the amount of venture capital in the market by relaxing investment restrictions placed on institutional investors such as banks, pension funds and insurance companies.[105] For example, when restrictions on pension

[100] See Leamon et al (n 23) 14; Avnimelech et al, 'Building Venture Capital Industries' (n 60) 21; Duruflé (n 58) 18.

[101] OECD, 'Government Venture Capital for Technology-Based Firms' (n 26) 5; Wilson and Silva (n 11) 45.

[102] Leamon et al (n 23) 38; Keith Fletcher, 'Incorporated Limited Partnerships: Venture Capital's Contribution to Legal Development' (2004) 17(2) *Australian Journal of Corporate Law* 157, 170. See also OECD, 'Government Venture Capital for Technology-Based Firms' (n 26) 5.

[103] See European Commission, 'Effectiveness of Tax Incentives' (n 2) 62.

[104] Income Tax Assessment Act 1936 (Australia), s 94D. Limited partnerships can also receive flow-through taxation treatment if they are Australian Fund of Funds or Venture Capital Management Partnerships. See Barkoczy et al (n 16) 268–69; Fletcher (n 102) 160.

[105] Jeng and Wells (n 42) 257; Wilson (n 2) 19; O'Shea and Stevens (n 53) 28–29; United Nations Economic Commission for Europe (n 12) 23. Due to the long-term investment horizons of many institutional investors, it has been suggested that their investments can also act as 'counter-cyclical stabilisers' in the market, as they can wait out poor economic conditions: Ständer (n 6) 8. See Barkoczy et al (n 16) 156–58 for some pro and con arguments around mandating pension fund investments in venture capital.

funds investing in venture capital were removed in the USA in 1978, the level of venture capital activity in the country reportedly increased significantly.[106] Likewise, when Finland reformed its rules for institutional investors in 1994, the contribution of banks and pension funds to venture capital reportedly increased nationally from 20 per cent in 1994 to 79 per cent in 1995.[107] An OECD questionnaire conducted in 2012 reported that countries including Canada, Hungary, Israel, Korea, Mexico, the Netherlands, Slovakia, Slovenia and the USA imposed restrictions on banks in relation to investment in 'alternative assets' (including private equity).[108] Countries including Austria, Canada, Chile, Estonia, Greece, Hungary, Israel, Korea, the Netherlands, Slovakia, Slovenia and Turkey imposed investment restrictions on pension funds, while countries including Austria, Canada, Chile, Estonia, Germany, Hungary, Israel, Korea, Mexico, the Netherlands, Slovakia and Slovenia imposed investment restrictions in relation to insurance companies.[109] While it is important to recognise that these restrictions were likely put in place to protect the integrity and financial security of these investors (which have important public functions), there do not seem to have arisen negative consequences from those countries that have relaxed their restrictions. Given the niche, small-scale and risky nature of venture capital investment, it is unlikely that many institutional investors would devote a significant part of their portfolios to venture capital. However, even a small amount of institutional investment in venture capital has the capacity to make a difference to the industry, precisely because it is so small.

Providing Clarity on Taxation and Reducing Taxation Barriers

Every country's baseline tax system inherently provides a range of built-in incentives and disincentives for venture capital investment[110] because different taxes and tax structures have the capacity to impact cultural attitudes around innovation and investment. Chapter three examines the ways that tax systems can be specifically used to encourage additional venture capital investment through the provision of tax incentives, but the discussion in this section takes a broader focus, looking instead at the ways that the taxation environment in a country impedes or enables the supply of, and demand for, venture capital investment more generally.[111]

Exit taxes – the taxes imposed on the profits made on successful investments – are among the most important taxes in terms of their impact on investment attitudes.[112] The most common form of exit tax is a tax on capital gains, with many

[106] Wilson (n 2) 19; Avnimelech et al, 'Building Venture Capital Industries' (n 60) 25.
[107] O'Shea and Stevens (n 53) 29.
[108] Wilson and Silva (n 11) 44.
[109] ibid.
[110] European Commission, 'Effectiveness of Tax Incentives' (n 2) 68.
[111] See ibid 62.
[112] ibid 11.

countries around the world having some form of capital gains tax (New Zealand and Singapore being two notable exceptions).[113] Research indicates that where venture capitalists have to pay higher capital gains taxes, they decrease both their investment levels and their value-adding behaviours.[114] The existence of an exit tax has also unsurprisingly been found to indirectly decrease incentives for entrepreneurial behaviour.[115] Consistent with these findings, lowering the rate of exit taxes or removing them altogether reduces investment risk by increasing net investment returns and may therefore encourage increased investment.[116] Interestingly, the effect of exit taxes on the provision of value-adding activities by venture capital investors is quite unclear. It has been suggested that exit taxes may reduce value-adding activities by reducing after-tax profits, thereby creating a disincentive for investors to undertake the hard work of finding, investing in, supporting and monitoring investees.[117] However, it has conversely been suggested that exit taxes may have the opposite effect of encouraging the provision of value-adding services and increasing startup survival rates,[118] presumably by motivating investors to achieve a higher after-tax return. As will be seen in chapter three, a common way for governments to encourage venture capital investment is to introduce incentives that lower or remove exit taxes. These kinds of incentives, which fall under the category of profit-related incentives, are discussed in detail in [3.3].

In some countries, it is not necessarily clear whether investment profits will be taxed as capital gains or as income. This is problematic where the tax consequences differ (eg where the capital gains tax regime is more concessional than the income tax regime), and the resulting uncertainty is likely to deter investment. This is the situation in Australia, where resident venture capital investors generally do not know for sure whether their gains will be taxed on income account

[113] But note that both countries may tax certain investment profits made by certain investors (eg share traders who are deemed to make their profits on income account).

[114] Lora Dimitrova and Sapnoti K Eswar, 'Capital Gains Tax, Venture Capital, and Innovation in Start-Ups' (2023) 27(4) *Review of Finance* 1471, 1474.

[115] Christian Keuschnigg and Søren Bo Nielsen, 'Tax Policy, Venture Capital, and Entrepreneurship' (2002) 87(1) *Journal of Public Economics* 175, 192, 198. Interestingly, wage taxes have been found to increase incentives for entrepreneurial behaviour; it is suggested that where the capital gains tax rate is lower than the personal income/wage tax rate, salaried employees will have an incentive to become entrepreneurs, because entrepreneurs make most of their gains through the capital growth of the equity they hold in their companies (meaning that becoming an entrepreneur in this circumstance will potentially be more tax effective than being a salaried employee): see European Commission, 'Effectiveness of Tax Incentives' (n 2) 63; Christofidis and Debande (n 21) 45. This effect has reportedly been seen in the USA and Europe: Leamon et al (n 23) 40.

[116] United Nations Economic Commission for Europe (n 12) 92; Carolin Bock and Martin Watzinger, 'The Capital Gains Tax: A Curse but also a Blessing for Venture Capital Investment' (2019) 57(4) *Journal of Small Business Management* 1200, 1203, 1226; Da Rin et al (n 59) 1704. *cf* James M Poterba, 'Venture Capital and Capital Gains Taxation' (1989) 3 *Tax Policy and the Economy* 47, 48, 55–56.

[117] Callagher et al (n 60) 383; Bock and Watzinger (n 116) 1204; European Commission, 'Effectiveness of Tax Incentives' (n 2) 58–59. Lowering exit taxes may therefore increase venture capitalists' incentives to monitor entrepreneurial behaviour, leading to improved success rates: Christian Keuschnigg, 'Taxation of a Venture Capitalist with a Portfolio of Firms' (2004) 56 *Oxford Economic Papers* 285, 303.

[118] Keuschnigg and Nielsen (n 115) 190–91.

or capital account.[119] If the gains are taxed on capital account, individual investors can generally reduce the gain they include in their assessable income by 50 per cent due to Australia's 'capital gains tax discount'.[120] No similar concession applies to investment gains taxed on income account, making the income tax regime less concessional in this regard. While the Australian government could easily resolve this uncertainty by providing deemed capital treatment for venture capital investments (which is how these investments are usually taxed), to date it has only done this in relation to investments made under its angel tax incentive, the early stage investor tax incentive.[121] Providing certainty as to how venture capital investments will be taxed in a jurisdiction is a simple step that governments can and should take to help improve the climate for venture capital investment.

A final taxation-related issue to consider is the way in which taxes and tax treatment apply supranationally. Even in places where cross-border investments are common, such as Europe, different jurisdictions may tax venture capital investments, investors and funds differently.[122] This can be a barrier to foreign investment. Furthermore, if there is a chance that investors may be taxed twice in a cross-border investment (once in the investor's jurisdiction and once in the investee's jurisdiction), they are likely to avoid making cross-border investments. Governments that take steps to harmonise the tax treatment of funds with their neighbours (including by implementing favourable double tax treaties) may therefore see an increase in certainty that could lead to increased local investment.

Creating a Positive Culture Around Venture Capital Investment

The supply of venture capital within a jurisdiction requires the presence of angel investors, venture capital funds and passive investors willing to commit capital to these funds. The incentives discussed in this book aim to attract and encourage investment in startups by these entities. However, incentives are not the only way to help boost the supply of venture capital within a jurisdiction. Governments can also work towards creating cultural change that will lead to a supportive environment in which venture capital can flourish.[123] Some of the ways they can do this include: proactively sharing and publicising venture capital success stories (which can increase reputational benefits for the industry);[124] implementing training programmes for venture capital investors (including institutional investors) and fund managers to upskill the industry and attract capital;[125] and creating angel and venture capital associations and matchmaking services to create links between investors and investees.[126] The Brazilian government's INOVAR programme,

[119] See Ollivierre (n 91) 34.
[120] See Barkoczy et al (n 16) 234–36; Income Tax Assessment Act 1997 (Australia), Division 115.
[121] See Income Tax Assessment Act 1997 (Australia), s 360–50.
[122] European Commission, 'Effectiveness of Tax Incentives' (n 2) 62.
[123] Avnimelech et al, 'Evolutionary Interpretation of Venture Capital Policy' (n 8) 110.
[124] Harding, 'Plugging the Knowledge Gap' (n 20) 75.
[125] It has been noted that very few countries have programmes such as these in place: Wilson (n 2) 25.
[126] Wilson (n 2) 25; Leamon et al (n 23) 58.

introduced in 2000, incorporated many of these elements. It was introduced in order to stimulate Brazil's small and underdeveloped venture capital market, and was developed in close consultation with stakeholders over almost two years.[127] INOVAR played an important educative and networking role.[128] It used INOVAR 'Funds Panels' to bring together potential fund investors and general partners, with the aim of attracting investment from pension funds (a strategy that finally paid off after several years).[129] It also used INOVAR 'Forums' to educate entrepreneurs and general partners (and, later, angels) about fundraising, pitching, business plans and the characteristics of the asset class.[130] Finally, INOVAR also trained local general partners and investors on best practices for investment and due diligence issues.[131] INOVAR 'Awards' were given to funds exhibiting instances of best practice, which helped reward and publicise good behaviour.[132] Although Brazil's venture capital industry still faces some challenging background conditions,[133] the educative and networking services provided through INOVAR are considered to have stimulated increased fundraising, generated awareness and forged connections between investors, startups and venture capitalists.[134]

Facilitating Exits

Evidence shows that a range of viable investment exit mechanisms is vital for a flourishing venture capital market[135] because, regardless of the demand for venture capital, venture capital investors will be reluctant to invest if they cannot identify a viable way to exit their investments in future (as this is how they make money for themselves and/or their investors).[136] Even aside from the creation of profits, exiting is important because it frees up both capital and investor expertise to be reinvested in new startups,[137] and also provides positive signalling effects to the market about the venture capital sector.[138]

[127] Leamon et al (n 23) 49–50; Ann Leamon and Josh Lerner, 'Creating a Venture Ecosystem in Brazil: FINEP's INOVAR Project' (Harvard Business School, 8 May 2012) Working Paper 12-099, 2, 6–7; Sophia Sciabica, 'Brazil's INOVAR: Building an Entrepreneurship Ecosystem' (*Americas Quarterly*, 5 August 2014) www.americasquarterly.org/content/brazils-inovar-building-entrepreneurship-ecosystem.

[128] Sciabica (n 127); Tuomi and De Castro Neto (n 64) 42.

[129] Leamon et al (n 23) 50; Leamon and Lerner (n 127) 9–11, 14.

[130] Leamon et al (n 23) 50; Leamon and Lerner (n 127) 12, 15.

[131] Leamon et al (n 23) 50; Leamon and Lerner (n 127) 12.

[132] Leamon et al (n 23) 51; Leamon and Lerner (n 127) 15–16.

[133] Sciabica (n 127).

[134] Leamon et al (n 23) 51; Leamon and Lerner (n 127) 12–14, 17; LAVCA, 'FINEP Celebrates 10 Years of INOVAR, Nearly R$5b Committed to VC in Brazil' (11 November 2010) lavca.org/2010/11/11/finep-celebrates-10-years-of-inovar-nearly-r5b-committed-to-vc-in-brazil/; Tuomi and De Castro Neto (n 64) 42.

[135] See United Nations Economic Commission for Europe (n 12) 19, 27; Bravo-Biosca (n 6) 4–5.

[136] European Commission, 'Effectiveness of Tax Incentives' (n 2) 50.

[137] ibid 20; Da Rin et al (n 59) 1705; Christofidis and Debande (n 21) 44; United Nations Economic Commission for Europe (n 12) 19; Jeng and Wells (n 42) 254; Colombo et al (n 63) 20.

[138] Wilson and Silva (n 11) 38.

One way that governments can facilitate venture capital exits is by setting up strong primary and secondary markets.[139] Although not all (or even most) venture capital investments are exited through initial public offerings (IPOs),[140] exiting through an IPO is often seen as a marker of success.[141] There is a large body of evidence suggesting that the 'presence of an active stock market open to issuance of new securities is essential for a well functioning early-stage equity financing industry'.[142] Furthermore, the presence of primary and secondary markets in a country can reportedly increase the scale of venture capital investment and business creation.[143] The USA's NASDAQ stock exchange, for instance, which was created in 1971 and has a focus on young tech companies, has been extremely successful and has been described as the 'underpinning' of the US venture capital industry (although listing on the NASDAQ is now far beyond the realm of what most early-stage startups could aspire to).[144] It was reported in 2007 that the NASDAQ had, since its creation, outpaced all other US markets in IPO listings; that it was the most successful secondary market in the OECD by far; and that at its height in 1999, it listed nearly 5000 firms and had a market capitalisation of over 50 per cent of GDP.[145] Second-tier markets in Sweden, the UK and, more recently, China have also reportedly played important roles in their respective countries' venture capital industries.[146] Sweden's second-tier 'over the counter' markets, established in the 1980s and 1990s, helped finance growth companies by facilitating exits, and the capitalisation of these markets relative to GDP at one point surpassed that of the USA.[147] Likewise, the UK's Alternative Investment Market, established in 1995, is the world's most active second-tier stock market, and was designed to attract young, high-growth companies by offering less stringent admission

[139] Wilson (n 2) 22.

[140] A study of 138 US funds that closed between 1990 and 2000 found that 19% of portfolio companies were exited via an IPO, 7% through a sale of listed equity and 23% through M&A transactions: Markus Laine and Sami Torstila, 'The Exit Rates of Liquidated Venture Capital Funds' (2005) 10(1) *The Journal of Entrepreneurial Finance* 53, 64. In contrast, a study of 1044 UK-based startups that received venture capital investment between 1999 and 2005 found that only 6% of them were exited through an IPO, with 33% exited via M&A transactions: Albert Banal-Estañol, Inés Macho-Stadler, Jonás Nieto-Postigo and David Pérez-Castrillo, 'Early Individual Stakeholders, First Venture Capital Investment, and Exit in the UK Startup Ecosystem' (2023) 80 *Journal of Corporate Finance* 102420, 8.

[141] See Barkoczy et al (n 16) 66, 68–69; European Commission, 'Effectiveness of Tax Incentives' (n 2) 38; Jeng and Wells (n 42) 254.

[142] United Nations Economic Commission for Europe (n 12) 34. See also European Commission, 'Effectiveness of Tax Incentives' (n 2) 50; Milosevic and Fendt (n 43) 662; Massimo G Colombo, Douglas J Cumming and Silvio Vismara, 'Governmental Venture Capital for Innovative Young Firms' (2016) 41(1) *Journal of Technology Transfer* 10, 21.

[143] United Nations Economic Commission for Europe (n 12) 35; Da Rin et al (n 59) 1704. See also Christofidis and Debande (n 21) 45.

[144] United Nations Economic Commission for Europe (n 12) 47. See also Wilson (n 2) 22.

[145] United Nations Economic Commission for Europe (n 12) 47.

[146] See Maria Pinelli and Uschi Schreiber, 'Funding the Future: Access to Finance for Entrepreneurs in the G20' (Ernst & Young, 2013) 30.

[147] United Nations Economic Commission for Europe (n 12) 70. Over the counter markets are decentralised markets and therefore operate somewhat different to exchanges.

requirements and lower costs.[148] China's ChiNext junior market, launched by the Shenzhen Stock Exchange in 2009, has reportedly helped develop a strong pipeline of venture capital activity in China by facilitating access to finance for local companies, reducing the number of local companies listing on overseas exchanges and attracting capital to China by increasing the chances of IPO exits (although the quality of these IPOs remains in question).[149]

Unfortunately, however, many government efforts to create secondary markets have faced significant challenges over the years.[150] Smaller economies are likely to struggle to successfully create their own local secondary markets because of a lack of critical mass, and small secondary markets can easily suffer from low liquidity and insufficient listings.[151] For example, New Zealand has made several unsuccessful attempts to establish alternative markets for early-stage investments over the past three decades. The first attempt, introduced in 2000, was replaced in 2003 by the NZX Alternative Market (NZAX), which offered lower listing fees and simpler listing requirements than the main exchange.[152] However, trading on the exchange was sluggish, due in part to a lack of risk appetite in the market.[153] The NZAX was replaced by the NXT Market in 2015.[154] However, it was announced in 2017 that the NXT and its listed companies would be amalgamated into the main NZX exchange, and would become subject to the general NZX listing rules.[155] The NXT was not seen to have met the needs of the targeted firms or to have developed as quickly or effectively as hoped.[156] In a similar story, Germany introduced the Geregelter Markt in 1987 specifically for venture capital-backed firms, but the market had 'virtually no effect on the development of a venture capital industry'.[157] It was not until 1997 that the German venture capital market truly began to take off, driven at least in part by changing attitudes to entrepreneurship and risk, but also supported by continuing government programmes and incentives (including a new junior market called Neuer Markt, which unfortunately turned out to be short-lived) and the emergence of the internet.[158]

[148] ibid 71.

[149] Pinelli and Schreiber (n 146) 30.

[150] See Avnimelech et al, 'Building Venture Capital Industries' (n 60) 16–17.

[151] See ibid 36; Wilson (n 2) 22; Pinelli and Schreiber (n 146) 30.

[152] Ellen Read, 'Celebrating the Alternative Stock Exchange' *New Zealand Herald* (17 November 2004) www.nzherald.co.nz/business/news/article.cfm?c_id=3&objectid=3610916.

[153] ibid; 'NZX's Alternative Market Trading Dwindles' *New Zealand Herald* (5 October 2010) www.nzherald.co.nz/business/news/article.cfm?c_id=3&objectid=10678299.

[154] Reuters, 'NZX Plans to Scrap Junior Markets NXT and NZAX' (27 June 2017) www.reuters.com/article/us-nzx-exchange/nzx-plans-to-scrap-junior-markets-nxt-and-nzax-idUSKBN19H2MR.

[155] ibid; NZX, 'Migrating to the Main Board and NZX Listing Rules from 1 January 2019' (2019) www.nzx.com/regulation/nzx-rules-guidance/nzx-listing-rules-review/nxt-and-ax-issuer-migration.

[156] Reuters (n 154); Chapman Tripp, 'Chapman Tripp Supports Consolidation of NZX Boards' (4 July 2017) www.mondaq.com/pressrelease/24878/chapman-tripp-supports-consolidation-of-nzx-boards.

[157] Ralf Becker and Thomas Hellmann, 'The Genesis of Venture Capital – Lessons from the German Experience' (CESifo Conference on Venture Capital, Entrepreneurship, and Public Policy, November 2002) CESifo Working Paper No 883, 36. See also Jeng and Wells (n 42) 284.

[158] Avnimelech et al, 'Evolutionary Interpretation of Venture Capital Policy' (n 8) 105; Gilson (n 11) 1102; Becker and Hellmann (n 157) 37. See also Arnd Plagge, *Public Policy for Venture Capital:*

2.5. Formulating Appropriate Policy Aims

Once governments have identified an addressable market need and considered the presence of supportive policies for venture capital investment, the next step in the introduction of a new incentive is to decide on what, exactly, the incentive will be aimed at achieving. It is essential for governments to articulate clear, rational policy aims to guide their venture capital incentives,[159] because an incentive's policy aims guide every aspect of its subsequent design and implementation, from form and targeting (discussed in chapters three and four) to implementation and evaluation (discussed in chapters five and six).[160]

An incentive's policy aims implicitly or explicitly indicate what the expected outputs and impacts of the policy are and therefore also define how the incentive's success will be evaluated.[161] As such, while governments may be tempted to commit to wide-ranging policy aims in order to attract support for their incentives,[162] they should ensure that an incentive's aims are not vague or unrealistically broad.[163] For example, one of Australia's early venture capital incentives, the Innovation Investment Fund programme, had objectives ranging from achievable to near-impossible. These included: developing fund managers with experience in the early-stage venture capital industry; encouraging the development of new companies commercialising R&D; establishing a 'revolving' or 'self-funding' scheme by reinvesting any profits made by the government through the programme; and developing a self-sustaining Australian early-stage venture capital market.[164] A 2010 review of the incentive found that it was realistically unlikely that it would ever succeed in achieving its policy objectives (particularly the last one), and a recommendation to change the incentive's objectives was put forward shortly before its termination in 2014.[165] The incentive was consequently branded a failure by some commentators,[166] despite the important contributions it made to the venture capital industry in Australia.[167] In a similar vein, Canada's

A Comparison of the United States and Germany (Deutscher Universitätsverlag, 2006) 47; Lars Abraham, *Venture Capital in Germany and the US: Differences and the Influence of Culture* (Freiberg TU Bergakademie, 2009) 40.

[159] See Stone (n 64) 195.

[160] United Nations Economic Commission for Europe (n 12) 41.

[161] Stone (n 64) 195.

[162] Murray et al (n 35) 9; ibid.

[163] See Luca de Angelis, 'Italy and Startups: Harnessing a Country of Innovators' (Master of Public Policy, Harvard University, 2017) 12; Munari and Toschi (n 7) 207.

[164] Innovation Investment Fund Program Round Three Guidelines No 1 of 2011 (Australia), cl 6.

[165] Gordon Murray, Marc Cowling and Weixi Lui, 'An Independent Econometric Analysis of the "Innovation Investment Fund" Programme (IIF) of the Australian Commonwealth Government: Findings and Implications' (Department of Innovation, Industry, Science and Research, 2010) 22, 29–30; Treasury and Department of Industry, Innovation, Science, Research and Tertiary Education, 'Review of Venture Capital and Entrepreneurial Skills' (2012) 23.

[166] Bronwen Clune, 'The Innovation Investment Fund Branded a Failure' (*SmartCompany*, 28 April 2014) www.smartcompany.com.au/startupsmart/advice/startupsmart-funding/the-industry-innovation-fund-branded-a-failure/.

[167] See Barkoczy et al (n 16) 351–55.

Venture Capital Catalyst Initiative has aims that include: translating innovation into economic growth; increasing the availability of late-stage venture capital to help high-potential companies grow; bolstering the growth and success of the Canadian life sciences sector; enhancing access to venture capital for underrepresented groups, such as women and racialised communities; enhancing and promoting diversity, equity and inclusion in Canadian venture capital; improving the sustainability of the Canadian venture capital ecosystem and spurring private sector investment by generating market-aligned financial returns; and attracting participation from private sector investors in venture capital funds.[168] This is quite the range of aims for one incentive, which is not problematic in and of itself, but may make it unlikely that the incentive will be considered a 'success' in all these areas (as with the Australian example above). Interestingly, the previous iteration of the programme aimed to achieve 'world-class financial returns', as opposed to the 'market-aligned financial returns' it now hopes for.[169] This is perhaps a more realistic expectation to strive towards.

At the heart of most incentives is the long-term aim of encouraging private sector venture capital and eventually reducing the need for government support[170] – in other words, creating a self-sustaining venture capital industry. Other common themes include addressing equity gaps, supporting innovative businesses and activities, increasing venture capital investment and attracting investors.[171] Policy aims can be stated informally, such as on government incentive websites, through media statements or in information statements, or formally, such as through a purpose statement in legislation or official programme guidelines. Unfortunately, in many cases, policy aims are not explicitly stated at all. This means that it can be surprisingly difficult to ascertain what, precisely, many incentives aim to do (other than broadly encouraging venture capital). For instance, it has been noted that China's Venture Capital Guiding Funds 'commonly have multiple aims that are never defined as clear, measurable objectives'.[172] This reinforces the argument made in the preceding paragraphs, which is that it is essential for governments to formulate and clearly express incentive policy aims. The incentives represented in Table 3 have, to a large extent, done this. The examples provide a useful illustration of the diversity of policy aims that incentives can have, and the different ways that these aims can be expressed. Each of the incentives represented in the table below is either current or has recently closed.

[168] Innovation, Science and Economic Development Canada, 'Venture Capital Catalyst Initiative: Performance Measurement Framework' (2022) 9.

[169] Innovation, Science and Economic Development Canada, 'Venture Capital Catalyst Initiative: Performance Measurement Framework' (April 2019) 5.

[170] OECD, 'Government Venture Capital for Technology-Based Firms' (n 26) 11.

[171] See ibid 12; United Nations Economic Commission for Europe (n 12) 41; Cumming, 'Government Policy' (n 26) 197–98; Brander et al, 'Government Sponsored Versus Private Venture Capital' (n 6) 18; Munari and Toschi (n 7) 206–07; Wilson (n 2) 17.

[172] Jun Li, 'Government-Backed Venture Capital as a Science, Technology and Innovation (STI) Policy Instrument: A Chinese Perspective' (2016) 7(1) *STI Policy Review* 66, 82.

Table 3 Examples of incentive policy aims

Incentive/programme	Policy aim
Australia's Venture Capital Limited Partnership programme	To stimulate Australia's venture capital sector by attracting foreign investors[a]
Belgium's Tax Shelter Start-Up – Petites Entreprises Débutantes	To mobilise private capital to provide risk capital in small, unlisted companies that are suffering from a funding gap[b]
Chile's Fondo Etapas Tempranas Tecnológicas (Early-Stage Tech Fund)	To promote the development of venture capital investment funds, focusing on Chilean companies that are in early stages of development and have potential for growth and innovation with sectors linked to technologies[c]
Denmark's Export and Investment Fund	To create the greatest possible social return by: promoting growth and renewal in Danish business life; promoting opportunities for Danish business to export and internationalise, participate in the global value chain and cultivate new markets; and contributing to a sustainable and green transition[d]
France's former Investissement Garantie scheme	To attract new investments to venture capital funds by improving their overall returns (thereby creating reputational benefits for fund managers – particularly new ones) and direct investments towards risky, early-stage companies[e]
Germany's INVEST Venture Capital Grant	To provide young, innovative companies with access to venture capital, encourage new investors to invest and encourage existing angel investors to invest more capital in young, innovative companies[f]
Hong Kong's Innovation and Technology Venture Fund	To attract more venture capital funds to co-invest in local innovation and technology startups in Hong Kong[g]
New Zealand Growth Capital Partners (NZGCP)	To help build a vibrant venture capital market in New Zealand by supporting early-stage tech companies and stimulating private investment[h]
Poland's former National Capital Fund (Krajowy Fundusz Kapitałowy)	To provide financial support to entrepreneurs through capital funds[i]
Singapore's former Section 13H incentive	To continue to encourage the inflow of local and foreign venture capital funds into Singapore and catalyse more financing options for locally based enterprises (especially startups and small- and medium-enterprises); to further boost the vibrancy of the startup ecosystem in Singapore[j]

(continued)

Table 3 ***(Continued)***

Incentive/programme	Policy aim
The UK's Enterprise Investment Scheme	To help smaller higher-risk trading companies raise finance by offering a range of tax reliefs to investors who purchase new shares in those companies[k]
The UK's Enterprise Capital Funds programme	To increase the supply of equity to UK growth companies that are affected by the equity gap and to lower the barriers to entry for fund managers looking to operate in the venture capital market[l]

[a] Department of Industry, Science, Energy and Resources, 'Venture Capital Limited Partnerships (VCLPs) Customer Information Guide' (February 2020) 6.

[b] 'Circulaire 2020/C/75 sur la Réduction Tax Shelter pour des Entreprises (Sociétés) qui Débutent' (*MinFin*, 2020) cl 1.1, eservices.minfin.fgov.be/myminfin-web/pages/public/fisconet/document/d28beac8-7b60-4a2d-9fed-bb026e269306?_ga=2.196813610.748963670.1591597718–924005305.1588834086 [tr author].

[c] Corfo, 'Fondo Etapas Tempranas Perfil Empresa Perfil Administradoras: Inversión y Financiamiento', www.corfo.cl/sites/cpp/convocatorias/fondo_etapas_tempranas_tecnologicas_perfil_administradoras.

[d] *Lov om Danmarks Eksport- og Investeringsfond* (Denmark) § 1 [tr author].

[e] Jasper Deuten, 'Venture Capital Investment Guarantee Programme by OSEO' (INNO Partnering Forum Peer Review Report, 2011) 8–9.

[f] Federal Ministry for Economic Affairs and Energy, 'INVEST – Venture Capital Grant' (December 2016) 2.

[g] Innovation and Technology Commission, 'Innovation and Technology Venture Fund (ITVF)' (1 November 2021) www.itf.gov.hk/l-eng/ITVF.asp.

[h] NZ Growth Capital Partners, 'About NZGCP' (2020) www.nzgcp.co.nz/about-us/.

[i] *Ustawa z dnia 4 marca 2005 r o Krajowym Funduszu Kapitałowym* (Poland) Art 1 [tr author].

[j] Ministry of Trade and Industry, 'Section 13H and the Fund Management Incentive', 1, www.mti.gov.sg/-/media/MTI/COS-2020/Microsite/Factsheets/ESG-Media-Fact-Sheet-on-Section-13H-and-Fund-Management-Incentive-at-MTI-COS.pdf?la=en&hash=EF5F623133EA06A08AC6BC8204CEAEA2CA376B09#:~:text=S13H%20provides%20tax%20exemption%20for,concessionary%20tax%20rate%20of%205%25. Note that this incentive is now the 'Section 13G' incentive.

[k] HM Revenue and Customs, 'Enterprise Investment Scheme: Overview of EIS Reliefs' (14 September 2020) www.gov.uk/hmrc-internal-manuals/venture-capital-schemes-manual/vcm10010.

[l] British Business Bank, 'The Enterprise Capital Fund Programme' (September 2019) www.british-business-bank.co.uk/wp-content/uploads/2019/09/ECF_Brochure_Version2_Sep2019_FINAL.pdf 1; British Business Bank, 'Enterprise Capital Funds: Guidance for Prospective Managers' (November 2014) 3.

While there is no one way to 'rank' the appropriateness of different policy aims, the more directly a policy aim is expressed in both substance and form, the easier it will be to judge whether that incentive has been successful or not. For instance, Australia's Venture Capital Limited Partnership programme aims to increase foreign investment, which is an easy outcome to measure. Likewise, Hong Kong's Innovation and Technology Venture Fund aims to attract more venture capital funds to co-invest in local startups – also an easy outcome to measure. In contrast, the UK's Enterprise Capital Funds programme aims to increase venture capital investment in local companies that are affected by the equity gap and to lower the barriers to entry for fund managers. This aim is problematic for two reasons. First, it is not necessarily straightforward to identify which companies are affected by the equity gap – it is not clear how these companies are defined. Second, it is difficult to measure the extent to which entry barriers for fund managers are lowered, because this is a subjective concept (unlike Hong Kong's aim of attracting more funds, which can be judged by the number of new funds entering the market). While this does not mean that the Enterprise Capital Funds programme has an inappropriate policy aim (especially because it is relatively clearly expressed compared with some other policy aims), it does mean that more consideration has to be given to how the programme's success will subsequently be measured at the evaluation stage. To the extent that governments can be direct and objective in the formulation of their policy aims, this is likely to make the task of evaluation easier. Unfortunately, few incentives are ever actually evaluated to gauge the extent to which they achieve their varied aims (as will be seen from the discussion in chapter six).

2.6. Assessing Net Benefits

A final thing for governments to consider before they introduce a new incentive is whether that incentive will, in achieving its policy aims, produce a 'net benefit'. Ideally, the incentive's intended positive impacts and outcomes (such as addressing market failure and increasing venture capital investment) should outweigh its expected costs, including the actual cost of providing the incentive, and any costs arising from unintended negative consequences such as distortions to the market.[173] Assessing the extent to which this is the case involves undertaking a 'cost–benefit' analysis (see further [6.3.5]).[174] The following table represents a simplified version of what this analysis looks like.

Table 4 Simplified example of a cost–benefit analysis

<table>
<tr><th>Potential benefits (put into monetary terms)</th><th>If ></th><th>Potential costs (put into monetary terms)</th></tr>
<tr><td rowspan="2">Addressing market failure
Increased funding of startups
Increased innovation
Spillover benefits such as job creation, increased productivity, etc</td><td>The incentive produces a net benefit</td><td rowspan="2">The cost of providing and administering the incentive
The cost of distortions that reduce the efficient functioning of the market (venture capital or otherwise)</td></tr>
<tr><td>If <
The incentive produces a net cost</td></tr>
</table>

[173] James (n 62) 3; Brown et al (n 68) 209; Stephen Barkoczy and Daniel Sandler, *Government Venture Capital Incentives: A Multi-Jurisdiction Comparative Analysis* (Australian Tax Research Foundation, 2007) 36; Stone (n 64) 187; Windholz (n 49) 38; Chen (n 60) 6; World Bank (n 74) 97.

[174] See Robert Litan, 'Regulation', *The Library of Economics and Liberty*, www.econlib.org/library/Enc/Regulation.html; Committee for Economic Development of the Conference Board, 'Regulation and the Economy: The Relationship and How to Improve It' (27 September 2017) www.ced.org/reports/regulation-and-the-economy.

There are several ways that the net benefits of an incentive can be reduced, even where the incentive is actually effective at encouraging increased venture capital investment and addressing market need. These include, primarily, market distortions and redundancy, both of which are concepts related to efficiency. Market distortions can take a number of forms. For instance, the presence of an incentive for venture capital investment in a jurisdiction might increase the amount of capital in the market, leading to increased competition for startup investments, leading, in turn, to prices for these investments rising and eventually becoming overvalued (see [2.3] above). This situation, known as the 'capitalisation effect', creates economic inefficiency and the potential for detrimental price corrections.[175] Investment displacement is another form of market distortion, and occurs when the introduction of an incentive for one sector diverts resources away from other sectors, potentially also reducing economic efficiency.[176] In this situation, a venture capital incentive could have its intended aim of changing investor behaviour[177] but still lead to an overall loss of efficiency. A distortion known as a 'race to the bottom' can occur when different countries compete to attract a finite pool of resources (such as venture capital investment). Countries may implement increasingly generous incentives (at increasing costs to their budgets) in order to attract foreign venture capital, for instance, and may end up spending a lot of money but producing little change in overall investment levels.[178]

Finally, a common form of distortion that is of particular concern in relation to investment incentives is the 'crowding out' of the private sector from the market as a consequence of incentives.[179] Crowding out is more likely to occur when governments introduce an oversupply of subsidised capital to a market.[180] For instance, the private sector was reportedly crowded out of the Hungarian venture capital market as a result of the introduction of the JEREMIE co-investment funds (see [2.3] above).[181] One of the best-known examples of an incentive that has triggered crowding out is Canada's Labour-Sponsored Venture Capital Corporation (LSVCC) Tax Credit. This incentive, which was introduced in 1984, provides tax benefits to investors who purchase shares in venture capital funds known as

[175] See Brooks (n 22) 41–42.

[176] See International Monetary Fund, Organisation for Economic Co-operation and Development, United Nations and World Bank, 'Options for Low Income Countries' Effective and Efficient Use of Tax Incentives for Investment' (Report to the G-20 Development Working Group, October 2015) 19; John Lester, 'Managing Tax Expenditures and Government Program Spending: Proposals for Reform' (2012) 35(5) *The School of Public Policy Publications* 1, 21; Chen (n 60) 9; European Commission, *Evaluating EU Activities: A Practical Guide for the Commission Service* (European Communities, 2004) 104.

[177] See Stanley Surrey, 'Tax Incentives as a Device for Implementing Government Policy: A Comparison with Direct Government Expenditures' (1970) 83(4) *Harvard Law Review* 705, 725.

[178] See International Monetary Fund et al (n 176) 29; James (n 62) 24; World Bank (n 74) 108.

[179] See Brander et al, 'Government Sponsored Versus Private Venture Capital' (n 6) 9–10.

[180] See OECD, 'Government Venture Capital for Technology-Based Firms' (n 26) 13, 15; O'Shea and Stevens (n 53) 29.

[181] See Becsky-Nagy (n 55) 31, 43, 45; Kállay and Jáki (n 51) 1143.

LSVCCs.[182] LSVCCs manage a large proportion of Canada's total venture capital, but have historically demonstrated below-market returns and high administrative costs.[183] Because the funds handle so much capital (which is subsidised for investors through the tax benefits), they can outbid private investors, with whom they compete for deal flow, in relation to investments.[184] Evaluations of the incentive have shown that this has driven up investment prices, lowered overall market returns and pushed private investors out of the market to such an extent that there has been a reduction in the overall amount of venture capital available in the country.[185] The LSVCC Tax Credit has therefore weakened, rather than stimulated, the Canadian venture capital industry.[186] Incentives that produce strong negative distortions, such as has occurred in the case of the LSVCC Tax Credit, are unlikely to be objectively justified because their negative effects outweigh the benefits they may produce.[187]

When the provision of incentives involves governments spending money to achieve an aim that would have occurred regardless, this is known as redundancy. An incentives redundancy 'ratio' is essentially a measure of its inefficiency, in that the more redundant an incentive is, the less efficient it is. Incentives can be redundant in a couple of different ways. First, they may provide an incentive for an investment that investors would have made anyway. In this case, the incentive has simply provided a 'windfall benefit' to the investors (a benefit they received without actually changing their behaviour). Profit-related incentives are often seen to provide windfalls to investors (see [3.3]). Windfall losses can also occur when incentives are removed (ie investors lose access to a benefit without changing their investment behaviour). Second, incentives can be redundant where they introduce new capital to a market but push out existing capital (crowding out).[188] In this situation, the incentives have failed to provide 'additionality', so are not efficient. Additionality refers to an increase in something (eg investment levels) above what it otherwise would have been, and is therefore a measure of effectiveness/efficiency (see [6.3.3]).

In undertaking the cost–benefit analysis for a new incentive, governments need to weigh up whether the efficiency losses caused by distortions and redundancy

[182] United Nations Economic Commission for Europe (n 12) 45; Cumming, 'Public Policy' (n 65) 82; European Commission, 'Effectiveness of Tax Incentives' (n 2) 85.

[183] United Nations Economic Commission for Europe (n 12) 45; Douglas J Cumming and Jeffrey G MacIntosh, 'Crowding Out Private Equity: Canadian Evidence' (2006) 21(5) *Journal of Business Venturing* 569, 571; Cumming, 'Public Policy' (n 65) 82–83.

[184] United Nations Economic Commission for Europe (n 12) 45; Cumming, 'Public Policy' (n 65) 84.

[185] Cumming and MacIntosh (n 183) 570–71. See also Josh Lerner, *Boulevard of Broken Dreams: Why Public Efforts to Boost Entrepreneurship and Venture Capital Have Failed – and What to Do About It* (Princeton University Press, 2009) 119–22.

[186] Cumming and MacIntosh (n 183) 571.

[187] Harding, 'Venture Capital' (n 18) 53. See, eg de Angelis (n 163) 49.

[188] See European Commission, 'Effectiveness of Tax Incentives' (n 2) 84; Brander et al, 'The Effects of Government-Sponsored Venture Capital' (n 7) 572–73; Bravo-Biosca (n 6) 9.

are outweighed by the benefits that may be produced by the incentive.[189] Because many unknowns exist before an incentive is introduced, even the most scrupulous consideration of benefits and costs is likely to be inaccurate in various ways and can sometimes be no better than a loose estimate.[190] Nevertheless, assessing an incentive's proposed net benefit is an important step in the decision-making process. Where an incentive is likely to produce a net benefit, its introduction will be considered justified and should be pursued; where it is likely to produce a net cost, it represents a waste of public capital and should not be introduced. In the latter situation, if the government still believes that an intervention is necessary, it should consider whether the market would be better served by an alternative policy option (such as another kind of supply-side incentive, or even one of the demand-side incentives mentioned above at [2.4.1]).[191] In some cases, the best solution may be for governments not to intervene at all. However, while not intervening in the market may be a valid policy choice,[192] it is not necessarily costless, as costs may arise in the form of 'forgone benefits' (ie benefits that would have arisen if the government had intervened).

2.7. Summary

This chapter has explored the process that governments should follow when thinking about introducing a new venture capital incentive in response to under-investment by the market. First, governments should identify an addressable market need through quantitative and qualitative research and engagement with stakeholders in order to find out what form of intervention would best serve the market. Second, governments should ensure that policies are in place to support (and not hinder) venture capital investment. Third, governments should formulate an appropriate policy aim (or aims) for their incentive, keeping in mind that these aims will be used to measure the success of the incentive in the future. To this end, policy aims that are direct and clearly expressed will be beneficial. Fourth, governments should assess the net benefit of their proposed incentive by considering whether the benefits it is intended to produce are likely to outweigh its projected costs. If the costs outweigh the benefits, the incentive is unlikely to be justified and

[189] See Hana Polackova Brixi, Christian MA Valenduc and Zhicheng Li Swift (eds), *Tax Expenditures – Shedding Light on Government Spending Through the Tax System: Lessons from Developed and Transition Economies* (World Bank, 2004) 23.

[190] Hans M van de Kar and Barbara L Wolfe (eds), *The Relevance of Public Finance for Policy-Making: Proceedings of the 41st Congress of the International Institute of Public Finance* (Wayne State University Press, 1987) 3, 52.

[191] See Committee for Economic Development of the Conference Board (n 174); Stone (n 64) 185, 187; Department of Prime Minister and Cabinet, *The Australian Government Guide to Regulation* (Australian Government, 2014) 26; Polackova Brixi et al (n 189) 23.

[192] Department of Prime Minister and Cabinet (n 192) 24.

should not be introduced. If the benefits outweigh the costs, on the other hand, the incentive may provide a valuable contribution to a country's innovation policy and should be pursued.

It should be recognised that creating successful government venture capital incentives is a long-term endeavour that is likely to involve trial and error, uncertainty and the need for adaptability.[193] The decision to implement an incentive is merely the first step in addressing venture capital market failure. The following chapters explore the next steps of incentive development, with chapter three looking at incentive form, chapter four looking at incentive targeting and chapter five looking at incentive implementation. These design considerations are crucial in helping incentives address and achieve their intended policy aims.

[193] Avnimelech et al, 'Evolutionary Interpretation of Venture Capital Policy' (n 8) 110.

3

Incentive Form

3.1. Introduction

The previous chapter highlighted the importance of governments formulating clear policy aims to direct their incentives. One of the reasons that this first step in incentive design is so important is that the form an incentive takes will depend, in large part, on what precisely governments want that incentive to achieve. Just as it is important for an incentive to be guided by an appropriate policy objective, the form that an incentive takes must also be appropriate to achieve the desired objective because an incentive's form is, at its most basic level, the mechanism used to deliver its benefits to recipients. As discussed in this chapter, venture capital incentives employ a wide variety of forms, some of which are delivered through the tax system (tax incentives), some of which are delivered through other financial mechanisms (direct incentives) and some rare few of which involve the provision of non-financial benefits (non-financial incentives). Each of these delivery methods has its own benefits and downsides, and meets different policy aims. Both tax and direct incentives generally operate by improving the risk–reward balance for investors in order to encourage investment,[1] for instance by lowering investment costs, increasing investors' profits or protecting against investment downside. Although the delivery methods of tax and direct incentives differ, their underlying purposes are broadly consistent, as both kinds of incentive 'provide financial assistance to achieve a particular objective'.[2]

This chapter groups incentives according to whether they provide 'investment-related' benefits, 'profit-related' benefits or 'loss-related' benefits (the latter two kinds of incentive can be collectively termed 'exit-related' incentives). These groups and the specific venture capital incentives they include are represented in

[1] See Colin M Mason, 'Public Policy Support for the Informal Venture Capital Market in Europe: A Critical Review' (2009) 27(5) *International Small Business Journal* 536, 541.

[2] Stanley S Surrey and Paul R McDaniel, *Tax Expenditures* (Harvard University Press, 1985) 99. See also Neil Brooks, 'The Logic, Policy and Politics of Tax Law' in Tim Edgar, Daniel Sandler and Arthur Cockfield (eds), *Materials on Canadian Income Tax*, 14th edn (Carswell, 2010) 1, 74; Stephen Barkoczy and Daniel Sandler, *Government Venture Capital Incentives: A Multi-Jurisdiction Comparative Analysis* (Australian Tax Research Foundation, 2007) 29; European Commission, 'Effectiveness of Tax Incentives for Venture Capital and Business Angels to Foster the Investment of SMEs and Start-ups: Final Report' (Taxation and Customs Union, 2017) Working Paper No 68, 12.

Table 5. Grouping incentives in this way allows comparisons to be made between incentives that differ in operation but are aimed at achieving the same or similar policy outcomes. Both investment-related and exit-related incentives aim to stimulate risk-taking by the private sector,[3] but they achieve this in different ways. Investment-related incentives provide benefits in relation to the initial investments made by investors, either by lowering the cost of making investments or by allowing the temporary use of government capital; both these mechanisms reduce investment risk and encourage increased investment.[4] Exit-related incentives, in contrast, provide benefits in relation to investment exits, generally by either increasing the investment upside (profit-related incentives) or decreasing the investment downside (loss-related incentives).

Table 5 Incentive forms

	Exit-related incentives	
Investment-related incentives [3.2]	**Profit-related incentives [3.3]**	**Loss-related incentives [3.4]**
• Tax credits (tax) [3.2.1] • Tax deductions (tax) [3.2.2] • Grants (direct) [3.2.3] • Equity co-investment (direct) [3.2.4] • Loans (direct) [3.2.5] • Visa incentives (non-financial) [3.2.6]	• Tax exemptions (tax) [3.3.1] • Reduced tax rates (tax) [3.3.2] • Grants (direct) [3.3.3] • Reinvestment relief (tax) [3.3.4] • Preferential returns (direct) [3.3.5]	• Tax-based loss relief (tax) [3.4.1] • Investment guarantees (direct) [3.4.2]

As represented in Table 5, this chapter discusses 13 different incentive forms that are used to encourage venture capital investment: six investment-related incentive forms (see [3.2]); five profit-related incentive forms (see [3.3]); and two loss-related incentive forms (see [3.4]). These incentive forms, which are set out in the table (along with their delivery methods), are explained in detail in the remainder of this chapter. The chapter concludes by making some overarching observations about when each kind of incentive form is likely to be particularly useful (see [3.5]), which is an area that has received little prior research attention.[5]

[3] Massimo Colombo, Fabio Bertoni and Terttu Luukkonen, 'Venture Capital: Policy Lessons from the VICO Project' (European Commission, 2011) 25.

[4] European Commission, 'Effectiveness of Tax Incentives' (n 2) 70. See also Alex Easson, *Tax Incentives for Foreign Direct Investment* (Kluwer Law International, 2004) 131–32.

[5] See European Commission, 'Effectiveness of Tax Incentives' (n 2) 70.

3.2. Investment-Related Incentives

Investment-related incentives enjoy popular use as venture capital incentives because they represent an effective way to increase the amount of additional venture capital invested in the market.[6] They present a strong incentive to investors because they provide them with an immediate reward for investing and arise regardless of whether the underlying investment is successful or not.[7] Incentives that lower upfront investment costs (such as tax credits, tax deductions and grants) 'make a greater number of investment projects more profitable at the margin', because investments can remain profitable for investors even if they produce lower returns, due to the reduced initial cost.[8] Likewise, investment-related incentives that allow the temporary use of government capital (such as equity co-investment and loans) help leverage private sector investment by allowing private investors to invest in a wider portfolio of companies and hopefully reap better investment rewards than they would otherwise be able to.[9] Both kinds of investment-related incentive therefore facilitate investments that may not otherwise have been made (ie they stimulate additionality).[10]

However, there are three main downsides to using investment-related incentives. First, investment-related incentives can represent a substantial cost for governments because they are paid in relation to initial investments, meaning both that they have an upfront cost and that they are available in relation to all eligible investments (unlike exit-related incentives, which have a delayed cost and only arise in relation to either profitable or loss-making investments, depending on their form).[11] This cost can be difficult for governments to justify, especially where the incentive has not resulted in obvious cases of investee success.[12]

Second, investment-related incentives may reduce positive investor behaviour. Because attaining an investment-related incentive does not require an investment to be successful (as is the case with profit-related incentives), investors may have little motivation to engage in the kind of beneficial value-adding behaviours that they would ordinarily undertake (such as careful due diligence and close ongoing

[6] Constantin Christofidis and Olivier Debande, 'Financing Innovative Firms Through Venture Capital' (European Investment Bank, February 2001) 45; Gilles Duruflé, 'Government Involvement in the Venture Capital Industry: International Comparisons' (CVCA, May 2010) 16.

[7] Barkoczy and Sandler (n 2) 33; Stephen Barkoczy and Peter Edmundson, 'Australasian and South East Asian Venture Capital Tax Expenditure Programs (2009) 37(1) *Intertax* 56, 57.

[8] International Monetary Fund, Organisation for Economic Co-operation and Development, United Nations and World Bank, 'Options for Low Income Countries' Effective and Efficient Use of Tax Incentives for Investment' (Report to the G-20 Development Working Group, October 2015) 20. See also European Commission, 'Effectiveness of Tax Incentives' (n 2) 62; Duanjie Chen, 'The Framework for Assessing Tax Incentives: A Cost–Benefit Analysis Approach' (Workshop on Tax Incentives and Base Protection, United Nations, 23–24 April 2015) 4.

[9] See Christofidis and Debande (n 6) 51; Mason (n 1) 549.

[10] International Monetary Fund et al (n 8) 20.

[11] Barkoczy and Sandler (n 2) 33–34.

[12] Barkoczy and Sandler (n 2) 34.

monitoring of investments) because they have already received the benefit of the incentive.[13] Furthermore, investment-related incentives may lead investors to invest without necessarily considering the long-term and high-risk nature of these investments.[14] In particular, investment-related incentives delivered through the tax system may encourage investors to make investments purely (or mainly) for tax minimisation purposes. This may, in turn, result in lower quality, disengaged investors and have negative effects on business success. This situation is exacerbated by the fact that investment-related incentives decrease the risk of investments, meaning that investors are somewhat protected from poor investment outcomes (because they paid less for their investments). In this way, investment-related incentives may worsen adverse selection and moral hazard risks, misalign the interests of investors, investees and governments, and create market distortions that impact the efficiency of incentives and reduce their economic benefits,[15] all of which are quite serious downsides.

Third, investment-related incentives have the potential to trigger an oversupply of capital where they result in the introduction of large amounts of new capital into the venture capital sector. As discussed in chapter two, oversupply can lead to overvalued investment, poor-quality investees and crowding out of the private sector (see [2.3]). Nevertheless, there will be instances where markets will benefit from an influx of capital – such as in the case of underdeveloped, nascent or severely capital-starved markets, including those in developing countries. In these cases, exit-related incentives will be unlikely to stimulate increased investment because of insufficient liquidity in the system, and investment-related incentives may be the only viable option to increase capital and counteract market imperfections.[16]

Interestingly, a report by the European Commission on the effectiveness of tax incentives for venture capital investment has recommended the use of tax-based investment-related incentives (primarily tax credits) as a matter of good practice.[17] While the report acknowledged the negative aspects of investment-related incentives discussed above, it emphasised the strong incentive effect provided by these incentives, as well as their propensity to encourage new investments (rather than providing windfalls to existing investors, as exit-related

[13] European Commission, 'Effectiveness of Tax Incentives' (n 2) 70. See also Christian Keuschnigg and Søren Bo Nielsen, 'Tax Policy, Venture Capital, and Entrepreneurship' (2002) 87(1) *Journal of Public Economics* 175, 190.

[14] OECD, 'Government Venture Capital for Technology-Based Firms' (1997) OCDE/GD(97)201, 14; Barkoczy and Sandler (n 2) 33. Milosevic and Fendt note that in France, investment-related tax relief is so generous that 'investors receive significant returns even if the fund does not generate any return': Miona Milosevic and Jacqueline Fendt, 'Venture Capital and Its French Exception: Explaining Performance through Human Capital, Policy and Institutional Failures' (2016) 43(5) *Science and Public Policy* 660, 664.

[15] See European Commission, 'Effectiveness of Tax Incentives' (n 2) 70.

[16] See Margaret O'Shea and Candice Stevens, 'Governments as Venture Capitalists' (1998) 213 *OECD Observer* 26.

[17] European Commission, 'Effectiveness of Tax Incentives' (n 2) 87.

incentives are sometimes seen to do – see below).[18] In a similar vein, research by Keuschnigg and Nielsen has indicated that while the provision of investment-related investment incentives does tend to discourage the provision of managerial advice and negatively impact the success of investees, these incentives also have a positive effect on the expansion of the entrepreneurial sector.[19] The use of investment incentives may therefore correlate to increased venture capital investment, but not necessarily the highest quality investment.

The discussion below elaborates on the six kinds of investment-related incentives that are used to encourage venture capital investment: tax credits (see [3.2.1]) and tax deductions (see [3.2.2]), both of which are tax incentives; grants (see [3.2.3]), equity co-investment (see [3.2.4]) and loans (see [3.2.5]), all of which are direct incentives; and visa incentives (see [3.2.6]), which are non-financial incentives. The discussion provides a number of examples of how these incentives have been used to encourage venture capital investment in different countries.

3.2.1. Tax Credits

Tax credits (also known as tax offsets) are the most common tax incentive form used to encourage venture capital investment,[20] with tax credit incentives available in countries including Australia (early-stage investor tax incentive and Early Stage Venture Capital Limited Partnership programme), Belgium (Tax Shelter Start-Up), Canada (Labour-Sponsored Venture Capital Corporation programme), Ireland (Employment and Investment Incentive), Italy (tax incentives for investment in innovative startups and small and medium enterprises (SMEs)), Malta (Seed Investment Scheme) and the UK (Enterprise Investment Scheme, Seed Enterprise Investment Scheme and Venture Capital Trusts scheme).[21] Tax credits are amounts that can be offset against an entity's tax liability, thereby reducing the tax they have to pay.[22] Tax credits are therefore only valuable to entities that have a tax liability against which to apply them, although taxpayers are often able to carry their credits forward to future income years (eg under Australia's early stage investor tax incentive, where unused credits can be carried forward indefinitely)[23] or back to past years (eg the UK's Seed Enterprise Investment Scheme, where credits can be carried back to the previous income year by treating the investment as having been acquired in that year).[24] In rare cases, tax credits may also

[18] ibid 175.
[19] Keuschnigg and Nielsen, 'Tax Policy, Venture Capital, and Entrepreneurship' (n 13) 193.
[20] EBAN and BOFIDI, 'Compendium of Fiscal Incentives: Tax Outlook in Europe – Business Angels Perspective' (2017) 82; European Commission, 'Effectiveness of Tax Incentives' (n 2) 103.
[21] European Commission, 'Effectiveness of Tax Incentives' (n 2) 98–103.
[22] ibid 69.
[23] Income Tax Assessment Act 1997 (Australia), s 63-10.
[24] Income Tax Act 2007 (UK), s 257AB.

be 'refundable' to a taxpayer if they cannot be fully utilised in the current income year.[25] An example of an incentive that provides a refundable tax credit is British Columbia's Venture Capital Program, which provides individual investors with a 30 per cent refundable tax credit, up to an annual maximum tax credit of CAD 120,000.[26] Where investors invest within the first 60 days of a calendar year, they can even elect to apply their credit to the previous year's tax liability.[27] Refundable tax credits are seen as one of the most equitable forms of tax incentive, as they provide the same benefit to all entities regardless of their tax liability. They effectively operate in the same way as a cash grant.[28] Because tax credits are applied after an entity's tax liability has been calculated, their value is not dependent on a taxpayer's marginal tax rate. In other words, taxpayers with different marginal rates of tax will obtain the same benefit from a tax credit (provided that they have a tax liability against which to apply it).[29] This makes them a more equitable form of incentive than tax deductions (see [3.2.2] below), which are tied to an entity's tax rate (meaning that deductions are more valuable for entities that have higher rates of tax). Furthermore, because tax credits are not tied to an entity's tax rate, the value of tax credits does not fluctuate if the underlying tax rate changes. This makes tax credits a more stable form of incentive than tax deductions.

Tax credits can be used to encourage direct investment in startups and/or passive investment in venture capital funds. For example, the UK's Venture Capital Trusts scheme, introduced in 1995, provides 'income tax relief' (tax credit) at the rate of 30 per cent of an investment, up to a maximum annual investment of GBP 200,000, to investors who purchase new shares in Venture Capital Trusts (which are venture capital funds structured as companies).[30] In contrast, the UK's Seed Enterprise Investment Scheme provides income tax relief at the rate of 50 per cent of an investment, up to a maximum annual investment of GBP 200,000, to individuals who invest directly in 'qualifying companies'.[31] The former incentive is therefore aimed at encouraging investment in (and by) venture capital funds, while the latter is aimed at encouraging investment by angels.

Tax credits are normatively seen as one of the most generous forms of tax relief, giving them a strong incentive effect, although the rates at which they are

[25] John R Hendon, Joseph R Bell, Brittany Blair and Don K Martin, 'State-Funded Angel Investor Tax Credits: Implementation and Perceived Effectiveness in a Sample of States Within the United States' (2012) 1(1) *Journal of Entrepreneurship and Public Policy* 50, 52.

[26] British Columbia, 'Tax Credits', www2.gov.bc.ca/gov/content/employment-business/investment-capital/venture-capital-programs/eligible-business-corporation/tax-credits#:~:text=Individual%20investors%20are%20entitled%20to,previous%20calendar%20year's%20tax%20return.

[27] ibid.

[28] Surrey and McDaniel (n 2) 109–10.

[29] Stanley S Surrey, *Pathways to Tax Reform: The Concept of Tax Expenditures* (Harvard University Press, 1973) 97–98.

[30] HM Revenue & Customs, 'Tax Relief for Investors Using Venture Capital Schemes' (7 July 2021) www.gov.uk/guidance/venture-capital-schemes-tax-relief-for-investors.

[31] Income Tax Act 2007 (UK), s 257AB.

granted impact their value.[32] Credit rates generally range from around 10 per cent (which is considered too low) to 100 per cent (which is extremely generous as it offsets the entire cost of an investment). It was reported in 2017 that more than 26 US states had tax credits for angel investors in place, offering rates of between 10 per cent and 50 per cent, with the majority offering rates of between 25 per cent and 40 per cent.[33] Governments set tax credit rates according to how strongly they want to encourage investment, and rates may be increased or decreased as necessary (see [5.2.3]).[34] However, like all forms of incentive, venture capital incentives structured as tax credits are rarely carefully evaluated, so it is difficult to know how well they work. Tax credits for angel investors used in the UK, France, Canada and the USA have reportedly been impactful in increasing angel investment in these countries,[35] although concerns remain around the impact of investment-related incentives, such as tax credits, on investment quality.[36] The UK's Venture Capital Trusts scheme, which has been evaluated more than once, reportedly created 27,000 jobs and generated GBP 1.4 billion of exports between 1995 and 2016.[37] However, the generous upfront tax relief provided through the scheme means that investments need only have 'average performance' in order for investors to end up with 'a very respectable result'.[38] This may mean that there is less focus than there would otherwise be on investment performance. It has been noted that there is a 'real danger that some people are being attracted to [Venture Capital Trusts] based solely on the tax benefits and past performance'.[39] The 30 per cent tax credit provided under British Columbia's Venture Capital Program has likewise been seen to help produce positive returns for some funds operating under the programme, which have otherwise produced relatively poor returns (all falling short of the returns made on investments in Toronto Stock Exchange and Toronto Stock Exchange Venture portfolios in the long term).[40] The 30 per cent tax credit is therefore seen to 'substantially increases the attractiveness of investing' in funds,[41] but the cost of this increase on investment quality is not necessarily clear.

Some tax credit incentives take measures to ensure that their investment-related mechanism does not impede investment quality. For example, Ireland's Employment and Investment Incentive, launched in 2011, provides income tax

[32] European Commission, 'Effectiveness of Tax Incentives' (n 2) 69.
[33] EBAN and BOFIDI (n 20) 82.
[34] See ibid.
[35] Duruflé (n 6) 16.
[36] EBAN and BOFIDI (n 20) 82.
[37] The Association of Investment Companies, 'Transforming Small Business: VCT Investment Review' (August 2017) 22, 24.
[38] Emma Agyemang, 'Are VCTs Worth the Risk for Higher Earners?' *Financial Times* (11 October 2019) www.ft.com/content/28c30bea-e9bc-11e9-85f4-d00e5018f061.
[39] ibid.
[40] Thomas Hellmann and Paul Schure, 'An Evaluation of the Venture Capital Program in British Columbia' (Ministry of Small Business, Technology and Economic Development, June 2010) 39.
[41] ibid.

relief of up to 40 per cent on investments made in qualifying companies either directly or through a 'designated investment fund'.[42] Until 2019, the incentive included a performance component to help control investment quality.[43] Income tax relief was initially granted in the year the investment was made at the fractional rate of 30/40. Four years after the investment was made, the investor could receive relief on the remaining 10/40 of the investment, but only provided that there was an increase in the number of the company's qualifying employees and the amount of wages paid to qualifying employees increased by the wages of at least one qualifying employee or there was an increase in the company's spend on qualifying R&D activities.[44] This performance incentive helped motivate investors to ensure that their investment was 'used to create positive macroeconomic outcomes',[45] and may therefore have gone some way towards mitigating the motivation and misalignment issues raised by the use of an investment-related incentive form. The reason for the removal of the performance component is unknown, but the removal is likely to have made the Employment and Investment Incentive more attractive to investors. For investments made after 2019, the Employment and Investment Incentive provides more relief for investments that are held for a longer time period (see [4.3.3]).[46] It seems that this concession was introduced as a replacement for the performance component, perhaps as a simpler way to ensure that investors remain committed over the long term.

3.2.2. Tax Deductions

Tax deductions (also known as tax allowances) are, like tax credits, investment-related incentives delivered through the tax system. However, they are both less popular and less appropriate than tax credits for use as venture capital incentives because of a range of equity, stability and accessibility issues (discussed below).

Tax deductions are amounts that an entity can deduct from their gross income when they calculate their taxable income.[47] Like tax credits, they can be used to encourage direct investment in startups and/or passive investment through venture capital funds. For example, Malaysia offers 100 per cent deductions to individuals and companies that invest in eligible venture companies (startups) or venture capital companies (venture capital funds).[48] Interestingly, deductions are

[42] Irish Tax and Customs, 'Relief for Investment in Corporate Trades' in *Tax and Duty Manual* (April 2023) Part 16-00-02, 5–6, www.revenue.ie/en/tax-professionals/tdm/income-tax-capital-gains-tax-corporation-tax/part-16/16-00-02.pdf.

[43] See European Commission, 'Effectiveness of Tax Incentives' (n 2) 194–95.

[44] Irish Tax and Customs (n 42) 7, 36.

[45] European Commission, 'Effectiveness of Tax Incentives' (n 2) 195.

[46] Irish Tax and Customs (n 42) 8–9.

[47] See Surrey (n 29) 93.

[48] Inland Revenue Board of Malaysia, *Venture Capital Tax Incentives* (9 May 2016) Public Ruling No 2/2016, 7; Income Tax (Deduction for Investment in a Venture Company or Venture Capital Company) Rules 2022 (Malaysia).

only granted under this incentive when the investor disposes of their shares – ie at the end of the investment period.[49] In a similar vein, China offers deductions at the rate of 70 per cent to venture capital enterprises (funds) and individuals that make new equity investments in 'start-up technological enterprises', with investors able to apply their deductions against their taxable income after a two-year holding period has passed.[50] Although Malaysia and China's deductions cannot be utilised by investors until some time after they make their investments (at the exit stage in the case of Malaysia), they are nevertheless investment-related incentives (albeit with some characteristics of profit-related incentives) because both deductions arise in relation to the initial investment amount. It is worth noting that tying the provision of the deductions to the eventual exit of investments may go some way to helping ensure investment quality because investors can only utilise their deductions if they make profitable exits.

Deduction rates vary between incentives, and sometimes even within incentives. For example, Turkey's Business Angels Law, introduced in 2012, provides deductions for angel investors who make eligible investments in qualifying 'venture companies' (startups).[51] Investors can deduct 75 per cent of the amount of the cost of their shares from their income and earnings in the relevant period, or 100 per cent if their investment is in a company that has been supported in the past five years by an eligible government R&D or innovation programme.[52] While deduction rates may even exceed 100 per cent in relation to some incentives (such as under Québec's former Business Investment Company tax incentive, which offered investors deductions of up to 150 per cent of their investments),[53] deductions are seen as being a less generous form of incentive than tax credits and exemptions (see [3.3.1] below).[54] Unlike a tax credit, the value of a deduction is tied to an entity's tax rate,[55] because deductions apply only to reduce the amount of income that is taxed, rather than reducing an entity's tax liability (like a tax credit does). This means that deductions are more valuable to entities that pay tax at higher rates, which makes deductions a less equitable form of incentive than tax credits, as discussed above.[56] Because the value of a deduction is tied to an entity's tax rate, the value of the deduction can also fluctuate if tax rates change, which can create instability and uncertainty for investors. Finally, deductions cannot be utilised by an entity unless they have a tax liability (or will have one in

[49] Inland Revenue Board of Malaysia (n 48) 8.

[50] PwC, 'People's Republic of China' (*Worldwide Tax Summaries*, 15 January 2024) taxsummaries.pwc.com/peoples-republic-of-china/corporate/tax-credits-and-incentives.

[51] Republic of Turkey, Ministry of Treasury and Finance, Regulation on Business Angels (2018), Art 4(2).

[52] ibid.

[53] Finances Québec, 'Adjustments to Certain Measures Announced in the Budget Speech of June 12, 2003' (18 July 2003) 2003–3 *Bulletin d'Information* 2.

[54] European Commission, 'Effectiveness of Tax Incentives' (n 2) 69.

[55] Barkoczy and Sandler (n 2) 32.

[56] See Surrey and McDaniel (n 2) 108.

future years, as excess deductions can often also be carried forward).[57] This makes deductions a less accessible form of incentive than many direct incentives, such as grants.

3.2.3. Grants

Although grants are often used as demand-side incentives for entrepreneurs, they are not commonly used as venture capital incentives. This is surprising given that they are stable, equitable and do not rely on an entity having a tax liability to be valuable. Grants are direct financial incentives that involve governments giving a sum of money to recipients to use for a specific purpose.[58] Because they are not delivered through the tax system, grants are likely to be more suitable than tax incentives for encouraging cross-border investment (because they avoid the difficulties of claiming and using tax credits in cross-border transactions).[59]

Grants are used as venture capital incentives in two main ways: as a way to encourage investment in startups; and as a way to subsidise the operating costs of venture capital funds (which may otherwise consume a significant proportion of a fund's capital, particularly if it is a small fund).[60] For example, Germany's INVEST incentive provides qualifying individual investors with a tax-free acquisition grant of 25 per cent of the amount of their investment in a qualifying company up to a maximum of €200,000 per company, and €400,000 in total per investor per year.[61] This is essentially the same as providing a 25 per cent refundable tax offset. The grant is intended to reduce the risk for investors when they invest in 'bold ideas' and improve the 'prospects for innovative firms to find a private investor'.[62] A report by the European Commission has noted that the INVEST incentive is the only incentive identified that structures upfront investment relief as a grant.[63] In contrast, Poland's National Capital Fund (KFK), a fund of funds that co-invested in private venture capital funds until 2017 and provided

[57] ibid 103.

[58] Stephen Barkoczy, Tamara Wilkinson, Ann L Monotti and Mark Davison, *Innovation and Venture Capital Law and Policy* (Federation Press, 2016) 375.

[59] European Commission, 'Effectiveness of Tax Incentives' (n 2) 194; Philipp Ständer, 'Public Policies to Promote Venture Capital: How to Get National and EU Measures in Sync' (Jacques Delors Institut, 31 August 2017) 16.

[60] Christofidis and Debande (n 6) 51; Gordon Murray, 'Early-stage Venture Capital Funds, Scale Economies and Public Support' (1999) 1(4) *Venture Capital* 351, 368–69.

[61] Federal Ministry for Economic Affairs and Climate Action, 'INVEST – Venture Capital Grant' (April 2023) 3. Eligible equity investment companies (venture capital funds) can also access the grant for investments up to €800,000 over three years (ibid 7).

[62] Federal Ministry of Economic Affairs and Energy, 'Financing for Start-ups, Company Growth, and Innovations', www.bmwi.de/Redaktion/EN/Dossier/financing-for-start-ups-company-growth-and-innovations.html.

[63] European Commission, 'Appendix 2: Good Practice Fiches' (June 2017) Final Report TAXUD/2015/DE/330, 5–6.

grants to its investee funds to help them cover the costs of preparing and monitoring investments (allowing them to invest more of their capital in startups).[64] This has historically been the more common way that grants have been used to encourage venture capital investment.

It is unclear why more governments do not use grants as venture capital incentives. It is possible that the issue comes down to perceived cost. The fact that governments have to pay grants out in cash, as opposed to accounting for the cost of tax credits as revenue that was not collected, means that grant expenditures are more 'visible' than tax expenditures, which may be a deterrent to governments (albeit a meaningless one to the extent that the costs of the different kinds of incentive are comparable – see further at [5.2.3]).[65] However, given the comparative advantages of grants and their lack of any serious downsides, their use as venture capital incentives is recommended.

3.2.4. Equity Co-investment

Equity co-investment involves governments and private sector investors pooling their funds to purchase shares in startup companies. Governments frequently use equity co-investment to develop nascent venture capital markets,[66] because by investing in partnership with the private sector, governments can address funding gaps, investor risk aversion, scarce capital and a lack of skilled investors. Government contributions are particularly valuable for smaller venture capital funds, as they help increase the size of small funds towards 'optimal operating scale', which gives funds greater capacity to cover fixed establishment and transaction costs.[67] However, while equity co-investment models are among the best designs for public support of early-stage venture capital funds,[68] a consensus as to how to best structure co-investment arrangements remains elusive.[69]

Co-investment differs from direct government investment in startups (which, as discussed at [1.3.1], does not constitute a venture capital incentive) because of the involvement of the private sector. The role that the private sector plays in

[64] Ustawa z dnia 4 marca 2005 r o Krajowym Funduszu Kapitałowym (Poland), Art 11. See also Francis J Skrobiszewski, 'Market Making: How Enterprise Funds Can Jump-Start Stagnant Economies (Innovations Case Narrative: Enterprise Funds)' (2012) 7(2) *Innovations: Technology, Governance, Globalization* 33, 55.

[65] Peter D Enrich, 'Saving the States from Themselves: Commerce Clause Constraints on State Tax Incentives for Business' (1996) 110(2) *Harvard Law Review* 337, 395–96; Surrey and McDaniel (n 2) 100, 104.

[66] Gordon Murray, Marc Cowling, Weixi Liu and Olga Kalinowska-Beszczynska, 'Government Co-Financed "Hybrid" Venture Capital Programmes: Generalizing Developed Economy Experience and its Relevance to Emerging Nations' (Kauffman International Research and Policy Roundtable, 11–12 March 2012) 2, 12.

[67] ibid 8; Christofidis and Debande (n 6) 51.

[68] OECD, 'Business Innovation Policies: Selected Country Comparisons' (2011) 18; Duruflé (n 6) 16.

[69] Josh Lerner, 'When Bureaucrats Meet Entrepreneurs: The Design of Effective "Public Venture Capital" Programmes' (2002) 112(477) *Economic Journal* F73, F73. See also Duruflé (n 6) 17.

co-investment varies according to the investment arrangement. Common arrangements include governments 'matching' the capital contributions of passive investors in a venture capital fund (indirect co-investment) or matching the capital contributions of angels when they invest in startups (direct co-investment). Government contributions will often be channelled through a specially formed 'fund of funds' (ie a fund that invests in other funds). New Zealand, as an example, provides both kinds of co-investment incentive. Through its NZD 300 million Elevate fund of funds, created in 2019, the government indirectly invests in privately managed venture capital funds on a matching basis alongside private sector co-investors.[70] Through its Aspire Fund, created in 2006, the government invests directly in small and medium-sized businesses alongside co-investors.[71]

Governments generally match private sector investment at a specific ratio in order to leverage private investment participation and help investors increase their investment capacity.[72] A commonly accepted view is that governments should not contribute more than 50 per cent of an investment, lest they skew the risk balance and reduce incentives for private investors to remain active and engaged.[73] However, ratios may need to be more generous in new markets, or where co-investments are required to be made in commercially unattractive investees. For example, under Australia's 2001 Pre-Seed Fund programme, the government committed capital to specially licensed funds at a ratio of 3:1. The licensed funds were required to invest in university-developed early-stage companies and projects that were far too nascent to otherwise attract private sector investment.[74] In order to reward investors who contributed to the licensed funds, the government forewent any share of profits returned by the funds.[75] However, the Pre-Seed Fund programme was financially unsuccessful and very little of the government's capital contributions were ever returned.[76] While the precise reasons for this remain unknown (but likely have a lot to do with the early stage of investments), it is possible that the generosity of the co-investment arrangement skewed the risk–reward balance and removed incentives for the private sector fund managers to make careful and well-managed investments. Interestingly, investments made through New Zealand's Aspire Fund, mentioned above, were previously made at a 1:1 ratio. However, recognising the detrimental effects of COVID-19 on the early-stage ecosystem, the government temporarily

[70] NZ Growth Capital Partners, 'Elevate NZ Venture Fund' (2020) www.nzgcp.co.nz/funding/elevate-venture-fund/.

[71] NZ Growth Capital Partners, 'Aspire NZ Seed Fund' (2020) www.nzgcp.co.nz/funding/aspire-seed-fund/.

[72] O'Shea and Stevens (n 16); United Nations Economic Commission for Europe, *Financing Innovative Development: Comparative Review of the Experiences of UNECE Countries in Early Stage Financing* (United Nations Publications, 2007) 84.

[73] See Karen Wilson, 'Policy Lessons from Financing Young Innovative Firms' (OECD, June 2015) OECD Science, Technology and Industry Policy Papers No 24, 14.

[74] Pre-Seed Fund Program Guidelines No 1 of 2003 (Australia), cl 49.

[75] ibid cl 148.

[76] See Barkoczy et al (n 58) 357.

relaxed this ratio to a maximum of 2:1 (public capital to private capital) in order to 'help establish investments'.[77] The ratio has now reverted to 1:1.[78]

In both direct and indirect co-investments, the private sector is generally in charge of finding, making and monitoring investments.[79] This means that governments do not bear the responsibility of sourcing deal flow, conducting due diligence, negotiating deals, identifying strategic investors, managing investments or identifying and negotiating exits – they are merely passive investors.[80] This is appropriate, as governments generally do not possess these skills. Governments do, however, still need to monitor the private sector co-investors to ensure that they comply with the incentive's rules and investment criteria (see [5.4]).[81] An example of how the co-investment process can be managed in practice can be seen in the European Angels Fund, which is a co-investment incentive for business angels and other non-institutional investors. The European Angels Fund enters 'long-term contractual relationships' with angels in the form of 'co-investment framework agreements'.[82] Under these agreements, the European Angels Fund grants a predefined amount to each angel (typically ranging from EUR 250,000 to EUR 5 million) on an upfront basis.[83] The angels have the freedom to make investment decisions, and have the responsibility for managing investments (which are made on a *pari passu* basis, with investment costs shared pro rata).[84] This is a light-touch approach that avoids the European Angels Fund having to commit to co-investments on a deal-by-deal basis.

Placing private sector investors (whether angels or fund managers) in charge of investment decisions gives these entities the opportunity to increase their management skills, scale up and develop a track record that may help them raise subsequent capital. This is particularly valuable for fund managers; it has been noted that participating in co-investment is one of the few ways that new fund managers can enter the venture capital industry.[85] Co-investment incentives can therefore diversify and deepen the market by bringing in new fund managers

[77] Aspire NZ Seed Fund, 'Aspire NZ Seed Fund Is Set to Increase Support for Tech Start-Ups' (25 June 2020) www.nzgcp.co.nz/assets/Media/Aspire-release_250620.pdf.

[78] NZ Growth Capital Partners, 'Aspire NZ Seed Fund – FAQs' (November 2022) www.nzgcp.co.nz/assets/Uploads/NZGCP-Aspire-FAQ_Nov22.pdf.

[79] Murray et al (n 66) 2.

[80] Cromwell Schmisseur, 'Information and Observations on State Venture Capital Programs: Report for the US Department of the Treasury and Interested Parties in the State Small Business Credit Initiative (SSBCI)' (February 2013) 21; Lisa Callagher, Peter Smith and Saskia Ruscoe, 'Government Roles in Venture Capital Development: A Review of Current Literature' (2015) 4(3) *Journal of Entrepreneurship and Public Policy* 367, 381.

[81] See O'Shea and Stevens (n 16) 29.

[82] European Investment Fund, 'European Angels Fund' (December 2016) 3, www.eif.org/news_centre/publications/eaf/eaf_en.pdf. As of 2024, the initiative is operational in Germany, Spain, Austria, the Netherlands, Ireland, Denmark, Finland, Italy and Flanders (Belgium), and also has a pan-European arm that supports cross-border investments within the European Union: EIF, 'European Angels Fund (EAF)' (2021) www.eif.org/what_we_do/equity/eaf/index.htm.

[83] European Investment Fund (n 82) 3.

[84] ibid.

[85] Murray et al (n 66) 6.

to the sector.[86] Examples of co-investment incentives that have played important roles in venture capital market development include Israel's 1993 Yozma programme and Australia's 1997 Innovation Investment Fund programme, both of which are credited with helping kick start their respective countries' venture capital industries by upskilling new generations of venture capital fund managers.[87] Likewise, a survey of angels operating under the European Angels Fund, published in 2019, reported that Fund commitments helped the respondents increase their investments (in terms of amounts and number of investees), that respondents became more active in follow-on investment rounds, and that a majority of the respondents did not decrease their personal contribution to investments as a result of Fund commitments (indicating additionality and minimal crowding out).[88] While the European Angels Fund reportedly helps angels improve and professionalise their investment activities, only a minority of respondents hired more employees for their investment activities or assumed a more active role in their portfolio companies.[89] However, approximately one-third of the respondents reported that the European Angels Fund has helped them prepare to manage a venture capital fund in the future,[90] indicating that the Fund may be having an impact on increasing the skills and experience of its recipients.

An attractive feature of co-investment is that as passive investors, governments are usually entitled to a share of investment returns and may even be able to recoup some of their investment costs in this way (although they may also share losses). This differs from many other investment-related incentives such as tax credits, deductions and grants, where governments do not receive any direct returns and can only hope to indirectly recoup their costs through the tax imposed on successful investments and/or investee companies. It is suggested that allowing the government to share in returns is beneficial for two reasons: first, it helps align the interests of the government with the interests of investors and fund managers; and second, it can provide capital for the continued provision of incentives.[91] In fact, some co-investment incentives may be intended to be 'revolving' or 'evergreen' incentives, whereby any returns received by the government are reinvested back into the incentive, allowing it to continue without an ongoing financial commitment by the government (see further [5.2.3]). Australia's Innovation Investment Fund co-investment programme, mentioned at [2.5], was intended to

[86] See Duruflé (n 6) 16.

[87] Gil Avnimelech, Martin Kenney and Morris Teubal, 'Building Venture Capital Industries: Understanding the US and Israeli Experiences' (Berkeley Roundtable on the International Economy, March 2004) Working Paper No 160, 33–35; Douglas Cumming and Sofia Johan, 'Venture's Economic Impact in Australia' (2016) 41(1) *Journal of Technology Transfer* 25, 56; Barkoczy et al (n 58) 355.

[88] Helmut Kraemer-Eis, Antonia Botsari, Julien Brault and Frank Lang, 'EIF Business Angels Survey 2019: Market Sentiment, Public Intervention and EIF's Value Added' (EIF, 2019) EIF Working Paper No 2019/60, 33.

[89] ibid. The survey indicated that around one-third of angels surveyed hire employees to undertake their investment activities: at 13.

[90] ibid.

[91] Cromwell Schmisseur (n 80) 6.

be a revolving programme, and the New Zealand Aspire fund was intended to be an evergreen fund when it was introduced, although the necessity of this is to be re-evaluated in the future.[92]

While many co-investment incentives allow the government to share in investment returns on a pro rata basis, governments sometimes agree to give preferential returns to the private sector co-investors (eg as was mentioned above in relation to Australia's Pre-Seed Fund programme). They may be more likely to do this when co-investment is targeted at particularly risky (and therefore unattractive) startups, such as those at a very early stage of development.[93] Preferential returns are discussed in detail as a separate form of incentive at [3.3.5]. Co-investment arrangements may also include other benefits for the private sector, such as a stipulation that government capital be drawn down prior to private capital (thereby shortening the duration of the private investors' investment and increasing their internal rate of return).[94] All of these 'extra' benefits are intended to make co-investments more attractive to the private sector, thereby increasing their incentive effect.

Co-investment funds are a 'major part' of the global early-stage venture capital market.[95] Between 1999 and 2012, the UK alone implemented at least six separate co-investment incentives,[96] while Australia has likewise implemented seven incentives at the federal level since 1997 (with a number of additional state initiatives also recently introduced).[97] However, although hundreds of millions of dollars have reportedly been invested in co-investment incentives internationally,[98] their success (or otherwise) generally receives little attention. Wilson and Silva reported in 2013 that of 21 OECD countries that had direct co-investment incentives and/or fund-of-funds incentives in place, fewer than 11 countries indicated that they had evaluated their incentives.[99] This makes it difficult to come to a conclusion on which of the various kinds of co-investment arrangements work well and which do not; more research in this area would undoubtedly be beneficial, but this depends in large part on the robust evaluation of the success of existing and past co-investment incentives.

[92] NZ Growth Capital Partners (n 78) 6.

[93] See Murray et al (n 66) 3–4; Mason (n 1) 538.

[94] Murray et al (n 66) 5.

[95] Murray et al (n 66) 8.

[96] These include the UK High Technology Fund (1999), the Regional Venture Capital Funds (2002), the Early Growth Funds (2002), the Aspire Fund (2008), the UK Innovation Investment Fund (2009) and the Angel CoFund (2011).

[97] The federal incentives are the Innovation Investment Fund programme (1997), the Pre-Seed Fund programme (2001), the Renewable Energy Equity Fund programme (2000), the Innovation Investment Follow on Fund (2009), the Renewable Energy Venture Capital Fund (2011), the Biomedical Translation Fund (2016) and the CSIRO Innovation Fund (2016).

[98] See Maria Pinelli and Uschi Schreiber, 'Funding the Future: Access to Finance for Entrepreneurs in the G20' (Ernst & Young, 2013) 24.

[99] Karen E Wilson and Filipe Silva, 'Policies for Seed and Early Stage Finance: Findings from the 2012 OECD Financing Questionnaire' (OECD, October 2013) OECD Science, Technology and Industry Policy Papers No 9, 27.

3.2.5. Loans

Loans are not considered to be a particularly popular or appropriate way to incentivise venture capital investment, and the use of loans to finance venture capital funds is seen to have had 'limited success'.[100] Loan incentives operate in a similar way to equity co-investment incentives (and can be described as debt co-investments) as they provide investors with government capital to use on a temporary basis to augment their own investment capital or subsidise their investment costs. Some incentives provide loans for both purposes – for example, Innovation Norway's venture capital loan programme, introduced in 2006, made loans to nationwide and regional venture capital funds for investment purposes, and also partly covered the administrative costs of the regional funds over 15 years.[101]

However, loans have a number of downsides that equity co-investment incentives do not share. For instance, loans can involve interest repayments that investors may struggle to meet until they begin making returns. This pressure could lead investors to make later-stage and/or less risky investments that have the capacity to quickly generate cash – a problem which reportedly arose in relation to the USA's Small Business Investment Companies programme.[102] In order to make loan incentives more attractive to the private sector, governments may defer loan repayments and impose low (or no) interest rates. For example, under the Norwegian government's venture capital loan programme, mentioned above, loans made to nationwide and regional venture capital funds did not need to be repaid for 15 years, and interest was not payable on an ongoing basis, but instead accumulated and was added to the principal annually (ie the interest was deferred).[103] Interest was imposed at the Norwegian Inter-bank Offered Rate plus 2 per cent for nationwide funds, and at the Inter-bank Offered Rate plus 0.5 per cent for regional funds.[104] The difference in interest rates reflected the greater investment difficulties faced by funds operating regionally (see [4.4.3]).

The conditions of a loan may also include repayment requirements that prejudice private sector investors' returns where investments produce little or no profit. For instance, loan amounts may have to be repaid to the government before any returns are distributed to the private sector, leaving private investors with little or no profit.[105] However, loans can actually benefit the private sector

[100] Timothy Bates, 'Government as Venture Capital Catalyst: Pitfalls and Promising Approaches' (2002) 16(1) *Economic Development Quarterly* 49, 49. See also Royal Norwegian Ministry of Trade and Industry, 'National Seed Capital Scheme' (December 2012) 5, investinor.no/wp-content/uploads/nhd-notifisering-nye-landsdekkende-sakornfond_jan-2013.pdf.

[101] OECD, *OECD Territorial Reviews: Norway* (OECD, 2007) 129; EFTA Surveillance Authority, 'Two New Norwegian Seed Capital Schemes Approved by the EFTA Surveillance Authority' (15 July 2005) www.eftasurv.int/newsroom/updates/two-new-norwegian-seed-capital-schemes-approved-efta-surveillance-authority.

[102] United Nations Economic Commission for Europe (n 72) 84.

[103] Innovasjon Norge, 'Annual Accounts Innovasjon Norge 2018' (29 March 2019).

[104] EFTA Surveillance Authority (n 101).

[105] This was a criticism levelled against Norway's 2006 venture capital fund loan incentive: see Royal Norwegian Ministry of Trade and Industry (n 100) 6.

when investments are profitable. Because the government's return, in a loan scenario, is capped at the loan amount plus interest, the private sector will be able to capture the majority of the investment upside in the case of a successful investment.[106] This is good for the private investors but not for the government, which will not share in the upside of the investment, even though in making the loan it has exposed itself to a similar risk as an equity investor.[107] To address this imbalance, governments may also sometimes claim a share of profits made on successful investments; the UK's Enterprise Capital Funds programme, for instance, provides for the government to take a share of investment profits (albeit a smaller share than the private sector – see further [3.3.5]). While this helps increase the return paid to the government (because it potentially receives interest, loan repayments and a share of profits), it leaves few positive incentives for the private sector investors. Essentially, loans that operate in this way penalise investors for bad investment decisions but also reduce their rewards for making good decisions.

As with equity co-investment incentives, loan incentives can also be used to encourage both angel investment and investment through funds. For example, the previous iteration of Denmark's business angel matching loan initiative, which ran from 2019 until it was replaced in 2023, provided that where an angel invested in an eligible young entrepreneurial enterprise at the pre-seed or seed stage, the investment could be matched on a 1:1 basis by a loan from the state investment fund, Vaekstfonden.[108] Vaekstfonden did not vet investments on a deal-by-deal basis; instead, angels (and/or angel syndicates) who were approved by Vaekstfonden received an individual line of credit that they could use to make investments.[109] The loan capital contributed to each investee company could range from DKK 250,000 to DKK 3,750,000, and loans matured in six years[110] (which was not a particularly long time frame given the average length of early-stage investments). It is not clear how the current iteration of Denmark's matching loan initiative operates, as the Export and Investment fund of Denmark (which replaced Vaekstfonden) does not currently make this information publicly available. In contrast to Denmark's angel loan incentive, Chile's CORFO agency provides lines of credit to early-stage venture capital funds under its Fondo Etapas Tempranas Tecnológicas (Early Stage Tech Fund), which has been in operation since 2012.[111] CORFO approves lines of credit of between UF 50,000 and UF 300,000, with the maximum amount not being more than 300 per cent of a fund's paid and committed capital (ie a maximum debt to capital ratio of 3:1).[112]

[106] See Murray et al (n 66) 5.
[107] Ann Leamon, Maria Susana Garcia-Robles and Josh Lerner, 'Best Practices in Creating a Venture Capital Ecosystem' (Multilateral Investment Fund of Inter-American Development Bank, December 2012) 43.
[108] Vaekstfonden, 'Investor Framework Agreement' (22 September 2022) cl 4.3.
[109] ibid cl 2.2.
[110] ibid cl 4.2.
[111] OECD, *Financing SMEs and Entrepreneurs 2015: An OECD Scoreboard* (OECD, 2015) 127.
[112] CORFO, 'What Is the Early Stage Tech Fund', wapp4.corfo.cl/fondoetapastempranas/investors.html.

Credit lines have a maximum term of 12 years, and credit accrues interest at the 10-year Banco Central de Chile rate plus five per cent. As can be seen from these examples, governments generally contribute loan capital, like equity co-investment capital, in proportion to the capital contributed by the private sector. For instance, Denmark contributed to investments under its business angel matching loan incentive on a 1:1 basis, Chile contributes loan capital to venture capital funds on up to a 3:1 basis and Norway, under its 2006 incentive discussed above, contributed loans to venture capital funds on a 1:1 basis for nationwide funds and on a 7:3 basis for regional funds.[113]

Whether they are provided to angels or venture capital funds (or both), loan incentives can help private sectors investors make additional (ie larger in size and/or quantity) investments and diversify their portfolios, thereby mitigating investment risk. They can also play a role in helping industry development (like equity co-investment incentives). For example, it has been recognised that the USA's Small Business Investment Companies programme (which was ostensibly the world's first government venture capital incentive) contributed to creating a large and valuable economic legacy as a major national source of industry recruitment and training.[114] The Small Business Investment Companies programme used loans and debentures as a way to provide government funding to specially licensed venture capital funds (SBICs) – SBICs could borrow from the US Small Business Administration at a ratio of 3:1 for every dollar of equity capital they raised.[115] The programme helped fund companies such as AOL, Apple, Intel and Sun Microsystems,[116] and is credited with shaping the modern US venture capital industry.[117] Nevertheless, the programme's shortcomings have also been recognised. Lerner notes that the SBICs often operated outside the scope of the programme and that there was widespread flouting of incentive rules (see further [5.4.2]).[118] Even though this has more to do with the poor administration of the Small Business Investment Companies programme than the use of a loan incentive form, loans are not recommended as venture capital incentive because their need to pay back capital and interest to governments creates perverse incentives for investors. Equity co-investment incentives provide many of the same market development benefits as loans, but do not share the same downsides, so are more appropriate (although it is recognised that they are less likely to lead to a guaranteed return for governments).

[113] Vaekstfonden (n 108) cl 5.2; CORFO (n 112); OECD, *OECD Territorial Reviews: Norway* (n 101) 129; EFTA Surveillance Authority (n 101).

[114] Murray et al (n 66) 11.

[115] James M Poterba, 'Venture Capital and Capital Gains Taxation' (1989) 3 *Tax Policy and the Economy* 47, 52.

[116] Congressional Research Service, 'SBA Small Business Investment Company Program' (3 September 2021) Report R41456, 22.

[117] See Federal Research Division, Library of Congress, 'Measuring the Role of the SBIC Program in Financing Small Businesses' (July 2017) 41.

[118] Josh Lerner, *Boulevard of Broken Dreams: Why Public Efforts to Boost Entrepreneurship and Venture Capital Have Failed – and What to Do About It* (Princeton University Press, 2009) 38.

3.2.6. Visa Incentives

Visa incentives are investment-related incentives that provide non-financial benefits to investors (in contrast to all the incentives discussed above). Visa incentives offer immigration visas to individuals who make eligible venture capital investments, in order to bring capital into a country. While many countries around the world offer so-called 'golden visas' to wealthy investors who make significant local investments, not all of these countries require investments to be made in venture capital. Examples of countries with venture capital-specific investment visa pathways include Australia, Canada and Portugal.[119]

Visa incentives include different conditions depending on their country of issue, but generally require venture capital investments to be held for the duration of the visa. For example, Australia's Business Innovation and Investment (Provisional) Visa (subclass 188) Significant Investor stream allows investors to stay in Australia for five years and apply for permanent residency if eligible when they make a 'complying significant investment' of at least AUD 5 million and hold it for the life of the visa.[120] At least AUD 1 million of this amount must be invested in venture capital and growth private equity funds that invest in startups and small private companies.[121] If venture capital investments are realised during the visa term, the returns must be reinvested.[122] Canada's Immigrant Investor Venture Capital Program, on the other hand, requires investors to have a legally acquired net worth of at least CAD 10 million, and to invest CAD 2 million in the Immigrant Investor Venture Capital Fund for a period of 15 years with no guarantee of a return.[123] Provided all language and education conditions are met, investors will then receive permanent residency.[124] Canada's visa incentive therefore has a longer investment period, but a lesser investment amount and an easier road to permanent residency, than Australia's incentive.

Visa incentives are relevant only to a small subcategory of investors (those who are wealthy, have a desire to immigrate and have no more convenient immigration pathways). In addition, given that investors obtaining visas in this way do not necessarily have any experience or familiarity with venture capital investment, they may not necessarily be the highest quality investors, or have a genuine interest in venture capital (although this may also be the case for investors using other

[119] Australian Government, Department of Home Affairs, 'Business Innovation and Investment (Provisional) Visa (subclass 188) Significant Investor Stream' (1 October 2021) immi.homeaffairs.gov.au/visas/getting-a-visa/visa-listing/business-innovation-and-investment-188/significant-investor-stream#; 'Immigrant Investor Venture Capital (IIVC) Program' (*Immigration.ca*, 26 October 2018) www.immigration.ca/immigrant-investor-venture-capital-iivc-program; 'Portugal Golden Visa – Invest in Portugal and Get the Residence Permit' (*Schengen Visa Info*, 2021) www.schengenvisainfo.com/eu-golden-visas/portugal-golden-visa/.

[120] 'Business Innovation and Investment (Provisional) Visa' (n 119).

[121] ibid.

[122] Migration Regulations 1994 (Australia), reg 5.19C.

[123] 'Immigrant Investor Venture Capital (IIVC) Program' (n 119).

[124] ibid.

kinds of investment-related incentives such as tax credits and deductions). The use of visa incentives therefore does not appear to have any specific major downsides provided that these incentives are implemented strictly and incentive rules are complied with (although there is always a risk that the investors allowed into a country may be of bad character).

3.3. Profit-Related Incentives

Profit-related incentives, which are a form of exit-related incentive, differ significantly from the investment-related incentives covered in the preceding discussion. Profit-related incentives operate by increasing the profits that can be made from successful venture capital investments, helping investors to 'reap the benefits' of their investment efforts.[125] Importantly, profit-related incentives have a range of positive benefits associated with their use that investment-related incentives do not share. First, because they do not provide an upfront benefit, profit-related incentives do not tend to be used for tax minimisation purposes,[126] and may be more likely than investment-related incentives to attract committed, patient investors. Second, unlike investment-related incentives, profit-related incentives are highly unlikely to trigger an oversupply of capital, because they generally do not result in a large influx of new capital entering the market.[127] Third, because profit-related incentives are contingent on the attainment of profits, investors who hope to benefit from these incentives may actually increase the time and effort they put into selecting their investee companies and proving value-adding services.[128] This, in turn, could also increase the quality of investments.[129] This stands in direct contrast to investment-related incentives, which, as noted at [3.2] above, are seen to have potentially negative effects on both investment quality and investor behaviour. Fourth, while they do not involve any direct returns to government (like, for instance, co-investments do), profit-related incentives do involve indirect returns. Because profit-related incentives only arise in relation to 'winners', or successful investments, governments stand to indirectly recoup some of the cost of providing the incentives 'to the extent that they collect tax from the successful investee companies' and their employees.[130] This may make profit-related incentives easier to justify, from a governmental perspective, than

[125] Marco Da Rin, Giovanna Nicodano and Alessandro Sembenelli, 'Public Policy and the Creation of Active Venture Capital Markets' (2006) 90(8) *Journal of Public Economics* 1699, 1701.

[126] See, eg Josh Lerner and Brian Watson, 'The Public Venture Capital Challenge: The Australian Case' (2008) 10(1) *Venture Capital* 1, 17.

[127] See John Armour and Douglas Cumming, 'The Legislative Road to Silicon Valley' (2006) 58(4) *Oxford Economic Papers* 596, 631.

[128] European Commission, 'Effectiveness of Tax Incentives' (n 2) 71. See also Keuschnigg and Nielsen, 'Tax Policy, Venture Capital, and Entrepreneurship' (n 13) 192; Da Rin et al (n 125) 1701; Lerner and Watson (126) 17.

[129] European Commission, 'Effectiveness of Tax Incentives' (n 2) 71.

[130] Barkoczy and Sandler (n 2) 34. See also OECD, 'Government Venture Capital' (n 14) 14.

investment-related incentives, which do not necessarily result in successful investees. Investors who benefit from profit-related incentives effectively 'earn' their benefit by contributing to investee success.[131]

A downside to profit-related incentives, however, is that they tend to provide less of an incentive effect to investors than investment-related incentives.[132] This is because venture capital investments take a long time to mature (meaning that investors have to wait a long time for profit-related incentive benefits to arise) and have a high risk of failure (which means that in many cases, incentive benefits will not arise at all). Profit-related incentives may therefore be less effective at increasing venture capital investment than investment-related incentives. Profit-related incentives may also act as windfalls to investors who would have invested anyway, meaning that they may provide less additionality and higher redundancy than investment-related incentives.[133] It has been suggested that profit-related incentives forgo government revenue in order to make investments that would already have been profitable (and hence would probably have been undertaken without the incentive) even more attractive.[134] The question of whether to use investment-related incentives or profit-related incentives may therefore come down to a determination of whether governments would prefer to increase investment quantity or investment quality in their jurisdictions.[135] If they want to increase investment quantity, investment-related incentives are likely to be more effective; if they want to increase quality, profit-related incentives are likely to be more effective.

The following discussion sets out the profit-related incentives that are commonly used to encourage venture capital investment. These include: tax exemptions (see [3.3.1]), tax reductions (see [3.3.2]) and reinvestment relief (see [3.3.4]), all of which are tax incentives; and exit grants (see [3.3.3]) and preferential returns (see [3.3.5]), both of which are direct incentives.

3.3.1. Tax Exemptions

Tax exemptions (also known as tax exclusions) are the second most popular form of tax-based venture capital incentive after tax credits.[136] They are also considered the most normatively generous form of incentive, 'as they serve to remove the entire tax base from the scope of tax, either permanently or temporarily' (ie they exclude an amount from gross income).[137] Like tax credits, tax exemptions are not

[131] Barkoczy and Sandler (n 2) 34.
[132] International Monetary Fund et al (n 8) 20; European Commission, 'Effectiveness of Tax Incentives' (n 2) 87.
[133] See Barkoczy and Sandler (n 2) 36.
[134] International Monetary Fund et al (n 8) 20.
[135] See European Commission, 'Effectiveness of Tax Incentives' (n 2) 205.
[136] ibid 16.
[137] ibid 69.

tied to an entity's tax rate, although they are generally more valuable to entities that pay tax at higher rates. Also like tax credits and deductions, tax exemptions are only valuable to entities that pay tax. It has been noted that venture capital profits in Malaysia are 'basically not taxed' thanks to the generous incentives provided by the Malaysian government, discussed below. However, the majority of venture capital groups in Malaysia have not benefited from these incentives because they have not been profitable, and 'profits are necessary for taxes'.[138] This is one of the downsides to using tax-based incentives in industries that have nascent and/or unprofitable venture capital industries – their benefit is often lost, and therefore provides little inducement to increase investment.

Tax exemptions can be used as venture capital incentives in three main ways: to exempt the profits made on venture capital investment from exit taxes (such as capital gains tax); to exempt any income received in relation to venture capital investments held by an investor (ie interest and dividends) from tax;[139] and to exempt the income and gains received by venture capital fund managers (particularly carried interest payments) from tax.[140] The first two kinds of exemptions may benefit direct or passive investors (or both), while the third kind benefits fund managers.

Exemptions from exit taxes provide an attractive benefit to investors (see [2.4.2]) and are likely to encourage venture capital investment by allowing investors to retain a higher proportion of returns after tax.[141] Exit tax exemptions may apply to either the investments investors or funds make in startup companies or the investments that passive investors make in venture capital funds, and they take various forms because of the different kinds of exit taxes imposed. For example, Australia's Venture Capital Limited Partnership and Early Stage Venture Capital Limited Partnership programmes provide eligible investors with both income and capital gains tax exemptions in relation to the profits made on the disposal of eligible investments, because these profits may be taxed on either income or capital account depending on their character (see [2.4.2]).[142] Other incentives that provide exit tax exemptions include: the UK's Venture Capital Trusts scheme, which provides capital gains tax exemptions when investors sell their shares in a Venture Capital Trust,[143] and Seed Enterprise Investment Scheme, which provides capital gains tax exemptions when investors sell their qualifying shares in a startup company that have been held for at least three years;[144] Australia's Pooled

[138] Syed Adil Hussain, 'Growing the Malaysian Venture Capital and Private Equity Industry' (2010) 1(4) *Islam and Civilisational Renewal* 629, 643.
[139] European Commission, 'Effectiveness of Tax Incentives' (n 2) 56, 70–71; Barkoczy and Sandler (n 2) 34.
[140] Barkoczy and Edmundson (n 7) 73.
[141] See Carolin Bock and Martin Watzinger, 'The Capital Gains Tax: A Curse but also a Blessing for Venture Capital Investment' (2019) 57(4) *Journal of Small Business Management* 1200, 1200–01.
[142] Income Tax Assessment Act 1997 (Australia), ss 51-54, 118-407.
[143] HM Revenue & Customs, 'Tax Relief for Investors Using Venture Capital Schemes' (n 30).
[144] Taxation of Chargeable Gains Act 1992 (UK), s 150E.

Development Fund programme, which provides income and capital gains tax exemptions when investors sell their shares in a Pooled Development Fund;[145] and Luxembourg's société d'investissement en capital à risque (SICAR) regime, which provides income tax exemptions when SICARs – collective investment vehicles – sell shares in their at-risk investments (eg investments in startup companies).[146]

Just as exit tax exemptions can apply either to exiting an investment in a startup (eg the UK's Seed Enterprise Investment Scheme and Luxembourg's SICAR regime) or exiting an investment in a venture capital fund (eg Australia's Pooled Development Fund programme and the UK's Venture Capital Trusts scheme), exemptions on the income received from held investments can apply to either investments in a startup, or investments in a venture capital fund. For example, Australia's Early Stage Venture Capital Limited Partnership and Pooled Development Fund programmes provide income tax exemptions for the dividends paid by startups that flow through to the investors in a registered limited partnership[147] and the dividends paid by a Pooled Development Fund to investors,[148] respectively, while the UK's Venture Capital Trusts scheme provides income tax exemptions on dividends paid by a Venture Capital Trust to investors[149] and Luxembourg's SICAR regime exempts both the income derived by SICARs on the securities they hold and the income they may receive from the capital they hold before making risk capital investments (but only for a period of 12 months).[150]

Incentives that exempt the dividends paid by startups from tax are less likely to stimulate increased investment than exit tax exemptions, because startups rarely distribute dividends, generally choosing instead to reinvest their profits into growing their businesses.[151] This means that these kinds of exemptions are unlikely to be a major motivator for investors.[152] It is also suggested that dividend

[145] Income Tax Assessment Act 1936 (Australia), ss 124ZM, 124ZN, 128B, 128D; Income Tax Assessment Act 1997 (Australia), s 118-13. See also Barkoczy et al (n 58) 295–98.

[146] Law of 15 June 2004 Relating to the Investment Company in Risk Capital ('SICAR') (Luxembourg), Art 34(2).

[147] Income Tax Assessment Act 1997 (Australia), s 51-52.

[148] Income Tax Assessment Act 1936 (Australia), s 124ZM. The PDF programme has a unique incentive that applies to dividends paid by a PDF to a 'relevant venture capital investor' (broadly, certain kinds of widely held superannuation funds). This incentive operates by allowing PDFs to generate special notional 'venture capital franking credits' in relation to the tax paid on their investments in eligible SMEs. The funds can allocate these venture capital franking credits to the dividends paid to their relevant investors, which gives rise to corresponding tax credits. Relevant venture capital investors are exempt from tax in relation to the dividends paid to them by a PDF, but still receive the tax credit in relation to the franked part of the dividend. The practical outcome of this incentive is that relevant venture capital investors recoup the underlying tax paid by the PDF on its investments. The incentive was introduced specifically to encourage superannuation funds to invest in PDFs: Income Tax Assessment Act 1997 (Australia), ss 210-1, 210-40, 210-100, 210-105, 210-120, 210-160–75. See also Barkoczy et al (n 58) 296–97.

[149] HM Revenue & Customs, 'Tax Relief for Investors Using Venture Capital Schemes' (n 30).

[150] Law of 15 June 2004 Relating to the Investment Company in Risk Capital ('SICAR') (Luxembourg), Art 34(2).

[151] European Commission, 'Effectiveness of Tax Incentives' (n 2) 71.

[152] ibid.

exemptions may put detrimental pressure on startups to make distributions that they would not otherwise make, because they should (initially at least) be focused on growing their businesses.[153] These kinds of exemptions are therefore not particularly appropriate (note that there are no comparable issues with providing exemptions on the dividends paid by venture capital funds to their investors as a way of distributing their profits).

Finally, exemptions on the income and gains received by venture capital fund managers are unlikely to strongly encourage increased venture capital investment because they do not benefit investors. They can also be seen as providing windfalls by making generally well-remunerated fund managers even better off. Nevertheless, it is suggested that exemptions for fund managers may help attract new participants to the venture capital industry,[154] and may help encourage active and engaged investment behaviour by raising after-tax profits for fund managers. Malaysia is one of few countries that offer tax exemptions for fund managers on their gains; it provides that the management and performance fees paid to fund managers of Venture Capital Companies (funds) are tax exempt (as well as conditionally exempting the gains made by the Venture Capital Companies themselves).[155] As will be seen below, it is more common for incentives to reduce the tax paid by fund managers on their income and gains, rather than exempting it completely.

3.3.2. Reduced Tax Rates

Reduced tax rates operate in materially the same way as tax exemptions but are less generous (because they merely reduce the tax payable, rather than exempting amounts completely). As with most tax incentives, reduced tax rates are only valuable to entities that pay tax. Like tax exemptions, reduced tax rates may apply in relation to the profits made on venture capital investments and/or to the management fees and carried interest payments received by fund managers.[156] In some cases, tax rates may be reduced to zero (which essentially gives the same result as a tax exemption) or to very low nominal amounts. For instance, Slovenia reportedly imposes a zero per cent tax rate in relation to venture capital funds and investments in high-risk companies (provided they meet certain requirements),[157]

[153] ibid.

[154] Barkoczy and Edmundson (n 7) 66, 73.

[155] Income Tax (Exemption) (No 3) Order 2022 (Malaysia), cl 2; Income Tax (Exemption) (No 2) Order 2022 (Malaysia), cl 3. Venture Capital Companies can also claim a deduction for investing in venture companies, but not if they have applied for and been certified for the tax exemption; the incentives are mutually exclusive: Income Tax (Deduction for Investment in a Venture Company or Venture Capital Company) Rules 2022 (Malaysia), cl 3.

[156] Reduced tax rates may also theoretically be imposed in relation to the dividends paid by startups, but no incentives have been identified that operate in this way.

[157] See Deloitte, 'International Tax: Slovenia Highlights 2020' (January 2020) 1; EBAN and BOFIDI (n 20) 60.

while Ghana reportedly imposes a one per cent tax rate in relation to profits arising from investments in venture capital companies for the first 10 years after investment.[158]

As with tax exemptions, reducing the tax rates on the gains made on venture capital investments has the capacity to encourage investors to actively nurture their investees (presumably because investors are able to capture a greater return of any eventual profits).[159] This monitoring helps raise investees' success rates.[160] However, the incentive effect of reduced tax rates is likely to be less significant than that of exemptions (because they are a less generous form of incentive). Australia's Pooled Development Fund programme is an example of an incentive that uses reduced tax rates to encourage venture capital investment. Pooled Development Funds, which are specially registered corporate venture capital funds, pay tax at the rate of 15 per cent in relation to their 'SME investments' and at the rate of 25 per cent in relation to their 'unregulated investments' (generally investments in banks or the short-term money market).[161] Both rates are concessional when compared with Australia's general corporate tax rate of 30 per cent.[162]

Reduced tax rates for the gains received by venture capital fund managers are more common than exemptions for these gains, probably because of the windfall issue discussed above (reduced tax rates, being less generous than exemptions, provide less of a windfall). For example, Ireland grants reduced tax rates to venture capital fund managers in respect of their carried interest payments. Broadly speaking, carried interest payments are treated as capital gains, and taxed at the rate of 15 per cent (for payments received by individuals or partnerships) or 12.5 per cent (for payments received by companies).[163] In contrast, the general capital gains tax rate in Ireland is 33 per cent.[164] Australia also treats carried interest payments received by the managers of Venture Capital Limited Partnerships and Early Stage Venture Capital Limited Partnerships as capital gains, which allows them to benefit from a 50 per cent discount on capital gains (provided the partnership agreement was entered into at least 12 months prior and the fund

[158] PwC, 'Ghana: Corporate – Tax Credits and Incentives' (*Worldwide Tax Summaries*, 29 July 2021) taxsummaries.pwc.com/ghana/corporate/tax-credits-and-incentives#:~:text=Interest%20and%20dividends%20from%20investment,after%20the%20year%20of%20disposal.

[159] See Christian Keuschnigg and Søren Bo Nielsen, 'Taxation and Venture Capital Backed Entrepreneurship' (2004) 11(4) *International Tax and Public Finance* 369, 386–87.

[160] See ibid.

[161] Pooled Development Funds Act 1992 (Australia), ss 4(1), 23(1), 24(21); Pooled Development Funds Regulations 1992 (Australia), reg 3(1); Income Tax Rates Act 1986 (Australia), s 23(5). See also Barkoczy et al (n 58) 292–97; Stephen Barkoczy, Don Maloney and Wayne Ngo, *Pooled Development Funds Handbook* (Australian Tax Practice, 2001) 73. New PDFs have not been able to be registered since 21 June 2007: Pooled Development Funds Act 1992 (Australia), s 4(1).

[162] Income Tax Rates Act 1986 (Australia), s 23(2).

[163] Taxes Consolidation Act 1997 (Ireland), s 541C.

[164] See Irish Tax and Customs, 'Capital Gains Tax (CGT) on the Sale, Gift or Exchange of an Asset' (24 June 2021) www.revenue.ie/en/gains-gifts-and-inheritance/transfering-an-asset/how-to-calculate-cgt.aspx.

manager is not a company).[165] Singapore, in contrast, provides that management fees and performance bonuses (carried interest payments) derived by an approved Singaporean fund manager from managing authorised investments of an approved Section 13G venture company (a fund) are taxed at the concessional rate of five per cent, rather than at the general corporate income tax rate of 17 per cent.[166] This concessional tax rate applies for 10 years initially, with extensions of five years allowed.

An issue that relates to both reduced tax rates and tax exemptions is that governments implementing these kinds of incentives need to ensure compliance with the OECD's Base Erosion and Profit Sharing (BEPS) Project Action 5, which is designed to cut down on the use of harmful tax practices globally.[167] An incentive that provides preferential tax treatment may be assessed against five key criteria as 'harmful' if it:

1. imposes no or low effective tax rates on income from geographically mobile financial and other service activities;
2. is ring-fenced from the domestic economy;
3. lacks transparency;
4. has no effective exchange of information; and
5. fails to require substantial activities.[168]

Although the first part of the first criterion – no or low effective tax rates – is a feature of tax exemptions and reduced tax rates, most tax-based venture capital investment incentives should not be at risk of meeting the rest of these criteria, primarily because incentives of this kind are rarely ring-fenced from the domestic economy (although see the discussion of Australia's Venture Capital Limited Partnership scheme at [4.2.2.6]). Many venture capital incentives also impose specific location requirements for investments and fund management activities (meaning they do not apply to geographically mobile activities), and require substantial activities (ie active investment and/or fund management). Nevertheless, governments should be cognisant of these minimum standards when designing their tax incentives in order to ensure that they are not considered harmful.

3.3.3. Exit Grants

Exit grants are amounts given to increase the profits received by venture capital investors – essentially like tax exemptions or reductions that are delivered directly.

[165] Income Tax Assessment Act 1997 (Australia), ss 61-760, 115-25(2A), 115-100.
[166] Income Tax Act 1947 (Singapore), ss 13G, 43V.
[167] See OECD, 'Harmful Tax Practices – 2018 Progress Report on Preferential Regimes: Inclusive Framework On BEPS: Action 5' (OECD/G20 Base Erosion and Profit Shifting Project, 2019) 9.
[168] ibid 13.

Exits grants are rare; the best example is Germany's INVEST incentive (which, it will be recalled from [3.2.3] above, also provides investment-related grants). Since 2017, the INVEST incentive has provided angel investors with exit-related tax relief in the form of a tax-free grant. When investors dispose of their qualifying investments, they receive a grant of an amount equivalent to 25 per cent of the capital gains from the sale, provided that their capital gains amount to at least EUR 2000.[169] From 2023, the exit grant is limited to the amount of the investment grant (ie 25 per cent of the initial investment amount);[170] previously, the exit grant was limited to 80 per cent of the initial investment amount.[171] It is unclear why the amount of the exit grant has been lowered, but potential reasons may be to control the cost of the incentive or to adjust the risk–reward balance for investors. It is also unclear why Germany has chosen to structure their profit-related incentive as a grant, rather than as a partial or complete exit tax exemption. One reason may be that, unlike tax-based forms of relief, grants can be utilised by all entities, regardless of whether they pay tax or not, and are therefore more equitable.

3.3.4. Reinvestment Relief

Reinvestment relief (sometimes referred to as a tax deferral or tax rollover) reduces or delays the payment of a tax liability to a future date when gains or profits are put into a new investment within a certain time period.[172] Because reinvestment relief applies in relation to the profits made on exit, but also involves the 'rolling over' of a gain into a new investment, it actually combines elements of both investment-related and exit-related incentives.[173] Reinvestment relief has the capacity to encourage increased investment because it is an attractive way for investors to minimise the tax incurred on their prior investments.[174] When the gains made on previous venture capital investments are rolled over into new venture capital investments, this serial investment can help support the deepening of venture capital markets.[175] On the other hand, the investment-related element of reinvestment relief comes with the same downside as other forms of investment-related tax incentives – it may attract disinterested investors who are merely investing to gain a tax benefit (thereby reducing investor, and possibly investment, quality).

[169] Federal Ministry for Economic Affairs and Climate Action (n 61) 4.
[170] ibid 3.
[171] Bundesministerium für Wirtschaft und Klimaschutz, 'INVEST – Zuschuss für Wagniskapital', www.bmwk.de/Redaktion/DE/Dossier/invest.html.
[172] European Commission, 'Effectiveness of Tax Incentives' (n 2) 97.
[173] ibid 70.
[174] Stephen Barkoczy and Tamara Wilkinson, *Incentivising Angels: A Comparative Framework of Tax Incentives for Start-Up Investors* (Springer, 2019) 95.
[175] European Commission, 'Effectiveness of Tax Incentives' (n 2) 70.

Another downside to reinvestment relief is that it has the capacity to be quite complicated (which can reduce its incentive effect). For example, France's reinvestment regime allows an entrepreneur who transfers the shares in their company to a holding company to defer the payment of capital gains tax on that transfer. The capital gain will be exempt from tax if, when the holding company sells the shares, it reinvests at least 60 per cent of the sale price into either an eligible company or certain kinds of venture capital funds within two years (otherwise the deferral will be lost and the gain will be taxed).[176] Among the funds that can receive investments under this regime are venture capital funds known as fonds commun de placement à risques.[177] While France's reinvestment regime incentivises reinvestment by experienced entrepreneurs, 'which helps to create a powerful network of business angels',[178] the scheme contains a lot of timing and other conditions that may not be easy for an entrepreneur or investor to meet or understand.

The USA also previously used reinvestment relief to encourage investment in its Specialized Small Business Investment Companies (privately owned companies that provided patient capital to minority-owned small businesses).[179] Individuals or companies who made gains on the sale of publicly traded securities could defer the taxation of these gains provided they reinvested the sale amount in an Specialized Small Business Investment Company within 60 days.[180] Tax was deferred until the interest in the Specialized Small Business Investment Company was eventually sold (when the deferral amount was generally taken into account in calculating the basis of the shares).[181] However, investments in Specialized Small Business Investment Companies were illiquid and risky, and most investors would have had to spend a great deal of time (likely far more than 60 days) learning about the industry and particular Specialized Small Business Investment Companies, and identifying exit strategies, before investing.[182] Furthermore, limits on the amount that could be deferred meant that the rollover provided little extra incentive to investors.[183]

Interestingly, some incentives allow gains to be reinvested/deferred retrospectively (as opposed to the basic situation, where an exit is made and a new investment is subsequently made). For example, under the UK's Seed Enterprise Investment Scheme, individuals can invest gains they have made on the disposal of an asset in shares that qualify for Seed Enterprise Investment Scheme income tax relief. When they do this, 50 per cent of the invested amount (up to GBP 200,000)

[176] Code Général des Impôts (France), Art 150-0B.
[177] ibid.
[178] Ständer (n 59) 14.
[179] Bates, 'Government as Venture Capital Catalyst' (n 100) 51, 57.
[180] John W McKinley and Craig J Wright, 'Rollover of Gains on Certain Property Dispositions' [1 July 2014] *Journal of Accountancy*, www.journalofaccountancy.com/issues/2014/jul/201410000.html.
[181] ibid.
[182] Bates, 'Government as Venture Capital Catalyst' (n 100) 57.
[183] ibid 57–58.

is exempt from capital gains tax in relation to the original disposal.[184] However, the original disposal need not actually have been made prior to the investment in qualifying shares. An investor can claim reinvestment relief on an ex post facto basis, provided that they still hold the Seed Enterprise Investment Scheme-qualifying shares.[185] The European Commission has suggested the ability to retrospectively roll investments over may 'act as an incentive to increase the rate and frequency of reinvestment',[186] although it may also constitute a windfall for investors who receive a tax benefit for making an investment they would have made in any case.

3.3.5. Preferential Returns

Preferential returns (also sometimes known as asymmetric returns or upside leverage) are a kind of profit-related incentive that only apply in relation to co-investment incentives (whether equity or debt). They involve the government forgoing a share of its own profits on an investment in order to increase the returns to private sector investors.[187] As noted above at [3.2.4], preferential returns can help encourage private sector investment where the provision of the co-investment alone is not enough (ie where investments are particularly risky/unattractive) and may also help governments attract more competent and experienced investors/fund managers to their incentives.[188]

Because preferential returns 'multiply the financial benefits of success to the disproportionate advantage' of venture capital funds and their private investors[189] whilst 'limiting the profits for the public investor',[190] they improve the risk–reward ratio for private investors.[191] However, because the preferential returns are still tied to profits, they do not protect investors against the cost of failed investments,[192] and therefore do 'not insulate management from the consequences of unsound decision making'.[193] In other words, they encourage investors to take care with the making and development of high-quality investments.[194] This positive effect can be reduced, however, where preferential returns are structured in a way that is too favourable to the private sector. Australia's Productivity Commission, which recommends against the use of preferential returns, has noted that they can lead to a poor return on the use of government funds, and that allocating returns on

[184] Taxation of Chargeable Gains Act 1992 (UK), s 150G, Sch 5BB.
[185] HM Revenue & Customs, 'HS393 Seed Enterprise Investment Scheme – Income Tax and Capital Gains Tax Reliefs (2018)' (6 April 2021).
[186] European Commission, 'Effectiveness of Tax Incentives' (n 2) 71.
[187] See Murray et al (n 66) 5.
[188] See ibid 6; United Nations Economic Commission for Europe (n 72) 85, 89.
[189] Murray (n 60) 367.
[190] Murray et al (n 66) 5.
[191] Leamon et al (n 107) 43.
[192] Christofidis and Debande (n 6) 51; Murray (n 60) 367.
[193] OECD, 'Business Innovation Policies' (n 68) 54.
[194] United Nations Economic Commission for Europe (n 72) 89.

a pro rata basis (ie with no preference) is more likely to 'reduce distortions to investment behaviour'.[195] It should also be noted that preferential returns reduce the amount of returns governments can expect to receive from their share of a co-investment; in the case of an evergreen or revolving incentive (see [3.2.4]), this means less capital is available to subsequently reinvest.

There are three main ways that governments can structure preferential returns.[196] The first is to split the distribution of returns (or profits) unevenly, with the larger portion going to the private sector.[197] Australia's Biomedical Translation Fund equity co-investment programme operates in this way. The government co-invests on a 1:1 basis in specially licensed venture capital funds, but receives only 40 per cent of any profits.[198] This can be compared with Australia's former Innovation Investment Fund programme (under which the government co-invested on a 1:1 basis but was only entitled to 10 per cent of profits) and Pre-Seed Fund programme (under which the government co-invested up to 75 per cent of funds and forewent any share of profits).[199] The UK's Enterprise Capital Funds loan co-investment programme also operates in a similar way, but does not use a defined percentage to govern return distribution. The government contributes loans of up to three-fifths of a fund's capital (or up to two-thirds in an Enterprise Capital Fund that targets SMEs prior to their first commercial sale) and receives interest on this amount (with the rate agreed between the parties) as a prioritised return.[200] After the interest has been paid, investment capital is repaid to private investors and the British Business Bank, and any remaining profits are divided between the British Business Bank and all other parties according to a fixed profit-sharing ratio that is agreed between the parties.[201] Essentially, through the profit-sharing ratio, the British Business Bank allocates part (but not all) of its profits above the prioritised return to the private sector investors and the fund manager.[202] Because the prioritised return is paid to the British Business Bank before any other disbursements are made, private investors only receive preferential returns if the fund is profitable; if the fund underperforms, the prioritised returns actually mean that the private sector investors bear deeper losses than they otherwise would (as discussed above at [3.2.5]).[203]

[195] Productivity Commission, *Business Set-up, Transfer and Closure* (Productivity Commission, 30 September 2015) Productivity Commission Inquiry Report No 75, 174.

[196] Murray et al (n 66) 5.

[197] United Nations Economic Commission for Europe (n 72) 44, 97; Leamon et al (n 107) 43.

[198] Australian Government, Department of Industry Innovation and Science and Department of Health, 'Biomedical Translation Fund Programme Guidelines' (3 August 2016) cls 4.1, 8.10.

[199] Innovation Investment Fund Program Round Three Guidelines No 1 of 2011 (Australia), cls 49, 89; Pre-Seed Fund Program Guidelines No 1 of 2003 (Australia), cls 49, 148.

[200] British Business Bank, 'Enterprise Capital Funds: Guidance for Prospective Managers' (November 2014) 5; United Nations Economic Commission for Europe (n 78) 74.

[201] British Business Bank (n 200) 5, 22–23.

[202] Duruflé (n 6) 17.

[203] ibid.

The second way that governments can structure preferential returns is to grant private investors an optional buyout clause.[204] Buyout clauses do not grant preferential returns per se, but instead allow investors the possibility of obtaining greater returns in the case of a successful investment (therefore functioning in materially the same way as the preferential returns discussed above). Buyout clauses (usually in the form of call options) allow investors to claim an additional upside on an investment that they predict will be successful by buying out the government's shares at a predetermined price (and usually within a predetermined time). When an investment is not likely to be successful, investors will generally not choose to exercise their buyout options, and any losses will be shared between the government and the private sector pro rata. Israel's successful Yozma equity co-investment programme is a well-known example of an incentive that used a buyout clause to good effect.[205] Through the programme, the Israeli government provided up to 40 per cent of the capital for 10 specially established funds.[206] The private investors in Yozma funds were granted a call option over the government's portion of investments for five years, which could be exercised at cost plus 5–7 per cent interest.[207] The private investors bore their share of any losses. The call option reportedly helped leverage fund returns and provided effective incentives for investment and close investee monitoring.[208] The increased upside provided by the call option reportedly also helped attract professional venture capital teams to the programme, which is seen to be a key factor in its success.[209] It has been noted that the design of the Yozma programme, with its use of buyout options,

> ensured that successes should be highly profitable, while failure would be subsidized only to the extent that the government investments were lost. This encouraged Israeli venture capitalists to exert considerable effort in firms with great potential for success while presumably more quickly terminating less successful investments.[210]

The third way that governments can structure preferential returns is for them to take a subordinated position, whereby returns and/or profits are paid to the private sector investors before the government (ie the opposite of the Enterprise Capital Funds example mentioned above).[211] A subordinated position may also involve governments taking first losses (although this is really more of a loss-related

[204] United Nations Economic Commission for Europe (n 72) 97; Duruflé (n 6) 17.
[205] Avnimelech et al (n 87) 34; Gil Avnimelech and Morris Teubal, 'Creating Venture Capital Industries that Co-Evolve with High Tech: Insights from an Extended Industry Life Cycle Perspective on the Israeli Experience' (2006) 35(10) *Research Policy* 1477, 1489–90.
[206] Günseli Baygan, 'Venture Capital Policy Review: Israel' (OECD, 28 January 2003) STI Working Paper 2003/3, 14.
[207] Avnimelech et al (n 87) 34; Ronald J Gilson, 'Engineering a Venture Capital Market: Lessons from the American Experience' (2003) 55 *Stanford Law Review* 1067, 1097.
[208] Gilson (n 207) 1097.
[209] See Avnimelech and Teubal (n 205) 1489–90.
[210] Avnimelech et al (n 87) 35.
[211] Murray et al (n 66) 19.

incentive – see below).[212] Subordinated return arrangements are more valuable to private investors where investments are not anticipated to make good profits. An example of an incentive that operated in this way is Poland's KFK, a fund of funds that invested up to 50 per cent of the capital in private funds. The KFK took a subordinated position in relation to returns, which were distributed in the following order:

1. Private investors were returned their initial investment capital.
2. The KFK was returned its initial investment capital.
3. Private investors received returns up to a hurdle rate (minimum investment return).
4. The KFK received returns up to a hurdle rate.
5. Any remaining capital was distributed to the fund managers, the private investors and the KFK according to the funding agreement. Fund managers generally had a right to receive 20 per cent of this amount as a part of their 'motivating salary' (carried interest).[213]

This system of returns is not very different to the way that returns are commonly distributed to limited partners in venture capital funds. However, the fact that private investors were repaid first lessened their risk, particularly in relation to investments that were not particularly financially successful.

3.4. Loss-Related Incentives

Loss-related incentives are the second form of exit-related incentive. Their use is generally not recommended because while they may play a role in incentivising increased venture capital investment by lessening the risk of investment losses,[214] they have a number of significant downsides.[215] Most importantly, loss-related incentives are seen to decrease investment monitoring and the careful selection of investees because they insulate investors from risk and help 'reduce the pain of bad decisions'.[216] They can also be expensive for governments to provide;[217] given the frequency of losses in the venture capital sector, governments that offer loss relief may incur large, uncontrollable and hard-to-forecast costs. These costs can

[212] ibid 5; Wilson (n 73) 18.

[213] KFK was subsumed into a larger fund of funds and ceased independent operation in 2019: see PFR Ventures, 'National Capital Fund', pfrventures.pl/en/kfk.html. See also Ilona Fałat-Kilijańska, 'How to Strengthen the Polish Venture Capital Market? An Analysis of the Solutions in Selected Countries' (2015) 4(25) *Financial Sciences* 9, 20.

[214] See European Commission, 'Effectiveness of Tax Incentives' (n 2) 11, 71, 87; Barkoczy and Sandler (n 2) 34.

[215] Leamon et al (n 107) 44.

[216] ibid 15, 44. See also Murray (n 60) 367; European Commission, 'Effectiveness of Tax Incentives' (n 2) 87.

[217] European Commission, 'Effectiveness of Tax Incentives' (n 2) 72.

be particularly difficult to justify, given that they are incurred in subsidising failed investments.[218]

Loss-related incentives come in two main forms: various kinds of tax-based loss reliefs (see [3.4.1]), which are tax incentives; and investment guarantees (see [3.4.2]), which are direct incentives. Each of these forms is discussed below.

3.4.1. Tax-Based Loss Relief

Tax-based loss relief allows a taxpayer 'to offset losses realised on the disposal of assets against specified categories of taxable income or capital gains'.[219] However, because different countries have very different tax systems, and impose varied rules in relation to how losses are treated, different kinds of loss relief can look very different.[220] Tax-based loss relief will only constitute a specific incentive for venture capital investment where it provides more favourable treatment of venture capital losses than the baseline tax system. This can be confusing, as some countries' baseline tax system might already allow for generous treatment of losses. For instance, a country's baseline tax system may allow losses on venture capital investments to be utilised without limitation, while another country's baseline tax system may quarantine or 'ring-fence' venture capital losses so that they can only be deducted against certain types of income,[221] or may even deny the use of these losses altogether. Some countries allow losses to be carried forward or back to other income years, while others require them to be used in the year when they are incurred.[222] This can lead to a situation where one country's tax-based loss relief for venture capital may appear less generous than another country's baseline tax treatment of losses. For example, Japan's baseline tax system generally requires losses made on the sale of unlisted shares to be set off against the gains made on the sale of unlisted shares in the year when they are incurred (ie the losses are quarantined). Japan's Angel Tax System (known as Enjeru Zei'sei), however, allows these losses to be carried forward three years.[223] In comparison, France's baseline tax system allows losses to be carried back one year or carried forward indefinitely (subject to annual caps).[224] This treatment of losses is very generous, but because it is built into France's baseline tax system, it does not specifically constitute a venture capital incentive.

The provision of loss relief is complicated by the concept of 'symmetric' tax treatment of gains and losses. Symmetric treatment occurs where gains and losses

[218] See Barkoczy and Sandler (n 2) 34.
[219] ibid 97.
[220] See Pamela Palazzi, 'Taxation and Innovation' (OECD, 2011) OECD Taxation Working Papers No 9, 58.
[221] ibid.
[222] ibid.
[223] European Commission, 'Effectiveness of Tax Incentives' (n 2) 196.
[224] See Code Général des Impôts (France), Arts 209, 220d.

are treated the same way (eg gains are subject to tax and losses can be deducted at the same rate, or gains are exempt from tax and losses cannot be deducted). Symmetric tax treatment is seen to reduce the variance of expected investment returns, and to therefore stimulate the 'optimal' degree of risk taking.[225] In contrast, providing more favourable loss relief has the capacity to trigger 'excessive' risk-taking.[226] Many countries therefore design their incentives to have symmetric treatment of gains or losses, which stops investors from 'double dipping' by benefiting both from investment incentives and from investment losses.[227] For example, Luxembourg's SICAR regime exempts the returns made by eligible SICARs from tax and does not allow any losses (realised or unrealised) to be claimed against a SICAR's taxable income.[228] Likewise, investors who receive tax exemptions under Australia's Venture Capital Limited Partnership and Early Stage Venture Capital Limited Partnership programmes and its early-stage investor tax incentive are also generally denied access to their losses.[229] This denial of losses can be seen as punitive or overly harsh, given that investors under these programmes incur losses frequently but cannot gain a tax benefit from them, while the same is not true of the losses made by investors outside these programmes.[230] However, it is important to remember that investors who invest through these programmes generally do not pay any tax on their investment returns, so gain a considerable benefit if they make a profit.

The implication of the symmetric tax treatment argument is that governments should only provide tax-based loss relief where gains are taxed, and only to the extent necessary to bring the treatment of gains and losses into balance.[231] Interestingly, and in contrast to the research on symmetric tax treatment, the European Commission has recommended the use of loss relief 'on more favourable terms than the baseline tax system' to venture capital investors as a matter of good practice in order to stimulate investment and risk-taking.[232] However, the extent to which the provision of tax-based loss relief actually provides an incentive for increased venture capital investment remains unclear.[233] Where investors do not have a tax liability (eg where their gains are exempt from tax), it is seen to be unlikely that making loss rules more generous would materially increase high-risk investments.[234] The incentive effective of tax-based loss relief is also

[225] Palazzi (n 220) 61–62.

[226] ibid.

[227] Barkoczy and Sandler (n 2) 171.

[228] Law of 15 June 2004 Relating to the Investment Company in Risk Capital ('SICAR') (Luxembourg), Arts 34(2), 34(3).

[229] Income Tax Assessment Act 1997 (Australia), s 26-68. See also Barkoczy and Wilkinson (n 174) 101–02.

[230] See Barkoczy et al (n 58) 296, 304.

[231] Palazzi (n 220) 62.

[232] European Commission, 'Effectiveness of Tax Incentives' (n 2) 87, 176.

[233] Matt Colahan, John Higton, Lucy Royce, Rebecca Klahr, Jayesh Navin Shah and Marc Cowling, 'The Use and Impact of Venture Capital Schemes' (HM Revenue & Customs, February 2016) Research Report 355, 7. *cf* See Barkoczy and Wilkinson (n 174) 102; Barkoczy and Sandler (n 2) 34.

[234] Palazzi (n 220) 63.

likely to be weaker for experienced investors (presumably as they anticipate making fewer losses).[235]

Given that tax-based loss relief may reduce the provision of investor monitoring and value-adding activities, is expensive to provide and could potentially be used for tax minimisation purposes rather than genuine investment purposes (particularly if losses can be set off against any kind of income and/or if front-end tax benefits are also provided),[236] it is unsurprising that only a couple of governments provide loss relief to venture capital investors on a more favourable basis than that afforded to other taxpayers. These include Japan, which, as discussed above, allows losses to be carried forward and utilised in future years. This form of loss relief is symmetric because gains are also taxed in Japan; the carry-forward loss relief provided under the Angel Tax System merely provides investors with more opportunities to use their losses in future years. Singapore previously provided loss relief under its former Enterprise Investment Incentive (discontinued in 2009) by allowing investors to deduct losses of up to SGD 3 million incurred on the sale of qualifying shares in startup companies from their taxable income.[237] The incentive was 'designed to cushion investors from the effect of losses, which would otherwise not be deductible to them when they exit their investments', and therefore operated as a de facto form of loss insurance that was subsidised through the tax system.[238]

The UK approaches the issue of loss relief in a clever way under its Enterprise Investment Scheme (as well as its smaller Seed Enterprise Investment Scheme).[239] When investors purchase shares in startups that qualify for investment-related income tax relief under the Enterprise Investment Scheme, they have the option of setting any loss they incur on the sale of these shares off against their income in the current or previous income year (instead of only setting the amount off against their capital gains).[240] However, in working out the amount of the loss, the initial investment amount is reduced by the amount of income tax relief the investor received in relation to the shares, meaning that the investor does not benefit twice in relation to the same investment (ie they do not receive income tax relief and then full access to their losses). Allowing investors to claim losses after taking into account any reduction for income tax relief ensures that they are not penalised for making failed investments and puts them in a similar position to ordinary investors, who can claim losses.[241] However, because investors receive partial capital gains tax exemptions on the sale of their shares, the treatment of

[235] European Commission, 'Effectiveness of Tax Incentives' (n 2) 72.

[236] See Palazzi (n 220) 62–63; Australian Government, The Board of Taxation, 'Review of Taxation Arrangements Under the Venture Capital Limited Partnership Regime' (June 2011) 38.

[237] Harold Siow Song Teng, *Government Policy and Critical Success Factors of Small Businesses in Singapore* (Cambridge Scholars Publishing, 2011) 35. See also Barkoczy and Edmundson (n 7) 69.

[238] Barkoczy and Edmundson (n 7) 70.

[239] HM Revenue & Customs, 'Tax Relief for Investors Using Venture Capital Schemes' (n 30).

[240] ibid.

[241] Barkoczy and Wilkinson (n 174) 94.

gains and losses under the Enterprise Investment Scheme and Seed Enterprise Investment Scheme is not symmetrical, and the provision of loss relief is therefore concessional because investors may benefit whether they make a gain or a loss. Interestingly, however, a 2016 evaluation of the Enterprise Investment Scheme indicated that loss relief may not actually be a strong motivating factor for investors. Investors saw income tax relief as the most important element of the scheme (with 42 per cent of investors rating it as 'essential' to their decision to invest), followed by capital gains tax relief (with 32 per cent of investors rating it as essential to their investment decision).[242] In contrast, only 11 per cent of investors rated loss relief as essential to their investment decision.[243] This suggests that to a large extent, the provision of loss relief might provide a windfall to investors who would already have invested. The 2016 evaluation also noted that although investors were concerned about losses, the tax relief provided under the scheme helped address this concern; investors reported that tax relief (including income and capital gains tax relief) 'meant that the value of their investment could effectively fall by a substantial amount before investors would start to lose money, which made them more willing to invest'.[244] Again, this suggests that the provision of loss relief may be unnecessary as a motivator. This lends support to the idea that loss relief is not a particularly appropriate form of venture capital incentive.[245]

3.4.2. Investment Guarantees

Investment guarantees are a form of loss-related incentive that are delivered directly, rather than through the tax system. Like loss relief, investment guarantees encourage venture capital investment by protecting against investment downside.[246] Guarantees generally involve governments covering a percentage of a fund or investor's losses and can be provided either in relation to individual investments or in relation to portfolios. The former clearly entails more effort and costs for governments, but gives them more control over their risk exposure.[247] Private investors often pay a fee to governments in consideration of a guarantee, and may also grant governments the right to share in any profits that arise (in order to compensate for losses).[248] For example, Austria introduced two forms of

[242] Colahan et al (n 233) 7.
[243] ibid.
[244] ibid 8.
[245] Note that the author took a different view on the merits of loss relief in earlier work (see Barkoczy and Wilkinson (n 174) 102) but has since changed their view on the basis of further consideration of Palazzi's theoretical research and Colahan et al's findings in relation to the UK's Enterprise Investment Scheme loss relief.
[246] OECD, 'Government Venture Capital for Technology-Based Firms' (n 14) 14; Murray et al (n 66) 5; Murray (n 60) 366.
[247] OECD, 'Government Venture Capital for Technology-Based Firms' (n 14) 18.
[248] See Murray (n 60) 375.

guarantees in the late 1990s that incorporated profit sharing.[249] The first, which was available to venture capital funds, provided a 100 per cent guarantee on the capital of a fund in return for a premium of 1–3 per cent per annum and a profit share of up to 20 per cent. Each investment was approved on an individual basis.[250] The second guarantee was available to the investors in approved venture capital funds, who could choose to purchase a guarantee that provided them with a put option exercisable at fund maturity (normally 6–8 years). The cost of a 100 per cent guarantee was an initial fee of 6–10 per cent, plus a 5–10 per cent share of any profits. Investors could also choose to buy an 80 per cent guarantee for a lower price.[251]

There are several reasons for governments to be cautious about the use of investment guarantees. By lowering investment risk, they may lessen investor effort, increase adverse selection of investments, encourage early write-offs of marginal investments and consequently reduce returns.[252] Like tax-based loss relief, guarantees are likely to stimulate little additionality, instead acting as windfalls to investors who would have invested anyway.[253] Guarantees are also likely to be expensive to provide.[254] Furthermore, it has been suggested that loss protection may also give rise to a 'self-fulfilling prophecy' regarding losses,[255] which could deter private sector investors. Some governments attempt to mitigate these downsides by limiting the percentage of losses that the guarantees cover.[256] For example, the Netherlands' Garantieregeling Particuliere Participatiemaatschappijen (PPM), introduced in 1981, covered up to 50 per cent of the losses incurred on early-stage investments by private 'venture capital companies'.[257] The scheme was amended in 1988 to exclude the first 'critically vulnerable' investment year from the guarantee. A guarantee under the scheme lasted five years from initial investment in a company; after this time, the guarantee was reduced by 10 per cent a year, disappearing completely at the tenth year.[258] This arrangement reflected the fact that as companies continue their development, their risk factor and chance of failure generally decline. France's Garantie de Fonds Propres Relance scheme also takes steps to limit costs. The scheme provides guarantees at the portfolio level to both

[249] Bannock Consulting, 'Innovative Instruments for Raising Equity For SMEs in Europe' (June 2001) Study ContractETD/00/503116, 18.

[250] ibid.

[251] ibid 18–19.

[252] See OECD, 'Government Venture Capital for Technology-Based Firms' (n 14) 18; Christofidis and Debande (n 6) 51; OECD, 'Business Innovation Policies' (n 68) 54; Hussain (n 138) 646; Callagher et al (n 80) 382.

[253] See OECD, 'Government Venture Capital for Technology-Based Firms' (n 14) 18.

[254] See Rebecca Urban, 'Venture Capitalists Call for Guarantee on Funds' *The Australian* (5 January 2013); Duruflé (n 6) 17.

[255] Duruflé (n 6) 17.

[256] See OECD, 'Government Venture Capital for Technology-Based Firms' (n 14) 18.

[257] Leslie Ann Jeng and Philippe C Wells, 'The Determinants of Venture Capital Funding: Evidence Across Countries' (2000) 6(3) *Journal of Entrepreneurship and Public Policy* 241, 280.

[258] Murray (n 60) 367.

venture capital funds and angel investors who make eligible investments through specific vehicles.[259] Guarantees last for 10 years from the time of the first investment in a company, and the guaranteed portion of an investment is 50 per cent in the general case and 70 per cent for companies that are under three years old.[260] The cost of the guarantee includes an annual commission on the invested amount of 0.45 per cent (for equity) or 0.6 per cent (for quasi-equity), and a capped 12 per cent share of any capital gains that arise.[261] A maximum loss ceiling ('stop loss') of 30 per cent is also imposed in relation to each agreement (ie in relation to the investments guaranteed in a portfolio).[262] This limit was introduced under the former iteration of the scheme, the Investissement Garantie, in response to a proliferation of losses in the early 2000s.[263] Neither iteration of the scheme has been thoroughly evaluated, and there is little evidence of its broader and indirect effects, societal returns or behavioural change,[264] although anecdotal evidence reported in 2011 was that two-thirds of the investments made through the Investissement Garantie scheme would not have been made in the absence of the guarantees, indicating some additionality.[265] It is also not clear the extent to which the quality of investors was improved through the guarantee scheme.[266] The guarantee fees and upside remuneration generated through the Investissement Garantie scheme were reportedly not sufficient to cover compensation payouts, requiring continual funding of the scheme.[267]

To the extent that France's investment guarantee has not had its intended effect, it is not alone; history suggests that, in general, guarantee programmes have not been particularly impactful.[268] The provision of downside protection has been described as 'counterproductive' in some instances, particularly where it encourages poor investor behaviour.[269] For instance, the USA's Small Business Investment Companies programme, which provides funds with federally guaranteed debt capital, has been criticised because the presence of guarantees in the past reportedly reduced managers' incentives to screen or monitor portfolio firms by limiting their exposure to unsuccessful investments.[270] The result was that many Small Business Investment Companies made investments in 'ineffective or corrupt firms'.[271] Likewise, Israel's former Inbal programme, which guaranteed

[259] Bpifrance, 'Garantie de Fonds Propres Relance: Dispositif Doté par l'État et Géré par Bpifrance 2021–2024' (June 2022) 5.
[260] ibid 9, 16.
[261] ibid 9.
[262] ibid 9.
[263] Jasper Deuten, 'Venture Capital Investment Guarantee Programme by OSEO' (INNO Partnering Forum, 2011) 12.
[264] ibid 16.
[265] ibid.
[266] ibid.
[267] ibid.
[268] See Avnimelech et al (n 87) 32; Mason (n 1) 542.
[269] United Nations Economic Commission for Europe (n 72) 84, 89, 97.
[270] Lerner (n 69) F75.
[271] ibid.

up to 70 per cent of approved funds' initial capital, is said to have encouraged the participation of non-professional venture capitalists through its downside protection, which in turn contributed to the poor performance of funds and investees.[272] Germany's former Deutsche Wagnisfinanzierungs-Gesellschaft (WFG) co-investment fund, which was introduced in 1975, provided a generous 75 per cent downside guarantee to investors as a way to induce the commitment of banks to the project.[273] It is suggested that this feature of the incentive may have contributed to its failure; the fund had a reported rate of return of below –25 per cent, and was not successful in stimulating market development.[274] The fund also provided call options for entrepreneurs whose companies received investment to buy back WFG's share of their company at cost plus interest.[275] This feature of the WFG was also highly criticised, as it was noted that the capped returns for the fund gave the fund managers little incentive to make good investments.[276] Finally, the Netherlands' PPM, mentioned above, may have played a role in increasing venture capital investment over its 14 years of operation,[277] but it is suggested that the PPM may also have encouraged quicker recognition of guaranteed losses (thereby increasing government expenditure).[278] Furthermore, a 1994 evaluation of the PPM found that the funding problems experienced by startups and fledgling companies had not been significantly reduced by the scheme, and that it did not appear to be the appropriate instrument for serving the lower end of the market.[279] In light of the lack of clear impact of investment guarantees, and the other downsides associated with their use, guarantees are not recommended for use as venture capital incentives. As with tax-based loss relief, it is suggested that governments avoid structuring their incentives in this way.

3.5. Summary

This chapter has looked at 13 distinct venture capital incentive forms, demonstrating the great variety of approaches that can be taken to encourage venture capital investment. While ranking these incentive forms according to their appropriateness for use is a subjective exercise that is unlikely to be particularly helpful (because of the range of pros and cons that attend each kind of incentive form), some broad takeaways on form suitability do emerge from the research undertaken here.

[272] See Avnimelech and Teubal (n 205) 1491; United Nations Economic Commission for Europe (n 72) 77.

[273] Ralf Becker and Thomas Hellmann, 'The Genesis of Venture Capital – Lessons from the German Experience' (CESifo, November 2002) Working Paper No 883, 14.

[274] See ibid 3, 25; Gilson (n 207) 1096.

[275] Gilson (n 207) 1095.

[276] ibid 1096.

[277] See OECD, 'Venture Capital and Innovation' (1996) 84.

[278] United Nations Economic Commission for Europe (n 72) 66.

[279] OECD, 'Venture Capital and Innovation' (n 277) 84.

First, as to the choice between tax and direct incentives, it can be said that while the two delivery methods are generally similar in most respects, tax incentives may be less equitable than direct incentives because they are usually only useful where entities have a tax liability. Direct incentives, on the other hand, generally allow for easier tracking and prediction of incentive costs, though they may be less politically attractive to governments for this reason. It is recommended that governments consider direct incentives over tax incentives in order to increase equity, encourage cross-border investment and help control incentive costs, although the use of tax incentives is generally acceptable (particularly refundable tax credits, which avoid equity issues).

Second, as to the choice between investment-related incentives and exit-related incentives, each group has its own benefits depending on the circumstances. As the discussion above highlighted, investment-related incentives are likely to better incentivise investment than exit-related incentives and may therefore be more appropriate in nascent venture capital markets. However, investment-related incentives may be detrimental to investor behaviour and investment quality, and may be used for tax minimisation or other ancillary purposes. Furthermore, co-investment incentives may lead to an oversupply situation if they introduce too much government capital to a market. Governments should temper these risks against the need to increase investment. Exit-related incentives, as discussed above, can be divided into the categories of profit-related incentives and loss-related incentives. Profit-related incentives are likely to encourage high-quality investment and positive post-investment behaviour because they only reward successful investments. They are also likely to be relatively cheap to provide and are not particularly vulnerable to abuse. However, they may provide less additionality than investment-related incentives and can provide windfalls to investors who would have invested anyway. It is recommended that profit-related incentives be used in more mature venture capital markets where governments want to help encourage investment quality (rather than quantity). In contrast, loss-related incentives are not recommended for use as venture capital incentives for a variety of reasons: they are likely to skew the risk–reward balance too far in favour of the private sector (which may encourage poor investment behaviour and low-quality investments); they tend to be expensive for governments to provide; they may create a negative perception of the venture capital sector; and they are unlikely to have a strong incentive effect. Instead of offering loss-related incentives, it is recommended that governments provide investors with symmetrical tax treatment in relation to their investments.

Third, as to the choice of specific incentive forms, a range of considerations arise. For instance, tax credits are generally recommended (although could be more equitable and appropriate if structured as grants instead).[280] Tax deductions are not generally recommended because of their instability and inequity. Grants

[280] Surrey (n 29) 99.

are recommended as being an equitable and stable form of direct incentive, while equity co-investment can be useful as a market development tool but needs to be structured well to avoid market flooding and other issues. Loans are not recommended because of the issues with repayments and interest discussed above. Visa incentives may be appropriate, provided they are structured so as not to encourage low-quality investors.

Of the exit-related incentives, tax exemptions are generally recommended as providing an attractive incentive, and reduced tax rates provide a similar, if less generous, alternative. Exit grants function in a similar way and are considered equitable, but are likely to be unfamiliar to many investors. Reinvestment relief can be complex and, like investment-related incentives, may be used for tax minimisation purposes, so should be approached with caution, and preferential returns should likewise be treated carefully to ensure that they do not skew the risk–reward balance too far in favour of private investors or unduly reduce government returns (which can prejudice the funding of future incentives). Loss-related incentives, as discussed above, are not recommended. These considerations and recommendations are explored in further detail and set out in tabular form in chapter seven.

The selection of an appropriate venture capital incentive form represents an important step in the design process and is followed by an equally important step: targeting. In targeting their incentives, governments must decide who can access their incentives and in what circumstances. These issues are discussed in chapter four, which also looks at common targeting conditions, criteria and strategies in detail. As will be seen in the following chapter, targeting requirements may vary depending on the form of incentive selected, but also share many broad commonalities across all venture capital incentive forms.

4

Targeting

4.1. Introduction

Building on the discussion in chapter three about selecting an appropriate incentive form, this chapter continues to look at incentive design but with a focus on the issue of targeting. Targeting an incentive is a multifaceted exercise that is achieved through the use of 'eligibility' or 'qualifying' criteria that restrict the entities and/or activities for which an incentive is available.[1] Eligibility criteria can either be prescriptive (ie an entity must meet certain conditions in order to receive an incentive) or exclusionary (ie an entity can receive an incentive unless they meet certain conditions). They can be objective (eg an investee company must not be more than five years old) or subjective (eg an investee company must have high growth potential). In some cases, decision-makers will need to exercise discretion to decide whether (or how well) criteria have been met, particularly if there is an assessment of 'merit' involved (see further [5.3.3]).

Targeting is a highly nuanced area of policy design, with a number of (sometimes competing) objectives. The most important of these objectives is to help incentives achieve their policy aims by directing them to the most appropriate recipients and activities.[2] Targeting also plays important roles in limiting incentive cost (by limiting the number of recipients) and increasing incentive efficiency (by reducing redundancy and focusing incentives on recipients/activities that are likely to produce additionality).[3] However, while targeting helps with incentive effectiveness, cost and efficiency, particularly where it is precise and tightly controlled, it can also have negative implications on incentive complexity, compliance costs

[1] European Commission, 'Effectiveness of Tax Incentives for Venture Capital and Business Angels to Foster the Investment of SMEs and Start-ups: Final Report' (Taxation and Customs Union, 2017) Working Paper No 68, 73.

[2] OECD, 'Government Venture Capital for Technology-Based Firms' (1997) OCDE/GD(97)201, 15.

[3] See International Monetary Fund, Organisation for Economic Co-operation and Development, United Nations and World Bank, 'Options for Low Income Countries' Effective and Efficient Use of Tax Incentives for Investment' (Report to the G-20 Development Working Group, October 2015) 21; Alex Easson, *Tax Incentives for Foreign Direct Investment* (Kluwer Law International, 2004) 199; European Commission, 'Effectiveness of Tax Incentives' (n 1) 73, 204; OECD, 'Business Innovation Policies: Selected Country Comparisons' (2011) 53; Albert Bravo-Biosca, 'Access to Finance for Innovation: Rationales and Risks of Public Intervention' (The Innovation Policy Platform, 2014) 13.

and uptake (see further [5.2]).[4] Strict targeting can also create barriers to innovation where it excludes new or innovative recipients and activities from being eligible for incentives.[5] Governments therefore need to strike a balance between 'simple' or light-touch conditions that could allow incentives to be used for 'very different aims than those originally intended' and 'complex and overengineered rules' that may improve incentive integrity but limit effectiveness.[6]

The process of targeting requires governments to make a range of decisions on eligibility, which are examined in this chapter. Among other things, governments must decide:

- what kinds of investors can receive an incentive and what characteristics they must demonstrate (see [4.2]);[7]
- what kinds of restrictions should be placed on investments and the investment process (see [4.3]);[8] and
- what kinds of criteria investees must meet in order to receive investment under an incentive (see [4.4]).[9]

This chapter concludes at [4.5] with some key takeaways as to how governments can best approach the task of targeting their incentives.

4.2. Targeting Investors

The process of targeting investors requires governments to determine the kinds of entities that are able to access an incentive. There are three main reasons why governments might choose to impose eligibility criteria on investors. First, governments may want to control the qualities of the investors who can participate in incentives. For instance, they may want to ensure that only investors exhibiting particular characteristics (eg having sufficient financial resources or prior investment experience) can participate, or they may want to target certain kinds of investors (eg individual investors/angels, venture capital funds and their passive investors, or some combination of these groups).[10] Second, governments are often mindful of the need to protect investors from the risk of venture capital investment;

[4] See Easson (n 3) 199; OECD, 'Government Venture Capital' (n 2) 15; European Commission, 'Effectiveness of Tax Incentives' (n 1) 73, 204.

[5] Deborah A Stone, *Policy Paradox and Political Reason* (HarperCollins, 1988) 236. See also European Commission, 'Effectiveness of Tax Incentives' (n 1) 205.

[6] Bravo-Biosca (n 3) 14.

[7] See United Nations Economic Commission for Europe, *Financing Innovative Development: Comparative Review of the Experiences of UNECE Countries in Early Stage Financing* (United Nations Publications, 2007) 42.

[8] See Stephen Barkoczy and Daniel Sandler, *Government Venture Capital Incentives: A Multi-Jurisdiction Comparative Analysis* (Australian Tax Research Foundation, 2007) 37–38.

[9] See Bravo-Biosca (n 3) 14; ibid.

[10] OECD, 'Government Venture Capital' (n 2) 14.

to this end, they may impose eligibility criteria on investors in order to limit the extent to which inexperienced 'everyday' or 'retail' investors can participate in incentives.[11] Finally, governments may impose eligibility criteria on investors in order to help control the costs of providing an incentive. Investor eligibility criteria, particularly those which allow governments to proactively select the investors that can participate, offer a way to control incentive costs by limiting the number of investors who can participate.

The following discussion breaks down and explores matters of investor targeting according to whether incentives target direct investors, such as angels (see [4.2.1]), or indirect investors, such as passive investors who invest through venture capital funds (see [4.2.2]) – although it should be noted that some incentives target both kinds of investors. As will be seen, the issues of investor characteristics, investor protection and cost limiting provide the impetus for many of the targeting criteria set out below.

4.2.1. Direct Investors

As demonstrated in the examples explored in chapter three, some incentives are aimed at encouraging investment by direct investors (ie angels). In order to achieve this aim, these incentives target direct investors through various eligibility criteria, such as entity criteria (see [4.2.1.1]), wealth and experience criteria (see [4.2.1.2]), residence criteria (see [4.2.1.3]) and independence criteria (see [4.2.1.4]). While some incentives impose no (or very limited) criteria on direct investors, others impose strict criteria. For example, Australia's early-stage investor tax incentive, which provides angel investors with special tax benefits in relation to their investments in eligible early-stage companies, imposes entity criteria (investors must not be a trust or partnership, an Early Stage Venture Capital Limited Partnership, a widely held company or a 100 per cent subsidiary of a widely held company),[12] wealth and experience criteria (investors that are not 'sophisticated' or 'professional' investors are limited in the tax benefits they are eligible to receive)[13] and independence criteria (investors must not be 'affiliates' of the proposed investee company at the time when the investment is made).[14] These criteria limit the number of investors who can participate in the incentive.

[11] Although different jurisdictions have varying rules for classifying investors, broad distinctions can be drawn between 'wholesale' or 'sophisticated' investors (who are generally wealthy and/or experienced) and everyday 'retail' investors.

[12] But note that the partners in a partnership and beneficiaries in a trust may nevertheless benefit from the incentive in certain circumstances: Income Tax Assessment Act 1997 (Australia), s 360-15; see also Stephen Barkoczy and Tamara Wilkinson, *Incentivising Angels: A Comparative Framework of Tax Incentives for Start-Up Investors* (Springer, 2019) 69–70.

[13] Income Tax Assessment Act 1997 (Australia), s 360-20.

[14] ibid s 360-15.

The criteria used to target direct investors under Australia's early stage investor tax incentive, along with residence criteria, are the most commonly used investor criteria for these kinds of incentives.[15] Research by the European Commission in 2017 found that of 46 venture capital tax incentives identified in 19 countries, 36 targeted natural persons (entity criteria), 23 required investors to be residents for tax purposes (residence criteria), five specifically permitted investors to be connected with the investee business and eight specifically did not permit investors to be connected (independence criteria).[16] The details of each of the different eligibility criteria for direct investors, along with the rationale for imposing them and comments on their appropriateness, are set out below.

4.2.1.1. Entity Criteria

As seen in the example of Australia's early stage investor tax incentive above, governments may require direct investors to be a certain kind of entity (such as an individual) in order to participate in an incentive. Belgium's Tax Shelter Start-Up takes this approach, requiring investors to be natural persons.[17] Alternatively, they may exclude certain kinds of entities from receiving an incentive (such as companies or partnerships). Requiring investors to be individuals may help ensure that the entities that benefit from an incentive are 'genuine' angels that will focus on early-stage investment. However, given that many angels choose to invest through partnerships or syndicates, excluding these entities from being able to participate in incentives for direct investment may be overly restrictive and may artificially limit the uptake of the incentive. It is also worth noting that entity criteria alone do not guarantee that investors will be high-quality, active or engaged.[18] For this reason, entity criteria are often combined with wealth and experience criteria (see below) in order to increase investor quality.[19]

Italy takes an interesting approach to entities under its tax incentives for investment in innovative startups and small and medium enterprises (SMEs). The incentives allow both individuals and companies that invest in innovative startups to claim tax benefits and do not place any particular eligibility criteria on these entities, making the incentives widely available. However, there is a distinction in the benefits offered to individuals and companies. Individuals receive a tax credit of 30 per cent of their investment amount up to EUR 1 million per year. In comparison, companies receive a deduction of 30 per cent on their investment amount up to EUR 1.8 million per year, which they can apply against their taxable

[15] See European Commission, 'Effectiveness of Tax Incentives' (n 1) 77–78.

[16] ibid 135–40.

[17] Spreds, 'Frequently Asked Questions: What Is the Tax Shelter and Who Benefits from It?', www.spreds.com/en/faq/tax-shelter/200.

[18] See European Commission, 'Effectiveness of Tax Incentives' (n 1) 77. *cf* OECD, 'Government Venture Capital' (n 2) 15.

[19] See European Commission, 'Effectiveness of Tax Incentives' (n 1) 77.

corporate income.[20] The incentive for individuals is therefore more generous, indicating that Italy may be particularly keen to encourage investment by individual direct investors. This example illustrates one way that governments can indirectly encourage participation by certain kinds of investors without imposing strict entity criteria.

4.2.1.2. Wealth and Experience Criteria

Governments may require direct investors to meet wealth and/or experience criteria for two main reasons. First, these criteria help protect inexperienced and/or financially constrained investors from the risks of venture capital investment. Wealthy and experienced investors are often judged to be more able to deal with 'the complex nature of investing in young firms' than other investors, and may have the resources to bear failed investments.[21] For this reason, Australia's early stage investor tax incentive limits the participation of 'retail' investors (ie investors that are not 'sophisticated' or 'professional' investors) in the incentive to ensure they do not overcommit to risky early-stage investments.[22] While sophisticated and professional investors can invest an unlimited amount in early-stage investments under the incentive (subject to a maximum annual tax credit of AUD 200,000), retail investors will lose any entitlement to a tax credit (and the incentive's profit-related tax benefits) if they invest more than AUD 50,000 per year in qualifying companies under the incentive.[23] As with the example of Italy above, this example demonstrates an incentive of a government prioritising investment by certain entities without specifically excluding others from being able to participate.

Second, wealth and experience criteria may contribute to investor quality, as experienced 'wholesale' investors should be well placed to provide value-adding services to their investees and may have better chances of producing successful

[20] Italian Ministry of Economic Development, Directorate General for Industrial Policy, Competitiveness and SMEs, 'The Italian Startup Act: Italy's Policy Framework to Support Innovative Startups' (8 July 2019) 16, www.mise.gov.it/images/stories/documenti/Executive%20summary%20ISA%2007_2019.pdf.

[21] Karen E Wilson and Filipe Silva, 'Policies for Seed and Early Stage Finance: Findings from the 2012 OECD Financing Questionnaire' (OECD, October 2013) OECD Science, Technology and Industry Policy Papers No 9, 47.

[22] Australian Taxation Office, 'Tax Incentives for Early Stage Investors: Qualifying for the Tax Incentives' (7 April 2021) www.ato.gov.au/Business/Tax-incentives-for-innovation/In-detail/Tax-incentives-for-early-stage-investors/?anchor=Thesophisticatedinvestortest#Thesophisticatedinvestortest.

[23] Income Tax Assessment Act 1997 (Australia), ss 360-15, 360-20. Broadly speaking, an individual may qualify as a sophisticated investor if they meet one of several wealth criteria (eg investing at least A$500,000) or are deemed by a 'financial services licensee' to have sufficient previous investment experience: see Corporations Act 2001 (Australia), ss 708(8), (10). They may qualify as a professional investor if they specifically fall under the prescriptive definition contained in the Corporations Act or if they have or control gross assets of at least A$10 million: see Corporations Act 2001 (Australia), ss 9, 708(11).

investments than less experienced investors. Turkey's Business Angels Law, for example, which provides deductions for angels who invest in qualifying companies, only allows wealthy or experienced investors to acquire and hold a 'BA Licence' that allows them to benefit from the tax incentive.[24] This requirement has the potential to 'promote investment quality by reducing the ability for non-professional or passive investors to participate'.[25] Denmark's business angel matching loan incentive also included an experience requirement as part of its merit assessment process. During the approval process, Vaekstfonden (the regulator) looked at whether angels had experienced at least one successful exit from a portfolio company (or a company they established or worked for), had at least two portfolio companies or active investments at the time of application and presented a convincing pre-seed and seed investment strategy.[26] It is not clear whether the current iteration of the incentive uses the same criteria or not.

The use of wealth and experience criteria to target direct investors is generally appropriate. The private venture capital market is predominantly a wholesale market, rather than a retail one,[27] so imposing restrictions on the participation of retail investors is unlikely to significantly shrink the pool of eligible investors. However, experience criteria can be detrimental where they introduce a bias against new or marginalised investors. For instance, high-net-worth individuals with the capacity to become angels may be deterred from investing in the sector if they need to have prior investment experience in order to benefit from incentives. Furthermore, it is suggested that the imposition of experience criteria on direct investors could potentially exacerbate the angel gender gap, as angels generally tend to be middle-aged males with a strong entrepreneurial background, with female angels being noted as less experienced, on average, than their male counterparts.[28] Interestingly, it is recognised that female investors are more likely

[24] Wealthy investors have gross income or annual wages of at least £200,000 within the last two years or total wealth of £1 million at the time of application. Experienced investors have: at least two years' experience as a fund or portfolio manager in banks or financial institutions, manager or equivalent in SME finance, project finance or corporate finance departments of a bank or financial institution, or manager or equivalent in a venture company; been working for at least two years as deputy general managers or equivalent in an enterprise with annual turnover of at least £25 million for at least two years within the last five years; been members of a business angels network for at least one year before obtaining a licence and have been shareholders as a business angel in at least one or more non-public companies whose net sales are below £5 million in the previous fiscal year; or at least two years' work experience in the domestic incubator or technology development centres which are established for supporting the start-ups and growth phase companies and have invested at least £20,000 in one of the companies operating in these centres: Republic of Turkey, Ministry of Treasury and Finance, *Regulation on Business Angels* (Regulation, 2018) Article 5.

[25] European Commission, 'Effectiveness of Tax Incentives' (n 1) 198.

[26] See Vaekstfonden, 'Investor Framework Agreement' (22 September 2022), cl 1.3.

[27] Jennifer Payne, 'Private Equity and Its Regulation in Europe' (2011) 12(4) *European Business Organization Law Review* 559, 571.

[28] Salome Gvetadze, Kristian Pal and Wouter Torfs, 'The Business Angel Portfolio Under the European Angels Fund: An Empirical Analysis' (European Investment Fund, January 2020) Research and Market Analysis Working Paper 2020/62, www.eif.org/news_centre/publications/eif_working_paper_2020_62.pdf 35.

to place greater emphasis on a venture's social impact, to invest locally (thereby contributing to local economic development) and to finance female entrepreneurs (which may help close the 'entrepreneurial gender gap' and therefore lead to more female angels),[29] making it a worthwhile endeavour to specifically encourage investment by female angels. Unfortunately, the research for this book did not identify any current incentives that specifically target female angels, despite the fact that in the UK only 15 to 18 per cent of angel investors are women (and only approximately 11 per cent are from ethnic minorities).[30] In order not to exclude certain angels, it is suggested that incentives should not use experience criteria alone to define eligible investors; instead, it is recommended that experience and wealth criteria be used as alternatives, so that both wealthy and/or experienced investors can qualify for incentives. In this way, incentives can promote investor quality and protect retail investors while not excluding new entrants.

4.2.1.3. Residence Criteria

It is not uncommon for governments to restrict their incentives for direct investment to investors who reside domestically. This ensures that incentive benefits accrue locally and prioritises investment by investors who are familiar with the local market.[31] The European Commission recommends against this practice, advocating for incentives rules to permit investment by cross-border investors.[32] However, this may be more relevant within the European Union than in other countries around the world, given the high degree of mutual trust and cooperation found in Europe's common market. The author therefore raises no particular objection to residence criteria. Indeed, residence criteria are likely to help keep additionality within a jurisdiction, making them appropriate in many circumstances.

Governments may also choose to actively prioritise investment by foreign investors, in order to draw in foreign expertise. However, it is more likely that governments will seek to encourage investment by foreign funds or passive investors (as in the examples at [4.2.2.6] below) rather than by foreign individuals, as angel investors tend to primarily invest locally, given their relatively limited resources.[33]

4.2.1.4. Independence Criteria

Some incentives require investors to be at 'arm's length' from their investees, or, alternatively, may impose exclusionary criteria to prohibit entities that are

[29] ibid.

[30] House of Commons Treasury Committee, 'Venture Capital' (Nineteenth Report of Session 2022–23, 24 July 2023) 12.

[31] European Commission, 'Effectiveness of Tax Incentives' (n 1) 78.

[32] ibid 14.

[33] ibid 78.

'connected' to or 'related parties' of a startup from participating in an incentive.[34] These kinds of criteria help target incentives towards genuine third-party investments and their effect is often to exclude company management from participating in incentives.[35] For instance, Tax Shelter Start-Up excludes company directors from gaining a tax credit under the incentive, because 'a company director does not need an additional incentive' to invest in their own company.[36] The incentive also excludes other corporate officers, such as managers and liquidators.[37] These exclusions are generally seen as appropriate as, while directors and managers may make significant investments in a startup, they usually do not face the same information asymmetries as third-party investors (see [2.2.1]).[38] Furthermore, they are likely to make their investments regardless of the existence of an incentive.[39] By excluding related parties from an incentive, governments can therefore minimise deadweight costs (particularly those related to the use of incentives for tax-planning purposes).[40]

However, independence requirements can cause problems for angel investors, as angels may often take a seat on the board of their investee companies or become directors (making them a related party of the company).[41] Allowances should ideally be made so that angels do not become ineligible investors in this situation, as this would discourage the provision of value-adding activities (eg taking a seat on the board to facilitate monitoring).[42] The UK's Seed Enterprise Investment Scheme, for instance, excludes investee company employees from participating in the incentive, but makes an exception for directors (thereby allowing angels to avoid the restriction where they are directors).[43] Alternatively, arm's-length criteria can be implemented such that they only apply when an investment is made, and not afterwards (as is done in relation to Australia's early stage investor tax incentive, mentioned above).

4.2.2. Indirect Investors (Funds, Fund Managers and Passive Investors)

Where incentives target indirect investment in startups (ie investments through funds), eligibility criteria can be imposed in relation to venture capital funds, fund managers and/or passive investors. These criteria are varied and may

[34] ibid 77.
[35] OECD, 'Government Venture Capital' (n 2) 15.
[36] 'Frequently Asked Questions' (n 17).
[37] ibid.
[38] European Commission, 'Effectiveness of Tax Incentives' (n 1) 88.
[39] ibid.
[40] ibid 77.
[41] ibid 77–78.
[42] ibid.
[43] Income Tax Act 2007 (UK), s 257BA.

involve both objective criteria such as fund size (see [4.2.2.1]), fund structure and lifetime (see [4.2.2.2]), passive investor character (see [4.2.2.5]) and investor residence (see [4.2.2.6]), as well as subjective criteria such as fund manager experience (see [4.2.2.3]) and fund manager investment strategy, activities and compensation (see [4.2.2.4]). All of these different kinds of criteria are discussed in detail below.

4.2.2.1. Fund Size

The size of a venture capital fund can impact its performance in a number of ways, and there are disadvantages to both funds that are too small and those that are too large. For this reason, governments commonly include minimum and/or maximum fund size criteria in their incentive rules.

Small funds are often at a disadvantage to large funds because of fixed investment costs (see [2.2.2]): once investment costs are accounted for, smaller funds have less capital to invest than larger ones (which also prejudices their ability to make follow-on investments that support their investees over the long term).[44] Smaller funds are therefore more likely to require government support in order to produce profitable investments and remain commercially viable,[45] which is why small funds can particularly benefit from government co-investment. In order to ensure that the funds participating in incentives have sufficient size to cover costs and support investees through multiple funding rounds,[46] governments may place minimum size restrictions on funds participating in incentives. For example, Australia's Venture Capital Limited Partnership and Early Stage Venture Capital Limited Partnership programmes (which provide tax benefits to investors in registered venture capital funds) require that registered funds have at least AUD 10 million of committed capital (and no more than AUD 200 million of committed capital in the case of Early Stage Venture Capital Limited Partnerships).[47] The UK's Enterprise Capital Funds programme (a debt co-investment incentive that makes loans to venture capital funds), on the other hand, places neither upper nor lower limits on the size of its funds. Instead, it simply requires funds to demonstrate that they are 'viable' in light of their proposed investment strategy.[48] This requirement is therefore subjective, unlike most fund size requirements (which are objective), and is therefore more uncertain. However, the programme

[44] OECD, 'Government Venture Capital' (n 2) 13; United Nations Economic Commission for Europe (n 7) 43.

[45] Gordon Murray, Marc Cowling, Weixi Liu and Olga Kalinowska-Beszczynska, 'Government Co-Financed "Hybrid" Venture Capital Programmes: Generalizing Developed Economy Experience and its Relevance to Emerging Nations' (Kauffman International Research and Policy Roundtable, 11–12 March 2012) 10.

[46] Karen Wilson, 'Policy Lessons from Financing Young Innovative Firms' (OECD, June 2015) OECD Science, Technology and Industry Policy Papers No 24, 10.

[47] Venture Capital Act 2002 (Australia), ss 9-1, 9-3.

[48] British Business Bank, 'Enterprise Capital Funds: Guidance for Prospective Managers' (November 2014) Part 1 (iv)(a).

will not contribute more than GBP 50 million per fund and, interestingly, some fund managers under the programme have reported that this limit is overly rigid and has constrained the levels of funding raised.[49]

Large funds have their own associated problems. Research suggests that at a certain size, fund investment returns begin to decline,[50] perhaps as a result of 'diseconomies of scale' and attention problems whereby fund managers have too many investees to monitor and manage.[51] Funds with larger portfolios per manager reportedly add less value to investees because the actual value added by venture capitalists is strongly correlated to the amount of time devoted to investees, and larger portfolios mean managers have less time for each investee.[52] For example, it has been estimated that funds with one extra investee per manager in their portfolio provide an average of two to three less hours of support per month and 20 per cent less advice to entrepreneurs.[53] This issue has been seen with Canada's Labour-Sponsored Venture Capital Corporations (LSVCCs), which are large tax-advantaged funds with a high number of investees per manager (in 2011 the portfolio size per manager of LSVCCs was reportedly double that of private funds).[54] The size and large portfolios of the LSVCCs reportedly make it difficult for managers to provide value-adding services effectively, which has likely contributed to the programme's poor outcomes.[55] Larger venture capital funds also tend to make larger investments for efficiency reasons, lessening the focus on early-stage investments and potentially leading to investment drift.[56] For these reasons, it is also common for governments to place maximum size restrictions on the funds participating in incentives (as in the example of Australia's Early Stage Venture Capital Limited Partnership programme above). Provided that they are proportionate and broadly in line with the size of commercial funds, both minimum and maximum fund size criteria are recommended for the reasons discussed here.

4.2.2.2. Fund Structure and Lifetime

Some incentives require venture capital funds to be structured as a specific kind of entity, such as a limited partnership (eg Australia's Venture Capital Limited

[49] Ipsos MORI and George Barrett, 'Enterprise Capital Funds: Interim Evaluation' (November 2021) 30.

[50] Wilson (n 46) 10.

[51] Douglas J Cumming, Luca Grilli and Samuele Murtinu, 'Government and Independent Venture Capital Investments in Europe: A Firm-Level Performance Analysis' (2017) 42 *Journal of Corporate Finance* 439, 442.

[52] Terttu Luukkonen, Matthias Deschryvere and Fabio Bertoni, 'The Value Added by Government Venture Capital Funds Compared with Independent Venture Capital Funds' (2013) 33 *Technovation* 154, 155.

[53] Douglas Cumming and Sofia Johan, 'Pre-Seed Government Venture Capital Funds' (2009) 7(1) *Journal of International Entrepreneurship* 26, 33.

[54] Douglas Cumming, 'Public Policy and the Creation of Active Venture Capital Markets' (2011) 13(1) *Venture Capital* 75, 84.

[55] ibid 82–85.

[56] See United Nations Economic Commission for Europe (n 7) 43.

Partnership and Early Stage Venture Capital Limited Partnership programmes, mentioned above) or a company (eg Malaysia's tax incentives for venture capital investors).[57] Other incentives are more flexible. For instance, Poland's National Capital Fund (KFK) (a co-investment fund) invested in funds that were companies, limited partnerships, limited joint-stock partnerships or other organisational units without legal personality.[58] As noted at [2.4.2], limited partnerships (with flow-through taxation) are the industry standard for venture capital funds (particularly in the USA, although perhaps less so in other places), so incentives that require or allow the use of this structure may encourage participation.

Regardless of the fund structure, funds that have a 'fixed lifetime' (ie a predetermined end or closing date) are particularly attractive to both investors and governments. Investors generally want to know when they can expect to have their investment capital repaid and when they can expect to receive their returns. In contrast, governments generally prefer funds with fixed lifetimes so that the provision of incentives to these funds has a set duration. The difficulty of 'ending' an incentive given in relation to open-ended funds can be seen in the example of Australia's Pooled Development Funds programme. This programme used an open-ended corporate venture capital fund form, and although the programme was 'frozen' in 2007 so that new funds have not been able to be registered since that date, as at January 2024, 18 funds are still registered under the programme and continue to receive tax benefits.[59] Although some discussion has been had regarding 'deregistering' the remaining funds, this would have equity implications for the fund managers and investors.[60] As such, the provision of incentives to these funds will continue for the foreseeable future even though the Pooled Development Funds programme has been superseded by the Early Stage Venture Capital Limited Partnership programme for some time. Using a fund structure with a fixed lifetime (such as a limited partnership) or imposing a fixed-lifetime requirement on funds is therefore a functional way to avoid this problem.

In order to enhance certainty, governments often impose finite lifetime criteria on funds participating in their incentives, regardless of the fund structure used. Nevertheless, it is also important for funds to have some timing flexibility, as economic conditions and other factors might make it impractical for funds to divest all their investments by a certain date.[61] For this reason, incentives may allow an optional fund lifetime extension that can be utilised as necessary. For instance,

[57] Income Tax Assessment Act 1997 (Australia), ss 118-405, 118-407; Inland Revenue Board of Malaysia, *Venture Capital Tax Incentives* (9 May 2016) Public Ruling No 2/2016, cl 4.2. See also Stephen Barkoczy and Peter Edmundson, 'Australasian and South East Asian Venture Capital Tax Expenditure Programs' (2009) 37(1) *Intertax* 56, 72.

[58] Ustawa z dnia 4 marca 2005 r o Krajowym Funduszu Kapitałowym (Poland), Art 11.

[59] 'List of Pooled Development Funds' (*Business*, 18 January 2024) business.gov.au/grants-and-programs/pooled-development-funds/list-of-pooled-development-funds.

[60] See Stephen Barkoczy, Tamara Wilkinson, Ann L Monotti and Mark Davison, *Innovation and Venture Capital Law and Policy* (Federation Press, 2016) 291.

[61] Robert Baldock, 'An Assessment of the Business Impacts of the UK's Enterprise Capital Funds' (2016) 34(8) *Environment and Planning C: Government and Policy* 1556, 1561.

Australia's former Innovation Investment Fund programme (an equity co-investment programme) required funds to have a 10-year lifespan, with an optional three-year divestment extension.[62] In contrast, Australia's current Biomedical Translation Fund co-investment programme requires funds to have a longer 15-year lifespan, but with no optional extension.[63] Likewise, Australia's Venture Capital Limited Partnership tax incentive programme requires registered funds to remain in existence for between five and 15 years.[64] The UK's Enterprise Capital Funds programme expects that funds will have a fixed 10-year lifespan with an optional two-year extension, in line with industry standards, but also states that it will consider alternative time frames where 'suitable justification' is provided by the fund manager.[65] As can be seen from these examples, lifetime criteria are particularly popular under equity and loan co-investment incentives (although they are also often used in relation to tax incentives). The use of lifetime criteria is recommended for the reasons discussed here, provided that the length of fund lifetimes is reasonable and there is a degree of flexibility to facilitate optimal divestment.

4.2.2.3. Fund Manager Experience

The characteristics of a fund manager can have important impacts on the success of venture capital investments.[66] Recognising this, governments often use competitive selection processes, including 'merit' criteria, to target certain fund manager characteristics.[67] These commonly include either: experience in managing funds and early-stage investment and a strong reputation; or being new entrants to the venture capital market.

Requiring fund managers to have prior experience is a good way to ensure their competency and increase the chances of investment success and other positive outcomes (although it may also exclude new entrants to the market, as discussed in relation to direct investors at [4.2.1.2]).[68] Competence is especially important for fund managers considering they invest other peoples' money (including the government's, in the case of co-investment incentives). Fund managers that have specialised skills, such as technical experience in business, management and entrepreneurship, specialised industry experience and strong networks are more likely to have increased capabilities for identifying

[62] Innovation Investment Fund Program Round Three Guidelines No 1 of 2011 (Australia), cl 88.

[63] Australian Government, Department of Industry Innovation and Science and Department of Health, 'Biomedical Translation Fund Programme Guidelines' (3 August 2016) cl 8.10.

[64] Venture Capital Act 2002 (Australia), s 9-1.

[65] British Business Bank (n 48) Part 2 (i)(a).

[66] See Cumming and Johan (n 53) 52; Federico Munari and Laura Toschi, 'Assessing the Impact of Public Venture Capital Programmes in the United Kingdom: Do Regional Characteristics Matter?' (2015) 30(2) *Journal of Business Venturing* 205, 208.

[67] See United Nations Economic Commission for Europe (n 7) 88.

[68] See Massimo Colombo, Fabio Bertoni and Terttu Luukkonen, 'Venture Capital: Policy Lessons from the VICO Project' (European Commission, 2011) 10.

investment opportunities, evaluating deals and conducting due diligence, and are more likely to be active investors who add value to their investees and stimulate investee growth.[69] Fund manager reputation can also impact investee success, with well-reputed fund managers potentially providing more effective managerial support,[70] generating greater increases in total factor productivity for their investees and achieving higher priced and more successful exits.[71] Unfortunately, high-quality, experienced and successful fund managers can be scarce, and may also be difficult to recruit into incentives.[72] This is particularly likely to be the case where incentive rules require funds to be based regionally or to focus on extremely early-stage investments (see [4.4]).[73]

Poland's KFK was an example of a co-investment incentive that looked for experienced and professional fund managers with prior success in venture capital investments (measured by number of deals and internal rates of return) to run its funds. Special attention was paid to prior experience in managing venture capital projects (especially innovative projects and those at early stages), investment exits and establishing and managing enterprises.[74] The incentive used a competitive selection process to select high-quality fund managers who would ideally increase the value of portfolio companies and produce high rates of return for investors.[75] Likewise, the UK's Enterprise Capital Funds programme assesses prospective recipients on their strength, expertise and experience as a management team, looking at factors including their ability to raise capital from the private sector, attract high-quality deal flow, carry out due diligence, negotiate investments, provide value-adding activities to investees, comply with reporting requirements and realise returns from investments.[76]

Governments that are looking to diversify and grow the number of venture capital funds operating in their jurisdictions might target new fund managers with little or no venture capital investment experience, rather than targeting experienced fund managers. For instance, France's Investissement Garantie (now the Garantie de Fonds Propres Relance) had a preference for new fund managers, as

[69] Miona Milosevic and Jacqueline Fendt, 'Venture Capital and its French Exception: Explaining Performance through Human Capital, Policy and Institutional Failures' (2016) 43(5) *Science and Public Policy* 660, 664; Dirk De Clercq and Sophie Manigart, 'The Venture Capital Post-Investment Phase: Opening the Black Box of Involvement' in Hans Landström (ed), *Handbook of Research on Venture Capital* (Edward Elgar, 2007) 193, 203–04; United Nations Economic Commission for Europe (n 7) 31, 33; Colombo et al (n 68) 10.

[70] *cf* De Clerq and Manigart (n 69) 202.

[71] Thomas J Chemmanur, Karthik Krishnan and Debarshi K Nandy, 'How Does Venture Capital Financing Improve Efficiency in Private Firms? A Look Beneath the Surface' (2011) 24(12) *The Review of Financial Studies* 4037, 4038, 4042, 4079; Christian Keuschnigg and Søren Bo Nielsen, 'Tax Policy, Venture Capital, and Entrepreneurship' (2002) 87(1) *Journal of Public Economics* 175, 182.

[72] Murray et al (n 45) 10.

[73] Munari and Toschi (n 66) 208.

[74] See Ustawa z dnia 4 marca 2005 r o Krajowym Funduszu Kapitałowym (Poland), Art 12.

[75] Although KFK has now closed, information about the venture capital funds it invested in can be found at: PFR Ventures, 'PFR Ventures Portfolio', pfrventures.pl/en/portfolio.html?Tab=database.

[76] British Business Bank (n 48) Part 4 (i).

it aimed to stimulate the development of the venture capital market in France.[77] Canada's Venture Capital Catalyst Initiative (a co-investment incentive) strikes a balance, expressing a preference for 'experienced or high-potential fund managers' that have managed venture capital or private equity funds or that have relevant entrepreneurial experience in the sector, but acknowledging and welcoming applications by new funds/management teams as well as diverse applications.[78] In some ways, targeting new fund managers makes sense, as it is recognised that venture capital investment has a steep learning curve and new fund managers often find it difficult to raise capital and break into the industry (see [3.2.4]).[79] By allowing and encouraging new fund managers to participate in incentives, governments may be able to play a 'certifying' role, helping fund managers establish relationships with institutional investors.[80] This can help fund managers increase their skills and develop a track record, eventually contributing to deeper venture capital markets (although it may come at the expense of other incentive outcomes, such as investor returns, being poorer). Where an incentive targets new fund managers, it remains important to ensure that these entities are still 'professionals whose success in prior endeavours will support their current efforts'.[81] Ultimately, the question of whether incentives should target experienced or new fund managers depends in large part on their policy aims (ie whether they are intended to improve fund quality or quantity).

4.2.2.4. Fund Manager Investment Strategy and Activities

The ways that fund managers approach investments can also be the subject of eligibility or merit criteria. In particular, it is not uncommon for governments to require fund managers to have a specific investment strategy in place that details prospective investees and portfolio size. An investment strategy requirement may be used to help governments select the best fund managers and ensure that fund managers are making the 'right' kinds of investments. Examples of incentives that have investment strategy requirements include:

- **Australia's Biomedical Translation Fund programme.** In deciding whether to license a fund manager under the programme, the regulator considers a range of merit criteria, one of which is the applicant's 'proposed investment strategy'. This includes, among other things: the extent to which the fund's proposed investment strategy is consistent with the programme's objectives,

[77] See Jasper Deuten, 'Venture Capital Investment Guarantee Programme by OSEO' (INNO Partnering Forum, 2011) 10.

[78] Innovation, Science and Economic Development Canada, 'Venture Capital Catalyst Initiative: Call for Expressions of Interest' (2022) 25, 28.

[79] See United Nations Economic Commission for Europe (n 7) 33.

[80] ibid 84, 92.

[81] Ann Leamon, Maria Susana Garcia-Robles and Josh Lerner, 'Best Practices in Creating a Venture Capital Ecosystem' (Multilateral Investment Fund of Inter-American Development Bank, December 2012) 45. See also Colombo et al (n 68) 10.

including the establishment and management of a balanced portfolio of investments that meets the programme's policy objectives; the number and the size of investments the fund proposes to make and the proposed investment focus; and the level and structure of management fees and distribution arrangements proposed.[82]

- **Australia's Early Stage Venture Capital Limited Partnership programme.** Early Stage Venture Capital Limited Partnerships are required to have an appropriate investment plan in order to be registered under the programme.[83] In deciding whether to approve an investment plan, the regulator must consider the extent to which the partnership focuses on early-stage venture capital, including: the stages of development, levels of cash flow, levels of technology, proportions of intellectual property to total assets, levels of risk and return, amount of tangible assets and collateral against which borrowing can be secured of the proposed investees, and the extent to which the partnership plans to comply with the Early Stage Venture Capital Limited Partnership programme requirements (among other things).[84]
- **The UK's Enterprise Capital Funds programme.** Under the Enterprise Capital Funds programme, the regulator must select funds to receive debt co-investment. As part of this process, one of the things the regulator considers is each applicant's investment strategy. In assessing a fund's proposed investment strategy, the regulator requires prospective fund managers to demonstrate that their strategy is consistent with the programme rules, targets an equity gap and is commercially viable. Fund managers should show that the fund has good prospects of delivering a high financial return, that potential conflicts of interest will be satisfactorily resolved and that the fund manager will be suitably resourced. Other things being equal, the regulator favours approaches that demonstrate that the proposed fund would target a particularly acute part of the equity gap. The regulator will also consider the fund's capacity to make non-financial contributions to the performance of the investee businesses (ie by providing value-adding activities).[85]
- **Poland's KFK co-investment fund.** As with the Enterprise Capital Funds programme above, the regulator of Poland's KFK co-investment fund had to select funds to receive co-investment and considered, among other things, the funds' investment strategies.[86] In assessing investment strategies, the regulator looked in particular for those that forecast high rates of return and were compatible with the management team's experience (including knowledge of the Polish market and potential to realise the investment strategy).

[82] Australian Government, Department of Industry Innovation and Science and Department of Health (n 63) cl 4.2.
[83] Venture Capital Act 2002 (Australia), s 13-1(1A).
[84] ibid ss 13-15, 13-20.
[85] British Business Bank (n 48) Part 4 (ii).
[86] Ustawa z dnia 4 marca 2005 r o Krajowym Funduszu Kapitałowym (Poland), Art 12.

Governments often want to ensure that fund managers operating under their incentives provide a high level of value-adding activities. This is because the level of value-adding activities contributed by fund managers correlates with the overall 'quality' of venture capital finance (ie the greater the level of value-adding activities provided, the higher the quality of the venture capital finance).[87] Value-adding activities become more important the earlier the stage of investment.[88] However, there is a 'wide variation' in how much particular fund managers engage in these activities,[89] and incentives may also unintentionally demotivate fund managers from providing value-adding activities.[90] For instance, fund sizes under Canada's Labour-Sponsored Venture Capital Corporation programme have at times been so large that fund managers were reportedly unable to devote sufficient time to their investees (due to their large portfolios), contributing to poor results for the programme.[91] It is therefore worth considering how governments can actively motivate fund managers to provide value-adding activities.[92] This may be done by imposing specific active investor requirements (although these can be hard to define, monitor and enforce), providing profit-related incentives so that incentives only arise where investments succeed (see [3.3]) and structuring compensation in ways that are primarily linked to investment performance (for instance, by paying fund managers lower management fees and higher carried interest payments).[93] For this reason, when selecting fund managers to participate in an incentive, some governments may look at the level and structure of compensation a fund manager proposed that they be entitled to receive for managing a fund (this is particularly relevant in relation to co-investment incentives).[94] For example, the regulator of the UK's Enterprise Capital Funds programme selects fund managers on a competitive basis and requires prospective fund managers to ensure that management costs will not be 'excessive'.[95] The British Business Bank (the regulator) has regard to the 'strength of the link between the financial performance of the fund and the remuneration of those individuals responsible for taking the investment decisions and otherwise managing the fund'.[96] As mentioned above, Australia's Biomedical Translation Fund co-investment programme also looks at 'the level and structure of management fees and distribution arrangements proposed' as one of its merit criteria for selecting fund managers,[97] as does

[87] See Keuschnigg and Nielsen (n 71) 177.
[88] European Commission, 'Effectiveness of Tax Incentives' (n 1) 35.
[89] United Nations Economic Commission for Europe (n 7) 33.
[90] ibid 88.
[91] ibid.
[92] OECD, 'Government Venture Capital' (n 2) 13.
[93] See Bravo-Biosca (n 3) 8; United Nations Economic Commission for Europe (n 7) 88; Milosevic and Fendt (n 69) 666.
[94] See De Clerq and Manigart (n 69) 212.
[95] British Business Bank (n 48) Part 4 (iv).
[96] ibid.
[97] Australian Government, Department of Industry Innovation and Science and Department of Health (n 82) cl 4.2.

Canada's Venture Capital Catalyst Initiative, which requires management fees to be 'competitive and based on comparable terms' in the Canadian venture capital market.[98] Competitive selection processes such as these help ensure that fund managers licensed under the programmes have the right kinds of performance incentives to provide value-adding activities.

Requiring fund managers to invest an amount of their own capital in their fund can also help to encourage active investment and the provision of value-adding activities.[99] For example, Chile's former loan co-investment programme reportedly required fund managers to invest at least 15 per cent of their assets (as opposed to the funds' assets) in the funds they managed in order to align their interests with those of the other investors.[100] Likewise, Poland's KFK looked specifically for fund managers that contributed to the fund's share capital when selecting recipients, and the UK's Enterprise Capital Funds programme also encourages fund managers to contribute to the fund as 'this would be viewed as a positive signal of the manager's commitment and belief in the likely success of the fund'.[101]

Of the various criteria discussed in this section, it is suggested that investment plan requirements may help focus investments on the desired targets and ensure that fund managers operate within the scope of an incentive; however, they also add to incentive uncertainty and administrative and compliance costs. It is therefore difficult to know whether the use of these criteria is justified or not. The criteria that help encourage the provision of value-adding activities, on the other hand, are recommended. In particular, it is suggested that incentives should ensure that fund manager remuneration is structured so as to incentivise successful investments and should also require fund managers to contribute some small amount of their own capital to their funds.

4.2.2.5. Passive Investor Character

While it may seem counterintuitive to impose eligibility criteria on passive investors (as this limits the pool of available investors), the characteristics of passive investors can actually play a role in the 'success, selection and post-investment activism' of venture capitalists.[102] For instance, funds that receive investment from insurance companies and corporations reportedly tend to invest more

[98] Innovation, Science and Economic Development Canada (n 78) 12. Interestingly, the previous 2017 iteration of the programme requires management fees to be at 'the minimum, market-based rate' and to give preference to applications with 'lower proposed incentive structures': Innovation, Science and Economic Development Canada, 'Venture Capital Catalyst Initiative: Call for Expressions of Interest' (2017) 16.

[99] Colombo et al (n 68) 25.

[100] Ronald J Gilson, 'Engineering a Venture Capital Market: Lessons from the American Experience' (2003) 55 *Stanford Law Review* 1067, 1098.

[101] British Business Bank (n 48) Part 2 (i)(a).

[102] Milosevic and Fendt (n 69) 662.

internationally, while those financed by banks tend to invest locally and in later stage (lower risk) investments.[103] Venture capital funds backed by government capital are more likely to invest in earlier stage, high-tech investments, in line with government venture capital policy, and institutional investors such as pension funds are generally willing to make long-term investments (unlike most banks).[104]

Incentives may also use eligibility criteria to exclude certain passive investors, such as inexperienced retail investors, in order to protect them. For example, only 'well-informed' investors (ie investors who are 'able to adequately assess the risks associated with an investment in such a vehicle') can acquire securities or partnership interests in Luxembourg's reserved alternative investment funds (RAIFs) (which are collective investment vehicles that invest in venture capital and private equity).[105] For the purposes of the RAIF regime, a well-informed investor is taken to include:

- an institutional investor (eg banks, insurance companies, pension funds);
- a professional investor (eg 'high-net worth' individuals); and
- any other investor who confirms in writing that they adhere to the status of a well-informed investor and who either invests at least EUR 125,000 in a RAIF or has been subject to a qualifying assessment by a credit institution certifying their expertise, experience and knowledge in adequately appraising an investment in risk capital.[106]

By limiting participation in RAIFs to well-informed investors, the regime avoids investor protection issues that may otherwise arise, given the risky investments that these vehicles make. This kind of restriction is unlikely to significantly impact the pool of available investors, as not many retail investors are likely to have the capital or desire to invest in venture capital funds.

4.2.2.6. Passive Investor Residence

Some incentives specifically target foreign passive investors, as they have the capacity to bring 'large amounts of money, awareness of best practices, and wide networks' into the local market.[107] Companies backed by a syndicate of domestic and international investors reportedly experience 'more vibrant growth' than other venture capital-backed companies in both the short and long term.[108] A suggested

[103] ibid.
[104] ibid.
[105] Law of 23 July 2016 on Reserved Alternative Investment Funds (Luxembourg), Art 1; Association of the Luxembourg Fund Industry, 'RAIF (Luxembourg Reserved Alternative Investment Fund)' (2021) www.alfi.lu/en-GB/Pages/Setting-up-in-Luxembourg/Alternative-investment-funds-legal-vehicles/RAIF-(Luxembourg-Reserved-Alternative-Investment-F.
[106] Law of 23 July 2016 on Reserved Alternative Investment Funds (Luxembourg), Art 2.
[107] Leamon et al (n 81) 15.
[108] Colombo et al (n 68) 13.

explanation for this is that domestic investors are seen to provide 'close counselling' to investees, while international investors provide access to international skills and networks.[109] An example of an incentive that specifically targeted foreign investors was Israel's 1993 Yozma co-investment programme, which required fund managers to attract a reputable foreign venture capital fund or financial institution to invest in their funds (alongside a domestic partner and the government). This feature of the programme was designed to help integrate Israeli venture capitalists into an international network,[110] with the participation of foreign investors seen to play an important role in the 'training and development of local investors'.[111]

In a similar vein, Australia's Venture Capital Limited Partnership programme, introduced in 2002, aims to stimulate Australia's venture capital sector by attracting foreign investors.[112] It does this by providing that eligible foreign investors who invest in a Venture Capital Limited Partnership (a specially registered venture capital fund) are broadly exempt from paying tax on the profits made from the sale of eligible venture capital investments that have been held by the Venture Capital Limited Partnership for at least 12 months.[113] Eligible foreign investors include: tax-exempt foreign residents; foreign venture capital funds of funds (provided that their committed capital does not exceed 30 per cent of the Venture Capital Limited Partnership's total committed capital); and taxable foreign residents who are not the general partners of a Venture Capital Limited Partnership (or an Early Stage Venture Capital Limited Partnership) and whose committed capital is less than 10 per cent of the Venture Capital Limited Partnership's total committed capital.[114] The Venture Capital Limited Partnership programme's tax exemptions for foreign investors reduce the risks of double taxation associated with cross-border investment, which may encourage investment by these entities.[115] Facilitating cross-border investment may, in turn, potentially help increase local investment volume and stimulate the

[109] ibid.

[110] Gil Avnimelech, Martin Kenney and Morris Teubal, 'Building Venture Capital Industries: Understanding the US and Israeli Experiences' (Berkeley Roundtable on the International Economy, March 2004) Working Paper No 160, 33; United Nations Economic Commission for Europe (n 7) 88. The programme also required fund managers to attend the board meetings of all Yozma funds, which stimulated participatory learning, increased networks and stimulated co-investment between funds (34).

[111] Wilson and Silva (n 21) 52.

[112] Australian Government, Innovation and Science Australia, 'Annual Report 2018–19' (2019) 28.

[113] Income Tax Assessment Act 1997 (Australia), ss 51-54, 118-405.

[114] Income Tax Assessment Act 1997 (Australia), s 118-420. Australian residents can and do invest in Venture Capital Limited Partnerships; however, they are not entitled to any specific tax incentives for doing so.

[115] European Commission, 'Effectiveness of Tax Incentives' (n 1) 198. It should be noted, however, that following changes made in 2006, foreign investors who purchase shares in Australian companies are unlikely to be taxed on the disposal of these shares anyway, making the Venture Capital Limited Partnership exemptions less important. However, the Venture Capital Limited Partnership exemptions do still reduce any tax uncertainty for eligible foreign investors investing through a Venture Capital Limited Partnership: see Barkoczy et al (n 60) 234.

development of the domestic venture capital industry.[116] It was reported that the Venture Capital Limited Partnership programme increased foreign investment in Australian businesses by over half a billion Australian dollars in 2018–19,[117] and that foreign investors contributed over 11 billion dollars to funds registered under the programme in 2022–23.[118] The programme therefore seems to be making progress towards meeting its policy aim.

As with other criteria discussed in this chapter, the question of whether governments should use residence criteria to target foreign investors or not depends to a large extent on what they hope to achieve with their incentives (ie whether they are specifically interested in stimulating foreign investment). However, even if governments do not want to incentivise foreign investors in particular, it is recommended that they consider at least removing any tax or other barriers that may deter cross-border investments (see [2.4.2]). Where governments do specifically want to attract foreign investors and consequently provide tax benefits to these investors that local investors do not receive, they should be careful to ensure compliance with the BEPS Project Action 5 minimum standard, as in this case the incentive may be considered to be 'ring-fenced from the domestic economy' (see [3.3.2]).[119]

4.3. Targeting Investments

When targeting investments under an incentive, governments are required to decide what kinds of restrictions should be placed on investments and the investment process. Investment-targeting criteria involve a fine balance: they can help to align investor behaviour with incentive policy aims, but they can also operate to unduly constrain investors. In the worst cases, investment-targeting requirements may actually damage investment performance and investor competitiveness.[120] The following list of common investment criteria highlights positive and negative examples of investment targeting. It includes criteria dealing with investment character (ie equity versus debt, new versus second-hand investments and at-risk requirements; see [4.3.1]), size (see [4.3.2]) and timing (see [4.3.3]).

[116] European Commission, 'Effectiveness of Tax Incentives' (n 1) 198.

[117] ibid.

[118] Australian Government, Department of Industry, Science and Resources, 'Venture Capital Dashboard FY 2022/3' (2023) 14, www.industry.gov.au/sites/default/files/2020-02/venture-capital-dashboard.pdf.

[119] See OECD, 'Harmful Tax Practices – 2018 Progress Report on Preferential Regimes: Inclusive Framework On BEPS: Action 5' (OECD/G20 Base Erosion and Profit Shifting Project, 2019) 13.

[120] See Cromwell Schmisseur, 'Information and Observations on State Venture Capital Programs: Report for the US Department of the Treasury and Interested Parties in the State Small Business Credit Initiative (SSBCI)' (February 2013) 25.

4.3.1. Investment Character

Governments generally require investments under their incentives to be made in the form of equity (although small proportions of debt can also sometimes be allowed).[121] There are many reasons to prefer equity to debt for investments in innovative startups (see [1.2.2]). Among other things, equity investment is more likely to encourage active investment (because investors own a stake in the company and, unlike debt investors, will have subordinated interests if the investee company is wound up) and may facilitate knowledge spillovers between investors and investees.[122] Equity investment may therefore help produce high-quality investees, and the inclusion of criteria targeting equity investment is generally considered to represent leading practice.[123]

An example of a programme that prioritises equity investment but allows for some flexibility is Australia's Early Stage Venture Capital Limited Partnership programme. The programme requires Early Stage Venture Capital Limited Partnership investments in startups to be in the form of shares in a company or units in a unit trust, options to acquire either of these securities, or convertible notes in a company or unit trust that do not constitute debt interests.[124] Early Stage Venture Capital Limited Partnerships can also make 'permitted loans' to their investees if they own at least 10 per cent of all the equity interests and debt interests that can be converted into equity interests in the investee company or unit trust.[125] In a similar vein, Germany's INVEST incentive requires investors to purchase newly issued shares on their own account, but allows shares to be acquired through convertible loans (although the INVEST grant will not be paid until the conversion is made).[126] Likewise, Québec's former Business Investment Company tax incentive allowed investors a tax deduction when they purchased convertible preferred shares, but at a lower rate than when they purchased ordinary shares.[127] New Zealand's Aspire angel co-investment fund takes an even broader approach – it is willing to make co-investments in investees through the purchase of shares, preference shares, convertible loans or other such instruments.[128] It will not, however, invest through non-convertible debt instruments, tokens or derivatives, and will not provide grants or loans.

[121] See European Commission, 'Effectiveness of Tax Incentives' (n 1) 148.

[122] ibid 78, 89, 180; Barkoczy et al (n 60) 54.

[123] See European Commission, 'Effectiveness of Tax Incentives' (n 1) 180.

[124] Income Tax Assessment Act 1997 (Australia), ss 118-425(1), 118-427(1).

[125] A loan that is repaid within six months, or such longer period as Innovation Australia allows, is also deemed to be a permitted loan: Venture Capital Act 2002 (Australia), ss 9-1, 9-2, 9-10.

[126] Federal Ministry for Economic Affairs and Climate Action, 'INVEST – Venture Capital Grant' (April 2023) 6–7.

[127] Finances Québec, 'Adjustments to Certain Measures Announced in the Budget Speech of June 12, 2003' (18 July 2003) 2003-3 *Bulletin d'Information* 2.

[128] NZ Growth Capital Partners, 'Aspire NZ Seed Fund – FAQs' (November 2022) 7, www.nzgcp.co.nz/assets/Uploads/NZGCP-Aspire-FAQ_Nov22.pdf.

Incentives may also impose conditions requiring investments to be made in the form of newly issued shares in an investee company. For instance, Germany's INVEST grant incentive, Belgium's Tax Shelter Start-Up and Ireland's Employment and Investment Incentive (an investment-related incentive for direct and indirect investment) all require investors to subscribe for new shares in investees in order to be eligible for incentives.[129] Many other incentives have similar conditions. Requiring investors to purchase new shares is entirely appropriate and represents leading practice. It ensures that investment capital is channelled to the issuing startup, and reduces the chance of providing windfalls to investors, which, in turn, helps increase the additionality of incentives.[130] In contrast, the purchase of second-hand shares generally represents a deadweight cost for incentives, as it does not involve the channelling of new capital to startups.[131] The only reason to allow for the purchase of second-hand shares under an incentive is to provide flexibility and security for investors in being able to increase their ownership and control over an investee, although this is not a particularly compelling justification. Nevertheless, some incentives, such as Australia's Venture Capital Limited Partnership programme, discussed above, do allow for the purchase of pre-owned shares. This aspect of the Venture Capital Limited Partnership programme has been criticised, with commentators noting that it allows transactions that are more properly characterised as later-stage private equity.[132] In general, criteria limiting investments under incentives to the purchase of new equity is recommended as an efficiency measure.

Finally, some incentives only apply in relation to investments that are held 'at risk', meaning, in a broad sense, that they represent true venture capital investments, with no special arrangements in place – such as options or other derivatives – that remove risk to the investor. Risk criteria can improve the targeting of investments by ensuring that they are made for the purpose of helping investee companies grow and become successful (rather than for other purposes, such as obtaining tax benefits). In this sense, at-risk criteria fulfil an anti-avoidance purpose (see [5.4.2]), in that they only allow investors to benefit from incentives where they are subject to the full risks of the investment.

The UK introduced a 'risk to capital' condition in 2018 under its Seed Enterprise Investment Scheme, Enterprise Investment Scheme and Venture Capital Trusts scheme for this reason. Under the schemes, the risk to capital condition is met if, having regard to all the circumstances existing at the time of the issue of the shares, it would be reasonable to conclude that (i) the issuing company

[129] See Federal Ministry for Economic Affairs and Climate Action (n 126) 6; Code des Impôts sur les Revenus 1992 (Belgium), Art 145/26 § 1; Irish Tax and Customs, 'Relief for Investment in Corporate Trades' in *Tax and Duty Manual* (April 2023) Part 16-00-02, 44, www.revenue.ie/en/tax-professionals/tdm/income-tax-capital-gains-tax-corporation-tax/part-16/16-00-02.pdf; Taxes Consolidation Act 1997 (Ireland), ss 494, 495.

[130] European Commission, 'Effectiveness of Tax Incentives' (n 1) 14, 79.

[131] ibid 89.

[132] See Barkoczy et al (n 60) 312.

has objectives to grow and develop its trade in the long-term, and (ii) there is a significant risk that there will be a loss of capital of an amount greater than the net investment return.[133] The risk to capital condition is designed primarily to exclude tax-motivated investments from benefiting under the schemes, and to ensure that investments represent genuine venture capital.[134] Other examples of incentives that use risk criteria include the following:

- **Ireland's Employment and Investment Incentive.** This incentive provides that there can be no terms of the relevant shares or agreements with the company or its shareholders that substantially reduce the risk that the investor will get their capital back or any expected dividend.[135] If an individual acquires an option, enters into an agreement or grants an option that would bind any person to purchase their eligible shares or would bind the individual to dispose of their eligible shares to any person for a price other than the market value of the shares, they are not entitled to tax relief under the Employment and Investment Incentive in relation to those shares.[136]
- **Australia's Venture Capital Limited Partnership and Early Stage Venture Capital Limited Partnership programmes.** These programmes provide that investments must be held 'at risk', meaning there must be no arrangement as to the maintenance of the value of the investment or the maintenance of any earnings or other return that might be made from owning the investment.[137]
- **Germany's INVEST grant.** This incentive provides that investment must be made in all opportunities and risks carried by the business.[138] However, standard market liquidation preferences (agreements that set the payout order in the case of investee liquidation) and anti-dilution provisions (agreements that allow investors to purchase shares in future in order to maintain their ownership percentage in an investee) are permitted.[139]
- **Luxembourg's RAIF regime.** Under this regime, RAIFs must provide in their constitutive documents that their exclusive object is 'the investment of their funds in assets representing risk capital', with risk capital defined as the direct or indirect contribution of assets to entities in view of their launch, development or listing on a stock exchange.[140]

[133] Income Tax Act 2007 (UK), s 257AAA.
[134] HM Revenue & Customs, 'Income Tax: Venture Capital Schemes – Risk to Capital Condition' (22 November 2017) www.gov.uk/government/publications/income-tax-venture-capital-schemes-risk-to-capital-condition/income-tax-venture-capital-schemes-risk-to-capital-condition. See also Wilkinson and Barkoczy (n 12) 84.
[135] Irish Tax and Custom (n 129) 44.
[136] ibid; Taxes Consolidation Act 1997 (Ireland), s 498.
[137] Income Tax Assessment Act 1997 (Australia), ss 118-425(1), 118-427(1), 118-430.
[138] Federal Ministry for Economic Affairs and Climate Action (n 126) 7.
[139] ibid.
[140] Law of 23 July 2016 on Reserved Alternative Investment Funds (Luxembourg), Art 48.

In general, risk conditions fulfil important targeting and integrity functions, and their use is recommended. Their only downside is that they can increase incentive complexity, but this is likely to be outweighed by their benefits.

4.3.2. Maximum Investment Criteria

Maximum investment criteria can serve four purposes: they can limit the cost of providing incentives; they can help keep investments small (countering investment drift); they can help protect investors by limiting their risk exposure; and/or they can encourage investors to diversify their investments by spreading their capital between different investees. For these reasons, maximum investment limits are common.[141] Maximum investment limits can apply to both individual investments and individual investors. In other words, they can limit the amount of capital that can be committed to a particular investment or they can limit the aggregate amount of capital that an investor can invest under an incentive, usually per year. Maximum investment limits can also be 'hard' or 'soft' limits. When a hard limit applies, investments above the limit are prohibited under an incentive and may lead to incentive benefits being denied or rescinded. In contrast, when a soft limit applies, any investment above the limit will not usually attract additional incentive benefits. Generally speaking, soft limits are more often intended to control incentive costs, while hard limits are more often intended to protect investors. The following discussion looks first at maximum investment limits that apply to investments, then at maximum investment limits that apply to investors.

Maximum investment limits that apply per investment are almost always aimed at encouraging investment diversification (and therefore investor protection).[142] These limits can be calculated by reference to a specific investment amount, by reference to the ownership interests taken in an investee[143] or by reference to a percentage of a fund's committed capital. For example, Australia's Innovation Investment Fund co-investment programme provided that no more than 20 per cent of a licensed fund's committed capital could be invested in any one investee company.[144] In contrast, the UK's Seed Enterprise Investment Scheme and Australia's early stage investor tax incentive both limit investors to holding a

[141] European Commission, 'Effectiveness of Tax Incentives' (n 1) 79, 147.

[142] See, eg Explanatory Memorandum, Tax Laws Amendment (Tax Incentives for Innovation) Bill 2016 (Australia), 12.

[143] European Commission, 'Effectiveness of Tax Incentives' (n 1) 148.

[144] This limit was raised from 10% at the start of the programme's operation. See Innovation Investment Fund Program Round Three Guidelines No 1 of 2011 (Australia), cl 77. Australia's Biomedical Translation Fund has the same requirement: Australian Government, Department of Industry Innovation and Science and Department of Health (n 63) cl 8.7. Under Australia's Early Stage Venture Capital Limited Partnership programme, the total amount invested in any one investee must not exceed 30% of the Early Stage Venture Capital Limited Partnership's committed capital: Income Tax Assessment Act 1997 (Australia), ss 118-425(1), 118-427(1), 118-445.

maximum interest in their investees of 30 per cent (although the Seed Enterprise Investment Scheme requirement applies for three years, while the early stage investor requirement only applies at the time the investment is made).[145] Belgium's Tax Shelter Start-Up likewise provides that an investor may hold no more than 30 per cent of the shares in an investee company.[146] Straightforward investment amount limits applied under two former UK co-investment programmes, the Regional Venture Capital Funds (which only allowed investments up to GBP 660,000 per investee) and the Early Growth Funds (which only allowed investments up to GBP 200,000 per investee).[147] New Zealand's Aspire Fund (an angel co-investment fund) was originally limited to investing no more than NZD 1.5 million per portfolio company, with this limit raised to NZD 2.5 million as a result of the impact of COVID-19, then removed entirely in 2022.[148]

Although maximum investment limits are intended to help reduce the risk of venture capital investment, they can cause a number of problems, particularly when they are set too low. For instance, in the case of the Regional Venture Capital Funds and Early Growth Funds programmes, the low investment limits hampered the performance of the funds under the programmes and made it 'harder to demonstrate the commercial attractiveness of early-stage [venture capital] investments (a key government objective)'.[149] Low investment limits can require investors to make investments that are too small to be commercially efficient/attractive, or to spread their capital too thinly, making investors less able and inclined to provide value-adding services (as they have only a small stake in each company and a large number of investments to manage).[150] Low maximum investment limits may also prevent or discourage investors from making follow-on investments in their investees, which can lead to diluted investments and depressed investment returns.[151] For instance, once the investment limits were met under any of the co-investment programmes mentioned above, no further follow-on investments could be made in those investees, even if they were vitally necessary. It is very important, therefore, that governments are not overly restrictive when setting maximum investment limits. Most venture capital investors are already cognisant of the need to diversify their investments, and do not necessarily need limits such as these in order to do so. This is illustrated by the example of Luxembourg's RAIF regime, which does not impose any interest,

[145] Income Tax Act 2007 (UK), ss 257BB, 257BF; Income Tax Assessment Act 1997 (Australia), s 360-15. See also Wilkinson and Barkoczy (n 12) 65, 85.

[146] Code des Impôts sur les Revenus 1992 (Belgium), Art 145/26 § 2.

[147] See BVCA and NESTA, 'From Funding Gaps to Thin Markets: UK Government Support for Early-Stage Venture Capital' (September 2009) 25.

[148] NZ Growth Capital Partners, 'Aspire NZ Seed Fund is Set to Increase Support for Tech Start-ups' (25 June 2020) www.nzgcp.co.nz/news-and-media/new-blog/aspire-nz-seed-fund-settings-change/; NZ Growth Capital Partners, 'Aspire NZ Seed Fund – FAQs' (n 128) 7.

[149] BVCA and NESTA (n 147) 25.

[150] ibid.

[151] ibid; Colin M Mason, 'Public Policy Support for the Informal Venture Capital Market in Europe: A Critical Review' (2009) 27(5) *International Small Business Journal* 536, 539.

size or diversification requirements on investments. RAIFs may invest their entire capital in one investee company and may also take a majority stake in their investees.[152] One reason for this is that, as discussed above, only 'qualified investors' may invest in a RAIF, and these investors are presumed to be aware of the risks of the RAIF's investment policy.[153] Therefore, while maximum interest limits serve an investor protection purpose and are unlikely to be detrimental provided they are not too low, their use may be superfluous, particularly in regard to incentives that target experienced or sophisticated investors.

Like maximum investment limits per investment, maximum investment limits per investor are relatively common. They are most frequently used in regard to investment-related incentives such as tax credits and deductions, because they limit the amount of investment investors can make in a year, which, in turn, limits the cost of providing incentives.[154] Often these limits will be soft limits, with amounts invested above them simply not qualifying for incentives. For example, Ireland's Employment and Investment Incentive imposes a soft maximum investment limit of EUR 250,000 per year, or EUR 500,000 per year if investors commit to holding their shares for at least seven years; investments made above these amounts do not qualify for tax relief.[155] Likewise, Australia's early stage investor tax incentive allows investors to make investments above AUD 1 million per year, but will not provide a tax incentive in relation to investment amounts that exceed this limit.[156] However, as noted at [4.2.1] above, retail investors who invest more than AUD 50,000 per year under the early stage investor tax incentive will lose any entitlement to the incentive.[157] The former soft limit is therefore aimed at controlling the costs of the incentive, while the latter hard limit is aimed at investor protection. Investment limits per investor can differ widely under different incentives. For example, Belgium's Tax Shelter Start-Up (which provides tax credits) allows investors to invest up to EUR 100,000 per year under the shelter.[158] In contrast, Germany's INVEST incentive allows individuals to claim investment grants on investments up to EUR 400,000 per year.[159] Although both incentives provide investment-related benefits to individual investors, their maximum investment limits differ. This may be for several reasons: for example, governments may have lower budgets for their incentives, or the incentives may be designed to focus on earlier stage (and therefore smaller) investments.

Interestingly, both Ireland and Germany, among other countries, also impose minimum investment limits on individual investments. Ireland requires the

[152] See KPMG, 'Reserved Alternative Investment Fund' (2017) 3.
[153] ibid 2.
[154] European Commission, 'Effectiveness of Tax Incentives' (n 1) 79.
[155] Irish Tax and Custom (n 129) 8–9.
[156] Income Tax Assessment Act 1997 (Australia), s 360-25.
[157] ibid ss 360-15, 360-20.
[158] 'Frequently Asked Questions' (n 17); European Commission, 'Effectiveness of Tax Incentives' (n 1) 142, 149.
[159] Federal Ministry for Economic Affairs and Climate Action (n 126) 3.

minimum annual investment by an individual in a company to be at least EUR 250,[160] while Germany requires individual investments to be at least EUR 10,000 (again, a significant difference in limits).[161] Minimum investment limits can help ensure that investments make a meaningful contribution (although whether Ireland's very low limit achieves this aim is questionable), but may also exclude less well-resourced investors from participating (which could be desired for investor protection reasons). Minimum investment limit criteria are unlikely to be necessary in most situations, as investors generally tend to prefer larger investments due to the issues of fixed investment costs, and retail investors can be excluded from incentives in other ways (such as through the use of wealth and experience criteria).

4.3.3. Timing and Holding Period Criteria

Where incentives involve investment through venture capital funds, governments may require that the funds' capital be invested within a specific number of years. These kinds of 'timing criteria' are particularly common in relation to co-investment incentives, as they allow governments to recoup their co-investment contributions within a reasonable amount of time (and therefore fulfil a similar function to fixed-lifetime requirements discussed above at [4.2.2.2]). For example, Poland's KFK co-investment programme required funds to invest their capital within four years (with a possible one year extension), while British Columbia's Venture Capital Program generally requires 80 per cent of capital raised in a year to be invested within two years.[162] Australia's Biomedical Translation Fund co-investment programme requires its licenced funds to invest their capital within seven years, by providing that they may generally not make any new investments after the seventh anniversary of the grant of the licence (except for follow-on investments in an existing investee).[163] If this requirement is not complied with, fund managers may have their management fees reduced. Furthermore, fund managers under the programme are generally not paid management fees beyond the 10-year mark (despite the fact that licensed funds have a 15-year lifespan) in order to encourage them to make their investments and close their funds on time.[164]

While the reasons for timing criteria such as these are clear, they can also impose significant pressure on fund managers, who need time to identify, assess

[160] Irish Tax and Custom (n 129) 5; Taxes Consolidation Act 1997 (Ireland), s 490.

[161] Federal Ministry for Economic Affairs and Climate Action (n 126) 3.

[162] Thomas Hellmann and Paul Schure, 'An Evaluation of the Venture Capital Program in British Columbia' (Report for the Ministry of Small Business, Technology and Economic Development, June 2010) 35.

[163] Australian Government, Department of Industry Innovation and Science and Department of Health (n 82) cl 8.5.

[164] ibid cls 8.1, 8.10.

and make high-quality investments. Rushing investment decisions is likely to increase the chances of poor choices,[165] and the use of timing criteria that require capital to be invested within a certain amount of time has been described as 'a deeply suspect strategy', not least because these criteria force an artificially large amount of capital into the market[166] (which may lead to or exacerbate the crowding out of the private sector). Some of the problems that can be caused by strict timing criteria could be seen under Australia's Management and Investment Companies programme, which ran from 1983 to 1991. Funds licensed under the programme were required to invest 70 per cent of their capital in eligible early-stage investments within 18 months of raising it (a very short amount of time),[167] and it has been suggested that this requirement may have contributed to the programme's poor results.[168] It has been noted that 'in their hurry to invest within the period allowed', the newly licensed funds (which were among the first true venture capital funds operating in the Australian market) overpaid for investments and made poor investment decisions due to an overabundance of capital in the market.[169] The result was that many funds exited the programme, even though this meant forgoing tax benefits.[170] Interestingly, Australia's successor to the Management and Investment Companies programme, the Pooled Development Funds programme, features a far more relaxed timing criterion: its registered funds must invest 65 per cent of their capital in eligible SME investments within five years of raising it.[171] By not allowing the funds to 'park' their capital indefinitely, this requirement therefore helps ensure that Pooled Development Funds remain focused on making early-stage investments. Despite the upsides of this more relaxed approach, the use of investment timing criteria should be approached with caution for the reasons set out above. Ideally, using a fixed-end fund structure of 10–15 years to ensure the timely making of investments is preferable to the use of timing criteria, as this leaves the maximum amount of flexibility and discretion to fund managers while still imposing a time limit that is in line with that adopted by most commercial funds.

In contrast to investment timing criteria, minimum holding period requirements are used primarily as anti-abuse measures, because they stop investors from immediately withdrawing their capital from an investment after having gained the benefit of an incentive.[172] Minimum holding periods can also help combat short-termism, provide a measure of stability for investees, facilitate knowledge

[165] See OECD, 'Government Venture Capital' (n 2) 15; Leamon et al (n 81) 54.

[166] Leamon et al (n 81) 46. See also Sofia Johan, Denis Schweizer and Feng Zhan, 'The Changing Latitude: Labor-Sponsored Venture Capital Corporations in Canada' (2014) 22(2) *Corporate Governance: An International Review* 145, 146.

[167] Management and Investment Companies Act 1983 (Australia), s 37(3).

[168] See Barkoczy et al (n 60) 287–88; David Forsaith, 'Venture Capital in Australia: The MIC Program and Subsequent Developments' (1993) 2(1–2) *Small Enterprise Research* 36, 40, 45.

[169] Forsaith (n 168) 45.

[170] ibid.

[171] Pooled Development Funds Act 1992 (Australia), s 32. See also See Barkoczy et al (n 60) 295.

[172] See European Commission, 'Effectiveness of Tax Incentives' (n 1) 80.

transfer between investors and startups and alert potential investors to the fact that venture capital generally involves illiquid and long-term investments.[173] While they are primarily used in relation to incentives that provide investment-related benefits (particularly tax credits, deductions and grants), minimum holding period requirements may therefore be imposed under any kind of incentive.

As seen in Table 6, minimum holding period requirements are generally between one and five years, although there does not appear to have been any research conducted regarding the optimal length for a minimum holding period. Key questions that would be interesting to explore include whether a short (eg one year) holding period is sufficient to prevent misuse of incentives for tax purposes and whether a long (eg five year) holding period acts to deter investment. Minimum holding periods can be enforced in two ways: either, as in the case of Australia, Malaysia, Turkey and China's incentives, benefits may not be granted until the holding period is satisfied;[174] or, as in the case of Germany, Belgium and the UK, incentives may be reduced or withdrawn if the investment is disposed of before the holding period has passed (see further the discussion of clawback rules at [5.4.2]). It will be noted that all the examples in Table 6 are tax-related incentives (with the exception of Germany's INVEST grant), highlighting the fact that minimum holding periods are generally only necessary in relation to tax incentives (as tax incentives give rise to the possibility of misuse for tax purposes). Minimum holding periods act as a way for governments to counteract some of the distortions to investor behaviour caused by tax incentives (particularly investment-related tax incentives), and are therefore a recommended feature of these kinds of incentives.

Table 6 Examples of minimum holding period requirements

Incentive	Number of years	Holding period requirement
Australia's Venture Capital Limited Partnership and Early Stage Venture Capital Limited Partnership programmes	1	The limited partnership must hold its shares in an investee for at least 12 months in order for investors to benefit from tax exemptions and reductions[a]
Malaysia's deduction for venture capital investors	2	Investors must hold their shares in an investee for two years in order to benefit from tax deductions[b]
Turkey's Business Angels Law	2	Investors must hold their shares in an investee for two years in order to benefit from tax deductions[c]

(continued)

[173] ibid.
[174] Inland Revenue Board of Malaysia (n 57) cl 7.2(e).

Table 6 ***(Continued)***

Incentive	**Number of years**	**Holding period requirement**
Germany's INVEST incentive	3	Investors must hold their shares in an investee for a three-year 'lock-up' period or else the grant must be repaid[d]
The UK's Seed Enterprise Investment Scheme	3	Investors must hold their shares in an investee for at least three years or tax credit will be reduced or withdrawn[e]
Italy's tax incentives for investment in innovative start-ups and SMEs	3	Investors must hold their shares in an investee for three years in order to benefit from tax deductions or credits[f]
Belgium's Tax Shelter Start-Up	4	Investors must hold their shares in an investee for four years or the tax credit will be partially recouped[g]
The UK's Venture Capital Trusts scheme	5*	Investors must hold their shares in a Venture Capital Trust (*a venture capital fund, as opposed to an investee) for at least five years or tax credits will be reduced or withdrawn[h]
Ireland's Employment and Investment Incentive	4/7	Investors must hold their shares in an investee for at least four years in order to receive tax credits, but individual investors can make larger investments and consequently receive greater credits if they commit to holding shares for at least seven years[i]
Saskatchewan's iteration of Canada's Labour Sponsored Venture Capital Corporations tax incentive	8*	Investors must hold their shares in a Labour Sponsored Venture Capital Corporation (*a venture capital fund, as opposed to an investee) for at least eight years or the tax credit will be recouped[j]

[a] Income Tax Assessment Act 1997 (Australia) 1997, ss 51-54, 118-405, 118-407.

[b] Inland Revenue Board of Malaysia (n 57) cl 7.2(e).

[c] Republic of Turkey, Ministry of Treasury and Finance (n 24) Art 4(1).

[d] Federal Ministry for Economic Affairs and Climate Action (n 126) 4.

[e] Income Tax Act 2007 (UK), ss 257CA, 257FA, 257FB.

[f] Italian Ministry of Economic Development, Directorate General for Industrial Policy, Competitiveness and SMEs (n 20) 16.

[g] 'Frequently Asked Questions: What Is the Tax Shelter and Who Benefits from It?' (n 17).

[h] HM Revenue and Customs, 'VCT: Investor Income Tax Reliefs: "Front-end" Income Tax Relief: Who Can Claim Relief' (9 March 2016) www.gov.uk/hmrc-internal-manuals/venture-capital-schemes-manual/vcm51020.

[i] Irish Tax and Custom (n 129) 8–9.

[j] Saskatchewan, 'Labour-sponsored Venture Capital Corporation Funds', www.saskatchewan.ca/residents/taxes-and-investments/tax-credits/labour-sponsored-funds#:~:text=The%20tax%20credit%20is%2032.5,Savings%20Plan%20(RRSP)%20eligible.

Finally, governments may sometimes impose maximum holding periods under incentives, with benefits withdrawn or curtailed if investments are held beyond these periods (when the incentives provided in this situation are tax exemptions or reductions, they are often referred to as tax 'holidays'). Maximum holding periods can help reduce incentive costs, but may also encourage investors to exit their investments prematurely and/or select later stage investees to invest in (so they can exit sooner).[175] It has been noted that they may introduce 'a bias towards short-term projects with low upfront investment costs, which may be those least likely to generate spillover effects on the wider economy'.[176] An example of an incentive that previously included a maximum holding period requirement was Germany's INVEST incentive, which completely removed entitlement to its exit grant if investors did not sell their shares within 10 years.[177] Malaysia currently offers tax exemptions only for the lesser of 10 years or the lifetime of the fund.[178] This encourages funds to divest their investments within 10 years (or less where investments were made some time after the fund was established), as otherwise they will not benefit from the incentive. Although maximum holding periods do provide some benefits, given the long-term nature of venture capital and the fact that some investments take longer to mature than others, it is recommended that investors not be penalised for holding on to investments in this way.[179] Australia's Early Stage Venture Capital Limited Partnership programme takes a preferable approach. It provides that partnerships registered under the incentive have a maximum lifetime of 15 years (thereby limiting the provision of incentives without specifically removing the provision of incentive benefits),[180] and also provides that investors' gains (which are generally exempt) will be incrementally taxed once the assets of an investee and its connected entities exceed AUD 250 million.[181] This allows the government to recoup some tax revenue in relation to particularly successful investments while maintaining flexibility for investors. Australia's early stage investor tax incentive likewise generally provides eligible investors with tax exemptions on their gains, but curtails the exemption after 10 years, with gains made after this time taxed with reference to a modified cost base (ie only the gains made after the 10 year period are taxed).[182] Both the Early Stage Venture Capital Limited Partnership and the early stage investor tax incentive conditions provide the benefit of a maximum holding period requirement (by controlling and limiting the revenue forgone under the programme) but do not force investors to divest before they are ready (because they

[175] European Commission, 'Effectiveness of Tax Incentives' (n 1) 80.
[176] International Monetary Fund et al (n 3) 20–21.
[177] Federal Ministry for Economic Affairs and Energy, 'INVEST – Venture Capital Grant' (December 2016) 4.
[178] Inland Revenue Board of Malaysia (n 57) cl 6.1.
[179] European Commission, 'Effectiveness of Tax Incentives' (n 1) 89.
[180] Venture Capital Act 2002 (Australia), s 9-3(1).
[181] Income Tax Assessment Act 1997 (Australia), s 118-408.
[182] ibid s 360-50. See also Wilkinson and Barkoczy (n 12) 72.

merely curtail incentives rather than removing access to them). Either of these approaches is therefore more appropriate than imposing a maximum holding period requirement.

4.4. Targeting Investees

One of the most important aspects of targeting a government venture capital incentive, regardless of its form, is defining eligible – and ineligible – investees.[183] Incentives often aim to support those startups that are most likely to drive innovation, economic growth and job creation, as this is likely to stimulate maximum additionality. However, some proportion of these startups would likely receive investment even without government venture capital incentives in place (depending on the size of the local private venture capital market). This means that where incentives focus on the most promising potential investees (ie those also targeted by the private sector), they are likely to be at least partially redundant, and may even crowd out the private sector in a worst-case scenario.[184]

An alternative approach is for incentives to target investees that are not likely to receive private sector support, perhaps because they are too young, operate in underserviced sectors or are otherwise commercially unattractive.[185] Focusing on these potential investees is likely to reduce an incentive's redundancy ratio (as these investees would probably not have received investment in absence of the incentive) but may end up subsidising unviable firms, whilst incurring substantial public costs in the process.[186] For instance, where incentives target very early-stage or risky investees, investors' risk profiles are unlikely to align with incentive objectives.[187] This means that incentives will need to be more generous (and consequently expensive) in order to attract the participation of investors.[188] This situation is likely to decrease the efficiency of incentives.

Even well-targeted incentives may end up supporting some investees that would otherwise have received investment, and some investees that are not commercially viable. However, in order to minimise the number of unsuitable investees being supported under an incentive, governments often use a framework of multiple investee-targeting criteria,[189] including size, age and stage criteria

[183] See OECD, 'Government Venture Capital' (n 2) 20.

[184] See Leamon et al (n 81) 30–31, 42.

[185] See OECD, 'Government Venture Capital' (n 2) 12; Yan Alperovych, Alexander Peter Groh and Anita Quas, 'When Can Government Venture Capital Funds Bridge the Equity Gap?' (European Financial Management Association Conference, 2017) 2.

[186] See OECD, 'Government Venture Capital' (n 2) 20.

[187] Hans Landström and Colin Mason, 'Venture Capital Research: The Road Ahead' in Hans Landström and Colin Mason (eds), *Handbook of Research on Venture Capital, vol 2: A Globalizing Industry* (Edward Elgar, 2012) 283, 288.

[188] See Leamon et al (n 81) 45.

[189] See European Commission, 'Effectiveness of Tax Incentives' (n 1) 76; United Nations Economic Commission for Europe (n 7) 41.

(see [4.4.1]), sector criteria or exclusions (see [4.4.2]), domestic or regional location criteria (see [4.4.3]) and high growth potential and innovation criteria (see [4.4.4]). Almost all incentives also require investees to be incorporated as some form of company in order to receive investment (which makes sense as most incentives require investments to be made through the purchase of shares).[190]

4.4.1. Size, Age and Stage Criteria

Maximum size, age and stage are three of the most common criteria used to target investees,[191] which is appropriate as 'young and small firms are more likely to be financially constrained than older and larger ones'.[192] Companies at the earlier stages of development are therefore generally most in need of government support,[193] and are more likely to receive high value from venture capital investment than their later stage counterparts.[194] Research on the UK's Enterprise Investment Scheme and Venture Capital Trusts scheme has demonstrated that the deadweight costs of the incentives increase as company size increases – in other words, the smaller the investee company, the more likely the schemes are to enable it to access investment that it would not otherwise be able to access; conversely, the larger the investee, the more likely the schemes are to subsidise investment that would already have been made.[195] Earlier research on the same schemes also found that smaller companies supported under the schemes tended to outperform larger companies in terms of (real) gross profits and labour productivity.[196] Size, age and stage criteria can therefore help focus incentives on companies that are most likely to produce additionality, and can be a useful way to counter investment drift (the preference for and tendency to make later-stage investments).[197]

[190] Some incentives might include further integrity conditions, such as that investees must be independent entities that are not controlled by other companies: see, eg Republic of Turkey, Ministry of Treasury and Finance (n 24) Art 26. To the extent that incentives prescribe that investees use certain forms of corporation, the main concern is that these forms represent those used in the market to form startups ordinarily. In other words, incentives should not arbitrarily require startups to use a corporate form that they would not ordinarily use or that would not suit their needs.

[191] Size criteria seem to be implemented the most frequently: see European Commission, 'Effectiveness of Tax Incentives' (n 1) 124–33; Wilson and Silva (n 21) 27.

[192] Bravo-Biosca (n 3) 13. See also Wilson (n 46) 18; Wilson and Silva (n 21) 27.

[193] Colombo et al (n 68) 10; OECD, 'Government Venture Capital' (n 2) 8, 12.

[194] Luukkonen et al, 'The Value Added' (n 52) 154–55; De Clerq and Manigart (n 69) 201; Marco Da Rin, Giovanna Nicodano and Alessandro Sembenelli, 'Public Policy and the Creation of Active Venture Capital Markets' (2006) 90(8) *Journal of Public Economics* 1699, 1699–1700.

[195] Matt Colahan, John Higton, Lucy Royce, Rebecca Klahr, Jayesh Navin Shah and Marc Cowling, 'The Use and Impact of Venture Capital Schemes' (HM Revenue & Customs, February 2016) Research Report 355, 14.

[196] Although larger companies tended to have higher fixed asset accumulation and employment: Marc Cowling, Peter Bates, Nick Jagger and Gordon Murray, 'Study of the Impact of the Enterprise Investment Scheme (EIS) and Venture Capital Trusts (VCTs) on Company Performance' (HM Revenue & Customs, 2008) Research Report 44, 50.

[197] See Productivity Commission, *Business Set-up, Transfer and Closure* (Productivity Commission, 30 September 2015) Productivity Commission Inquiry Report No 75, 174–75; European Commission,

Size criteria are generally defined on an objective basis with reference to a company's financial resources (eg assets, revenue, turnover, profits) and/or human resources (eg number of employees).[198] For example, the European Union utilises a standard size-based definition of micro, small and medium-sized companies, as represented in Table 7.[199]

Table 7 European Union definition of micro, small and medium-sized companies

Company category	Staff headcount	Turnover	or	Balance sheet total
Medium-sized	<250	≤€50 m		≤€43 m
Small	<50	≤€10 m		≤€10 m
Micro	<10	≤€2 m		≤€2 m

Even within the European Union, different incentives use different elements of this standard definition (and sometimes diverge from it altogether). For instance, Germany's INVEST incentive requires investee companies to have fewer than 50 full-time equivalent employees and an annual turnover or annual balance sheet total that does not exceed EUR 10 million (ie it uses the European Union's definition of small companies).[200] Italy's tax incentives for investment in innovative startups and SMEs, on the other hand, requires investees to have annual turnover under EUR 5 million per annum (ie it uses only one element of the European Union definition, and places eligible companies between the European Union's definition of small and micro-sized companies).[201] Belgium's Tax Shelter Start-Up uses the same elements as the European Union to define size, but does not use the same limits; it provides that a company will constitute an eligible SME where it has a balance sheet of less than EUR 3.65 million, turnover of less than EUR 7.3 million and fewer than 100 employees; and an eligible startup where it has a balance sheet of less than EUR 350,000, turnover of less than EUR 700,000 and fewer than 10 employees.[202] Outside the European Union, Turkey's Business Angel law defines size according to headcount and turnover: it requires, among other things, that investees must have net annual sales not exceeding TL 5 million for the two fiscal years prior to the investment and have a maximum of 50 employees.[203] Finally, Australia's early stage investor tax incentive defines

'Effectiveness of Tax Incentives' (n 1) 74–75. In regard to investment drift, see Cromwell Schmisseur (n 120) 13.

[198] International Monetary Fund et al (n 3) 21.

[199] Commission of European Communities Recommendation of 6 May 2003 Concerning the Definition of Micro, Small and Medium-sized Enterprises (Recommendation 2003/361), Annex, Title I, Art 2.

[200] Federal Ministry for Economic Affairs and Climate Action (n 126) 5.

[201] Italian Ministry of Economic Development, Directorate General for Industrial Policy, Competitiveness and SMEs (n 20) 5.

[202] Spreds, 'Lower your Taxes by Investing in Startups and Scaleups', www.spreds.com/en/tax-shelter; Code des Impôts sur les Revenus 1992 (Belgium), Art 145/26.

[203] Republic of Turkey, Ministry of Treasury and Finance (n 24) Art 26.

size according to expenses and revenue: it provides that an investee and its 100 per cent subsidiaries must have incurred expenses of AUD 1 million or less and assessable income of AUD 200,000 or less in the previous income year.[204] The differences between the ways these incentives define size demonstrate that there is no one right way to structure size criteria; an appropriate size definition for an incentive will depend on the context of the relevant market and the incentive's policy aims.

Age-based criteria are also generally determined objectively and may relate to the number of years since a company's incorporation date, or alternatively, and perhaps more appropriately, to the number of years the company has been actively trading for. Most incentives impose an age limit of between two and 10 years (on one of these bases).[205] For example, Germany's INVEST incentive requires investee companies to be no more than seven years old (and also requires that they commence their business activities within one year after investment),[206] while Italy's tax incentives for investment in innovative startups and SMEs requires startups to be either newly incorporated or less than five years old[207] and Belgium's Tax Shelter Start-Up requires companies to be no more than four years old.[208] Australia's early stage investor tax incentive requires investees to be either less than three years old, or less than six years old but with total expenses of less than AUD 1 million over the past three years.[209] It will be noticed that the German, Italian, Belgium and Australian incentives discussed above all use a combination of size- and age-based criteria to target their investees, as do many other countries. For example, China's tax incentive for corporate venture capital enterprises is available for investment in 'start-up technological enterprises', which are defined as entities that are not more than five years old, do not have more than 200 employees and do not have more than RMB 30 million of total assets and annual sales revenue,[210] and Chile's Fondo Etapas Tempranas Tecnológicas requires investees, among other things, to have sales not exceeding UF 5000 per year and be three years old or less.[211] Interestingly, it has been observed that age limits may unintentionally discriminate against investees that are located regionally because 'regional firms tend to take longer to get established due to lower available resources'.[212] On this basis, it has been recommended that

[204] Income Tax Assessment Act 1997 (Australia), s 360-40.

[205] See European Commission, 'Effectiveness of Tax Incentives' (n 1) 124–33.

[206] See, eg Germany's INVEST incentive: Federal Ministry for Economic Affairs and Climate Action (n 126) 5.

[207] Italian Ministry of Economic Development, Directorate General for Industrial Policy, Competitiveness and SMEs (n 20) 5.

[208] Spreds, 'Lower your Taxes' (n 202); Code des Impôts sur les Revenus 1992 (Belgium), Art 145/26.

[209] Income Tax Assessment Act 1997 (Australia), s 360-40.

[210] KPMG, *China Tax Alert* (Issue 15, May 2017) 2 assets.kpmg.com/content/dam/kpmg/cn/pdf/en/2017/05/china-tax-alert-15.pdf.

[211] Vicerrectoría de Investigación y Estudios Avanzados, 'Fondo Etapas Tempranas Tecnológicas Perfil Empresas' (Pontificia Universidad Católica de Valparaíso) www.pucv.cl/uuaa/vriea/fondo-etapas-tempranas-tecnologicas-perfil-empresas.

[212] House of Commons Treasury Committee (n 30) 20.

the UK's Enterprise Investment Scheme age limit of seven years and the Venture Capital Trusts scheme's limit of 10 years be raised.[213] However, while this change could benefit regional startups, it also risks encouraging investment drift.

Finally, stage-based criteria are often determined on a more subjective basis. For example, Australia's former Pre-Seed Fund co-investment programme required its licensed funds to invest in eligible companies or projects at the 'pre-seed' stage, meaning that they had no sales revenue, they required funding for proof of concept research and/or market validation, and they had either no management team or a team just beginning to form, among other things.[214] In this particular instance, the targeting of the incentive was focused at such an early stage that funds struggled to produce returns.[215] New Zealand's Aspire angel co-investment fund looks to invest at the 'seed' stage, which it defines as the stage where a company is looking for an investment of between NZD 100,000 and NZD 2 million for the purposes of early-stage growth.[216] It will also make investments at the earlier pre-seed and 'proof of concept' stages, as it is focused on supporting investments that would not otherwise receive investment, in order to avoid crowding out the private sector.[217] In general, criteria related to investee stage appear to be less common than age- and size-based criteria based on the research undertaken for this book, most likely because there are no consistent definitions of the stages.[218] Far more common is that investees be required, regardless of stage, to be unlisted. Incentives that require investees to be unlisted include Australia's early stage investor tax incentive, Malaysia's deduction for venture capital investors, Turkey's Business Angels Law, the UK's Enterprise Capital Funds programme and Belgium's Tax Shelter Start-Up.[219] The use of unlisted criteria is recommended because these criteria help reduce redundancy levels and the deadweight costs associated with incentivising investment in companies that have other, easier means of raising capital.

[213] ibid 21.

[214] Pre-Seed Fund Program Guidelines No 1 of 2003 (Australia), cls 3, 27, 28.

[215] See Barkoczy et al (n 60) 357; Cumming and Johan (n 53) 30, 34, 46–47. The licensed funds under the programme were further constrained in their investments by a requirement that they invest at least 60% of their committed capital within five years of becoming licensed, and that they generally not invest more than A$1 million in any one investee: Pre-Seed Fund Program Guidelines No 1 of 2003 (Australia), cl 38.

[216] NZ Growth Capital Partners, 'Aspire NZ Seed Fund – FAQs' (n 128) 3, 5, 15.

[217] ibid.

[218] A survey of direct government funding, fund of funds and direct co-investment incentives in 32 OECD countries in 2013 reported that half of the incentives had a specific stage focus for investees. Of these, 83% focused on the seed stage and 79% on the early stage. This indicates that perhaps stage-based criteria are more common in relation to direct incentives than tax incentives. It is not clear, however, whether the incentives explicitly required investors to invest in companies at these stages, or whether this was merely one of their stated aims: Wilson and Silva (n 21) 27.

[219] Income Tax Assessment Act 1997 (Australia), s 360-40; Inland Revenue Board of Malaysia (n 57) cl 7.2; Republic of Turkey, Ministry of Treasury and Finance (n 24) Art 26; British Business Bank (n 48) Part 3 (i)(c); Code des Impôts sur les Revenus 1992 (Belgium), Art 145/26.

There are problems associated with the use of size, age and stage criteria. For instance, size- and age-based criteria might exclude startups in some industries that tend to grow slower or faster (for instance, biotech companies will usually be larger than tech startups at the same stage of development and take longer to develop, and will also generally have higher capital requirements). Combining size- and age-based criteria with other kinds of criteria (including stage-based criteria, provided that they are appropriately defined) can therefore be useful as it recognises that 'size is not a sole indicator of innovativeness or growth potential' and avoids making strong assumptions about company growth prospects based entirely on age.[220] For example, the UK's Enterprise Capital Funds programme requires investees to meet the European Union definition of an SME (see above), and to meet one of the following three conditions: the investee has not been operating in any market; it has been operating in any market for less than seven years following its first commercial sale (not including sales made to test the market); or it requires an initial risk finance investment, which, based on a business plan prepared in view of entering a new product or geographic market, is higher than 50 per cent of its average annual turnover in the preceding five years.[221] These alternative tests avoid basing eligibility entirely on size- or age-related factors.

4.4.2. Sector Criteria

Incentives may be targeted towards companies that operate in specific sectors, such as information technology (IT), biotechnology or clean technology.[222] Sectors may be targeted for a variety of reasons, including: because they are particularly innovative or likely to produce socially valuable spill-over effects;[223] because they are particularly likely to be influenced by incentives or are of strategic economic value;[224] because they have potential but are not yet competitive;[225] or because they experience underinvestment.[226]

However, sector-based targeting is not recommended for a range of reasons. For example, it is often seen as serving special interests or 'favouritism'; furthermore, prioritising certain sectors over others may increase inefficiency and market

[220] European Commission, 'Effectiveness of Tax Incentives' (n 1) 178.

[221] British Business Bank (n 48) Part 3 (i)(c).

[222] A 2012 survey of direct and co-investment programmes in 32 OECD countries found that 45% had sector requirements, with ICT, biotech and cleantech being the most frequent sectors targeted: Wilson and Silva (n 21) 27.

[223] International Monetary Fund et al (n 3) 21; European Commission, 'Effectiveness of Tax Incentives' (n 1) 75.

[224] International Monetary Fund et al (n 3) 21–22.

[225] Philipp Ständer, 'Public Policies to Promote Venture Capital: How to Get National and EU Measures in Sync' (Jacques Delors Institut, 31 August 2017) 10.

[226] See OECD, 'Government Venture Capital' (n 2) 9.

distortion.[227] For instance, sectoral targeting was used in the first two rounds of Australia's former Innovation Investment Fund co-investment programme, which was introduced in 1997, near the pinnacle of the IT boom. The programme required licensed funds to invest in IT startups, and channelled large amounts of capital into the IT sector.[228] However, when the tech-wreck occurred just three years later, many of the funds were disproportionately affected due to their heavy IT exposure.[229] Subsequent rounds of the programme therefore removed the sectoral targeting requirement.[230] Although it is reported that sectoral targeting can improve stakeholder involvement and buy-in (particularly from industry associations), and may be suitable for addressing advanced goals,[231] it is increasingly recognised that companies with high-growth potential can be found in any industry and that targeting specific industries may neglect important links and emerging high-growth opportunities in other industries or at the intersection between sectors.[232]

An appropriate (and popular) alternative to targeting investees by sector is to exclude investees operating in certain sectors from participating in incentives.[233] Commonly excluded sectors are those that involve capital preservation, rather than genuine venture capital investment (such as finance or real estate).[234] For example, the UK's Enterprise Capital Funds programme excludes potential investees that engage in dealing in land, commodities or financial instruments; financial activities, property development or the provision of legal or accountancy services; leasing; receiving royalties or licence fees (except where these arise from an intangible asset such as a patent); farming, market gardening or forestry; and operating or managing hotels, guest houses, hostels, or nursing or residential care homes.[235] Enterprise Capital Funds are also excluded from investing in synthetic fibres and yarns, motor vehicles, shipbuilding, steel, coal, transport and the production of certain agricultural and fisheries products.[236] Belgium's Tax Shelter Start-Up excludes investment, treasury or financing companies; companies that have the construction, acquisition, management, development, sale or rental of real estate for their own account as their main purpose or activity; and companies created in order to conclude management or administration contracts, or that obtain most of

[227] Ständer (n 225) 10; International Monetary Fund et al (n 3) 21–22.

[228] Innovation Investment Fund Program Guidelines No 1 of 1997 (Australia), cl 7; Barkoczy et al (n 60).

[229] Department of Innovation, Industry, Science and Research, *Innovation Investment Fund Program Progress Report* (2011) 20.

[230] See Innovation Investment Fund Program Round Three Guidelines No 1 of 2011 (Australia), cl 7; Barkoczy et al (n 60) 346–47, 349.

[231] Stefan Lilischkis, 'Policies in Support of High-Growth Innovative SMEs' (European Commission, June 2011) INNO-Grips Policy Brief No 2, 47–48.

[232] ibid 7; European Commission, 'Effectiveness of Tax Incentives' (n 1) 75.

[233] See Barkoczy and Edmundson (n 57) 72; European Commission, 'Effectiveness of Tax Incentives' (n 1) 76.

[234] European Commission, 'Effectiveness of Tax Incentives' (n 1) 18.

[235] British Business Bank (n 48) Annex D.

[236] ibid Annex C.

their profits from such contracts.[237] Allowing investment in sectors such as these is likely to increase incentive redundancy and deadweight costs, while excluding them can help target incentives more tightly on deserving sectors.[238] This is because these sectors are generally already profitable and commercially attractive, so do not struggle to attract capital in the way that innovative businesses often do.

However, it is important that exclusions not be overly restrictive to the point where they prevent genuinely innovative companies from receiving investment under incentives.[239] This occurred in relation to Australia's Venture Capital Limited Partnership and Early Stage Venture Capital Limited Partnership programmes, which originally disallowed investment in investees undertaking finance activities such as banking.[240] This targeting unintentionally excluded 'fintech' businesses (which experienced rapidly increasing popularity between 2008 and 2014) from receiving investment under the programmes. The exclusion was therefore modified in 2019 to make provision for investment in innovative fintech businesses. The new rules allow activities that involve developing technology for use in relation to finance, insurance or making investments (or activities that are ancillary to this).[241]

4.4.3. Location Criteria

Governments impose an array of location criteria on investees, ranging from relatively broad criteria (eg an investee must be a domestic resident) to specific ones (eg an investee must be located in a certain regional area). While there is some benefit to requiring investees to be located domestically, regional location criteria are more problematic, as discussed below.

Domestic location requirements may require investees to be domestic residents, to undertake the majority of their activities domestically or to produce a national benefit.[242] Domestic location requirements ensure that the benefits of incentives (and any associated spillovers) accrue locally.[243] This may be appropriate, particularly as funds that invest locally tend to add more value to their investees.[244] However, ongoing domestic location requirements may prevent investees from migrating internationally, which is often necessary for their continued growth.[245] Therefore, point-in-time domestic location requirements

[237] Code des Impôts sur les Revenus 1992 (Belgium), Art 145/26.
[238] European Commission, 'Effectiveness of Tax Incentives' (n 1) 18, 76.
[239] ibid 18.
[240] Income Tax Assessment Act 1997 (Australia), s 118-425(13).
[241] Income Tax Assessment Act 1997 (Australia), s 118-425(13A). See also Douglas Arner, Jànos Barberis and Ross Buckley, 'The Evolution of Fintech: A New Post-Crisis Paradigm?' [2016] *UNSWLRS* 62.
[242] See, eg Inland Revenue Board of Malaysia (n 57) cl 4.3; British Business Bank (n 48) Part 3 (i)(c).
[243] European Commission, 'Effectiveness of Tax Incentives' (n 1) 76, 132.
[244] Cumming and Johan (n 53) 33.
[245] See Barkoczy et al (n 60) 167.

(ie requirements that only apply at the time when an investment is made) may be a more appropriate solution. This is the approach taken under New Zealand's Aspire angel co-investment fund; the regulator notes that while investees must be New Zealand-based when they first receive investment, it often encourages investees to expand offshore later down the line as they grow.[246] Australia's Venture Capital Limited Partnership and Early Stage Venture Capital Limited Partnership programmes likewise only require investees to be located in Australia at the time when an investment is made (although they have some asset and performance location requirements that continue for 12 months).[247] These requirements ensure that some spill-over benefits accrue locally, while retaining flexibility for investees. In this vein, the Venture Capital Limited Partnership and Early Stage Venture Capital Limited Partnership programmes also allow registered funds to invest up to 20 per cent of their committed capital in investees that do not meet the location requirements, which allows for follow-on investments in companies that may have moved overseas. In contrast, the UK's Seed Enterprise Investment requires companies to have a permanent establishment in the UK for three years following an initial investment,[248] which is considerably less flexible but does increase the chances of spill-over benefits accruing in the UK rather than elsewhere.

Regional location requirements have been popular in the past, but have a history of mixed success and outright failure.[249] They have been used (and critiqued) in incentives including the European Seed Capital Fund scheme (which provided loans) and the UK's Regional Venture Capital Fund programmeme (which provided co-investment to funds).[250] The reasoning behind regional location requirements is that regions outside capital cities and financial centres are more likely to experience equity gaps or market failures, and startups in these areas can find it particularly difficult to access venture capital funding.[251] Furthermore, startups have the capacity to 'contribute disproportionately to job growth and positive spillover effects' in regional economies,[252] and governments may envisage a role for regionally based incentives to 'demonstrate that good investment opportunities exist in often-overlooked regions'.[253] However, the reality is that regional areas often lack high-quality deal flow, the critical mass necessary to

[246] NZ Growth Capital Partners, 'Aspire NZ Seed Fund – FAQs' (n 128) 7.

[247] Income Tax Assessment Act 1997 (Australia), ss 118-425(2), (12A), 118-427(3), (13).

[248] Income Tax Act 2007 (UK), s 257DD.

[249] See OECD, 'Government Venture Capital' (n 2) 6; International Monetary Fund et al (n 3) 22; Avnimelech et al (n 110) 15; Munari and Toschi (n 66) 219; Leamon et al (n 81) 47.

[250] See Gordon C Murray, 'A Policy Response to Regional Disparities in the Supply of Risk Capital to New Technology-based Forms in the European Union: The European Seed Capital Fund Scheme' (1998) 32(5) *Regional Studies* 405, 417; United Nations Economic Commission for Europe (n 7) 53; BVCA and NESTA (n 147) 25–26.

[251] See OECD, 'Business Innovation Policies' (n 3) 51; Munari and Toschi (n 66) 208–09; Murray et al (n 45) 10; Center for Regional Economic Competitiveness and Cromwell Schmisseur, 'Program Evaluation of the US Department of Treasury State Small Business Credit Initiative' (October 2016) 61; Gvetadze et al (n 28) 36.

[252] Center for Regional Economic Competitiveness and Cromwell Schmisseur (n 251) 61.

[253] Cromwell Schmisseur (n 120) 3.

sustain venture capital markets and/or the components of a functioning innovation system.[254] Funds that are required to invest in regional investees may find it difficult to make profitable investments, which can lead to poor investment results and/or investment drift.[255] In recent years, therefore, it has been recommended that a regional focus should be avoided,[256] and that investors should be allowed to invest where opportunities are most attractive.[257]

4.4.4. Diversity Criteria

Some incentives in the past have required incentives to target investees that have gender or ethnically/racially diverse management teams, and this trend may be increasing. A recent report by the UK's House of Commons Treasury Committee recognised that venture capital has a diversity problem: it was reported in 2022 that less than five per cent of total venture capital investment had been made in companies with female founders, and that for every GBP 1 of equity investment in the UK in 2021, all-male founder teams received GBP 0.84, mixed-gender founder teams received GBP 0.14 and all-female founder teams received GBP 0.02.[258] Furthermore, a 2020 market report showed that in the UK in 2019, less than 2 per cent of venture capital investment went to black and ethnic minority-led business (while 18.3 per cent of the population identified as an ethnicity other than white in the 2021 census).[259] In response to these figures, the Committee recommended that HM Treasury should make provision of diversity statistics a requirement for entities to be eligible to receive tax relief under the Enterprise Investment Scheme, Seed Enterprise Investment Scheme and Venture Capital Trusts scheme, with investors required to disclose the gender and ethnic breakdown of both investees and their own staff.[260] While this is a reporting requirement (see [5.4.1]) rather than a targeting requirement, it could nevertheless have some impact on increasing diversity. The Committee also recommended that the British Business Bank, which regulates the Enterprise Capital Funds programme (among other things), consider the creation of one or more venture capital funds with the specific purpose of promoting greater diversity in venture capital allocation.[261]

[254] See Munari and Toschi (n 66) 209; Rebecca Harding, 'Venture Capital and the Regions: Not Always the Most Appropriate Funding Mechanism' (2000) 7(1) *New Economy* 49, 51–52; Jun Li, 'Government-Backed Venture Capital as a Science, Technology and Innovation (STI) Policy Instrument: A Chinese Perspective' (2016) 7(1) *STI Policy Review* 66, 82; BVCA and NESTA (n 147) 25–26.

[255] Harding (n 254) 53; Avnimelech et al (n 110) 15. See also BVCA and NESTA (n 147) 26.

[256] Colombo et al (n 68) 25.

[257] Leamon et al (n 81) 47.

[258] House of Commons Treasury Committee (n 30) 12.

[259] ibid.

[260] ibid 15.

[261] ibid 17.

An example of an incentive that currently includes a focus on investee diversity, without going so far as to implement specific diversity criteria, is Canada's Venture Capital Catalyst Initiative (a co-investment incentive). The initiative requires funds to collect and report on gender and diversity metrics, as well as implement policies and practices that promote diversity in building their portfolios.[262] This aligns with the initiative's policy aims, which include enhancing access to venture capital for underrepresented groups, such as women and racialised communities, and enhancing and promoting diversity, equity and inclusion in Canadian venture capital (see [2.5]).[263] Past experience has shown that incentives that have required investee companies to be owned by a minority or member of a disadvantaged group in order to receive investment have not been particularly successful,[264] with the major issue being a lack of high-quality deal flow. In this sense, incentives that target diversity face similar challenges to incentives that target regional investment. Therefore, while Canada's approach under the Venture Capital Catalyst Initiative might be seen as too 'soft', because it does not mandate investments in diverse investees, it is nevertheless likely to be the most appropriate way to encourage greater investee diversity while not compromising the quality of investees. Interestingly, New Zealand's Aspire angel co-investment fund specifically notes that while it does have a 'higher risk tolerance for investments in under-served areas of the market eg certain sectors, regions, or founders with or addressing more diverse backgrounds or regions', it will not invest in companies just because they are 'founded by under-represented individuals or regions'.[265] In order to receive an angel co-investment through the fund, the investee still needs to 'have the potential to be a large, scalable technology company that other venture capital investors will potentially back in the future'.[266] Again, this goes some way towards supporting investee diversity while not sacrificing quality.

4.4.5. High Growth Potential and Innovation Criteria

In order to target high-quality investees and help produce positive outcomes, some incentives require investees to demonstrate their potential for high growth.[267] This is clearly quite a subjective concept, particularly because it refers to 'potential' and not to any concrete metrics that have already been achieved.

[262] Government of Canada, 'Venture Capital Catalyst Initiative', ised-isde.canada.ca/site/sme-research-statistics/en/venture-capital-catalyst-initiative.

[263] Innovation, Science and Economic Development Canada, 'Venture Capital Catalyst Initiative: Performance Measurement Framework' (2022) 9.

[264] See, eg the USA's Specialized Small Business Investment Companies programme: Timothy Bates, 'Government as Venture Capital Catalyst: Pitfalls and Promising Approaches' (2002) 16(1) *Economic Development Quarterly* 49, 51; and the UK's Aspire fund, which targeted investments in female-led businesses.

[265] NZ Growth Capital Partners, 'Aspire NZ Seed Fund – FAQs' (n 128) 5.

[266] ibid.

[267] European Commission, 'Effectiveness of Tax Incentives' (n 1) 73.

High growth potential is measured differently depending on an incentive's rules. For example, New Zealand's Aspire Fund (a co-investment fund) targets potential investees that are aiming to solve a problem for an addressable market, that have a differentiated product that is defensive against competitors and that have the potential for very high returns.[268] Chile's Fondo Etapas Tempranas Tecnológicas (a loan programme), on the other hand, requires investees to be developing specific projects with high potential for growth and innovation.[269] This programme also requires investees to be limited in developing their innovative project by insufficient capital (ie to demonstrate a need for funding).[270] High growth potential criteria, while subjective and difficult to measure, do help target incentives towards high-potential investees and are therefore useful. Need for funding criteria, on the other hand, may indirectly encourage adverse selection by focusing incentives too closely on unviable startups.[271] They are also likely to be superfluous, because investees that do not need funding generally do not seek out venture capital investment. Therefore, although need for funding criteria may increase additionality and reduce redundancy by not funding companies that could receive investment elsewhere,[272] their use is not recommended.

Given that most government venture capital incentives aim to support innovative enterprises,[273] it is surprising that only a few incentives impose explicit innovation criteria on investees. Innovation criteria can be a helpful form of targeting, even though, like high growth potential criteria, they are subjective and can be difficult to establish with certainty. For this reason, incentives often target proxies for innovation, such as R&D expenditure and patents. Some incentives might likewise require investees to originate out of a university or research institute,[274] in the thought that they may be more likely to be innovative. Examples of incentives that use innovation criteria include the following:

- **Italy's tax incentives for investment in innovative startups and SMEs.** This tax credit/ deduction-based incentive requires startups to meet one of three 'innovation'-related indicators: R&D expenditure corresponds to at least 15 per cent of the higher value between turnover and annual costs (as per the last statement of accounts); the total workforce includes at least one-third PhDs, PhD students or researchers, or at least two-thirds master's degrees; or the company is the owner or licensee of a registered patent (or it has filed an application for an industrial property right) or original registered software.[275]

[268] NZ Growth Capital Partners, 'Aspire NZ Seed Fund – FAQs' (n 128) 4–5.
[269] Vicerrectoría de Investigación y Estudios Avanzados (n 211).
[270] ibid.
[271] See Ralf Becker and Thomas Hellmann, 'The Genesis of Venture Capital – Lessons from the German Experience' (CESifo Conference on Venture Capital, Entrepreneurship, and Public Policy, November 2002) CESifo Working Paper No 883.
[272] ibid.
[273] United Nations Economic Commission for Europe (n 7) 41.
[274] ibid.
[275] Italian Ministry of Economic Development, Directorate General for Industrial Policy, Competitiveness and SMEs (n 20) 5.

- **Japan's Angel Tax Law.** This tax deduction/loss relief-based incentive takes a simpler approach, merely requiring investees to have a specific number of employees (which correlates to the company's age) engaged in research.[276]
- **Germany's INVEST grant.** Under this grant incentive, investee companies must have proven innovative capacity, which means that the company belongs to a sector that has been defined as innovative (according to a specific list), owns a patent or has claimed public funding for a research or innovation project in the two years before submitting an application. Proof of innovative capacity can also be provided in the form of a separate expert opinion from a nominated independent expert.[277]
- **Australia's early stage investor tax incentive.** This tax offset/exemption-based incentive imposes complex innovation criteria on investees, requiring them to meet either a '100 point' test or a 'principles based' test. The 100-point test is met if an investee company obtains 100 points from a list of innovation-related activities (eg having a certain level of R&D expenses, receiving an innovation-related grant, taking part in an incubator or accelerator programme, receiving third-party investment and holding an eligible patent).[278] The principles-based test is met if an investee company meets the five following conditions: the company is genuinely focused on developing one or more new, or significantly improved, products, processes, services or marketing or organisational methods for commercialisation; the business has a high growth potential; the company has the potential to successfully scale that business; the company has the potential to address a broader than local market; and the company has the potential to have competitive advantages.[279]
- **Turkey's Business Angels Law.** This incentive provides tax deductions at a more generous rate than normal for investment in companies whose projects have been supported within the past five years through specific government R&D and innovation programmes.[280]
- **China's tax incentive for corporate venture capital enterprises.** This deduction-based incentive requires investees to have R&D expenditure of at least 20 per cent of their total expenditure for the investment year and the following year.[281]

As with high growth potential criteria, innovation criteria may not be a perfect measure of a company's innovative potential, but they are likely to help improve targeting, even if only through a signalling effect. Their use is therefore recommended, provided they are not overly complex or restrictive.

[276] See John W Darcy, *Japan Master Tax Guide 2016/17*, 14th edn (Wolters Kluwer, 2016) 227–28.
[277] Federal Ministry for Economic Affairs and Climate Action (n 126) 5.
[278] Income Tax Assessment Act 1997 (Australia), s 360-45.
[279] ibid s 360-40.
[280] Republic of Turkey, Ministry of Treasury and Finance (n 24) Art 4(2).
[281] KPMG, *China Tax Alert* (n 210) 2–3.

4.5. Summary

This chapter has looked at the wide range of eligibility criteria that are commonly used to target venture capital incentives. It has considered these criteria according to how they target direct and indirect investors, investments and investees. Of the criteria that target direct investors, those that are recommended are: wealth and experience criteria (as alternatives) to increase investor quality and protect retail investors while not excluding new entrants; and independence criteria (imposed only at the time an investment is made) to avoid the deadweight costs of incentivising investment by related parties, while still allowing for investors to subsequently become involved with their investee companies. The criteria that may be appropriate in some cases depending on an incentive's policy aims are entity and residence criteria, which could be used to serve specific policy objectives if appropriate and relevant.

Of the criteria that target funds, fund managers and passive investors, those that are recommended are: minimum and maximum fund size criteria to ensure commercial viability while countering the risk of investment drift and poor investor behaviour; fixed-lifetime criteria to limit the provision of incentives and facilitate the timely return of capital; competitive fund manager compensation criteria so that fund managers are incentivised to provide value-adding activities; criteria requiring fund managers to commit a small amount of their own capital to the fund they manage to ensure buy-in; and criteria limiting passive investment by retail investors (although this may not be particularly necessary, given that not many retail investors are likely to invest in venture capital funds). The criteria that may be appropriate in some cases depending on an incentive's policy aims are fund structure criteria, fund manager experience or newness criteria (although fund managers selected to participate in incentives should always demonstrate a certain level of competence), criteria requiring funds to have approved investment plans (if necessary to ensure compliance with programme aims) and criteria dictating passive investor character and location.

Of the criteria that target investments, those that are recommended are: criteria requiring investments to be made primarily in the form of new equity in order to best serve the needs of startups and avoid deadweight costs; at-risk requirements that help prevent misuse of incentives; maximum investment amount criteria to help keep incentives focused on early-stage investments; and minimum holding period requirements (of a reasonable duration) to also help prevent misuse of tax incentives. A criterion that may be appropriate in some cases depending on an incentive's policy aims is a maximum interest criterion, which may encourage investors to spread their capital over multiple investments. The criteria that are not recommended for use are: minimum investment amount criteria, as they are unlikely to be necessary; investment timing criteria, as they risk flooding the market with capital and forcing investors to make investments within a predetermined time period; and maximum holding period criteria, as they may encourage investors to divest their investments before they are ready (although the curtailment of an incentive's benefits after a certain time remains reasonable).

Finally, of the criteria that target investees, those that are recommended are: size, age and stage criteria, used in combination to target investees that are likely to benefit most from venture capital investment; sector exclusion criteria, to help increase the additionality of incentives by preventing investment in non-deserving or inappropriate areas; domestic residence criteria that apply at the time of investment (to make sure benefits accrue nationally) but allow later flexibility for investees to move overseas; high growth potential and/or innovation criteria, which send a signalling effect about the kinds of investees targeted under an incentive (provided they are not too complex or hard to meet); and unlisted criteria, to help target incentives on companies that need investment. A criterion that may be appropriate in some cases, depending on the incentive's policy aims, is a diversity criterion, although a diversity preference (rather than a strict criterion) is likely to be more appropriate. The criteria that are not recommended are: sector-based criteria, which can be overly restrictive and inappropriate; regional location requirements, which can lead to detrimental market effects; and need-for-funding criteria, which may increase adverse selection issues.

The discussion above has highlighted that while eligibility criteria primarily serve a targeting function, helping incentives achieve their policy aims by reaching the intended recipients, investments and investees, they also have important roles to play in protecting certain investors, controlling the time frame and costs of incentives, and helping prevent incentive misuse. They are therefore a vital element of incentive design. Chapter five continues to build on these issues, as it looks particularly at incentive time frame, cost and value, the role of decision-makers in applying eligibility criteria and allowing access to incentives, and incentive abuse and misuse. It will be seen in chapter five that many of the eligibility criteria discussed in this chapter are also relevant and important in the context of incentive implementation, administration and monitoring.

5

Implementation, Administration and Monitoring

5.1. Introduction

Chapter four discussed the many different kinds of criteria that can be used to target incentives appropriately. Together, these criteria make up a large part of an incentive's rules. This chapter builds upon the concept of incentive rules to explore how these rules, and incentives themselves, are implemented (see [5.2]), how incentives are administered by a regulatory body in order to uphold their rules (see [5.3]) and how incentive use is monitored to ensure integrity and evaluability (see [5.4]). These processes – implementation, administration and monitoring – are essentially regulatory in nature[1] and have important impacts on recipient experience and the capacity of incentives to achieve their policy aims.[2] They can also influence an incentive's cost, uptake and efficiency, as will be seen from the discussion below.

5.2. Implementing Incentives

The implementation of an incentive should ideally be as simple, clear and streamlined as possible, in order to keep incentive costs down and increase accessibility for recipients.[3] This will allow the maximum number of eligible entities to access the incentive, rather than excluding some through cost or difficulty (which can result in a negative selection effect whereby the entities that most need incentives

[1] See Cary Coglianese, 'Measuring Regulatory Performance: Evaluating the Impact of Regulation and Regulatory Policy' (OECD, August 2012) Expert Paper No 1, 10.

[2] See Karen E Wilson and Filipe Silva, 'Policies for Seed and Early Stage Finance: Findings from the 2012 OECD Financing Questionnaire' (OECD, October 2013) OECD Science, Technology and Industry Policy Papers No 9, 59, 61; Alex Easson, *Tax Incentives for Foreign Direct Investment* (Kluwer Law International, 2004) 159; Eric L Windholz, *Governing Through Regulation: Public Policy, Regulation and the Law* (Routledge, 2018) 104.

[3] See Hana Polackova Brixi, Christian MA Valenduc and Zhicheng Li Swift (eds), *Tax Expenditures – Shedding Light on Government Spending Through the Tax System: Lessons from Developed and Transition Economies* (World Bank, 2004) 23.

may be unable to access them). There are a variety of ways that governments can help to ensure that their incentives are implemented effectively and efficiently, including by having clear incentive rules (see [5.2.1]), having certainty around incentive time frames and termination (see [5.2.2]) and maintaining control over incentive costs (see [5.2.3]).

5.2.1. Rules

An incentive's rules or guidelines are the first – and arguably most important – step in its implementation, as they set out what the incentive is and how it operates. Incentive rules can be legislative in character (ie they can take the form of laws), quasi-legislative (ie they can take the form of government directions or guidelines) or totally informal (ie they can be based on the 'say-so' of government). Legislation is commonly used to implement tax incentives (as this is generally the only way tax laws can be introduced and changed), while less formal methods are commonly used for direct incentives (which generally are not required to be legislatively implemented). In terms of certainty and equity for recipients, and transparency and accountability for government, legislative rules are preferable, as legislative amendments require formal processes, while government directions or guidelines can generally be changed on an ad hoc basis.[4] Both legislative and quasi-legislative rules are preferable to informal or non-existent rules.

However incentive rules are implemented, it is important that they are clear, precise, well drafted and written in plain language, in order to make them easy for recipients (and regulators) to understand and apply, and to promote equity, predictability and consistency.[5] This, in turn, will help promote incentive uptake.[6] The implementation of France's former Investissement Garantie scheme was commended in this respect, particularly for being simple and easy for recipients to understand, having a lean design and one clear policy objective, having rules that were 'simple, straightforward and attractive' for venture capital funds, having clear eligibility criteria and requirements, and being tailored to venture capitalists' need to move quickly.[7] The scheme also reportedly had low levels of bureaucracy and red tape, and quick, efficient and 'business-like' implementation that was appreciated by recipients.[8] In contrast, two of Australia's early venture capital tax incentive programmes, the Management and Investment Companies programme (1983)

[4] See Sebastian James, 'Tax and Non-Tax Incentives and Investments: Evidence and Policy Implications' (Investment Climate Advisory Services of the World Bank Group, September 2013) 38.

[5] Deborah A Stone, *Policy Paradox and Political Reason* (HarperCollins, 1988) 235; World Bank, *World Development Report 2005: A Better Investment Climate for Everyone* (Oxford University Press, 2004) 102.

[6] See World Bank (n 5) 103.

[7] Jasper Deuten, 'Venture Capital Investment Guarantee Programme by OSEO' (INNO Partnering Forum, 2011) 14–15.

[8] ibid 14.

and the Pooled Development Funds programme (1992), have been criticised for the complexity and onerousness of their rules. The Management and Investment Companies programme investment requirements were so strict as to 'virtually guarantee failure',[9] and the programme is seen to have had a 'high degree of regulation over almost every aspect of its operation, making it unwieldy and inflexible'.[10] Funds registered under the Pooled Development Fund programme have likewise reported the 'difficulties of compliance with the terms of the programme given the number and complexity of the various rules and restrictions',[11] and the programme's relatively tight investment restrictions have been seen by some to impair the widespread use of Pooled Development Funds.[12]

The less room that eligibility criteria leave for subjectivity or interpretation, the more certainty participants will have, and the more administrative costs for recipients and regulators will be minimised.[13] A key criticism of the USA's Specialized Small Business Investment Companies programme, which ran from 1969 until 1995, was that the 'extensive set of regulations' for administering the programme was vague and left room for discretionary decision-making by the regulator, and decisions were reportedly made 'on a case-by-case basis with little respect for precedent'.[14] The implementation of the programme was described as 'bureaucratic chaos'.[15] This illustrates the negative effects that uncertainty around incentive rules can have on recipient experience (as well as incentive effectiveness and efficiency). Even where eligibility is determined on a discretionary basis (see [5.3.3] below), subjectivity should be minimised as much as possible through the use of clear eligibility criteria, in order to help govern regulatory decision-making by limiting the arbitrary exercise of discretion.[16] Incentive rules should explain how various eligibility/merit criteria are weighted, as well as clearly identifying decision makers and the roles that they play.[17] Australia does this well under several of its venture capital incentives, including its Biomedical Translation Fund programme, where the 'Programme Delegate' is empowered under the Programme Guidelines to make decisions on the licensing of funds according to

[9] Bill Ferris, *Inside Private Equity*, 2nd edn (Allen & Unwin, 2013) 216.

[10] Stephen Barkoczy, Tamara Wilkinson, Ann L Monotti and Mark Davison, *Innovation and Venture Capital Law and Policy* (Federation Press, 2016) 287.

[11] Department of Industry, Tourism and Resources and AusIndustry, *Pooled Development Funds Registration Board: Annual Report 2004–2005* (2005) 1.

[12] Kon Mellos and Nick Wormald, 'Australia: Private Equity Trends and Developments' [2002] *International Financial Law Review* 51. See also Barkoczy et al (n 10) 303–04.

[13] International Monetary Fund, Organisation for Economic Co-operation and Development, United Nations and World Bank, 'Options for Low Income Countries' Effective and Efficient Use of Tax Incentives for Investment' (Report to the G-20 Development Working Group, October 2015) 24, 26. See also Mark Burton and Kerrie Sadiq, *Tax Expenditure Management: A Critical Assessment* (Cambridge University Press, 2013) 134–35.

[14] Timothy Bates, 'Government as Venture Capital Catalyst: Pitfalls and Promising Approaches' (2002) 16(1) *Economic Development Quarterly* 49, 52.

[15] ibid 51.

[16] International Monetary Fund et al (n 13) 24; Stone (n 5) 235; World Bank (n 5) 102.

[17] See Department of Finance, *Commonwealth Grants Rules and Guidelines 2017* (2017) 17, 21.

specific eligibility and merit criteria.[18] The Guidelines explain that licence applications are assessed first against the eligibility criteria and then against the merit criteria, which include things like fund size and structure, proposed investment strategy and experience of the management team.[19] The Programme Delegate makes the initial eligibility assessment before referring eligible applications to Industry Innovation and Science Australia (the regulator) for merit assessment. The Programme Delegate then makes the final decision about which fund managers to offer licences to.[20] This transparent and clear decision-making process increases certainty for applicants to the programme.

Governments can assist recipients to navigate incentives by making incentive rules accessible to the public, providing detailed guidance and resources, and making regulatory and administrative decisions publicly available in order to build a body of precedent.[21] The UK has been particularly good at this, as it provides extensive official guidance on its tax-based venture capital schemes through an online 'Venture Capital Manual'.[22] The Manual, which is available publicly and kept up-to-date, breaks the incentive's legislative rules down and provides practical examples of their application.[23] Malaysia also provides useful resources for understanding its venture capital incentives, providing a list of the incentives online, along with their key requirements and the relevant tax orders that implement them, with Malay and English translations.[24] Unfortunately, many other countries do not follow these examples. The research undertaken for this book has demonstrated that many countries make it difficult to access incentive rules at all, and often fail to provide accurate or up-to-date information. These failures make it difficult or impossible for investors and investees to access incentives, which is likely to detrimentally impact incentive uptake, equity and effectiveness.

Changes to incentive rules can decrease certainty for recipients by making it hard to know how particular investments will be treated in particular circumstances; in turn, this uncertainty may deter investors and make it difficult for incentives to achieve their policy aims.[25] For example, it has been noted in relation

[18] See Department of Industry Innovation and Science and Department of Health, 'Biomedical Translation Fund Programme Guidelines' (3 August 2016).

[19] ibid cl 4.

[20] ibid cl 5.

[21] World Bank (n 5) 102.

[22] HM Revenue & Customs, 'Venture Capital Schemes Manual' (22 March 2021) www.gov.uk/hmrc-internal-manuals/venture-capital-schemes-manual.

[23] In contrast, it has been noted that countries including Belgium, Spain, Sweden and the USA do not provide publicly available guidance manuals for their venture capital incentives: see European Commission, 'Effectiveness of Tax Incentives for Venture Capital and Business Angels to Foster the Investment of SMEs and Start-ups: Final Report' (Taxation and Customs Union, 2017) Working Paper No 68, 154–59; Philipp Ständer, 'Public Policies to Promote Venture Capital: How to Get National and EU Measures in Sync' (Jacques Delors Institut, 31 August 2017) 16.

[24] See Securities Commission Malaysia, 'Venture Capital Incentives', www.sc.com.my/development/vcpe/venture-capital-tax-incentives.

[25] See OECD, 'Government Venture Capital for Technology-Based Firms' (1997) OCDE/GD(97)201, 20; European Commission (n 23) 205.

to the USA's Specialized Small Business Investment Companies programme, which was implemented quasi-legislatively and changed frequently, that the incentives rules themselves, while not necessarily easy to comply with, were seen as 'less damaging than the uncertainty about what the rules actually were at any point in time'.[26] Unfortunately, changes to venture capital incentive rules are common. In some situations, change may be necessary and valid – for instance, different phases of market development require different policies (which often cannot be predicted in advance), and changing external conditions can necessitate changes to the way an incentive operates.[27] Evaluation of incentives may also demonstrate that improvements could be made to their effectiveness or efficiency (see [6.4]). In other situations, however, changes may merely reflect shifting political leadership and the desire for incoming politicians to put their 'stamp' on an incentive.[28] Where incentives are changed, renamed or replaced every few years (particularly if these changes impact incentive value), current and future recipients may lose confidence in them and incentive uptake may suffer.[29] Furthermore, incentive performance will be extremely difficult to measure and reliably evaluate.[30] For these reasons, 'cosmetic' changes to incentives (such as name changes)[31] should be avoided, and necessary changes should be carefully managed in a gradual way, with prior announcements, and with evaluation of their effects to ensure the intended outcome is achieved.[32]

5.2.2. Time Frame and Termination

Something that governments should carefully consider – ideally before they introduce an incentive, but certainly after doing so – is how long they want the incentive to remain in place for. The creation of meaningful change in investment behaviour and environmental conditions 'requires a persistent long-run commitment lasting decades', and incentives often need to be in place over one or more investment cycles (which generally outlast political cycles) in order to achieve their policy

[26] Bates (n 14) 52.

[27] Gil Avnimelech, Alessandro Rosiello and Morris Teubal, 'Evolutionary Interpretation of Venture Capital Policy in Israel, Germany, UK and Scotland' (2010) 37(2) *Science and Public Policy* 101, 110.

[28] See International Monetary Fund et al (n 13) 28; Karen Wilson, 'Policy Lessons from Financing Young Innovative Firms' (OECD, June 2015) OECD Science, Technology and Industry Policy Papers No 24, 13, 30.

[29] European Commission (n 23) 205.

[30] OECD, 'Business Innovation Policies: Selected Country Comparisons' (2011) 147.

[31] An example of a cosmetic name change has recently occurred in relation to Singapore's Section 13G funds, which until 2023 were known instead as Section 13H funds. The Act that legislates for the funds was amended, and as a consequence the name of the funds changed, which is confusing and could have been avoided: see Income Tax Act 1947 (Singapore), s 13G.

[32] See European Commission (n 23) 182, 198; Ann Leamon, Maria Susana Garcia-Robles and Josh Lerner, 'Best Practices in Creating a Venture Capital Ecosystem' (Multilateral Investment Fund of Inter-American Development Bank, December 2012) 47.

aims.[33] Interim indications of a venture capital fund's success can take five years to emerge, with full performance often not known for more than 10 years.[34] Likewise, the performance of an incentive can take just as long, if not longer, to become clear, which is something that governments should consider when thinking about the end dates of their incentives.[35] Incentives that are started and stopped within a short time frame will likely struggle to achieve their intended policy aims,[36] and the resources put into providing an incentive can therefore be wasted if it is terminated too early.

When governments introduce incentives, they can deal with the issue of time frame in two broad ways: they can introduce incentives on an open-ended basis, deferring the decision of when they will be terminated until some point in the future; or they can introduce incentives on a time-limited basis, with a specified date as to when the incentive will end. For example, New Zealand's Aspire fund (a fund of funds co-investment incentive) is currently open-ended, or 'evergreen', meaning it will continue investing indefinitely as long as it generates returns to reinvest.[37] In contrast, Singapore's Angel Investors Tax Deduction Scheme was only made available from 1 March 2010 to 31 March 2020. After this date, investors could no longer obtain new approvals or renewal of their angel investor status, but could continue to enjoy tax deductions in respect of their qualifying investments made while they remained approved.[38] Enterprise Singapore explained that the government chose not to extend the scheme after this date in order to 'maintain the resilience and progressivity of the tax system'.[39] The UK's Enterprise Investment Scheme and Venture Capital Trusts scheme both had sunset clauses of April 2025,[40] but were recently both extended to 2035. Interestingly, the Seed Enterprise Investment Scheme, which is closely related to the Enterprise Investment Scheme, is completely open ended.[41]

[33] Gordon Murray, Marc Cowling, Weixi Liu and Olga Kalinowska-Beszczynska, 'Government Co-Financed "Hybrid" Venture Capital Programmes: Generalizing Developed Economy Experience and Its Relevance to Emerging Nations' (Kauffman International Research and Policy Roundtable, 11–12 March 2012) 10–11, 22. See also Wilson and Silva (n 2) 59; United Nations Economic Commission for Europe, *Financing Innovative Development: Comparative Review of the Experiences of UNECE Countries in Early Stage Financing* (United Nations Publications, 2007) 92; Leamon et al (n 32) 9, 47; European Commission (n 23) 82; Avnimelech et al (n 27) 110.

[34] Murray et al (n 33) 10.

[35] Wilson and Silva (n 2) 59.

[36] ibid.

[37] NZ Growth Capital Partners, 'Aspire NZ Seed Fund – FAQs' (November 2022) 6, www.nzgcp.co.nz/assets/Uploads/NZGCP-Aspire-FAQ_Nov22.pdf.

[38] Inland Revenue Authority of Singapore, 'Angel Investors Tax Deduction Scheme (AITD)' (7 January 2022) www.iras.gov.sg/taxes/individual-income-tax/basics-of-individual-income-tax/special-tax-schemes/angel-investors-tax-deduction-scheme-(aitd).

[39] StartupSG and Enterprise Singapore, 'Angel Investor Tax Deduction (AITD) Frequently Asked Questions (FAQs)' (February 2020) ssn-core-prod-files.s3.ap-southeast-1.amazonaws.com/2020-02/AITD%20FAQs_site%20%28002%29.pdf.

[40] Income Tax Act 2007 (UK), ss 157, 261.

[41] Treasury Committee, *Venture Capital* (2022–23, HC 134) 10.

Time-limited incentives can provide certainty to recipients, which, as mentioned above, is important for investor confidence and uptake of incentives. Certainty around timing facilitates financial forward planning and can encourage investors to change their investment behaviour in order to take advantage of incentives.[42] In fact, the presence of end dates (or 'sunset clauses', as they are often referred to in regulatory theory)[43] may increase an incentive's impact; it has been noted that 'when foreseen to be phased out in the near future, the investment effects of an incentive tend to be bigger than of permanent incentives'.[44] However, the key problem with time-limited incentives is the risk that they will not have achieved their policy aims by the nominated end date. In order to address this risk, governments sometimes introduce time-limited incentives that include an explicit possibility of renewal if the incentive performs well or if its existence remains necessary.[45] For example, Singapore's Section 13G and Fund Management Incentive (which provides tax exemptions and reductions) was set to expire in 2020, but was extended for five years until the end of 2025.[46] Likewise, Ireland's Employment and Investment Incentive tax credit programme was slated to end in 2020, but was actually extended and made more accessible in 2019, and now appears to be open-ended.[47] Although the expiry of an incentive's term provides 'a natural point of evaluation'[48] and a 'trigger to reassess its utility',[49] ongoing renewals can also create long-term uncertainty around the future of the incentive, negating the positive effect of having an end date in the first place. For instance, it was reported that the approaching 2025 end date of the UK's Enterprise Investment Scheme and Venture Capital Trusts scheme created uncertainty that 'would affect founder and investor behaviour'.[50] The House of Commons Treasury Committee recommended in mid-2023 that 'HM Treasury should provide more certainty for founders and investors alike by announcing the length of the extension and a clear timeline for implementing it as soon as possible',[51] and the 11-year extension was effected in late 2023.

[42] See European Commission (n 23) 82.

[43] See Productivity Commission, 'Identifying and Evaluating Regulation Reforms' (Research Report, December 2011) 34.

[44] International Monetary Fund et al (n 13) 23, citing US Department of the Treasury, 'The Case for Temporary 100 Percent Expensing: Encouraging Business to Expand Now by Lowering the Cost of Investment' (29 October 2010) 6.

[45] See Burton and Sadiq (n 13) 222.

[46] Ministry of Trade and Industry Singapore, 'Section 13H and Fund Management Incentive' (2020) www.mti.gov.sg/-/media/MTI/COS-2020/Microsite/Factsheets/ESG-Media-Fact-Sheet-on-Section-13H-and-Fund-Management-Incentive-at-MTI-COS.pdf#:~:text=What%20is%20it%3F,Singapore%2Dbased%20businesses%20and%20startups.&text=Further%20boost%20the%20vibrancy%20of%20the%20startup%20ecosystem%20in%20Singapore.

[47] See Irish Tax and Customs, 'Relief for Investment in Corporate Trades' in *Tax and Duty Manual* (April 2023) Part 16-00-02, 8, www.revenue.ie/en/tax-professionals/tdm/income-tax-capital-gains-tax-corporation-tax/part-16/16-00-02.pdf.

[48] International Monetary Fund et al (n 13) 23.

[49] Productivity Commission (n 43) xviii.

[50] House of Commons Treasury Committee (n 41) 10–11.

[51] ibid.

There are a number of valid reasons why governments may choose to terminate their incentives, such as the incentive achieving its policy aim or there no longer being a market need to justify its continuation (see [2.3]).[52] For example, Israel's Yozma programme was privatised and sold following its success in catalysing an Israeli venture capital industry.[53] In fact, once participation by the private sector reaches an 'acceptable' level, continuing to provide incentives risks granting windfalls to investors or crowding out the private sector, and termination is therefore recommended. However, it is also important to recognise that some markets may never become self-sustaining and will require ongoing governmental support.[54] Removing an incentive in this situation can risk undoing any good work the incentive has achieved, as noted above.

Unintended problems can arise when an incentive is terminated. For instance, recipients often suffer windfall losses when an incentive is removed (ie they lose access to the benefit of an incentive even though they have not changed their investment behaviour).[55] This loss is compounded if the capitalisation effect of incentives has resulted in the cost of investment rising (see [2.6]).[56] Furthermore, the announcement that an incentive is going to be removed can often lead to distortions in investment behaviour as recipients flock to take advantage of it before it ceases. One of the only ways that governments can really address these issues is by giving clear advance notice of incentive termination, such as through a sunset clause.[57]

Both ongoing and time-limited incentives can be difficult to terminate, even where they are ineffective, because of policy inertia and the vested interests incentives create 'among businesses and within government'.[58] Inertia can lead governments to maintain and defend venture capital incentives that have become (or have always been) unnecessary and/or inefficient (a phenomenon known as 'lock-in').[59] This can be a particular problem in innovation systems, as 'heavy sunk costs and prior commitments' often make it difficult for governments to 'respond to changing elements in the underlying innovation ecology'.[60] For example, even

[52] Incentives can also be terminated for less valid reasons, such as for political gain: see Leamon et al (n 32) 30.

[53] Günseli Baygan, 'Venture Capital Policy Review: Israel' (OECD, 28 January 2003) STI Working Paper 2003/3, 13.

[54] Albert Bravo-Biosca, 'Access to Finance for Innovation: Rationales and Risks of Public Intervention' (The Innovation Policy Platform, 2014) 10.

[55] See Neil Brooks, 'The Logic, Policy and Politics of Tax Law' in Tim Edgar, Daniel Sandler and Arthur Cockfield (eds), *Materials on Canadian Income Tax*, 14th edn (Carswell, 2010) 1, 42.

[56] See ibid.

[57] See Productivity Commission (n 43) xx.

[58] International Monetary Fund et al (n 13) 28. See also European Commission (n 23) 83; James (n 4) 38.

[59] See International Monetary Fund et al (n 13) 6, 28; Gerhard Fuchs and Philip Shapira (eds), *Rethinking Regional Innovation and Change: Path Dependency or Regional Breakthrough?* (Springer, 2005) 5, 25.

[60] Mark Dodgson, Alan Hughes, John Foster and Stan Metcalfe, 'Systems Thinking, Market Failure, and the Development of Innovation Policy: The Case of Australia' (2011) 40(9) *Research Policy* 1145, 1153.

though funds operating under the USA's Specialized Small Business Investment Companies programme reportedly had 'extremely high' failure rates during the programme's first three decades, the programme itself 'proved almost impossible even to modify'.[61] Likewise, Canada's Labour-Sponsored Venture Capital Corporation (LSVCC) tax credit, which was introduced in the 1980s, has been accused of poor performance and crowding out the private sector for many years.[62] It was announced in 2013 that the incentive would be phased out over three years by reducing the tax credit available on the purchase of new shares in an LSVCC from 15 per cent to 10 per cent in 2015, five per cent in 2016 and 0 per cent from 2017 onwards.[63] However, in 2016, the Canadian government decided to reinstate the tax credit at the rate of 15 per cent for investment in new approved shares of prescribed provincial LSVCCs up to CAD 5000.[64] The government's rationale for reinstating the credit was to 'facilitate access to venture capital for small and medium-sized businesses and support saving by the middle class'.[65] However, given the wide-ranging criticism of the LSVCC tax credit, the reinstatement, without meaningful addressing of the programme's downsides, seems like a questionable decision, perhaps driven by regional entrenchment of the programme and rent-seeking behaviour on the part of investors (see further [5.4.2] below).[66] Governments should be aware of and on guard against these risks of entrenchment. Allowing for – and heeding the results of – transparent, independent evaluation should assist with this (as discussed in chapter six).

A final timing issue that particularly affects investment-related incentives has to do with the timing of incentive 'rollout' or 'rounds'. As highlighted in chapter three, investment-related incentives have the capacity to trigger an oversupply of capital where they introduce large amounts of capital to the venture capital sector, particularly if they do so within a short time period. For example, it will be recalled that the introduction of multiple JEREMIE funds in Hungary within a short timespan created an oversupply of capital that led to poor investment results (see [2.3]).

[61] Josh Lerner, *Boulevard of Broken Dreams: Why Public Efforts to Boost Entrepreneurship and Venture Capital Have Failed – and What to Do About It* (Princeton University Press, 2009) 39.

[62] See United Nations Economic Commission for Europe (n 33) 45; Douglas J Cumming and Jeffrey G MacIntosh, 'Crowding Out Private Equity: Canadian Evidence' (2006) 21(5) *Journal of Business Venturing* 569, 571; Douglas Cumming, 'Public Policy and the Creation of Active Venture Capital Markets' (2011) 13(1) *Venture Capital* 75, 82–84.

[63] Government of Canada, 'Budget 2013 – Labour Sponsored Venture Capital Corporations (LSVCC) Tax Credit' (15 July 2015) www.canada.ca/en/revenue-agency/programs/about-canada-revenue-agency-cra/federal-government-budgets/budget-2013/budget-2013-labour-sponsored-venture-capital-corporations-lsvcc-tax-credit.html.

[64] Department of Finance Canada, 'Growing the Middle Class: Budget 2016' (22 March 2016) 221; Government of Canada, 'Lines 41300 and 41400 – Labour-Sponsored Funds Tax Credit' (24 December 2021) www.canada.ca/en/revenue-agency/services/tax/individuals/topics/about-your-tax-return/tax-return/completing-a-tax-return/deductions-credits-expenses/lines-413-414-labour-sponsored-funds-tax-credit.html.

[65] Department of Finance Canada (n 64) 221.

[66] See Jack M Mintz, 'Equity-Based Incentives Are Not the Way to Encourage Innovation' *Financial Post* (26 February 2020) financialpost.com/opinion/jack-m-mintz-equity-based-incentives-are-not-the-way-to-encourage-innovation.

A similar effect appears to have occurred in relation to Australia's Innovation Investment Fund programme, where two rounds of new funds were licensed to receive co-investment within a couple of years.[67] Given that Australia's venture capital industry was extremely nascent, this created a glut of funds with relatively few promising investment opportunities to take up, leading to poor investment outcomes (particularly for funds licensed in the second round).[68] Recognising the problems this caused, the Australian government changed its approach in relation to the third round of the Innovation Investment Fund programme, instead licensing funds in this round over a period of seven years.[69] Although market flooding is most likely to be a problem in relation to co-investment incentives (both equity and debt), any investment-related incentive has the capacity to create an oversupply of capital. Governments should therefore be aware of how many entities are eligible and likely to participate in incentives and take steps to roll their investment-related incentives out on a slower basis, if necessary, to help with sustainable market development. This may involve registering or licensing fewer recipients within the first couple of years of an incentive (see [5.3.2] below).

5.2.3. Cost and Value

An incentive's cost is a major factor in its efficiency, because where the cost of providing the incentive outweighs the benefits it produces, it will not be efficient (see [6.3.5]). Two of the main contributors to incentive cost are the cost of providing the incentive's benefits (eg the monetary value of a tax credit or deduction in terms of revenue forgone, the amount of a grant or co-investment, the revenue forgone from a tax exemption, the returns forgone from preferential returns, etc) and the incentive's administrative costs. These administrative costs are influenced by many of the issues discussed in this chapter, including the complexity of incentive rules, how long the incentive is in place for, the relevant application and decision-making processes and the extent of incentive monitoring that occurs (see below).

It is important that governments control incentive costs, in order both to promote incentive efficiency and to protect incentive longevity. There are several ways that governments can do this, including:

- collecting information on incentive costs and having a clear budget set in advance;
- using targeting/eligibility criteria to limit the number of entities that can participate in an incentive, restrict uptake and control the kinds of investments that can be made (see chapter four);

[67] See Barkoczy et al (n 10) 347–48.
[68] See ibid 348–49.
[69] See ibid 349–50.

- requiring the use of closed-end fund structures (where relevant) (see [4.2.2.2]);
- imposing maximum investment limits (see [4.3.2]);
- reducing or curtailing the provision of incentives a certain amount of time after investment or when an investment exceeds a certain value (see [4.3.3]);
- minimising administrative/regulatory costs by having clear and simple incentive rules, as well as streamlined application, decision-making and monitoring processes (see [5.2.1] and [5.3]);
- imposing a clear incentive time frame to facilitate budgeting (see [5.2.2]);
- reducing the value of incentives where necessary (ie the rate or percentage of the benefit) (see below); and
- employing integrity measures such as clawback provisions and related-party restrictions to reduce incentive abuse and misuse (see [5.4.2] below).

Interestingly, tax incentives tend to be more expensive to provide than direct incentives. There are two key reasons for this. First, tax expenditure costs are often 'hidden' within the fiscal system, and may therefore not receive the same level of scrutiny as direct incentives.[70] Tax incentives may therefore be both easier to enact and easier for governments to fund than direct incentives.[71] While tax expenditure (or tax benchmark and variation) reporting is now common practice in most developed countries, it has been noted that 'the gap between the level of scrutiny and transparency of tax expenditures compared with direct spending remains wide'.[72] Second, the cost of providing tax incentives also tends to be more difficult to control than that of direct incentives, because tax incentives tend to be awarded to recipients 'as of right' (ie to any entity that satisfies the relevant eligibility criteria – see [5.3.3]). This makes it hard to control their uptake, and also makes their costs harder to reliably predict in advance.[73] Because of the difficulty of calculating forgone revenue, even cost calculations made on an ex post facto basis may be no better than a good estimate.[74] In comparison, direct incentives can often be fully

[70] See Peter D Enrich, 'Saving the States from Themselves: Commerce Clause Constraints on State Tax Incentives for Business' (1996) 110(2) *Harvard Law Review* 337, 395–96; Stephen Barkoczy and Daniel Sandler, *Government Venture Capital Incentives: A Multi-Jurisdiction Comparative Analysis* (Australian Tax Research Foundation, 2007) 32; Richard Krever, 'Taming Complexity in Australian Income Tax' (2003) 25(4) *Sydney Law Review* 467, 488.

[71] See Christopher Howard, 'Testing the Tools Approach: Tax Expenditures versus Direct Expenditures' (1995) 55(5) *Public Administration Review* 439, 442, 444; Burton and Sadiq (n 13) 21; Stanley S Surrey and Paul R McDaniel, *Tax Expenditures* (Harvard University Press, 1985) 100, 104.

[72] Polackova Brixi et al (n 3) 2. See also OECD, *Tax Expenditures in OECD Countries* (2010) 33.

[73] See OECD, *Tax Expenditures in OECD Countries* (n 72) 30; John Lester, 'Managing Tax Expenditures and Government Program Spending: Proposals for Reform' (2012) 35(5) *The School of Public Policy Publications* 1, 25; Stanley Surrey, 'Tax Incentives as a Device for Implementing Government Policy: A Comparison with Direct Government Expenditures' (1970) 83(4) *Harvard Law Review* 705, 726.

[74] Richard Krever, 'Tax Deductions for Charitable Donations: A Tax Expenditure Analysis' in Richard Krever and Gretchen Kewley (eds), *Charities and Philanthropic Institutions: Reforming the Tax Subsidy and Regulatory Regimes* (Australian Tax Research Foundation, 1991) 18.

costed in advance (although this is more difficult in the case of contingent liabilities such as guarantees). Unlike tax incentives (which have been referred to as 'open-ended', 'resistant to eradication' and 'uncontrollable spending'),[75] direct incentives are almost always subject to budgetary caps and may be more likely to have defined end dates (see [5.2.2] above). For these reasons, direct incentives are generally a more cost-efficient option than tax incentives, all else being equal. However, this is no concrete reason to recommend direct incentives over tax incentives, as this cost efficiency may be balanced out by lower administrative costs or more significant incentive effects for tax incentives (and is likely to differ in relation to different incentives anyway).

An issue that is closely related to incentive cost is that of incentive value/generosity. An incentive's value or generosity is determined by a combination of the form of its benefits, the rate of the incentive, maximum investment limits, the relevant local tax rates and the way that tax gains and losses are ordinarily treated.[76] The more valuable or generous an incentive is perceived to be, the more entities will want to take it up, which, in turn, will generally lead to increased costs (as more entities use the incentive).[77] While high uptake can be a good thing, as it can help incentives to achieve their policy aims, incentives that are too generous will not be efficient, as the same outcomes could have been achieved for a lower cost.[78] Incentives that are too generous may also represent a windfall to investors and/or increase the proportion of low-quality investments being made (both of which increase the redundancy and deadweight costs of the incentive). However, incentives will generally need to be more generous if the kind of investments targeted under an incentive are particularly risky or unattractive.[79] Several incentives explicitly take this into account; for instance:

- Belgium's Tax Shelter Start-Up provides a more generous incentive for investments in smaller companies (a 45 per cent tax credit for investments in startups, a 30 per cent tax credit for investments in small and medium enterprises (SMEs) and a 25 per cent credit for investments in scale-ups).[80] This differentiation 'recognises the difference in the scale of investment risk between SMEs and microenterprises'.[81]

[75] Howard (n 71) 442; Polackova Brixi et al (n 3) 5; OECD, *Tax Expenditures in OECD Countries* (n 72) 24; Brooks (n 55) 75–76.

[76] European Commission (n 23) 166–67. It has been noted in relation to tax incentives that the rate at which they are granted is the most important feature in encouraging uptake and consequent increases in investment: EBAN and BOFIDI, 'Compendium of Fiscal Incentives: Tax Outlook in Europe – Business Angels Perspective' (2017) 82.

[77] See European Commission (n 23) 69, 87.

[78] See Barkoczy and Sandler (n 70) 36.

[79] See broadly Leamon et al (n 32) 45.

[80] Code des Impôts sur les Revenus 1992 (Belgium), Art 145/26, § 3; Spreds, 'Lower your Taxes by Investing in Startups and Scaleups', www.spreds.com/en/tax-shelter.

[81] European Commission (n 23) 197.

- Norway's former Venture Capital Loan Program provided loans to both nationwide funds and regional funds, and while nationwide funds received loans of up to 50 per cent of their total capital, regional funds received more generous loans of up to 70 per cent of their total capital.[82]
- Australia's former Pre-Seed Fund programme required funds licensed under the programme to invest in very early-stage companies and projects coming out of universities that would ordinarily by far too nascent to attract private sector investment.[83] In order to attract recipients, it provided a generous 3:1 contribution of equity co-investment to funds, and gave up any share of profits returned by the funds (see [3.3.5]).[84]
- Québec's former Business Investment Company tax incentive granted investors a tax deduction of 150 per cent of the value of their investment when an investee's assets were below CAD 25 million and 125 per cent when an investee's assets were between CAD 25 million and CAD 50 million.[85]
- France's Garantie de Fonds Propres Relance guarantees 50 per cent of an investment in a startup that is three or more years old and 70 per cent of an investment in a startup that is less than three years old.[86]

In contrast, the UK's Venture Capital Trusts scheme has recently been adjusted so that it focuses on investments in riskier businesses. The scheme has experienced high levels of investment in recent years, due in part to strong financial performance, the reduction of tax relief on some other kinds of investments (making Venture Capital Trusts comparatively more attractive) and a 25-year track record.[87] However, a drop in demand for the incentive has reportedly already emerged since the rule change,[88] perhaps indicating that investors do not feel that the Venture Capital Trusts benefits are generous enough to justify more risky investments.

Governments may sometimes need to adjust the value of their incentives in order to increase uptake levels. For example, in 1999 the State of Hawai'i introduced a non-refundable angel investor tax credit at the rate of 10 per cent (up to

[82] EFTA Surveillance Authority, 'Two New Norwegian Seed Capital Schemes Approved by the EFTA Surveillance Authority' (15 July 2015) www.eftasurv.int/newsroom/updates/two-new-norwegian-seed-capital-schemes-approved-efta-surveillance-authority; OECD, *OECD Territorial Reviews: Norway* (OECD, 2007) 129.

[83] Pre-Seed Fund Program Guidelines No 1 of 2003 (Australia), cl 49.

[84] ibid cl 148.

[85] Finances Québec, 'Adjustments to Certain Measures Announced in the Budget Speech of June 12, 2003' (18 July 2003) 2003-3 *Bulletin d'Information* 2.

[86] Bpifrance, 'Garantie de Fonds Propres Relance: Dispositif Doté par l'État et Géré par Bpifrance 2021–2024' (June 2022) 9.

[87] HM Revenue & Customs, 'Venture Capital Trusts Statistics Commentary' (10 December 2019) 1–3, assets.publishing.service.gov.uk/government/uploads/system/uploads/attachment_data/file/850880/VCT_National_Statistics_2019_Commentary.pdf; Emma Agyemang, 'Are VCTs Worth the Risk for Higher Earners?' *Financial Times* (11 October 2019) www.ft.com/content/28c30bea-e9bc-11e9-85f4-d00e5018f061.

[88] Kate Beioley, 'Tax-Efficient VCT Market Suffers Drop in Demand After Rule Change' *Financial Times* (22 February 2019) www.ft.com/content/d25bfb48-3077-11e9-ba00-0251022932c8.

USD 500,000 per investment).[89] It quickly became clear that this 10 per cent rate was not generous enough to entice a significant increase in angel investment in Hawai'i (which is geographically isolated and has a relatively high cost of living).[90] As a result, the rate of the credit for investment in 'qualified high technology businesses' was drastically raised to 100 per cent (up to USD 2 million per investment) in 2001,[91] making it the USA's most generous business investment tax credit at the time.[92] While only 23 taxpayers claimed around USD 162,000 of credits in the incentive's first year of operation, over USD 26 million of credits were reportedly claimed in the year following the rate increase, showing a dramatic increase in uptake.[93] However, reports on the additionality of the credit are mixed.[94] Commentators have noted that the 100 per cent credit may have attracted poor-quality ventures with little chance of success, raised the risks of fraud for recipients and regulators and promoted abuse of the programme for tax purposes.[95] The 100 per cent credit rate was reduced in 2009 in response to budget concerns, and the credit ceased operation completely in 2010.[96] This example illustrates the difficulty of balancing incentive value, uptake and cost.

An incentive's value is highly context dependent and difficult to benchmark with other incentives (particularly those in other jurisdictions).[97] As such, when setting the value of their incentives, governments should not base their decision on the value of other incentives or what is done in other jurisdictions; instead, they should consider whether the value of the incentive is 'sufficient to achieve the desired goals or alternatively, too liberal and therefore unnecessarily costly'.[98] However, incentives do not exist in a vacuum, and the presence of generous incentives in nearby jurisdictions may necessitate increases in incentive value in order to attract recipients (see the example of Vermont at [6.3.2]), although this can also lead to a 'race to the bottom'.

A final issue related to incentive cost is that some incentives either directly or indirectly provide returns to government, which may lead to a certain portion of incentive costs being offset. The incentive forms that allow for the possibility of direct returns to the government are equity co-investment incentives and loans.

[89] John R Hendon, Joseph R Bell, Brittany Blair and Don K Martin, 'State-Funded Angel Investor Tax Credits: Implementation and Perceived Effectiveness in a Sample of States Within the United States' (2012) 1(1) *Journal of Entrepreneurship and Public Policy* 50, 52; Andrew Kato, Sumner LaCroix and James Mak, 'Small State, Giant Tax Credit: Hawaii's Leap into High Technology Development' (University of Hawai'i Economic Research Organisation, 27 October 2009) Working Paper No 2009-3, 5.

[90] Hendon et al (n 89) 52–53. See also EBAN and BOFIDI (n 76) 82.

[91] Hendon et al (n 89) 52.

[92] Kato et al (n 89) 4, 8.

[93] ibid 8. See also EBAN and BOFIDI (n 76) 82.

[94] Kato et al (n 89) 21–23; Hendon et al (n 89) 53.

[95] Kato et al (n 89) 27.

[96] Matthew Denes, Xinxin Wang and Ting Xu, 'Financing Entrepreneurship: Tax Incentives for Early-Stage Investors' (December 2019) 67; Kato et al (n 89) 11.

[97] See James (n 4) 21–22.

[98] Kerrie Sadiq, 'An Analysis of Tax Expenditures versus Direct Expenditures' (Australasian Tax Teachers Association Conference, 2008) 13.

Equity co-investment incentives generally provide for a portion of investment proceeds to be returned to the government as a co-investor. This portion may be reduced where an incentive also provides preferential returns to the private sector. In contrast, loans generally include repayments of capital and interest to the government, and may also provide for governments to take a share of investment profits. For both equity co-investment programmes and loans, governments might use the returns they receive to fund future rounds of the programmes. For example, New Zealand's Aspire Fund, discussed above, is currently an evergreen incentive, the profits from which will be used to finance the fund's future investments.[99] Australia's former Innovation Investment Fund co-investment programme was likewise a 'revolving' programme (in theory at least). Under the Innovation Investment Fund programme, the returns of capital received by the government from its investments in licensed funds were contributed to a revolving fund that was intended to (and, to a certain extent, did) fund later rounds of the programme.[100] Unfortunately, the capital held in the revolving fund was returned to consolidated revenue when the Innovation Investment Fund programme was cancelled in 2014.[101] In contrast, the incentive forms that allow for the possibility of indirect returns to the government are profit-related incentives such as tax exemptions, tax reductions, exit grants and reinvestment relief. Because these incentives arise in relation to profitable investment exits, they may allow governments to indirectly recoup some of the cost of providing the incentives through the tax they collect from successful investee companies and their employees (see [3.3]).[102]

Whether an incentive provides for direct returns to government, indirect returns to government or no returns at all (eg tax offsets, deductions, grants, visa incentives and all forms of loss-related incentives) does not indicate anything per se about the appropriateness of the incentive. This is particularly the case given that no incentive form can guarantee returns to the government, as they will only arise where investments are successful. Nevertheless, the anticipated and/or actual amount of any returns received should be taken into account in working out the actual cost of an incentive for the purposes of evaluating its efficiency (see [6.3.5]), although it is acknowledged that this can be a challenging exercise.[103]

5.3. Administering Incentives

The administration of incentives is undertaken by regulatory bodies and involves the day-to-day processes of making incentives function. A regulatory body, or

[99] 'NZ Growth Capital Partners (n 37) 6.
[100] See Barkoczy et al (n 10) 347–48, 361.
[101] Department of Industry, *Innovation Australia: Annual Report 2013–14* (2014) 46.
[102] Barkoczy and Sandler (n 70) 34; Stephen Barkoczy and Peter Edmundson, 'Australasian and South East Asian Venture Capital Tax Expenditure Programs' (2009) 37(1) *Intertax* 56, 72.
[103] See European Commission (n 23) 72.

regulator, can take a variety of forms, as discussed below (see [5.3.1]). Part of a regulator's function involves acting as a gatekeeper to incentives, by either checking that incentive recipients are eligible to participate in incentives or actively selecting recipients themselves (see [5.3.2] and [5.3.3]). The regulator will also often be responsible for monitoring incentives, collecting data and helping to avoid abuse (see [5.4]). All of these administrative processes are broken down in detail below.

5.3.1. Regulatory Body

Governments around the world appoint a range of different bodies to regulate their incentives, and sometimes there may even be multiple regulators managing different venture capital incentives within the same country – or even multiple regulators managing the same incentive (see below). Regulatory bodies that are commonly given oversight of venture capital incentives include:[104]

- **Tax authorities (where incentives are delivered through the tax system).** Examples include the Australian Tax Office, which regulates Australia's early-stage investor tax incentive, and the UK's HM Revenue & Customs, which implements the country's Enterprise Investment Scheme, Seed Enterprise Investment Scheme and Venture Capital Trusts scheme.
- **Government departments/agencies (particularly those that deal with finance or innovation).** Examples include the USA's Small Business Administration, which regulates the country's Small Business Investment Companies programme, and Luxembourg's Commission de Surveillance du Secteur Financier, which regulates the country's sociétés d'investissement en capital à risqué (SICAR) regime.
- **Other specially created bodies.** Examples include Industry Innovation and Science Australia, which regulates Australia's Biomedical Translation Fund programme and the British Business Bank, which regulates the UK's Enterprise Capital Funds programme.
- **A combination of the above.**

Despite the fact that tax incentives are commonly regulated by tax authorities, some commentators suggest that tax authorities are not the most appropriate regulators for venture capital incentives. This is because their primary function is to collect tax, and they may therefore lack the expertise needed to make decisions in regard to incentives (even where these incentives are delivered through the tax system).[105] Certainly it seems logical that a specially formed regulator that is

[104] See broadly Barkoczy and Sandler (n 70) 37.

[105] See Krever, 'Tax Deductions' (n 74) 16–17; Barkoczy and Sandler (n 70) 32; Burton and Sadiq (n 13) 7; Surrey (n 73) 728; Surrey and McDaniel (n 71) 106; OECD, *Tax Expenditures in OECD Countries* (n 72) 28.

tailored to administering innovation-related incentives would be better equipped to make policy-related decisions about incentives.[106] Furthermore, it makes sense that all of a country's venture capital incentives, whether they are tax or direct incentives, should be under the oversight of the same body. On the other hand, it is also arguable that tax authorities should be in charge of implementing and enforcing tax incentives, as only they have the 'unique authority, expertise and experience necessary for the execution of the tax law'.[107] Having tax-based incentives administered by the relevant tax authority also means that all the accounting and tax records are kept in one centralised location,[108] and may help prevent tax abuse.[109]

As a way of balancing these issues, some countries split the management of their tax-based incentives between two regulators.[110] For example, Australia's Venture Capital Limited Partnership and Early Stage Venture Capital Limited Partnership programmes are dually managed by Australia's tax regulator, the Australian Tax Office and its innovation body, Industry Innovation and Science Australia.[111] However, this kind of dual management approach has raised concerns about inefficiency and costly double handling.[112] Interestingly, Australia's newest venture capital incentive, the early stage investor tax incentive, is regulated solely by the Australian Tax Office, which has responsibility for assessing incentive eligibility and collecting information from recipients.[113] The Commissioner of Taxation has the power to make public and private rulings in relation to the application of the incentive's rules, and the Australian Tax Office will generally act in accordance with these rulings.[114] Industry Innovation and Science Australia is able to provide guidance on rulings,[115] but otherwise plays no part in the regulation of the incentive. It has been suggested that because Industry Innovation and Science Australia has 'the most appropriate specialist skills in assessing innovation criteria', granting it the power to make rulings may be more appropriate, and would allow the Australian Tax Office to focus on dealing with 'technical tax matters'.[116]

[106] See, eg Stephen Barkoczy and Tamara Wilkinson, *Incentivising Angels: A Comparative Framework of Tax Incentives for Start-Up Investors* (Springer, 2019) 63, 101.

[107] International Monetary Fund et al (n 13) 28. See also OECD, *Tax Expenditures in OECD Countries* (n 72) 45; European Commission (n 23) 81.

[108] Duanjie Chen, 'The Framework for Assessing Tax Incentives: A Cost–Benefit Analysis Approach' (Workshop on Tax Incentives and Base Protection, United Nations, 23–24 April 2015) 32.

[109] James (n 4) 35.

[110] See David A Weisbach and Jacob Nussim, 'The Integration of Tax and Spending Programs' (2004) 113(5) *Yale Law Journal* 955, 963; Barkoczy and Sandler (n 70) 32–33.

[111] See Barkoczy and Wilkinson (n 106) 101.

[112] See Kerrie Sadiq, 'Powering Innovation Through Tax Concessions: The Changing Research & Development Tax Incentives' (2014) 16(1) *Journal of Australian Taxation* 1, 26; Barkoczy and Sandler (n 70) 33; United Nations Economic Commission for Europe (n 33) 42.

[113] Tax Administration Act 1953 (Australia), s 396-55; Explanatory Memorandum, Tax Laws Amendment (Tax Incentives for Innovation) Bill 2016 (Australia) 1.15.

[114] See Tax Administration Act 1953 (Australia), Divs 358, 359, s 357-60; Barkoczy and Wilkinson (n 106) 62–63.

[115] See Barkoczy and Wilkinson (n 106) 63.

[116] ibid 101.

Ultimately, however, there is little cause to recommend either tax authorities or specialised departments or bodies over the other in the regulation of venture capital incentives. The reality is that both tax and direct incentives tend to be complex instruments that involve a high degree of regulation and administration, and in both cases, the relevant department administering the incentive will have to create tailored processes for application, decision-making, monitoring and distributing incentive benefits.[117]

Regardless of the body selected to regulate incentives, there are a number of baseline principles that regulators should conform to in order to ensure that incentives are delivered as effectively and efficiently as possible. These principles have been well explored by regulatory experts and theorists,[118] and the following list sets out some of the principles that are particularly relevant to regulators in charge of managing venture capital incentives.

- **Experienced staff.** Regulators should have appropriately qualified and experienced staff (ideally with private sector experience and a thorough understanding of early-stage investment, startups and the venture capital industry).[119] This may require training staff.[120] OSEO, the regulator of France's former Investissement Garantie scheme, was particularly commended in this respect, with a review of the scheme noting that OSEO staff were appropriately skilled and familiar with the French venture capital market, and that such skills and competencies are not typically common in innovation agencies.[121] Familiarity with markets is particularly important in relation to the decision-making process (see below), as regulators in many cases may need to select or approve investors, funds, fund managers and/or investees participating in incentives. This process will be difficult if regulators lack industry experience or familiarity with investment performance metrics.[122]
- **Appropriate relationship with the private sector.** There should be relationships between the regulator and the private sector in order to 'ensure that regulation serves the public interest and is informed by the legitimate needs' of those affected by it.[123] However, these relationships should be maintained at arm's length to minimise the risks posed by agency capture, rent-seeking behaviour, corruption and fraud. Again, France's regulator OSEO was

[117] See Weisbach and Nussim (n 110) 962–63.

[118] See, eg Ashley C Brown, Job Stern, Bernard Tenenbaum and Defne Gencer, *Handbook for Evaluating Infrastructure Regulatory Systems* (World Bank, 2006) 201–44.

[119] Murray et al (n 33) 22; Josh Lerner, 'When Bureaucrats Meet Entrepreneurs: The Design of Effective "Public Venture Capital" Programmes' (2002) 112(477) *Economic Journal* F73, F80.

[120] See, eg Cromwell Schmisseur, 'Information and Observations on State Venture Capital Programs: Report for the US Department of the Treasury and Interested Parties in the State Small Business Credit Initiative (SSBCI)' (February 2013) 6.

[121] Deuten (n 7) 14.

[122] Murray et al (n 33) 10.

[123] OECD Regulatory Policy Committee, 'Recommendation of the Council on Regulatory Policy and Governance' (2012) 4. See also Lerner, 'When Bureaucrats Meet Entrepreneurs' (n 119) F80.

commended for its relationship with Investissement Garantie scheme recipients, with a review of the scheme noting that the relationship was not the typical agency–client relationship, but resembled instead 'a partnership with a mutual interest' – increasing investments in French SMEs.[124] The Investissement Garantie scheme was reportedly implemented by 10 OSEO staff, with six or seven of these involved with managing the guarantee, and three to four involved in managing relationships with recipients.

- **Certainty and consistency.** Regulatory certainty and consistency are important for the effective and efficient functioning of incentives. In order to maximise certainty, regulatory bodies should ideally be created by law, and have their principles, practices, procedures and policies articulated in law.[125] Australia's regulator, Industry Innovation and Science Australia, for instance, is governed by the Venture Capital Act 2002 and has its rules articulated clearly within that legislation. However, the regulator has also experienced four name changes over the past 15 years, from the Venture Capital Registration Board to Innovation Australia to Innovation and Science Australia to its current iteration. These cosmetic changes do not foster certainty, but unfortunately are not uncommon. Regulatory bodies often change over time, particularly due to consolidation or political shifts,[126] and these changes can create confusion for recipients, complicate the gathering of data and risk the loss of important institutional knowledge. Such a change occurred, for instance, in 2013 when France's highly praised regulator, OSEO, was restructured into a new regulator, Bpifrance. Furthermore, continually changing those responsible for the oversight and implementation of an incentive has been described as a blueprint for limiting success.[127] One way to increase regulatory certainty and consistency is for regulators to have final decision-making authority over incentive decisions and fully enforce their decisions, standards and rules.[128] It has been noted that 'poor regulator practices can discourage compliance, waste government resources and add to business costs and delays', and even in the case of appropriate and well-designed regulation, 'poor enforcement practices can risk rendering it ineffective, or unduly burdensome, or both'.[129] For example, in the case of the USA's former Specialized Small Business Investment Companies programme, it has been reported that the regulator was extraordinarily unpredictable and inefficient, and the 'outcome of each routine transaction was always in doubt'.[130] These administrative failures are seen to have contributed to the programme's failure.[131]

[124] Deuten (n 7) 14–15.
[125] Brown et al (n 118) 185–87.
[126] See Wilson and Silva (n 2) 59.
[127] Bates (n 14) 52.
[128] Brown et al (n 118) 185–87, 192.
[129] Productivity Commission (n 43) xiv–xv.
[130] Bates (n 14) 52.
[131] ibid.

- **Transparency.** Regulators should be transparent in their policies and administration, and subject to scrutiny and evaluation to ensure that they are held accountable for their actions.[132] Transparency can serve to strengthen the trust of investors in government, enhance the confidence of the public and play an important role in helping avoid incentive abuse and corruption (see [5.4.2] below).[133] It can be particularly useful for regulators to make their decisions publicly available in order to build a body of precedent.[134] This transparency can help applicants predict the likely outcomes of their applications and increases certainty and consistency.
- **Resources.** Regulators are not generally in charge of the amount of resources that are allocated to them for the performance of their administrative functions. However, it is important for regulators to be adequately resourced so that they can perform their functions effectively. Even well-designed programmes can falter 'if adequate administrative resources are not available'.[135]

5.3.2. Application and Approval Processes

Most incentives require recipients to apply to be approved (ie registered, licensed or certified) in order to receive benefits. Some incentives require only investors to be approved, while others also require investees to be approved (although this is less common).[136] Approval processes fulfil a gatekeeping role in relation to incentives – they help ensure that only eligible entities that meet the relevant targeting requirements can participate, thereby protecting the integrity of incentives.[137] Formal approval processes also help regulators collect data about incentive and their recipients (see [5.4.1] below).

Examples of incentives that include approval processes include:

- Singapore's Fund Management Incentive, which requires 'fund management companies' (fund managers) that manage special Section 13G venture capital funds to be licensed by the Monetary Authority of Singapore in order to receive incentives;[138]

[132] International Monetary Fund et al (n 13) 23; Department of Finance (n 17) 35.
[133] International Monetary Fund et al (n 13) 23.
[134] ibid; World Bank (n 5) 102.
[135] Easson (n 2) 159. See also Brown et al (n 118) 217.
[136] See Barkoczy and Sandler (n 70) 37.
[137] See OECD, 'Tax Incentives for R&D and Innovation' (2016) 5.
[138] Startup Investor SG and Enterprise Singapore, 'Startup Investor SG: Section 13H and the Fund Management Incentive', 2, ssn-core-prod-files.s3.ap-southeast-1.amazonaws.com/2020-05/Factsheet_S13H_FMI_11%20May.pdf.

- the UK's Venture Capital Trusts scheme, which requires Venture Capital Trusts to be approved by HM Revenue & Customs to invest in and/or make loans to qualifying companies;[139]
- Australia's Early Stage Venture Capital Limited Partnership and Venture Capital Limited Partnership programmes, which require venture capital funds to be registered before their investors can claim tax incentives;[140]
- Turkey's Business Angels Scheme, which requires angel investors to obtain a five-year renewable licence before they can participate in the incentive;[141] and
- Malaysia's incentive for Venture Capital Companies, which require investments made by Venture Capital Companies (ie funds), other companies and investors in startups to be certified annually by the Malaysian Securities Commission.[142] Venture capital management corporations (fund managers) are also required to registered with the Securities Commission.[143]

The application processes that entities go through in order to be approved range in complexity from simple and straightforward to more opaque, confusing and uncertain. A common criticism of venture capital incentives 'is that some have unnecessarily elaborate or incomprehensible application procedures and that the award procedure is excessively long'.[144] Having an overly complex and cumbersome application process is a hallmark of poor incentive design, as it is likely to raise incentive administration costs (creating a burden on government) and compliance costs (creating a burden on recipients), thereby reducing incentive efficiency.[145] High costs and complex processes can lead to various selection effects, reducing incentive effectiveness. For instance, they might drive away high-quality recipients, who do not feel it worth the effort, relative to the benefits they could obtain, to engage with a complex incentive.[146] As noted above at [5.2], complex, costly or cumbersome application processes might also deter or exclude smaller or less-well-resourced entities from participating in incentives,[147] meaning that

[139] HM Revenue & Customs, 'Tax Relief for Investors Using Venture Capital Schemes' (7 July 2021) www.gov.uk/guidance/venture-capital-schemes-tax-relief-for-investors.

[140] See Venture Capital Act 2002 (Australia), Div 9; Income Tax Assessment Act 1997 (Australia), Subdiv 118-F.

[141] European Commission (n 23) 197; Republic of Turkey, Ministry of Treasury and Finance, 'Regulation on Business Angels' (2018) 5.

[142] Securities Commission Malaysia, 'Venture Capital Tax Incentives Guidelines' (18 April 2014) cl 4; Inland Revenue Board of Malaysia, *Venture Capital Tax Incentives* (9 May 2016) Public Ruling No 2/2016, 4, 11.

[143] Securities Commission Malaysia, 'Guidelines on Registration of Venture Capital and Private Equity Corporations and Management Corporations' (2020) SC-GL/1-2015 (R1-2020), cl 15; Inland Revenue Board of Malaysia (n 142) 11.

[144] OECD, 'Government Venture Capital for Technology-Based Firms' (n 25) 21.

[145] European Commission (n 23) 153; International Monetary Fund et al (n 13) 17; James (n 4) 26–27. See also Productivity Commission (n 43) 9.

[146] See Wilson and Silva (n 2) 59.

[147] See James (n 4) 31.

incentives may disproportionately benefit only the entities that have the capacity to take advantage of them (and not necessarily the most deserving entities).[148] This raises equity issues, as well as potentially stimulating less additionality. This effect reportedly occurred in relation to the European Union's Capital Risque pour les Enterprises d'Amorçage loan programme in the late 1990s, with smaller beneficiaries reportedly not finding it worth the effort to engage with the programme's administrative complexity and application rigidity.[149] In contrast, an evaluation of British Columbia's Venture Capital Program (a tax credit incentive) found 'very positive' feedback on the programme's registration and application processes, with over 80 per cent of surveyed respondents noting that they were aided by programme personnel and that the programme was easy to understand and complete.[150] Over 70 per cent of respondents noted that the cost of applying for and complying with the programme was less than CAD 5,000, which, the evaluation found, indicated a low cost of administration.[151]

It can be difficult to fully appreciate the complexity of different application processes on face value. For example, Australia's early stage investor tax incentive has a seemingly simple process for receiving incentive benefits, as it does not have an explicit application process or approval requirement. Instead, recipients claim tax incentives when they file their tax returns and are responsible for self-assessing their own eligibility and that of their investees.[152] In contrast, the application process for Germany's INVEST incentive has a four-step application and approval process that operates as follows:

1. Prospective investee companies submit an online application to the Federal Office of Economics and Export Control (BAFA) to certify their eligibility for funding under the incentive. Certification lasts for 12 months (recently increased from six months), highlighting the fast-changing nature of startups.
2. Using the application number of the relevant certified investee company, investors submit an online application to BAFA for approval to receive the INVEST grant. The approval is valid for three months.
3. Investors provide proof of their shareholding in an investee company and their payment for the shares to BAFA, and the INVEST grant is paid.
4. Investors provide proof of share disposal and realised capital gains (after the three-year holding period) to BAFA, and BAFA issues the exit grant.[153]

[148] OECD, *Tax Expenditures in OECD Countries* (n 72) 26. See also Burton and Sadiq (n 13) 116.

[149] United Nations Economic Commission for Europe (n 33) 52.

[150] Thomas Hellmann and Paul Schure, 'An Evaluation of the Venture Capital Program in British Columbia' (Ministry of Small Business, Technology and Economic Development, June 2010) 40.

[151] ibid.

[152] See Australian Taxation Office, 'Tax Incentives for Early Stage Investors: Qualifying for the Tax Incentives' (7 April 2021) www.ato.gov.au/Business/Tax-incentives-for-innovation/In-detail/Tax-incentives-for-early-stage-investors/?anchor=Thesophisticatedinvestortest#Thesophisticatedinvestortest.

[153] Bundesministerium für Wirtschaft und Energie, 'Richtlinie zur Bezuschussung von Wagniskapital privater Investoren für junge innovative Unternehmen INVEST – Zuschuss für Wagniskapital' (Federal Gazette, 21 December 2020) cl 7 [tr author].

Germany's process seems initially to be more complex that Australia's, despite the fact that both incentives provide both investment and profit-related relief. However, this is not the complete picture. Under Australia's incentive, investors bear the risk of incorrectly claiming the tax incentive.[154] Investee companies must meet a number of complex eligibility requirements, and the only way that investors can know for certain that a company is eligible is to obtain a ruling from the Commission of Taxation.[155] These rulings apply only until a company's circumstances change, and the onus is on investors to investigate whether this has happened or not. Germany's certification of investee companies under the first step of its process is actually therefore a more certain and straightforward way of addressing this issue. Furthermore, Australia's incentive places reporting obligations on eligible investees, requiring them to provide information on shares they issue that could give rise to an entitlement to incentive benefits (whether this actually occurred or not).[156] This imposes a burden on startup companies that could be avoided, for example by following the second step of Germany's process (linking an application to receive a grant to an already certified investee). While Australia's process for claiming the tax incentive may therefore appear simpler, it is likely that, in reality, it provides less work for regulators, but more work – and more uncertainty – for investors and startups than Germany's four-step process. In fact, Germany's INVEST incentive application process has been recognised as an example of leading practice for its clear requirements, the ability to apply online and the range of consistent, clear and up-to-date resources provided for recipients in both German and English by the Federal Ministry for Economic Affairs and Energy and BAFA.[157] Furthermore, by requiring investors to be approved before making their investment, Germany's process facilitates the prediction and control of incentive costs. In contrast, Australia's process means that it will be impossible for governments to know how many entities will claim the tax incentive until after they have claimed it.[158] Requiring recipients to be approved prior to claiming incentive benefits is therefore useful for governments from a cost management and data collection standpoint.

One simple step that governments can take to make their incentive application processes simpler and more accessible to recipients is to allow for online applications, as in the example of Germany's INVEST programme. A 2017 report by the European Commission on angel and venture capital tax incentives found that of 28 incentives where information on application processes was available, 22 incentives allowed applications to be made online.[159] Information on application processes was reportedly not available for a further 18 incentives (which is

[154] Barkoczy and Wilkinson (n 106) 61.
[155] ibid 62.
[156] See Tax Administration Act 1953 (Australia), s 396-55.
[157] See European Commission (n 23) 189, 192.
[158] See OECD, *Tax Expenditures in OECD Countries* (n 72) 28.
[159] European Commission (n 23) 154–59.

concerning, as it means that potential recipients are also likely to struggle to access this information).[160] It was also reported in 2017 that of 16 tax-based incentives provided by Europe's five largest venture capital markets (Germany, France, the UK, Spain and Sweden), only eight (50 per cent) provided for online applications.[161] Even where incentives already provide for online applications, improvements may still be able to be made; for instance, British Columbia's Venture Capital Program allows for online applications, but a 2010 evaluation recommended that the login system, which was seen to be inefficient, should be simplified.[162]

Other steps that governments can take to make application processes more streamlined include requiring regulators to communicate clearly and promptly with incentive recipients,[163] to process decisions as quickly as possible and to set a clear decision-making time frame. Poor administration, 'such as lengthy delays in determining whether an investment qualifies for an incentive, can nullify the attraction of the incentive and even act as a deterrent to investment'.[164] To combat this, some incentives make their approval time frames explicit. For instance, licensing applications under Singapore's Fund Management Incentive are stated to take around six months to be processed and approved (previously four months).[165] Licences are granted for up to five years and may be renewed after they expire.[166] While the approval timeline is quite long, at least recipients can forward plan for this, as they are given the timeline information in advance, and the licences have a long duration. In contrast, the registration application process for fund managers under Malaysia's incentives for Venture Capital Companies is stated to take just six weeks to process.[167] The decision-making timeline is similar under Australia's Venture Capital Limited Partnership and Early Stage Venture Capital Limited Partnership programmes, where Industry Innovation and Science Australia is empowered under the Venture Capital Act 2002 to make decisions on the registration of limited partnerships within 60 days.[168]

5.3.3. As-of-Right versus Discretionary Approval

Approval decisions can be made on an as-of-right (objective) basis or on a discretionary (subjective) basis.[169] In the former case, any entity that satisfies the relevant

[160] ibid.
[161] Ständer (n 23) 16.
[162] Hellmann and Schure (n 150) 7.
[163] Productivity Commission (n 43) xv.
[164] Easson (n 2) 159.
[165] Monetary Authority of Singapore, 'Securities and Futures Act (cap 289): Frequently Asked Questions (FAQs) on the Licensing and Registration of Fund Management Companies' (1 June 2023) 14.
[166] Startup Investor SG and Enterprise Singapore (n 138) 2.
[167] Securities Commission Malaysia, 'Guidelines on Registration (n 143) cl 21.
[168] See Venture Capital Act 2002 (Australia), Div 11.
[169] See James (n 4) 5.

eligibility criteria can participate in the incentive. In the latter case, the regulator must assess the extent to which an entity has satisfied the relevant eligibility or merit criteria and may judge the entity competitively against other applications. The regulator in this situation has discretion over which entities participate in the incentive. Figure 1 sets out the broad kinds of approval processes that may be used under venture capital incentives and highlights the degree of objectivity/subjectivity required for each one.

Figure 1 As-of-right versus discretionary approval processes

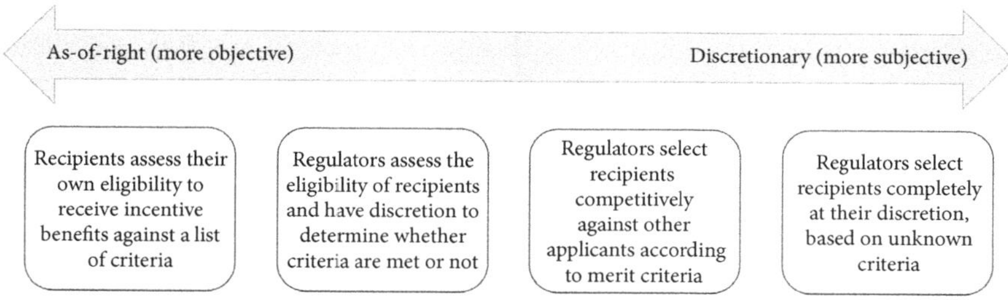

The following discussion outlines the reasons for preferring either the as-of-right or discretionary approval process with regard to incentive costs, administrative efficiency, recipient quality, certainty and the prevention of abuse and corruption.

Incentive Cost (Discretionary Preferred Over As-of-Right)

Discretionary approval processes are preferable to as-of-right processes from a budgetary and cost perspective because they allow regulators to select only the desired number of entities to participate in incentives (which makes their uptake very easy to control). Incentives with discretionary approval processes can adapt to changing budgetary circumstances, and do not face cost blow-outs as a consequence of rising demand.[170] For example, the UK's Enterprise Capital Funds programme has a highly competitive application process in place for prospective fund managers, and the regulator is not bound to accept any applications by fund managers.[171] This means that it has complete control over the number of fund managers selected. The regulator selects fund managers to participate in the Enterprise Capital Funds programme based on the 'findings of commercial, financial and legal due diligence and any other information or advice deemed necessary', as well as a range of assessment criteria that were discussed at [4.2.2].[172]

[170] Krever, 'Tax Deductions' (n 74) 19.
[171] British Business Bank, 'Enterprise Capital Funds: Guidance for Prospective Managers' (November 2014) 4.
[172] ibid 8, 28.

As-of-right incentives, on the other hand, have little protection against rising or fluctuating uptake levels because they are awarded to all eligible entities.[173] It is therefore particularly important that, in situations where as-of-right incentives are used, their eligibility criteria are tightly targeted towards the best recipients.

Administrative Efficiency (As-of-Right Preferred Over Discretionary)

From an administrative perspective, as-of-right approval processes are often seen as the quicker, cheaper, easier and more efficient option, because there is no need for regulators to assess recipients.[174] Such approval processes are often praised for involving 'less bureaucratic discretion', encouraging private decision-making and being simpler in design than discretionary processes.[175] They are also seen to be a more equitable way to provide incentives, because all entities that meet the eligibility criteria can participate in the incentive.[176]

'Self-declared' eligibility, as seen in Figure 1, is a very simple way to implement incentives.[177] In order for recipients to be able to assess their own eligibility, however, it is important that the eligibility criteria be clearly specified, 'with as little room as possible for subjective interpretation or negotiation'.[178] Where this is done, the process of granting incentives can be 'largely automatic by verification of stipulated criteria'.[179] In contrast, subjective or merit-based criteria will need to be assessed by a regulator, which increases the regulator's workload and may involve 'cumbersome and time-consuming processes'.[180] Therefore, while the cost of providing as-of-right incentives may be higher (because of the uptake issue mentioned above), the administration costs of discretionary incentives can be significant for both governments and recipients,[181] and as-of-right processes may be cheaper in this respect. However, one important administrative benefit of discretionary approval processes is that they generally result in a great deal more information being collected about incentive recipients and how they use incentives, which can be useful (see [5.4.1] below).[182] This is because applicants disclose information to regulators in order to support their applications.

[173] Krever, 'Tax Deductions' (n 74) 18.
[174] See Howard (n 71) 444; James (n 4) 34.
[175] See Brooks (n 55) 75. *cf* Surrey and McDaniel (n 71) 100–01.
[176] See Maria Pinelli and Uschi Schreiber, 'Funding the Future: Access to Finance for Entrepreneurs in the G20' (Ernst & Young, 2013) 35.
[177] Weisbach and Nussim (n 110) 980.
[178] International Monetary Fund et al (n 13) 26.
[179] ibid.
[180] European Commission (n 23) 81.
[181] See OECD, 'Business Innovation Policies' (n 30) 53; James (n 4) 27.
[182] See European Commission (n 23) 81.

Recipient Quality (Discretionary Preferred Over As-of-Right)

Discretionary incentives allow governments to control for recipient quality by selecting the best recipients (particularly where they use a competitive/merit-based selection process)[183] and to carefully tailor the provision of incentives,[184] including by being able to respond to changing circumstances.[185] In this way, discretionary incentives may potentially be better targeted than as-of-right incentives, consequently improving their effectiveness and efficiency.[186] As-of-right incentives generally do not have the same focus on recipient 'worthiness',[187] and are often accused of subsidising activities that would have occurred anyway (ie they provide windfalls).[188] However, the quality benefits associated with discretionary incentives will only realistically accrue if the relevant decision-maker is skilled, effective and acts with integrity in their role, which is not always the case.[189] In reality, the decision-making process is often seen as being 'prone to error'.[190]

Certainty (As-of-Right Preferred Over Discretionary)

From the perspective of incentive recipients, as-of-right approval processes provide far more certainty than discretionary ones, because they do not involve subjective decisions by a regulator. In contrast, discretionary approval processes often involve a great deal of uncertainty for applicants, which can take a long time to be resolved. For example, Poland's recently privatised National Capital Fund (KFK) selected high-quality fund managers to receive co-investments on a competitive basis through a multi-step selection process. Following an open tender, the best applicants were shortlisted and asked to present their investment offers in detail, and KFK carried out legal and financial due diligence on these applicants before entering investment agreements.[191] This kind of intensive selection process is quite common for competitive co-investment incentives because regulators want to select the highest quality fund managers to take part in their incentives (see [4.2.2]).

[183] See OECD, 'Business Innovation Policies' (n 30) 17.
[184] European Commission (n 23) 81.
[185] World Bank (n 5) 103.
[186] See European Commission (n 23) 81, 90; Department of Finance (n 17) 31; Easson (n 2) 108.
[187] Sadiq, 'An Analysis of Tax Expenditures' (n 98) 12–13. See also Howard (n 71) 444.
[188] See Pinelli and Schreiber (n 176) 35; Surrey and McDaniel (n 71) 102.
[189] European Commission (n 23) 90. See, eg Leamon et al (n 32) 31.
[190] James A Brander, Edward J Egan and Thomas F Hellmann, 'Government Sponsored versus Private Venture Capital: Canadian Evidence' (National Bureau of Economic Research, May 2008) Working Paper No 14029, 6.
[191] Ustawa z dnia 4 marca 2005 r o Krajowym Funduszu Kapitałowym (Poland), Arts 12, 13. KFK was subsumed into a larger fund of funds and ceased independent operation in 2019: see PFR Ventures, 'National Capital Fund', pfrventures.pl/en/kfk.html. See also Ilona Fałat-Kilijańska, 'How to Strengthen the Polish Venture Capital Market? An Analysis of the Solutions in Selected Countries' (2015) 4(25) *Financial Sciences* 9, 20.

Where incentives use discretionary processes to select recipients, regulators can increase certainty for applicants by ensuring that they apply their discretion consistently, so that similar entities receive similar and comparable treatment, and by publishing decisions. These actions increase equity and can help preserve confidence in the incentive and the regulator.[192] New Zealand's former Venture Investment Fund implemented a range of positive processes in this respect. Recognising the need to make a large number of subjective approval decisions quickly on a 'consistent and unbiased' basis, the regulator engaged an external consultancy to help them re-examine their approach to decision-making processes.[193] Part of the revamped decision-making process involved keeping practice notes on investments that were approved as meeting the programme's investment goals, but that did not fit into an established category of eligible investees.[194] This allowed flexibility of the approval process in a way that forward-fed into process improvements. Process and practice notes were kept on a staff intranet, and staff were expected to be familiar with them. This feature also helped train new staff, as they could access data on the decisions and processes. The improvements to the approval process, including the decision-making data retention, reportedly had the added benefit of helping more decisions to be made in a significantly reduced time frame, leading to overall gains in efficiency.[195]

Prevention of Abuse (No Clear Preference)

Both as-of-right and discretionary approval processes can become subject to abuse or corruption. As-of-right processes involve far less scrutiny of applicants than discretionary processes, which may facilitate the participation of ineligible entities. It has been noted that however tightly eligibility criteria are crafted, 'it is inevitable that they will be breached', which generally leads to a need for anti-avoidance measures (as will be discussed at [5.4.2] below).[196] This, in turn, can add to the deadweight costs of an incentive and reduce overall efficiency.[197]

That being said, discretionary incentives also present risks of corruption and abuse.[198] The exercise of discretion by governments is often seen as problematic because it 'introduces the risk of rent-seeking behavior on the part of the investors and corrupt behavior on the part of the public officials'.[199] For instance, it has been suggested that the selection process for USA's SBIC licences 'appeared to emphasise

[192] See James (n 4) 36.
[193] Controller and Auditor-General, 'New Zealand Venture Investment Fund' (2012) oag.parliament.nz/2012/efficiency-stories/corporate/new-zealand-venture-investment-fund.
[194] ibid.
[195] ibid.
[196] Krever, 'Taming Complexity' (n 70) 488. See also Brooks (n 55) 76.
[197] See Krever, 'Tax Deductions' (n 74) 16; Easson (n 2) 108.
[198] European Commission (n 23) 81, 90; James (n 4) 29, 36.
[199] International Monetary Fund et al (n 13) 26. See also World Bank (n 5) 102–03.

political connections over investment acumen',[200] which is unlikely to have helped the incentive's success. A report to the G20 has recommended that the exercise of discretion 'should be kept to a minimum' for these reasons.[201] In contrast, as-of-right expenditures may potentially be more resistant to rent-seeking behaviours (although not to other kinds of exploitation).

5.4. Monitoring Incentives

It is important for regulators to monitor incentives for two key reasons: to ensure that incentives are operating in an effective and efficient manner and are making progress towards their policy aims;[202] and to ensure that incentives are not being taken advantage of or otherwise abused (for instance, in the ways set out above). The first of these two tasks involves putting data collection processes in place, as a fundamental part of incentive management (see [5.4.1]). The second task is facilitated through the monitoring of incentives (as this makes it harder to 'get away' with poor behaviour), as well as through a number of specific anti-avoidance and targeting mechanisms (discussed at [5.4.2]), some of which were foreshadowed in chapters three and four.

5.4.1. Data Collection

Collecting data for the purpose of monitoring incentive costs, targeting and performance is recognised in regulatory theory, tax expenditure theory, programme evaluation theory and innovation policy as an element of leading practice in the administration of incentives.[203] The kinds of data that may be useful for the purpose of monitoring incentives include:

- the number of incentive applications and recipients;
- the cost of providing and administering the incentive;
- records of decisions made;
- the sector or industry investees operate in;
- investees' stage of development;

[200] Josh Lerner, 'Innovation, Entrepreneurship and Financial Market Cycles' (OECD, March 2010) OECD Science, Technology and Industry Working Paper No 2010/3, 33.

[201] International Monetary Fund et al (n 13) 26.

[202] See OECD, 'Government Venture Capital for Technology-Based Firms' (n 25) 2.

[203] See, eg Brown et al (n 118) 193, 197; James (n 4) 35; European Commission (n 23) 181; International Monetary Fund et al (n 13) 23; Department of Prime Minister and Cabinet, *The Australian Government Guide to Regulation* (Australian Government, 2014) 51–52; Jean-Michel Josselin and Benoît Le Maux, *Statistical Tools for Program Evaluation: Methods and Applications to Economic Policy, Public Health, and Education* (Springer, 2017) 4.

- the extent to which investments are staged and syndicated;
- the number of investments made per investor/fund manager;
- the location of the investments/investees; and
- how investments are exited.[204]

Regulators can collect some of this data from their own records. Some of the data, however, needs to come from incentive participants. For this purpose, many incentives impose 'reporting requirements' on incentive recipients and/or investees as a condition of participating. Although reporting requirements add to an incentive's administrative costs, and to recipients' and investees' compliance costs,[205] the OECD notes that where well-designed systems of data collection are built into incentives from their inception, they need not impose significant reporting burdens on recipients.[206] Governments should maintain consistency in reporting requirements and definitions to avoid generating confusion and extra work for recipients (including by having a consistent definition of the kind of investment that constitutes venture capital and the methodology used to calculate investment returns, etc),[207] and reporting requirements should be as streamlined as possible.[208] From a practical standpoint, the easier it is for incentive recipients and investees to comply with data reporting requirements, the more likely they are to willingly and thoroughly engage in this process and the lower their costs will be in doing so.

In some cases, regulators will need to responsively improve their reporting requirements. For example, an evaluation of British Columbia's Venture Capital Program examined 519 investee companies that had received investment under the programme, but could only access data on 317 of these, either because of missing data or because the companies were brand new investees that had not reported yet.[209] In response to this lack of data, the evaluation recommended that electronic reporting requirements be implemented to collect data on investees. It suggested collecting data at a minimum on investee employment and revenue figures, and ideally also on investee taxes and wages paid, the amount of equity they raise and any changes to status (eg initial public offering, acquisition, closure) they experience.[210] This data would help the regulator to know how well the incentive is working.

An example of an incentive that imposes quite a detailed disclosure and data-reporting regime on recipients is Luxembourg's SICAR regime. SICARs, which are

[204] See, eg Douglas Cumming and Sofia Johan, 'Pre-Seed Government Venture Capital Funds' (2009) 7(1) *Journal of International Entrepreneurship* 26, 32–33.
[205] James (n 4) 31.
[206] OECD, 'Business Innovation Policies' (n 30) 126.
[207] See Murray et al (n 33) 2; Wilson (n 28) 31.
[208] Productivity Commission (n 43) xiv–xv.
[209] Hellmann and Schure (n 150) 7.
[210] ibid 11.

special purpose investment funds, must prepare annual prospectuses and reports to enable the Luxembourg government to assess their activities.[211] Prospectuses must include the information necessary for prospective investors to be able to make an informed judgement on the risks and benefits of investing in a particular SICAR, and must be broadly up to date when new SICAR securities or partnership interests are issued to new investors.[212] Annual reports must include a balance sheet or a statement of assets and liabilities, an income and expenditure account for the financial year, a report on the activities of the past financial year, as well as any significant information enabling investors to make an informed judgement on the development of the activities and the results of the SICAR.[213] Reports must be finalised within six months of the end of the relevant financial period, and must be provided free of charge to investors.[214] A SICAR must also send both its prospectus and its annual report to the regulator, the Commission de Surveillance du Secteur Financier (CSSF).[215]

The data collected through monitoring also serves another purpose, which is that it may subsequently be used to evaluate incentives (see chapter six).[216] Better data on incentive uptake, reach and recipients will help governments gain a better understanding of how different incentives perform, which should, in turn, improve policy outcomes.[217] Conversely, without data, accurate evaluations cannot be undertaken.[218]

5.4.2. Avoiding Abuse and Corruption

The abuse of incentives has the capacity to add to both their direct and administrative costs. While the term 'abuse' is often used to broadly describe the situation where incentives are not used for their intended purposes or implemented as they should be, it is useful to break this concept down into more specific elements: abuse, misuse and corruption. In this part, incentive abuse refers to the situation where incentives are taken advantage of in a way that is inconsistent with their rules. Incentive misuse refers to the situation where incentives are used by recipients in a way that is inconsistent with achieving their policy aims (ie recipients obey the letter of the rules if not the spirit). Finally, incentive corruption refers to the situation where the regulators of incentives do not perform their roles and

[211] Law of 15 June 2004 Relating to the Investment Company in Risk Capital ('SICAR') (Luxembourg), Arts 24, 26.
[212] ibid.
[213] ibid art 24.
[214] ibid arts 23, 29.
[215] ibid art 28.
[216] Josselin and Le Maux (n 203) 3.
[217] See, eg What Works Centre for Local Economic Growth, 'Innovation: Grants, Loans and Subsidies' (October 2015) Evidence Review No 9, 37.
[218] See James (n 4) 5.

responsibilities as they should. These three elements, and the ways that governments might consider addressing them, are discussed below.

Incentive Abuse

The abuse of incentives is problematic because it increases incentive costs while also lessening their effectiveness.[219] This is because recipients who abuse incentives obtain incentive benefits, but do not contribute to achieving incentive policy aims. Any costs incurred in this situation are, by their nature, deadweight costs. There are myriad ways that recipients can abuse incentives, including lying or concealing information about themselves or their activities in order to access incentives when they should otherwise not be able to,[220] and flouting incentive rules once they have accessed them. The latter issue was reportedly a major problem in relation to the early days of the USA's Small Business Investment Companies co-investment programme. Under this programme, a large number of Small Business Investment Companies were financed, but were given minimal review.[221] Lerner notes that recipients reportedly undertook lines of business outside the scope of the programme (such as real estate development) and engaged in non-arm's-length transactions, and that nine out of 10 Small Business Investment Companies violated federal regulations in some way.[222]

The more oversight regulators have over incentive participants, the less opportunity these participants generally have to abuse the incentive (which is why incentives that are granted to recipients as of right tend to be more open to abuse than those that are granted on a discretionary basis). Therefore, imposing thorough reporting and data collection requirements on recipients and employing the kinds of licensing and registration requirements discussed above at [5.3.2] can help minimise incentive abuse. Luxembourg's SICAR regime, discussed above, imposes a range of requirements on SICARs to help avoid incentive abuse. For example, SICARs must have the accounting information provided in their annual reports audited by an approved statutory auditor (the réviseur d'entreprises agréé).[223] The auditor must alert the CSSF (the regulator) where they become aware of material breaches of the law or regulations, where the information contained in the prospectus or annual report does not truly describe the financial situation and the assets and liabilities of the SICAR, and where the assets of the SICAR are not invested according to the regulations set out by the law or the prospectus.[224] In order to ensure that SICARs comply with their obligations, the CSSF can request SICARs to provide any information relevant to the fulfilment of its duties and may

[219] See James (n 4) 26; International Monetary Fund et al (n 13) 16.
[220] Stone (n 5) 222.
[221] Lerner, *Boulevard of Broken Dreams* (n 61) 38.
[222] ibid.
[223] Law of 15 June 2004 Relating to the Investment Company in Risk Capital ('SICAR') (Luxembourg), Art 27.
[224] ibid.

also examine the books, accounts, registers or other records and documents of SICARs.[225] This oversight of the SICAR regime is likely to help prevent abuse of the incentive, but obviously also increases the regime's cost. Something regulators should attempt to do is tailor their monitoring and enforcement strategies to the level of risk present in particular situations (which, it is acknowledged, can be difficult to ascertain).[226]

Incentive Misuse

In contrast to incentive abuse, incentive misuse involves conduct by recipients that is not necessarily against incentive rules, but that does not help the incentive achieve its policy aims. For example, a common form of misuse involves recipients finding ways around eligibility criteria by 'recharacterising' their investments to fit,[227] thereby attempting to reap the benefits of incentives without changing their behaviour.[228] Incentive misuse therefore also increases deadweight costs and decreases effectiveness and efficiency.

The best way to guard against incentive misuse is through special targeting mechanisms, many of which were discussed in chapter four. These targeting mechanisms can include things such as:[229]

- **Arm's length criteria (see [4.2.1.4]).** Criteria that prevent related parties of investee companies from benefiting from incentives ensure that investments made under incentives are genuine third-party investments.
- **Fund manager investment criteria (see [4.2.2.4]).** Criteria that require fund managers to invest a certain amount of their own capital in a fund they manage help align fund manager interests with the interests of the government providing the incentive (thereby reducing agency risks) and are likely to encourage good investment behaviour.
- **New equity criteria (see [4.3.1]).** Criteria that require investments to be made in the form of new shares issued by the investee prevent the purchase of second-hand shares from being rewarded under an incentive, as this does not channel any money to startups.
- **Risk criteria (see [4.3.1]).** Criteria that require investments to be held 'at risk' prevent investments from attracting incentive benefits where there is some arrangement to protect against or lessen the risk of the investment.
- **Minimum holding period criteria (see [4.3.3]).** Holding period criteria prevent investors from withdrawing their capital within a certain amount of time and help ensure that incentives are not used primarily for tax purposes.

[225] ibid art 32.
[226] Productivity Commission (n 43) xv.
[227] See Krever, 'Taming Complexity' (n 70) 488.
[228] See Stone (n 5) 222.
[229] See European Commission (n 23) 202.

- **Maximum fund size criteria, maximum investment criteria, maximum investee size criteria, maximum investee age criteria, stage criteria (see [4.2.2.1], [4.3.2] and [4.4.1].** These criteria help address the risk of investment drift by ensuring that investors remain focused on supporting innovative early-stage companies, rather than less risky, later-stage companies.
- **Sector exclusion criteria (see [4.4.2]).** Criteria that exclude investees in certain non-innovative sectors from receiving investment under incentives prevent investors from investing in commercially attractive and less risky opportunities that do not fit within an incentive's policy aims.

Governments can also guard against the misuse of their incentives through the use of design features, many of which were discussed in chapter three. These include ensuring that the benefits provided under incentives are not so overly generous that they skew the risk–reward balance, as this can encourage poor investment behaviour, such as a failure to perform adequate due diligence on prospective investments or to adequately monitor investees. In particular, governments should be wary of providing incentives that offer loss relief or guarantees as they have a propensity to encourage these behaviours (see [3.4]).[230]

Governments can also use specific anti-avoidance mechanisms to ensure that recipients comply with incentive rules and targeting criteria. These anti-avoidance mechanisms often take the form of 'clawback' provisions, which retroactively remove a recipient's entitlement to a benefit if they cease to meet certain conditions (or if they never met them to begin with).[231] For example, Ireland's Employment and Investment Incentive uses a clawback mechanism to protect the integrity of the incentive by withdrawing entitlement to tax credits (either completely or partially) in the following circumstances:[232]

- where investors dispose of their shares within a four-year holding period;
- where conditions relating to qualifying companies, trades and subsidiaries do not continue to be met for four years following the share issue or the commencement of trading, including a company being listed on a stock exchange;
- where an investee company repays any debt to the individual (other than an ordinary trade debt), makes a loan to the individual or generally attempts to circumvent the requirements of the incentive by providing a benefit for the individual, etc (in which case, the individual is deemed to have received value from the company and their benefits under the incentive are reduced accordingly);

[230] Margaret O'Shea and Candice Stevens, 'Governments as Venture Capitalists' (1998) 213 *OECD Observer* 26, 29.

[231] See, eg Barkoczy and Wilkinson (n 106) 87.

[232] Taxes Consolidation Act 1997 (Ireland), ss 495, 496, 498, 499, 502. See also Irish Tax and Customs (n 47) 78.

- where an individual acquires an option or enters into an agreement which would bind any person to purchase any eligible shares for a price other than the market value of the shares;
- where an individual grants to any person an option within four years of the date of issue, or enters into an agreement which would bind the individual to dispose of any eligible shares to any person for a price other than the market value of the shares; or
- where an individual subscribes for shares for other than bona fide commercial purposes (ie to avoid tax).

Where relief is clawed back from an investor, the investor cannot lose more tax relief than they originally obtained but may have to pay interest and/or penalties to the Revenue Commissioner.[233]

While clawback mechanisms can be a useful tool, they also introduce an additional element of uncertainty for recipients (as they face the risk of having their benefits revoked even several years later). For this reason, perhaps, they are not particularly common. The European Commission found the use of clawback provisions in relation to just seven out of 46 tax-based angel and venture capital incentives that they identified in their 2017 report.[234] Four out of these seven were incentives based in the UK, where clawback provisions seem to be quite popular.

Incentive Corruption

Incentive administration becomes corrupted where governments or regulators do not perform their roles properly, either because they start to act in accordance with their own self-interest or because they fall prey to external lobbying (agency capture).[235] Self-interest and political factors have the capacity to negatively influence incentive policy formation, regulation and administration.[236] Events such as election cycles and promotional opportunities may induce politicians to implement policies that focus on the short term, while media scrutiny might 'discourage risk taking in favor of overly conservative policies (even when experimentation with new schemes would be welfare-enhancing)'.[237] Policies may likewise be rushed if there is a 'political need for government to be seen to be acting decisively'.[238] Similarly, regulators might improperly exercise their

[233] Irish Tax and Customs (n 47) 19.
[234] European Commission (n 23) 154–59.
[235] See Lerner, 'When Bureaucrats Meet Entrepreneurs' (n 119) F79; Windholz (n 2) 44–45.
[236] See What Works Centre for Local Economic Growth, 'Access to Finance' (November 2014) Evidence Review No 4, 8; Syed Adil Hussain, 'Growing the Malaysian Venture Capital and Private Equity Industry' (2010) 1(4) *Islam and Civilisational Renewal* 629, 634; United Nations Economic Commission for Europe (n 33) 91.
[237] Bravo-Biosca (n 54) 9.
[238] Windholz (n 2) 101.

discretion in approving recipients or administering incentives where they feel that they have something to gain personally from acting in a particular way.

Agency capture, on the other hand, occurs where interest groups lobby and successfully persuade governments or incentive regulators to act in their favour (known as 'rent-seeking behaviour').[239] Capture has the potential to increase the risk of distortion and reduce the effectiveness and efficiency of incentives,[240] and is seen to be a particular problem where there is a long history of government intervention.[241] In this situation, incentives can become entrenched, as seen in the examples at [5.2.2] above. Australia's Management and Investment Companies programme has been described as a 'classic case' of agency capture.[242] The programme provided tax deductions to investors, who contributed capital to specially licensed corporate venture capital funds known as MICs.[243] As a measure to control the cost of providing the tax incentives, all the MICs together could only raise up to AUD 40 million a year of 'tax concessional capital', with this amount apportioned between them based on their investment plan and performance.[244] Unsurprisingly, the MICs licensed at the beginning of the programme lobbied strongly against the grant of future licences (as this would reduce the annual amount of capital they could raise).[245] As a result, while seven licences were issued in the first year of the programme's operation, the number of MICs did not rise above 11 at any point over the programme's eight years of operation.[246] Furthermore, most of the approved fundraising was allegedly allocated to the original MICs.[247] Christopher Golis, who attended the first meeting of the original seven MICs, reported that

> [w]ithin five minutes the licensees were discussing how to prevent the issue of any more licences. What they failed to realise is that in a new market it is important to have as many new members as possible who act in an educative role and expand the size of the market.[248]

The result of the licensee's behaviour was that agency capture 'artificially limited the size of the market'.[249] It was further noted that 'with $160 million of capital allocations available' over the eight years of the programme, there was really no

[239] See Hussain (n 236) 634; Murray et al (n 33) 9; Sadiq, 'An Analysis of Tax Expenditures' (n 98) 9–10.

[240] Polackova Brixi et al (n 3) 5; World Bank (n 5) 97; Bravo-Biosca (n 54) 9.

[241] Dodgson et al (n 60) 1153; Leamon et al (n 32) 30–33.

[242] Kevin Hindle and Christopher Golis, 'Australia's Venture Capital Industry: Past Performance, Present Structure and Future Prospects' (Frontiers of Entrepreneurship Research, 2001) 17–18.

[243] Income Tax Assessment Act 1936 (Australia), former s 77F.

[244] Victor Wan, 'Financing High Technology: The Australian Venture Capital Market' (1989) 9 *Technovation* 337, 339.

[245] See Hindle and Golis (n 242) 18.

[246] See Barkoczy et al (n 10) 288; ibid.

[247] Christopher Golis, 'How to Make Risk Irresistible: Incentives for Venture Capital' (1991) 3 *JASSA: Finsia Journal of Applied Finance* 5, 7.

[248] ibid 7.

[249] ibid 8.

need for this behaviour.[250] Although the Management and Investment Companies programme's closure was recommended in 1988, lobbying by the programme's Licensing Board reportedly resulted in two extensions to its operation.[251] To a certain extent, this may also be the result of agency capture and/or self-interest.

While it is difficult to guard against regulators acting in self-interest or falling prey to agency capture (and almost impossible to avoid governments acting for political reasons), there are some measures that can be put in place to help avoid these outcomes. Regulatory transparency, as discussed above, particularly with regard to approval processes, helps limit opportunities for corruption, particularly where regulators are bound to report to the public the identity of recipients and the details and amounts of incentives provided.[252] Likewise, limiting the opportunities for regulators to exercise unfettered discretion in decision-making can also reduce opportunities for corruption.[253] Incentives should ideally also limit the opportunities for lobbying and rent-seeking behaviour by recipients and interest groups by preventing these entities from influencing approval and other decision-making processes, maintaining impartiality and avoiding favouring incumbent recipients.[254]

5.5. Summary

This chapter has explored issues around implementing government venture capital incentives (although many of the leading practices discussed here would also be appropriate in relation to other kinds of incentives). Unlike the more visible features of incentives, such as their policy aim, form and targeting, implementation, administration and monitoring often tend to 'fly under the radar'. This is unfortunate, as they can have a large impact on the effectiveness and efficiency of an incentive, and, consequently, on its ultimate success or failure. It has been noted that the 'potential exists for a great deal of public funds to be lost into the twin abysses of inefficiency/poor decision making and corruption'.[255] Increasing the focus on how incentives are administered – and by whom – is therefore an important goal. More sharing between policymakers and regulators about what works (and what does not) could materially help improve incentive implementation and administration.[256]

[250] Walker observed that the programme 'could have been four times the size for no change in tax revenue loss': Graham Walker, 'Can DCFs Succeed Where MICs Fail? $2bn of Development Funds: Here's How' (1991) 4 *JASSA: Finsia Journal of Applied Finance* 24, 25.

[251] David Forsaith, 'Venture Capital in Australia: The MIC Program and Subsequent Developments' (1993) 2(1–2) *Small Enterprise Research* 36, 41–42.

[252] International Monetary Fund et al (n 13) 23; James (n 4) 40. See, eg Leamon et al (n 32) 31.

[253] See James (n 4) 29.

[254] OECD, 'Business Innovation Policies' (n 30) 17; European Commission (n 23) 48.

[255] Murray et al (n 33) 21.

[256] Wilson and Silva (n 2) 61.

The discussion in this chapter has highlighted several important principles that are relevant to the implementation, administration and monitoring of incentives. These include appropriateness, effectiveness and efficiency, but also consistency, certainty, transparency, accessibility and equity. The various recommendations made in this chapter are aimed at achieving one or more of these principles. For instance, incentives should be implemented legislatively or quasi-legislatively in order to promote certainty, and should have clear, enforceable rules that are made publicly available in order to increase accessibility, consistency and efficiency. Providing guidance on the application of these rules promotes the same principles. Having a clear time frame for incentives (in line with a budget) and avoiding cosmetic and unnecessary changes both promote certainty and consistency, which can lead to increased uptake of incentives. Controlling incentive cost and setting appropriate incentive value are likewise both important factors in efficiency.

From an administrative perspective, having appropriate (and appropriately resourced) regulators is a key factor in helping incentives achieve their policy aims effectively and efficiently, and the same can be said of having appropriate approval processes to ensure that incentive targeting is achieved. Transparent and consistent regulator decision-making promotes certainty and equity, and is particularly important where decision-making involves subjective or discretionary elements. From a monitoring perspective, having appropriate data collection processes in place can aid incentive efficiency, and can provide information on incentive effectiveness. Implementing the various measures for minimising or preventing abuse, discussed above, is also likely to improve both incentive effectiveness and efficiency by helping cut deadweight costs. Where any of the measures discussed above are implemented in a way that minimises compliance costs and burdens placed on investors and investees, this is also likely to make incentives more accessible and equitable. All of these recommendations are discussed in detail in chapter seven.

This chapter has focused on ways of ensuring that incentives operate well. However, whilst knowing that an incentive is operating appropriately, effectively and efficiently is important, it is equally important to know whether the incentive is actually effective at achieving its policy aims or not, and the extent to which it achieves these aims in an efficient way. This is because even an incentive that is implemented, administered and monitored to the best standard will not be considered a success if it does not achieve its aims, or if it does so at an unjustifiable cost. With this in mind, chapter six builds on the principles outlined in this chapter to explore the ways in which incentive success is evaluated. It will be seen from the discussion in the following chapter that the processes of monitoring and data collection discussed in this chapter at [5.4.1] are vital preconditions to undertaking useful evaluations of incentives.

6

Evaluation and Measuring Success

6.1. Introduction

Chapters two to five have set out the various considerations and strategies that go into designing venture capital incentives. This chapter brings all of these previous steps together by looking at how incentive performance is evaluated. Evaluation is the process of measuring and assessing the 'impacts and merits' of an incentive,[1] and is vital to determining whether an incentive is effective (ie it achieves its policy aims), efficient (ie its benefits outweigh its costs) and appropriate (ie it remains necessary and relevant).[2] While evaluation is a useful tool that can be employed from the time an incentive is conceived (to gauge market need and quantify the incentive's proposed costs and benefits), this chapter is concerned with evaluations that take place during an incentive's operation (to assess its processes and allow for interim course correction) and once it has ended (to measure incentive outcomes and improve the design of future incentives). As will be discussed below at [6.2.1], these kinds of evaluations are known respectively as process and impact evaluations.

The evaluation of incentives is important because it helps governments and policymakers gauge the extent to which the earlier steps of incentive design, targeting and implementation have been successful.[3] Evaluation provides governments with the information they need to ensure that their limited resources are directed towards incentives that have the 'potential for the biggest impact',[4] and is an essential part of identifying leading practice in incentive design and operation. All significant incentives should ideally be 'required to develop a formal evaluation strategy', as it is recognised that preparing for and undertaking evaluation is 'a pedagogical exercise that has the potential to improve thinking about programme logic'.[5] Engaging in regular evaluation is acknowledged to be a necessary part of

[1] ACT Government, 'Evaluation Policy and Guidelines' (December 2010) 3.

[2] See John Lester, 'Managing Tax Expenditures and Government Program Spending: Proposals for Reform' (2012) 35(5) *The School of Public Policy Publications* 1, 16; OECD, 'Business Innovation Policies: Selected Country Comparisons' (2011) 116; OECD Regulatory Policy Committee, 'Recommendation of the Council on Regulatory Policy and Governance' (2012) 13, 29.

[3] See, eg ACT Government (n 1) 3.

[4] Maria Pinelli and Uschi Schreiber, 'Funding the Future: Access to Finance for Entrepreneurs in the G20' (Ernst & Young, 2013) 34.

[5] OECD, 'Business Innovation Policies' (n 2) 24.

achieving best practice in incentive administration according to the literature on venture capital incentives, as well as the literature on regulatory, tax expenditure and programme evaluation.[6] Neglecting to incorporate 'appropriate monitoring, evaluation and continuous improvement processes' into an incentive's design, on the other hand, can contribute to its failure.[7]

In practice, many governments avoid evaluating their venture capital incentives and do so only sporadically (if at all).[8] There are likely to be several reasons for this institutional resistance to evaluation on the part of governments and regulators, including:

- They may not want to be held accountable for their spending on, and administration of, incentives (particularly if incentives are expensive to provide and/or do not produce meaningful results).[9] Governments and regulators may be particularly reluctant to examine incentive performance where they are concerned that negative outcomes might reflect poorly on them. Furthermore, some incentives provide political value just through their existence or appearance of success, and in these cases, governments and regulators will have little incentive to engage in evaluation that might show otherwise.[10]
- They may be concerned about protecting recipients' and investees' confidential data, particularly as angels, venture capitalists and startups are notoriously private about their activities.[11]
- Evaluations of 'innovative and experimental' policies are both theoretically and practically difficult.[12] Evaluators must grapple with issues such as time lags (see

[6] See OECD, 'Government Venture Capital for Technology-Based Firms' (1997) OCDE/GD(97)201, 21; Leonard E Burman, 'Is the Tax Expenditure Concept Still Relevant?' (2003) 56(3) *National Tax Journal* 613, 621; What Works Centre for Local Economic Growth, 'Innovation: Grants, Loans and Subsidies' (October 2015) Evidence Review No 9, 3; Productivity Commission, 'Identifying and Evaluating Regulation Reforms' (Research Report, December 2011) x.

[7] See Eric L Windholz, *Governing Through Regulation: Public Policy, Regulation and the Law* (Routledge, 2018) 106.

[8] See OECD, 'Business Innovation Policies' (n 2) 15; Karen E Wilson and Filipe Silva, 'Policies for Seed and Early Stage Finance: Findings from the 2012 OECD Financing Questionnaire' (OECD, October 2013) OECD Science, Technology and Industry Policy Papers No 9, 22, 27; European Commission, 'Effectiveness of Tax Incentives for Venture Capital and Business Angels to Foster the Investment of SMEs and Start-ups: Final Report' (Taxation and Customs Union, 2017) Working Paper No 68, 5; Gordon Murray, Marc Cowling, Weixi Liu and Olga Kalinowska-Beszczynska, 'Government Co-Financed "Hybrid" Venture Capital Programmes: Generalizing Developed Economy Experience and its Relevance to Emerging Nations' (Kauffman International Research and Policy Roundtable, 11–12 March 2012) 6, 10.

[9] See, eg Department of Finance, *Commonwealth Grants Rules and Guidelines 2017* (2017) 29; Richard M Bird, 'Tax Challenges Facing Developing Countries' (Institute for International Business, March 2008) Working Paper No 9, 10.

[10] See Josh Lerner, 'Innovation, Entrepreneurship and Financial Market Cycles' (OECD, March 2010) OECD Science, Technology and Industry Working Paper No 2010/3, 35.

[11] See, eg Lester (n 2) 24.

[12] Luca de Angelis, 'Italy and Startups: Harnessing a Country of Innovators' (Policy Analysis, Master of Public Policy, Harvard University, 2017) 3; European Commission, 'Effectiveness of Tax Incentives' (n 8) 67.

[6.2.3]), data availability and quality (see [5.4.1] and [6.3.2]) and the difficulty of establishing causality (see [6.3.3]).[13] Furthermore, evaluation is a complex endeavour, and evaluators therefore need to have 'a significant level of expertise' that may be lacking.[14]
- Undertaking evaluations, particularly rigorous ones, is often a costly exercise (see [6.2.4]).[15]

However, despite the historical reluctance of government to evaluate their venture capital incentives, the OECD suggests that evaluation of venture capital incentives is becoming more common, particularly following the 2008 global financial crisis (one consequence of which was to limit discretionary public spending and produce a consequent focus on efficiency).[16] A handful of 'robust quantitative evaluations' have been undertaken since the early 2000s,[17] including evaluations of New Zealand's Venture Investment Fund (2009),[18] Australia's Innovation Investment Fund programme (2010),[19] British Columbia's Venture Capital Program (2010),[20] Scotland's Scottish Venture Fund programme (2012),[21] Finland's Finnish Industry Investment fund (2003 and 2014),[22] the UK's Enterprise Investment Scheme and Venture Capital Trusts scheme (2008 and 2016),[23] co-investment schemes (2011)[24] and the Enterprise Capital Funds programme (2021).[25]

The discussion in this chapter draws on regulatory evaluation, tax expenditure evaluation and programme evaluation theories to make recommendations for leading practice in evaluating government capital incentives. It also draws

[13] ACT Government (n 1) 6. See, eg Douglas Cumming, 'Government Policy Towards Entrepreneurial Finance: Innovation Investment Funds' (2007) 22(2) *Journal of Business Venturing* 193, 231.

[14] Jean-Michel Josselin and Benoît Le Maux, *Statistical Tools for Program Evaluation: Methods and Applications to Economic Policy, Public Health, and Education* (Springer, 2017) 1.

[15] OECD, 'Business Innovation Policies' (n 2) 146.

[16] ibid 15–16.

[17] Murray et al, 'Government Co-Financed "Hybrid" Venture Capital Programmes' (n 8) 6.

[18] Ministry of Economic Development, 'Evaluation of the Venture Investment Fund' (November 2009).

[19] Gordon Murray, Marc Cowling and Weixi Liu, 'An Independent Econometric Analysis of the "Innovation Investment Fund" Programme (IIF) of the Australian Commonwealth Government: Findings and Implications' (Department of Innovation, Industry, Science and Research, 2010).

[20] Thomas Hellmann and Paul Schure, 'An Evaluation of the Venture Capital Program in British Columbia' (Ministry of Small Business, Technology and Economic Development, June 2010).

[21] Public and Corporate Economic Consultants, 'Scottish Enterprise: Economic Impact of the Scottish Venture Fund' (December 2012).

[22] Markku Maula and Gordon Murray, *Finnish Industry Investment Ltd: An International Evaluation* (Ministry of Trade and Industry, January 2003); Matti Saarikoski, Pekka Roine, Juha Ruohonen, Antti Halonen, John Sulin and Herve Lebret, *Evaluation of Finnish Industry Investment Ltd* (Ministry of Employment and the Economy, January 2014).

[23] Marc Cowling, Peter Bates, Nick Jagger and Gordon Murray, 'Study of the Impact of the Enterprise Investment Scheme (EIS) and Venture Capital Trusts (VCTs) on Company Performance' (HM Revenue & Customs, 2008) Research Report 44; Matt Colahan, John Higton, Lucy Royce, Rebecca Klahr, Jayesh Navin Shah and Marc Cowling, 'The Use and Impact of Venture Capital Schemes' (HM Revenue & Customs, February 2016) Research Report 355.

[24] Marc Cowling, Weixi Liu, Gordon Murray, Josh Sieple and Paul Nightingale, 'BIS Equity Schemes Evaluation' (Department of Business Innovation and Skills, 2011).

[25] Ipsos MORI and George Barrett, 'Enterprise Capital Funds: Interim Evaluation' (November 2021).

on examples of actual evaluations of government venture capital incentives that have been undertaken, such as those mentioned above, in order to highlight some lessons from past experiences. The discussion focuses mainly on impact evaluations (ie evaluations that measure the effectiveness and efficiency of an incentive at achieving its outcomes) because these are the most commonly used benchmarks for incentive 'success'. The remainder of this chapter looks at the preliminary considerations for evaluations (see [6.2]), explores the methodology for undertaking impact evaluation (see [6.3]) and discusses the impacts of evaluation (see [6.4]). It concludes with a summary of the key principles arising from the chapter (see [6.5]).

6.2. Preliminary Considerations

Before engaging in evaluation of their venture capital incentives, governments need to turn their minds to a range of preliminary considerations, such as what kind of evaluation they want to undertake (see [6.2.1]), who the evaluator will be (see [6.2.2]), the timing of evaluations (see [6.2.3]) and the cost of evaluations (see [6.2.4]). As will be seen below, each of these considerations raises issues for how evaluations will be conducted and the scope of their results.

6.2.1. Types of Evaluation

There are two broad kinds of evaluation that can be used to assess government venture capital incentives. An evaluation that looks at how an incentive operates is generally known as a 'process evaluation', a 'formative evaluation' or a 'program evaluation'.[26] This kind of evaluation is generally narrow in scope and aims to help governments answer questions about how well an incentive's implementation and operation work in terms of effectiveness and efficiency. For example, a process evaluation might look at whether an incentive's regulator is performing their role efficiently by making fair decisions on a timely basis, or whether the incentive is monitoring its recipients effectively. Many of the issues that are commonly considered in a process evaluation (eg design, administration and regulation) were discussed in chapter five and earlier chapters.

In contrast, an evaluation that looks at an incentive's causal effects, outcomes and/or cost-effectiveness is often known as an 'impact evaluation', a 'summative evaluation' or an 'economic evaluation'.[27] Essentially, an impact evaluation aims

[26] See What Works Centre for Local Economic Growth, 'Innovation' (n 6) 3; ACT Government (n 1) 20; Karen Wilson, 'Policy Lessons from Financing Young Innovative Firms' (OECD, June 2015) OECD Science, Technology and Industry Policy Papers No 24, 29.

[27] See Wilson (n 26) 29; What Works Centre for Local Economic Growth, 'Innovation' (n 6) 3; ACT Government (n 1) 20.

to establish 'the extent to which planned outcomes are achieved as a result of the program' and identify 'the main factors behind success or failure'.[28] This kind of evaluation is broad in scope, and can help governments answer questions such as whether an incentive is achieving its objectives, whether it provides an appropriate solution to the problem at hand, whether it represents good value for money and, ultimately, whether the incentive should continue.[29] For example, an impact evaluation may look at whether an incentive is generous enough to create behavioural change, whether it reaches the intended targets or whether it creates unintended distortions to the market. The issues around impact evaluations are largely considered in this chapter.

Both process and impact evaluations are important, and together, they can present a complete picture of incentive performance.[30] While process evaluations are generally easier and cheaper to undertake, without an impact evaluation, it is difficult to gain a full understanding of whether the incentive is actually 'successful' or not. For example, in a process evaluation of France's former Investissement Garantie scheme, the scheme's implementation and administration received a very favourable report. However, the evaluation made a point of noting that, due to a lack of impact evaluation, there was 'little evidence on the broader and indirect effects of the scheme', including its additionality.[31] This made it difficult to comment on the success of the scheme in achieving its policy aims. Impact evaluations are therefore important because, as noted in chapter five, even an incentive that is implemented very well may be unsuccessful in practice.

Australia's former Innovation Investment Fund co-investment programme, which ran from 1998 to 2014, was subject to both kinds of evaluation: it was evaluated in 2002 by the Australian National Audit Office (a process evaluation); and in 2010 by independent econometricians from the UK, at the request of (and funded by) the programme's regulator (an impact evaluation).[32] The 2002 process evaluation aimed to determine whether the Innovation Investment Fund programme was being effectively managed by the Commonwealth.[33] The evaluation focused

[28] Josselin and Le Maux (n 14) 3.

[29] See Stanley S Surrey, *Pathways to Tax Reform: The Concept of Tax Expenditures* (Harvard University Press, 1973) 35–36; ACT Government (n 1) 3; Sebastian James, 'Tax and Non-Tax Incentives and Investments: Evidence and Policy Implications' (Investment Climate Advisory Services of the World Bank Group, September 2013) 35; Queensland Treasury, 'Queensland Government Program Evaluation Guidelines' (2020) 3; Peter H Rossi, Mark W Lipsey and Howard E Freeman, *Evaluation: A Systematic Approach*, 7th edn (Sage Publications, 2004) 40; What Works Centre for Local Economic Growth, 'Access to Finance' (November 2014) Evidence Review No 4, 1.

[30] See What Works Centre for Local Economic Growth, 'Innovation' (n 6) 3; Cary Coglianese, 'Measuring Regulatory Performance: Evaluating the Impact of Regulation and Regulatory Policy' (OECD, August 2012) Expert Paper No 1,7, 34–35.

[31] Jasper Deuten, 'Venture Capital Investment Guarantee Programme by OSEO' (INNO Partnering Forum, 2011) 16.

[32] Murray et al, 'An Independent Econometric Analysis' (n 19); Murray et al, 'Government Co-Financed "Hybrid" Venture Capital Programmes' (n 8) 7.

[33] The Auditor General, 'Management of the Innovation Investment Fund Program' (2003) Audit Report No 12, 13.

on whether there were robust corporate governance arrangements in place to support effective programme administration; whether the selection process to award licences to fund managers was fair and consistent with government requirements and recognised better practice; whether there were appropriate safeguards to protect the Commonwealth's financial interests; whether the monitoring of licence agreements was effective and provided appropriate assurance on compliance and performance; and whether programme performance management was sound.[34] The results of this process evaluation were generally favourable, with some suggestions made in relation to strengthening risk management and assurance of programme delivery against objectives.[35]

In contrast, the 2010 impact evaluation aimed to determine the quantitative impact of the Innovation Investment Fund programme on the young, high-potential Australian firms that received risk capital investments through the programme's licensed funds.[36] The evaluators found that while the programme had 'provided material and relevant support' to early-stage companies and 'raised substantial finance' that would not otherwise have been available, it was 'unlikely to engender by itself a viable and flourishing [venture capital] industry in Australia' (which was broadly one of its policy aims, as discussed at [2.5]).[37] As such, the programme's objectives were 'overly ambitious' and did not 'reflect fully the highly challenging environment for early-stage [venture capital] investment across the developed world'.[38] The results of this impact evaluation, undertaken after the programme had been in operation for a decade, allowed the Australian government to assess the programme's contributions to the sector. Consideration was paid to changing the programme's policy aims to better reflect its role, but the programme was ultimately cancelled in 2014 before these changes could take effect.[39] As discussed below at [6.4], termination of incentives is one possible response to the results of evaluation.

6.2.2. Choice of Evaluator

One of the important choices that governments must make when evaluating their incentives is who the evaluator will be. In particular, governments must decide whether an evaluation will be undertaken internally by the regulator responsible for the incentive, internally by another government department, agency or body, or externally by an independent third party.[40] All kinds of evaluation involve costs,

[34] ibid.
[35] ibid 16.
[36] Murray et al, 'An Independent Econometric Analysis' (n 19) 1.
[37] ibid.
[38] ibid.
[39] See Stephen Barkoczy, Tamara Wilkinson, Ann L Monotti and Mark Davison, *Innovation and Venture Capital Law and Policy* (Federation Press, 2016) 354.
[40] See European Commission, *Evaluating EU Activities: A Practical Guide for the Commission Service* (European Communities, 2004) 14.

with internal evaluations generally being cheaper to undertake than independent external evaluations. It is suggested that it may be appropriate for internal evaluations to focus mainly on process evaluations (rather than impact evaluations),[41] because internal evaluators will often be less impartial and skilled at impact evaluation than external evaluators. However, internal evaluators, such as regulators, should have the expertise and in-house knowledge to undertake process evaluations well. Furthermore, internal evaluations can strengthen organisational learning and facilitate 'direct feedback into the design' of the incentive.[42] External evaluations, while often more expensive, are often seen as more impartial, credible and reliable than internal evaluations because they are ideally designed and undertaken in a transparent fashion by independent evaluators.[43] They may help bring to light information on incentives that internal evaluators could miss because they are too close to problems (or because they directly contribute to the problems). For example, the external consultancy brought in to evaluate New Zealand's former Venture Investment Fund (discussed at [5.3.3]) was seen as 'invaluable' because it used a fresh pair of eyes to evaluate regulatory efficiency and undertook the review thoroughly, which the small regulatory team may otherwise have been unable to do.[44] Similarly, a recent evaluation of the UK's Enterprise Capital Funds programme was undertaken by market research firm Ipsos and George Barrett, a former chief economist of the Ecorys research consultancy, and the result was a comprehensive and robust analysis of the programme, with both econometric and cost–benefit analyses.[45]

Both internal and external evaluations of venture capital incentives are relatively rare, as mentioned above at [6.1]. Responses to the 2012 OECD Financing Questionnaire (a research project that investigated the role of public support in promoting seed and early-stage financing) revealed that of 32 OECD countries with seed and early-stage venture capital incentives in place, only 13 had evaluated their incentives at that time.[46] Of these, three countries had undertaken internal evaluations of five incentives, five countries had undertaken external-government evaluations (evaluations undertaken by another government agency) of six incentives and nine countries had undertaken fully external evaluations of 12 incentives (some countries undertook more than one kind of evaluation).[47] It is clear,

[41] See, eg Josh Lerner, David Moore and Stuart Shepherd, 'A Study of New Zealand's Venture Capital Market and Implications for Public Policy' (LECG, 2005) 142.

[42] European Commission, 'Evaluating EU Activities' (n 40) 53. See also OECD, 'Business Innovation Policies' (n 2) 148.

[43] European Commission, 'Evaluating EU Activities' (n 40) 53. Both tax expenditure and regulatory theorists note the benefits of third-party evaluations: see Lester (n 2) 24; Ashley C Brown, Jon Stern, Bernard Tenenbaum and Defne Gencer, *Handbook for Evaluating Infrastructure Regulatory Systems* (World Bank, 2006) 34.

[44] Controller and Auditor General, 'New Zealand Venture Investment Fund' (2012) oag.parliament.nz/2012/efficiency-stories/corporate/new-zealand-venture-investment-fund.

[45] See Ipsos MORI and George Barrett (n 25).

[46] Wilson and Silva (n 8) 57.

[47] ibid 58.

therefore, that there is still work to be done in creating a robust evaluation culture in relation to government venture capital incentives (and likely many other kinds of incentives too).

6.2.3. Evaluation Timing

It is well accepted that government venture capital incentives should be 'evaluated and assessed on a regular basis', rather than as a one-time event.[48] For instance, Lerner suggested that it would be appropriate to evaluate the progress of the former New Zealand Venture Innovation Fund towards achieving its policy aim every three years, which would strike a balance between giving the market sufficient time to respond and allowing the government to monitor the incentive's performance and 'modify its direction as required'.[49] Regular evaluation ensures that current and relevant information is available to governments when they need to make policy decisions about incentives,[50] and the OECD suggests the best generalisable and policy-relevant results will come from a smaller number of 'long-term well-designed evaluations' that use 'controlled samples of beneficiaries and non-beneficiaries' (see [6.3.3] below), rather than 'multiple evaluations of varied quality employing disparate methods'.[51] Essentially this requires governments to develop a formal evaluation and data collection strategy from the time an incentive is introduced.[52] Unfortunately, however, Murray et al note that it 'remains exceptional for governments to organise both the data collection and an agreed methodology for the formal evaluation of a programme at or near the time of its original introduction'.[53]

The time in an incentive's lifespan at which evaluations are undertaken can have significant effects on how the success of the incentive is perceived.[54] Angel and venture capital investments take a long time to mature, and a true picture of investment and incentive success may only appear a decade or more after an incentive is implemented (although some outcomes, like the number of investees supported and the amount of additional capital raised, will become evident sooner).[55] A 2015 evaluation of Germany's INVEST incentive (undertaken two

[48] OECD, 'Government Venture Capital for Technology-Based Firms' (n 6) 21. See also Ann Leamon, Maria Susana Garcia-Robles and Josh Lerner, 'Best Practices in Creating a Venture Capital Ecosystem' (Multilateral Investment Fund of Inter-American Development Bank, December 2012) 47; Wilson (n 26) 15; European Commission, 'Effectiveness of Tax Incentives' (n 8) 81; OECD, 'Business Innovation Policies' (n 2) 17; Mark Burton and Kerrie Sadiq, *Tax Expenditure Management: A Critical Assessment* (Cambridge University Press, 2013) 98; Brown et al (n 43) 35.

[49] Lerner et al (n 41) 146.

[50] See Burton and Sadiq (n 48) 98; OECD, 'Business Innovation Policies' (n 2) 147.

[51] OECD, 'Business Innovation Policies' (n 2) 24.

[52] ibid 24. See also Productivity Commission (n 6) xxv.

[53] Murray et al, 'Government Co-Financed "Hybrid" Venture Capital Programmes' (n 8) 6.

[54] OECD, 'Business Innovation Policies' (n 2) 125.

[55] See, eg Robert Baldock, 'An Assessment of the Business Impacts of the UK's Enterprise Capital Funds' (2016) 34(8) *Environment and Planning C: Government and Policy* 1556, 1569–70; Murray et al,

years after its introduction) noted this, commenting that 'An evaluation so soon after the start of the program cannot determine its sustainability' and that 'The question of whether growth and innovations are actually induced by INVEST can only be answered eight to ten years after starting the program'.[56] Nevertheless, the evaluation reported on the additional investment induced by the programme, the amount of grant funds that had been paid out and the characteristics of investors and investees, among other things.[57] Likewise, the 2021 evaluation of the UK's Enterprise Capital Funds programme, which looked at funds that first received co-investment in 2011, noted that it was arguably premature to undertake a cost–benefit analysis of the programme because most of the firms in the scope of the study were at an early stage of development, and estimates of impact based on their short-term expansion would understate the longer-term economic benefits involved.[58] In this vein, evaluating the success of an incentive too early can be problematic where it risks showing large amounts of capital invested but little in the way of positive investment outcome (which may not have had the chance to emerge yet). The results of early evaluations may therefore reduce support for an incentive and could lead to early termination, removing the chance for 'long-term positive effects' to emerge.[59] Unfortunately, a review of evaluations of innovation-related grants, loans and subsidies from around the world found that few evaluations considered the timing of incentive effects, and, in particular, their long-term impact (10 years plus).[60] Interestingly, the review found that where evaluations did consider the long-term effect of incentives, the results did not suggest that their effects increased over time.[61]

The timing of an evaluation can also have an impact on the reliability of its results. For example, where recipients and investees report on their expected/projected outcomes early in an incentive's life, they may be likely to optimistically overestimate these outcomes.[62] It can therefore be difficult to rely on the results of early projections.[63] However, waiting to report on incentive performance until

'Government Co-Financed "Hybrid" Venture Capital Programmes' (n 8) 2. See also Leamon et al (n 48) 47; Syed Adil Hussain, 'Growing the Malaysian Venture Capital and Private Equity Industry' (2010) 1(4) *Islam and Civilisational Renewal* 629, 630. It is also important to recognise that different incentives have different 'gestation periods', meaning that they may take a shorter or longer time to produce change: OECD, 'Business Innovation Policies' (n 2) 24.

[56] Sandra Gottschalk, Jürgen Egeln, Frank Herrmann, Silke Hupperts, Bettina Müller, Karsten Reuss, Mila Köhler, Johannes Bersch and Simona Wagner, 'Evaluation of the Public Funding Program "INVEST – Grant for Venture Capital": English Short Version' (BMWi, July 2016) 1.

[57] ibid 3–4, 7–8.

[58] See Ipsos MORI and George Barrett (n 25) 57.

[59] OECD, 'Business Innovation Policies' (n 2) 125.

[60] What Works Centre for Local Economic Growth, 'Innovation' (n 6) 36.

[61] ibid.

[62] See Hussain (n 55) 630.

[63] See broadly European Commission, 'Effectiveness of Tax Incentives' (n 8) 65. The evaluation of the UK's Enterprise Capital Funds noted this, explaining that the indirect nature of the programme's impacts means that some strong assumptions are needed to provide estimates of its likely net costs and benefits, and that there are 'major challenges in projecting the lifetime benefits of the programme based

after even one round of investments has been exited means that stakeholders have to wait a long time to see if an incentive is performing well, and this may represent a lost opportunity to make beneficial interim changes to the incentive's operation. This is one reason that periodic evaluation can be useful, as demonstrated in the case of Australia's Innovation Investment Fund programme (discussed at [6.2.1] above), where the early process evaluation undertaken by the Australian National Audit Office four years after the incentive's introduction allowed the government to make responsive improvements to the programme. New Zealand's Elevate Fund appears to be employing a similar strategy of periodic review. The Fund was introduced in early 2020, and the minister with oversight of the incentive was invited to comment on its operation within its first six months. While the document produced was by no means a full evaluation of the incentive's performance, it found that the fund 'has taken significant steps to be investment ready', reported on the state of the market and identified market gaps that needed additional government support.[64] Ongoing monitoring and evaluation of the Elevate Fund will continue to be important as the Fund matures, but it is encouraging to see the New Zealand government's proactive approach to monitoring incentive operation, and its transparent publication of this information.

6.2.4. Evaluation Cost

The issues discussed above all have impacts on evaluation cost, from the kind of evaluation that is undertaken (with process evaluations generally being easier and cheaper to undertake than impact evaluations, because of the ease of data collection and interpretation) and who the evaluator is (in-house evaluators are likely to be cheaper than external evaluators) to the timing of the evaluation (with one-off evaluations generally being cheaper than frequent periodic evaluations). In some cases, the thoroughness and depth of an evaluation will be compromised because of cost factors.

Governments should therefore consider whether evaluations can satisfy a cost–benefit analysis. Not all incentives are substantial enough to justify an in-depth evaluation, and in many cases it will not be efficient to perform large-scale evaluations of small incentives.[65] Furthermore, evaluation may not represent a 'good investment when the sample sizes of target and non-target groups are too small for statistical inference'.[66] Nevertheless, it is also important to recognise that there is a public benefit to evaluation where it facilitates policies being 'grounded upon

on the observed short-term growth of firms receiving investment in the short-term': Ipsos MORI and George Barrett (n 25) 57.

[64] Ministry of Business, Innovation and Employment, 'Update on the Venture Capital Fund's Progress and the Wider Capital Markets' (17 August 2020) 1.

[65] See Wilson and Silva (n 8) 60.

[66] OECD, 'Business Innovation Policies' (n 2) 148.

better information'.[67] These considerations will need to be weighed up for each incentive a government implements. Ideally, governments should factor the cost of planned evaluations into incentive budgets when they are introduced.

6.3. Methodology for Impact Evaluations

There is no consistent methodology that is employed in evaluating the impact of government venture capital incentives.[68] Evaluating incentives of this kind is an extremely complex endeavour because the 'likely economic outcomes are hard to predict, hard to measure and evaluate, and may differ substantially' at the local and national levels.[69] In addition, evaluation requires consideration of direct, indirect and external effects relating to the supply side, the demand side and the relevant local framework conditions.[70] As a result, very few evaluations 'can precisely identify the full range of policy effects' caused by incentives, and even fewer can attribute effects to specific aspects of incentive design.[71]

Despite these difficulties, it is suggested that establishing a basic methodology for evaluating government venture capital incentives does not need to be overly complicated. The following proposed methodology has six steps (which build and elaborate on a four-step evaluation process described by Hendon, Bell, Blair and Martin):[72]

1. Identify relevant measures of success (which should be tied to incentive policy aims) (see [6.3.1]).
2. Collect the necessary quantitative and qualitative data on incentive operation, outcomes and costs (see [6.3.2]).
3. Establish or estimate the extent to which outcomes represent an increase over what would have occurred in the absence of the incentive (additionality) and the extent to which outcomes can be attributed to the incentive (causality) (see [6.3.3]).
4. Evaluate the extent to which the incentive has been effective in meeting its policy aims (see [6.3.4]).
5. Evaluate the incentive's efficiency by comparing its benefits and costs (see [6.3.5]).

[67] Burton and Sadiq (n 48) 115.
[68] See Cromwell Schmisseur, 'Information and Observations on State Venture Capital Programs: Report for the US Department of the Treasury and Interested Parties in the State Small Business Credit Initiative (SSBCI)' (February 2013) 6; Murray et al, 'Government Co-Financed "Hybrid" Venture Capital Programmes' (n 8) 6.
[69] What Works Centre for Local Economic Growth, 'Innovation' (n 6) 11.
[70] Wilson and Silva (n 8) 56.
[71] What Works Centre for Local Economic Growth, 'Innovation' (n 6) 11.
[72] John R Hendon, Joseph R Bell, Brittany Blair and Don K Martin, 'State-Funded Angel Investor Tax Credits: Implementation and Perceived Effectiveness in a Sample of States Within the United States' (2012) 1(1) *Journal of Entrepreneurship and Public Policy* 50, 57–58.

6. Draw a conclusion on whether the incentive remains appropriate, based on its effectiveness and efficiency and a continuing market need (see [6.3.6]).

These steps are explored in more detail below.

6.3.1. Identifying Measures of Success

As discussed throughout this book, an incentive's effectiveness is judged with reference to how well it achieves its policy aims. The performance measures against which an incentive is evaluated should therefore be tied to these aims.[73] This is one reason that clear, relevant and well-articulated policy aims are such an important part of the incentive design process (see [2.5]).[74] Unfortunately, it will be recalled from chapter two that policy aims have a tendency to be ambiguous, conflicting and subject to change.[75] Without well-defined policy aims, it is considerably more difficult to assess incentive effectiveness.[76]

There are many specific performance measures that governments may want to employ in order to measure the effectiveness of their incentives. Different measures will give a different picture of success, and for this reason, the selection of performance measures can be 'highly nuanced and even at times controversial'.[77] However, one clear guideline is that whatever performance measures are selected, they should be explicitly stated. An example of an evaluation that did this well was Cumming's 2007 independent academic evaluation of Australia's Innovation Investment Fund programme, which looked at: the extent to which the co-investment funds licensed under the programme had engaged in start-up; early-stage, high-tech, staged and syndicated investments; the size of funds' portfolios; the exit mechanisms used; and the share price returns performance of initial public offering (IPO) exits.[78] These measures differ from those used in the 2010 evaluation of the Innovation Investment Fund programme, which focused on investee metrics, including: the types of entities that received investment; the scale of support; impacts on investee performance; and the subsequent outcomes produced by investees in relation to the Australian economy.[79] Both sets of performance measures provide a range of interesting and useful information, but neither fully measures the success of the Innovation Investment Fund programme against its policy aims.

Governments should avoid looking at particular performance measures in isolation, or they risk producing a distorted view of success. For example, measuring

[73] See Wilson (n 26) 31; Lerner et al (n 41) 140, 148–49; OECD, 'Business Innovation Policies' (n 2) 123.

[74] See Josselin and Le Maux (n 14) 7.

[75] Deborah A Stone, *Policy Paradox and Political Reason* (HarperCollins, 1988) 195.

[76] Lester (n 2) 17.

[77] Coglianese (n 30) 17.

[78] Cumming, 'Government Policy Towards Entrepreneurial Finance' (n 13) 201–03.

[79] See Murray et al, 'An Independent Econometric Analysis' (n 19) 1.

only the extent to which an incentive increases venture capital investment ignores the quality of the investments, the survival/success rate of investees, the extent to which investors provide value-adding services and the returns made on investments. Without this additional information, it is difficult to determine whether the incentive actually represents a good use of public funds.[80] As an illustration of this issue, a review of China's Venture Capital Guiding Funds co-investment programme, published in 2016, reported that CNY 309 million had been invested in 14 private funds to 2009, and that these funds had gone on to raise CNY 2.382 billion.[81] However, seed and early-stage financing in China from 2003 to 2012 reportedly did not increase in a significant and sustained way.[82] This indicates that while the Venture Capital Guiding Funds programme was apparently successful at leveraging private investment in funds, it was not necessarily as successful in increasing early-stage finance.

While policy aims differ between incentives, there are some performance measures that are commonly used to demonstrate incentive effectiveness. These include: the amount of venture capital investments made and the number of startups funded under an incentive; investee outcomes produced under an incentive, such as survival rates, the creation of new jobs, increases in patenting and innovative activities, and increases in sales, profitability and productivity;[83] and investment outcomes produced under an incentive, such as the number of successful exits and amount of investment returns, and the level of value-adding services provided to investees.[84] These measures are explored in more detail below.

Increased Investment

Most government venture capital incentives explicitly aim to increase venture capital investment, so investment levels are an oft-used measure of success for incentives.[85] As discussed below at [6.3.3], data on additional investment (rather than gross investment) is particularly useful when it comes to measuring incentive success, because it makes an estimate of the increase in investment levels that can realistically be attributed to an incentive (additionality). In contrast, data on changes to gross investment levels is less useful, because changes may be attributable to other causes.

[80] See European Commission, 'Effectiveness of Tax Incentives' (n 8) 21.

[81] Jun Li, 'Government-Backed Venture Capital as a Science, Technology and Innovation (STI) Policy Instrument: A Chinese Perspective' (2016) 7(1) *STI Policy Review* 66, 80.

[82] ibid 81.

[83] See OECD, 'Business Innovation Policies' (n 2) 124–25.

[84] See Miona Milosevic and Jacqueline Fendt, 'Venture Capital and its French Exception: Explaining Performance through Human Capital, Policy and Institutional Failures' (2016) 43(5) *Science and Public Policy* 660, 661; OECD, 'Government Venture Capital for Technology-Based Firms' (n 6) 21; Li (n 81) 70.

[85] See OECD, 'Government Venture Capital for Technology-Based Firms' (n 6) 21; Milosevic and Fendt (n 84) 663; James (n 29) 5.

An example of an evaluation that has considered increased investment as a measure of success is the 2010 evaluation of British Columbia's Venture Capital Program, which measured increased investment by calculating the incentive's 'equity leveraging factor'.[86] This figure was calculated by dividing the amount of equity raised by investee companies, excluding equity raised under the programme, by the amount of equity raised under the programme. The evaluation noted that the equity leveraging factor for the programme was 376 per cent, meaning that for every dollar of equity raised in the programme, an additional CAD 3.76 was raised outside the programme.[87] What this says about the programme's influence, however, is unclear (ie it is not clear whether the increased equity raised outside the programme is attributed to the programme's positive effects or, alternatively, whether the large amount of equity raised outside the programme indicates that the programme was not particularly effective).

In addition to looking at how investment levels have increased generally, some evaluations might also look at how investment levels have increased in relation to particular sectors or development stages. For example, Cumming reported in 2007 that funds operating under Australia's Innovation Investment Fund programme were 46 per cent more likely to invest in seed-stage companies than other types of private funds and were also more likely to invest in risky high-tech companies.[88] Data of this kind can help demonstrate an incentive's progress towards achieving its policy aims, and also the extent to which its targeting is functioning as intended.

Investee Survival Rates

Data on investee survival rates helps provide a picture of overall investment quality and, to a certain extent, may provide an indication of how well the investors/fund managers operating under an incentive nurture and support their investees. However, there are a couple of problems associated with the use of investee survival rates as a measure of incentive success. First, data on survival rates may not distinguish between truly successful investees and 'marginal survivors' that are still operating but have no genuine prospects of success.[89] Second, it is difficult to know when to measure survival rates, as they will generally be high in the years following investment but will begin to decline as time goes on, presenting a different picture. Third, high investee survival rates under an incentive may indicate that the incentive is performing well and making a meaningful contribution to the venture capital sector, but they may also indicate that the incentive's targeting is leading investors to focus on later-stage or less risky investees (rather than on the investees that are most in need of support). If this is the case, the incentive is likely

[86] Hellmann and Schure (n 20) 29.
[87] ibid.
[88] Cumming, 'Government Policy Towards Entrepreneurial Finance' (n 13) 197.
[89] See OECD, 'Business Innovation Policies' (n 2) 139.

to be at least partially redundant.[90] However, low investee survival rates (high rates of investee failure) can undermine incentives and discourage investors,[91] and may also indicate problems with incentive targeting. Quantitative data on survival rates can therefore be difficult to interpret and should be paired with qualitative data from investors and investees where possible in order to really understand what is happening.

Investee Growth

The growth of investees (in terms of revenue, assets, sales, productivity, etc) is often used as a measure of success for incentives, as it can indicate that incentives are spurring positive outcomes for investee companies.[92] Data on investee growth may present a more nuanced picture of success than investee survival rates, although it can be more difficult to measure. A 2020 evaluation of the European Angel Fund (an angel co-investment fund) looked at investee outcomes under the programme, reporting that investees supported under the Fund exhibit positive growth trajectories for employment, total assets and turnover (which was found to increase sharply in the post-investment period).[93] Likewise, the 2010 evaluation of British Columbia's Venture Capital Program, mentioned above, found that, compared with similar companies that were not supported under the programme, investees under the programme were larger, created more jobs and saw greater revenue growth.[94]

In contrast, evaluations of the UK's Enterprise Investment Scheme and Venture Capital Trusts scheme undertaken in 2008 and 2016 also looked at investee company outcomes, but showed mixed results. The evaluations focused particularly on investee profitability, sales, capital structure, labour productivity and survival.[95] The 2008 evaluation found that the Enterprise Investment Scheme and the Venture Capital Trusts scheme were generally positively associated with real fixed asset formation, real sales turnover and employment growth, but had, on average, little discernible impact on real gross profits or investment amounts. Furthermore, it reported that Enterprise Investment Scheme and Venture Capital Trusts-supported investments tended to be associated with companies exhibiting lower profit margins.[96] Survival rates for Enterprise Investment Scheme and

[90] See Margaret O'Shea and Candice Stevens, 'Governments as Venture Capitalists' (1998) 213 *OECD Observer* 26, 29.

[91] ibid.

[92] See, eg Hellmann and Schure (n 20) 26.

[93] Salome Gvetadze, Kristian Pal and Wouter Torfs, 'The Business Angel Portfolio Under the European Angels Fund: An Empirical Analysis' (European Investment Fund, January 2020) Research and Market Analysis Working Paper 2020/62, 34, 36. The report also noted that angels under the initiative 'almost exclusively' target innovative, high-tech startups, with a majority located in the ICT sector (35).

[94] Hellmann and Schure (n 20) 28.

[95] See OECD, 'Business Innovation Policies' (n 2) 136.

[96] Cowling et al, 'Study of the Impact' (n 23) 49.

Venture Capital Trust-supported companies were also significantly lower than those of the control group.[97] It is important to note, however, that both these outcomes may be accounted for in some part by the fact that the programmes support high-risk, early-stage innovative companies (of the kind that are likely to fail),[98] making it difficult to know what conclusions to draw from the data. In comparison, the 2016 evaluation found more positive outcomes. It reported, among other things, that 76 per cent of Enterprise Investment Scheme investees and 65 per cent of Venture Capital Trusts investees attributed an increase in sales to the schemes, 58 per cent of Enterprise Investment Scheme investees and 51 per cent of Venture Capital Trusts investees attributed an increase in productivity to the schemes, and 62 per cent of investees (for both schemes) reported that Enterprise Investment Scheme and Venture Capital Trusts funding resulted in 'significantly improved financial performance' for the company.[99] Seventy-one per cent of investees reported that their company had grown following Enterprise Investment Scheme or Venture Capital Trusts investment, and 90 per cent of this number attributed this to the schemes.[100] The evaluation also reported that Venture Capital Trusts investees were less likely than Enterprise Investment Scheme investees to have sought investment in order to start a new company or launch a new product, while Enterprise Investment Scheme investees were more likely to seek investment for business expansion purposes.[101] However, because the information collected in the 2016 evaluation was qualitative, rather than quantitative, it is not clear how reliable the information provided by recipients and investees actually was (see further [6.3.2]).

Increased Jobs

The number of jobs created by investee companies supported under an incentive is often used as a benchmark for incentive success, as seen in the example of the European Angel Fund above.[102] This is because increased jobs are politically attractive, help spur regional development and are 'the most common measure of local economic performance'.[103]

As with other measures of success, calculating the number of jobs created by investees under an incentive can be challenging.[104] When undertaking the

[97] ibid.
[98] See ibid 50.
[99] Colahan et al (n 23) 16–18.
[100] ibid 19.
[101] ibid 5.
[102] See, eg James A Brander, Edward J Egan and Thomas F Hellmann, 'Government Sponsored versus Private Venture Capital: Canadian Evidence' (National Bureau of Economic Research, May 2008) Working Paper No 14029, 18.
[103] Massimo G Colombo, Douglas J Cumming and Silvio Vismara, 'Governmental Venture Capital for Innovative Young Firms' (2016) 41(1) *Journal of Technology Transfer* 10, 19.
[104] See International Monetary Fund, Organisation for Economic Co-operation and Development, United Nations and World Bank, 'Options for Low Income Countries' Effective and Efficient Use of Tax Incentives for Investment' (Report to the G-20 Development Working Group, October 2015) 18.

calculation, evaluators should consider additionality (ie how many additional jobs have been created because of the incentive), causality (ie whether these jobs would have been created if the incentive did not exist) and 'displacement' (ie whether these jobs have been truly created, or have merely been displaced from other sectors).[105] If jobs have been displaced, the value of their social benefit depends on the 'productivity (and wage) differential between the new and old jobs'.[106] Evaluators should also consider the timing of their data collection as they may underestimate the number of jobs created if they count too early (when investees are still growing) or overestimate them if they count later (when investees may be contracting).[107] Furthermore, the longer the time taken to undertake the count, the more difficult it will be to causally attribute any jobs created to the effects of an incentive.[108]

Patenting Rates

Evaluations may consider investee patenting rates as a measure of incentive success because patenting rates are a common proxy for the innovativeness of investees.[109] Venture-backed companies tend to patent at higher rates than other companies,[110] so one measure of the success of an incentive in driving innovation might be an increase in patenting rates compared with previous performance and/or compared with similar investees that were not supported under the incentive.[111]

Positive Exits

Positive investment exits are often used as a proxy to help estimate the quality of investments made under an incentive,[112] and therefore can also be used as a measure of incentive success. Although data on investment exits does not provide the greatest depth of information (similar to investee survival rates),

[105] See Marie Howland, 'Measuring Capital Subsidy Costs and Job Creation: The Case of Rural UDAG Grants' (1990) 56(1) *Journal of the American Planning Association* 54, 55, 57; European Commission, 'Evaluating EU Activities' (n 40) 104.

[106] International Monetary Fund et al (n 104) 10.

[107] Howland (n 105) 55, 57.

[108] ibid 55.

[109] Fabio Bertoni and Tereza Tykvová, 'Does Governmental Venture Capital Spur Invention and Innovation? Evidence from Young European Biotech Companies' (2015) 44(4) *Research Policy* 925, 926; Brander et al, 'Government Sponsored versus Private Venture Capital' (n 102) 8.

[110] See Samuel Kortum and Josh Lerner, 'Assessing the Contribution of Venture Capital to Innovation' (2000) 31(4) *The RAND Journal of Economics* 674, 689; Bertoni and Tykvová (n 109) 926.

[111] See Brander et al, 'Government Sponsored versus Private Venture Capital' (n 102) 8.

[112] See ibid 7–8; Barry Bracewell-Milnes and JCL Huiskamp, *Investment Incentives: A Comparative Analysis of the Systems in the EEC, the USA and Sweden* (Kluwer, 1977) 122–23; Federico Munari and Laura Toschi, 'Assessing the Impact of Public Venture Capital Programmes in the United Kingdom: Do Regional Characteristics Matter?' (2015) 30(2) *Journal of Business Venturing* 205, 210.

it involves data that is often publicly available, and therefore quite easy to access (unlike data on investment returns, which is often not made public – see below).[113]

Investees that become listed through an IPO are often seen as being the most successful and highest quality investees.[114] For example, the 2010 evaluation of Australia's Innovation Investment Fund programme (discussed above) looked at the business outcomes of investees, such as IPOs, acquisitions, trade sales and failure, as an incentive performance measure.[115] Funds licensed under the Innovation Investment Fund programme reportedly produced a higher percentage of publicly listed investees (as well as investees that held greater market capitalisation) than those funded by private venture capital and private equity funds.[116] These outcomes are attributed to the positive investment behaviour demonstrated by fund managers under the programme, which had smaller portfolios per manager and more intensive staging and syndication of investments relative to non-government-subsidised private fund managers.[117]

Like data on investee survival rates, data on investment exits can be difficult to interpret (and may also be influenced by external factors, such as economic turmoil), so should be considered carefully. The number of exits achieved under an incentive is likely to differ depending on the incentive's targeting, with incentives that target earlier stage investment (such as many angel incentives) probably producing relatively fewer exits than incentives that target later-stage investments.[118] Similarly, the regional funds operating in the UK between 1998 and 2007 (including Regional Venture Capital Funds, University Challenge Seed Funds and some Early Growth Funds) were reportedly 17 per cent less effective at achieving positive exits than comparable private funds.[119] This is likely due to their explicit focus on regional locations, which can reduce investment quality because of a lack of deal flow (see [4.4.3]). In a situation like this, governments have the opportunity to decide whether they would like to refocus their incentives on more commercially viable investments that might produce better exits or whether the poor exit outcomes are an acceptable price to pay for the achievement of incentive policy aims.

Investment Returns

The amount of returns made on investments under an incentive provides more detailed information on investment success than data on investment exits alone

[113] Milosevic and Fendt (n 84) 661; Hellmann and Schure (n 20) 32.
[114] See Hellmann and Schure (n 20) 32.
[115] Murray et al, 'An Independent Econometric Analysis' (n 19) 2.
[116] Douglas Cumming and Sofia Johan, 'Venture's Economic Impact in Australia' (2016) 41(1) *Journal of Technology Transfer* 25, 56.
[117] ibid 31.
[118] See, eg Hellmann and Schure (n 20) 33.
[119] Munari and Toschi (n 112) 216.

and can be used as a valuable measure of incentive success.[120] High returns can indicate that high-quality investments have been made under an incentive and/or that investees have benefited from value-adding activities and mentoring. High returns also please investors, create reputational benefits for fund managers and can make the venture capital sector seem more attractive. Venture capitalists reportedly 'exhibit significant performance persistence over time', meaning that where they outperform the market with one fund, they are 'likely to do so with the next one'.[121] This positive performance can in turn 'generate a virtuous spiral of success breeding success'.[122] However, investment returns involve sensitive private data that is often difficult to access.[123] Investors may exaggerate successes and have strong incentives to conceal negative returns[124] because they often trade on their reputations. It has been noted that fund managers are 'generally loath to assist in any rigorous and independent evaluation where the data and subsequent results do not remain fully under their control'.[125] Even if data on returns can be accessed, finding a 'widely acceptable methodology' for calculating immensely complex fund investment returns 'is not a trivial task'.[126] Many venture capital funds work out their overall returns using the 'internal rate of return' method, which is acknowledged to have a range of problems, particularly in the context of private equity.[127]

In any case, the attainment of high returns under an incentive is not necessarily evidence of the incentive's success, as these returns may indicate investment drift, conflicts with incentive targeting or crowding out, all of which can impact the incentive's overall effectiveness.[128] This reportedly occurred, for instance, in relation to Finnish Industry Investment (a government-owned investment company established in Finland in 1995).[129] It was reported in 2007 that Finnish Industry Investment has been ineffective in addressing early-stage market failures because its focus on maintaining profitability has led it to invest in later-stage companies (although whether this problem persists is unclear).[130] Therefore, high returns may indicate that an incentive is performing well, but may also indicate that it is targeted inappropriately.[131] Investments in innovative startups are generally

[120] See broadly OECD, 'Government Venture Capital for Technology-Based Firms' (n 6) 21.
[121] Milosevic and Fendt (n 84) 664.
[122] ibid.
[123] Hellmann and Schure (n 20) 32; Munari and Toschi (n 112) 210.
[124] Hussain (n 55) 630.
[125] Murray et al, 'Government Co-Financed "Hybrid" Venture Capital Programmes' (n 8) 6.
[126] ibid 2.
[127] See Ludovic Phalippou, 'An Inconvenient Fact: Private Equity Returns & The Billionaire Factory' (2023) 30(1) *The Journal of Investing* 11, 12.
[128] See broadly Massimo Colombo, Fabio Bertoni and Terttu Luukkonen, 'Venture Capital: Policy Lessons from the VICO Project' (European Commission, 2011) 23.
[129] See United Nations Economic Commission for Europe, *Financing Innovative Development: Comparative Review of the Experiences of UNECE Countries in Early Stage Financing* (United Nations Publications, 2007) 58.
[130] ibid.
[131] See, eg Albert Bravo-Biosca, 'Access to Finance for Innovation: Rationales and Risks of Public Intervention' (The Innovation Policy Platform, 2014) 11.

illiquid, extremely risky and have higher due diligence costs than investments in more mature companies.[132] Failure rates for pre-seed investments in the USA can reportedly be as high as 80 per cent, with failure rates for seed and early-stage investments reportedly ranging from 40 per cent to 60 per cent.[133] For these reasons, investment in very early-stage innovative companies is unlikely to be profitable, which is why incentives are often necessary.

Where returns are low under an incentive, this may indicate that the incentive is targeting investees that would not otherwise be supported by the private sector (whether due to size, age, stage or quality).[134] However, even though failed investments can still produce social benefits (such as educating investors and entrepreneurs),[135] most investors make venture capital investments in order to reap profits, and poor returns therefore have the capacity to create a negative perception of the industry and drive investors away.[136] This can end up harming the sector, particularly where it decreases participation by institutional investors.[137] For this reason, an incentive is generally not considered successful merely because it 'elicits a large volume of low-quality investment yielding little or no return'.[138] A practical example of this situation is Canada's Labour-Sponsored Venture Capital Corporations tax incentive (see [2.6]), which has been accused of weakening the Canadian venture capital industry by 'transferring control of the supply of venture capital to an inferior organizational form' (ie a kind of fund that produced lower returns than the private sector, but nevertheless continued to attract capital).[139] Although the labour-sponsored venture capital corporations (LSVCCs) managed a large proportion of Canada's total venture capital, they demonstrated below-market returns and high administrative costs.[140] Because the LSVCCs handled such a large amount of capital, and because their investors were able to benefit from tax subsidies, they were able to outbid private investors, with whom they competed for deal flow, in relation to investments.[141] This, in turn, drove up investment prices and lowered overall market returns.[142] Ultimately, therefore, the returns produced under an incentive should be broadly in line with the returns produced by a healthy private sector. However, each incentive is

[132] European Commission, 'Effectiveness of Tax Incentives' (n 8) 35.
[133] Cromwell Schmisseur (n 68) 12.
[134] See Brander et al, 'Government Sponsored versus Private Venture Capital' (n 102) 15.
[135] See OECD, 'Business Innovation Policies' (n 2) 139.
[136] See OECD, 'Venture Capital and Innovation' (1996) 10.
[137] See ibid.
[138] See Bracewell-Milnes and Huiskamp (n 112) 127.
[139] Douglas J Cumming and Jeffrey G MacIntosh, 'Crowding Out Private Equity: Canadian Evidence' (2006) 21(5) *Journal of Business Venturing* 569, 571.
[140] ibid 605; United Nations Economic Commission for Europe (n 129) 45; Douglas Cumming, 'Public Policy and the Creation of Active Venture Capital Markets' (2011) 13(1) *Venture Capital* 75, 82–83.
[141] United Nations Economic Commission for Europe (n 129) 45; Cumming, 'Public Policy and the Creation of Active Venture Capital Markets' (n 140) 84.
[142] Cumming and MacIntosh (n 139) 605.

different, and incentives that target more risky investments are likely to produce poorer returns (which may be acceptable from a policy perspective). It is unlikely that many incentives will produce higher returns than would have otherwise been produced commercially, and where this occurs, it is quite likely to lead to a crowding out of the private sector.

6.3.2. Collecting the Necessary Data

Chapter five discussed the collection of data for the purposes of monitoring incentives. As mentioned at [5.4.1], monitoring data is often also useful for the purposes of evaluating incentives. However, specific evaluation data may also need to be collected in order to perform an evaluation. Unfortunately, there is often a serious lack of reliable data on the performance of government venture capital incentives.[143] For example, it was noted that the independent econometric evaluation of Australia's Innovation Investment Fund programme undertaken in 2010 was made more difficult by a lack of comprehensive 'time series' data from either the Innovation Investment Fund funds or the investee companies, and by the inability of the regulator to provide data on several Innovation Investment Fund funds.[144] This required the evaluators to seek data on a post hoc basis, with such data collection being 'invariably costly and inefficient', and the information obtained not always being reliable.[145]

In order to avoid this situation, evaluation data on an incentive should be collected from the time the incentive is implemented, and ideally, data on the state of the market the incentive is intended to address should be collected before an incentive starts.[146] This data can help demonstrate the impact of an incentive and may assist in establishing causality (see [6.3.3]).[147] In order for data collection processes to be in place from the time an incentive is introduced, however, regulators need to define credible performance measurement standards for incentives at the outset (so that they know what data to collect), and then measure results consistently.[148] This requires a degree of foresight and organisation, as well as clear incentive policy aims.

The kinds of data needed for an evaluation will depend on the performance measures being assessed. Both quantitative and qualitative data are useful when conducting an evaluation. Quantitative data helps to show what outcomes have

[143] See Wilson (n 26) 30.
[144] Murray et al, 'An Independent Econometric Analysis' (n 19) 2–3.
[145] ibid.
[146] Douglas Cumming and Sofia Johan, 'Government Venture Capital Research: Fake Science and Bad Public Policy' (2019) 21(1) *Venture Capital* 121, 125; Murray et al, 'Government Co-Financed "Hybrid" Venture Capital Programmes' (n 8) 10.
[147] Cumming and Johan, 'Government Venture Capital Research' (n 146) 126–27.
[148] Cromwell Schmisseur (n 68) 6. See also OECD, 'Business Innovation Policies' (n 2) 123–24; Wilson (n 26) 28.

occurred, while qualitative data helps to show why outcomes have occurred. In this sense, qualitative data can be extremely useful from a policymaking perspective, as it may help link particular design features with incentive outcomes.[149] While quantitative data is often collected through incentive reporting requirements and other information held by regulators, qualitative data is often gathered through case studies, surveys/questionnaires and interviews of recipients and investees.[150] These entities will naturally have more information than governments or regulators on how an incentive motivates or otherwise influences them.[151]

The kinds of quantitative and qualitative data shown in Table 8 may be relevant in relation to assessing the performance measures discussed above.

Table 8 Kinds of data that may be relevant to assessing various performance measures

	Quantitative data	**Qualitative data**
Increased investment	The number and amount of investments made under the incentive; the number of entities participating in the incentive	Information on the amount of increased investment that was made by recipients because of the incentive and the reasons that investments were made/increased[152]
Investee survival rates	The number of investees surviving a certain amount of time post-investment	Information on the extent to which investees are 'merely surviving' versus still actively growing or working towards success and whether the incentive improved their chances of survival
Investee growth	Increases in investee sales numbers, profitability and productivity	Information on how investees spent their investment capital; the extent to which the existence of the incentive increased investees' access to funding and/or improved their outcomes (such as employment rates, profits)
Increased jobs	Increases in job creation by investees	Information on the type and quality of jobs created, and whether they were displaced from other industries

(continued)

[149] See OECD, 'Business Innovation Policies' (n 2) 149.

[150] See Hana Polackova Brixi, Christian MA Valenduc and Zhicheng Li Swift (eds), *Tax Expenditures – Shedding Light on Government Spending Through the Tax System: Lessons from Developed and Transition Economies* (World Bank, 2004) 21, 24; European Commission, 'Evaluating EU Activities' (n 40) 103. See, eg Colahan et al (n 23) 3–4.

[151] World Bank, *World Development Report 2005: A Better Investment Climate for Everyone* (Oxford University Press, 2004) 97.

[152] See James (n 29) 16.

Table 8 *(Continued)*

	Quantitative data	**Qualitative data**
Patenting rates	The number of patents secured by investees	Information about the innovations patented and their market potential
Positive exits	The number of successful exits made, and the ways investments were exited	Information about the continuing growth prospects of exited investees
Investment returns	The amount of returns made by investors	Information about the level of value-adding services provided by fund managers and how this contributed to investee success and investment exits

An illustration of how qualitative data can be useful can be seen in the example of Vermont, in the USA. Vermont introduced an angel tax credit incentive in 2006, but during the incentive's two-year tenure, only one entity reportedly applied to use it.[153] Based on quantitative data alone, the reason for the incentive's low uptake cannot be ascertained. Qualitative data from local angels, however, indicated that the low rate of the tax credit under the incentive (10 per cent) was unattractive, particularly given that a more attractive incentive existed in the neighbouring state of Maine.[154] This qualitative data therefore helped policymakers respond to the problem of low uptake (in this case, by choosing to terminate the incentive – see [6.4] below).[155]

It is important to recognise that both quantitative and qualitative data can be subject to conscious or unconscious response bias and may be unreliable. This problem is likely to be worse for qualitative data, which is subjective, opinion-based and often self-reported.[156] For example, as noted at [6.3.1] above, investors who perform poorly have a natural incentive to conceal their returns,[157] while investors who perform well are more likely to publicise their success in order to reap the associated reputational benefits. There is an observable 'bias in available data towards funds with satisfactory performance',[158] and it has been noted that fund managers 'have little incentive to help in the publication and dissemination of accurate industry performance data'.[159] In many cases, investees may also be likely to present rosy pictures of their success out of self-interest. When

[153] Hendon et al (n 72) 56.
[154] ibid.
[155] ibid.
[156] See What Works Centre for Local Economic Growth, 'Innovation' (n 6) 20; James (n 29) 16.; OECD, 'Business Innovation Policies' (n 2) 121.
[157] See Murray et al, 'Government Co-Financed "Hybrid" Venture Capital Programmes' (n 8) 2.
[158] Hussain (n 55) 630.
[159] Murray et al, 'Government Co-Financed "Hybrid" Venture Capital Programmes' (n 8) 2.

recipients or investees are asked about the importance of incentives in the making of investment decisions, there is a recognised tendency for respondents to overstate the importance of incentives. This is because 'both investors and investees are likely to favour the continuation and expansion of schemes that benefit them'.[160] Furthermore, it may even be 'beyond the respondent's cognitive capacities' to separate the impact an incentive has had from the many other determinants of innovative performance.[161] Ultimately, the reality is that recipients and investees may be unable to provide accurate, reliable and complete data,[162] which has negative effects on the integrity of any evaluations undertaken in reliance on this data (see [6.3.6] below).[163]

6.3.3. Establishing Additionality and Causality

The ultimate aim of impact evaluation is to assess the extent to which changes have occurred as a result of an incentive's existence that would not otherwise have occurred (additionality), and to attribute these changes to the effects of that incentive (causality).[164] Additionality and causality are interlinked concepts that are difficult to measure but are important to take into account for a variety of reasons, not least because they ensure the robustness of evaluations.

Establishing Additionality

Additionality occurs when certain positive outcomes (eg investment levels, jobs created by investees) increase above what they would have been if an incentive did not exist. These increases are known as 'incremental' or 'additional' increases (as opposed to 'gross' or 'total' increases).[165] The reason it is important to estimate the additionality produced by an incentive is because any non-additional increases (ie increases that would have occurred with or without an incentive) are considered a 'deadweight' cost and a waste of money.[166] Where only non-additional increases occur, recipients have benefited from an incentive without producing extra positive outcomes, meaning that the incentive has not made progress towards meeting its policy aims and is therefore ineffective.[167] In this situation, the incentive has

[160] European Commission, 'Effectiveness of Tax Incentives' (n 8) 27. See also James (n 29) 16.
[161] OECD, 'Business Innovation Policies' (n 2) 121.
[162] Department of Finance (n 9) 27.
[163] See OECD, 'Business Innovation Policies' (n 2) 148.
[164] ibid 118.
[165] See Alex Easson, *Tax Incentives for Foreign Direct Investment* (Kluwer Law International, 2004) 66; Duanjie Chen, 'The Framework for Assessing Tax Incentives: A Cost–Benefit Analysis Approach' (Workshop on Tax Incentives and Base Protection, United Nations, 23–24 April 2015) 9; International Monetary Fund et al (n 104) 10.
[166] See European Commission, 'Evaluating EU Activities' (n 40) 103.
[167] Stephen Barkoczy and Daniel Sandler, *Government Venture Capital Incentives: A Multi-Jurisdiction Comparative Analysis* (Australian Tax Research Foundation, 2007) 36.

a high redundancy ratio, which means that it is also inefficient because its costs outweigh its benefits.[168] The more additionality stimulated by an incentive, the lower its redundancy ratio will be and the more efficient it will be.

Unfortunately, it can be difficult to identify additionality.[169] For example, gross investment levels may fluctuate due to changing economic conditions, rising and falling independently of the effects produced by an incentive.[170] This makes it hard to know whether any investment increases are due to an incentive or not (and if so, how much). Because additionality is hard to measure, the supporters of an incentive 'tend to base their claims on the assumption that all qualifying investment is incremental', while opponents 'assume that very little of it is'.[171] Similar issues arise with identifying additional increases to investment returns, employment numbers, investee survival rates, etc.

The main way that evaluations seek to identify additionality is through asking recipients and investees subjective questions about the impact an incentive has had on their activities and how it has affected their outcomes (see [6.3.2] above). For example, the 2016 evaluation of the UK's Enterprise Investment Scheme and Venture Capital Trusts scheme, mentioned above, asked a range of investees whether they thought the investments made in their companies would have gone ahead without the schemes' incentives. Of those surveyed, 35 per cent responded that their investments would definitely not have taken place, 28 per cent responded that their investments would probably not have gone ahead and 11 per cent responded that their investments definitely would have gone ahead without the incentive.[172] This indicates that the schemes are likely to be stimulating a reasonable amount of additionality, at least in the view of investees. The schemes' redundancy ratio/deadweight was also seen to be lower for smaller companies (likely because the smaller the company, the 'more likely it was that the schemes enabled them to secure investment they would otherwise not have received').[173] In contrast, Canada's Labour-Sponsored Venture Capital Corporations tax incentive is seen to have produced very little additionality, and has been accused of significantly crowding out the private sector as a result.[174] A 2006 study by Cumming and MacIntosh found evidence that LSVCCs crowded out private funds by more than 100 per cent, to the extent that they actually led to a reduction in the overall amount of venture capital available in the country.[175] As noted above, this effect occurred because LSVCCs were able to outbid private investors.

[168] See Chen (n 165) 9; Easson (n 165) 75–76.
[169] Easson (n 165) 75.
[170] Bracewell-Milnes and Huiskamp (n 112) 20.
[171] Easson (n 165) 75.
[172] Colahan et al (n 23) 14.
[173] ibid.
[174] See Cumming and Johan, 'Government Venture Capital Research' (n 146) 122; United Nations Economic Commission for Europe (n 129) 45.
[175] Cumming and MacIntosh (n 139) 604–05; Cumming, 'Public Policy and the Creation of Active Venture Capital Markets' (n 140) 84.

A wide-ranging study by Brander et al, published in 2015, looked at data from 20,446 enterprises based in 25 countries that received venture capital funding between 2000 and 2008.[176] The study found that when government-sponsored venture capital and private venture capital were both present in a market, the total amount of investment was higher, and the exit outcomes were better than if there were just private venture capital present (or just government venture capital).[177] The authors found additional investment at both the startup level (ie startups with mixed public and private investment received more private funding and more funding overall than startups with only one type of investment) and the market level (ie markets that received more government investment also received more private funding and more total funding).[178] This indicates that a certain amount of additionality has been achieved generally by government intervention, although this of course means little in relation to the evaluation of specific incentives.

Establishing Causality

Whereas the process of estimating additionality involves looking at how much 'extra' has been produced by an incentive, the process of establishing causality involves identifying an incentive's impact as the reason that these additional outcomes have been produced. The OECD recommends that robust evaluations should specifically 'seek to explain causality and rule out alternative explanations' for outcomes in order to elucidate not only whether an incentive has worked, by also why and how it worked.[179] Governments should be wary not to assume that the existence of an incentive automatically produces the desired outcomes, or that consuming incentive inputs necessarily results in the delivery of these outcomes.[180] However, establishing causality between an incentive and the changes it produces is acknowledged to be an extremely difficult task due to the 'confounding variables' involved,[181] the sensitivity of venture capital to macro- and micro-economic conditions and fluctuations in the business cycle,[182] and concurrent changes to policy and target populations.[183] The existence and size of changes produced by an incentive may also appear to differ depending on the data that is collected and measured in an evaluation, with issues such as data reliability and evaluation timing playing

[176] The authors note that approximately half the enterprises were based in the USA, with representation also from European and East Asian economies, along with Australia, Brazil, Canada, India, Israel and New Zealand. The enterprises covered a wide range of industries, but technology-intensive sectors were strongly represented: James A Brander, Qianqian Du and Thomas Hellmann, 'The Effects of Government-Sponsored Venture Capital: International Evidence' (2015) 19 *Review of Finance* 571, 574.

[177] ibid 574–75.

[178] ibid.

[179] OECD, 'Business Innovation Policies' (n 2) 147. See also Coglianese (n 30) 22.

[180] See Department of Finance (n 9) 27.

[181] See Josselin and Le Maux (n 14) 9.

[182] See What Works Centre for Local Economic Growth, 'Innovation' (n 6) 11; James (n 29) 5.

[183] OECD, 'Business Innovation Policies' (n 2) 118.

vexatious roles in establishing causality (see [6.2.3]).[184] However, estimates of an incentive's benefits are unfortunately 'of limited use to policy makers unless those benefits can be attributed, with a reasonable degree of certainty', to that particular incentive.[185]

The main way that evaluations seek to identify causality is through the use of 'counterfactual' scenarios, which illustrate how incentive recipients and investees would have acted or fared if an incentive had not existed.[186] Counterfactuals can be constructed in a variety of ways (and with varying levels of robustness), such as through the use of a 'control group' of entities that are similar to incentive recipients, but that did not participate in an incentive. An example of an evaluation that used a control group to establish causality is the independent econometric evaluation of Australia's Innovation Investment Fund programme undertaken in 2010 (mentioned at [6.2.1] above).[187] The evaluation used a 'matched sample' analysis to compare 102 companies that received investment through Innovation Investment Fund co-investment funds between 1997 and 2009, 106 similar companies that had received only private investment and 95 similar companies that received investment from funds affiliated with Innovation Investment Funds (ie funds that were run privately by the same fund managers that managed Innovation Investment Funds).[188] Another example of an evaluation that employed a robust methodology to establish causality through the use of a control group is Cowling et al's 2008 evaluation of the UK's Enterprise Investment Scheme and Venture Capital Trusts scheme.[189] The data used in the evaluation included full Enterprise Investment Scheme and Venture Capital Trusts scheme records for each company that received at least one investment under either scheme, collected from 1994 to 2006 (over 12,000 Enterprise Investment Scheme companies and 1000 Venture Capital Trusts-supported companies, and around 660 companies that benefited from both schemes), as well as a control group of over 80,000 companies that did not benefit from investment under either scheme.[190] The evaluators attempted to identify and account for missing information and differences in the control group where possible, in order to ensure the robustness of their evaluation.[191] The evaluation

[184] See ibid 118–19.

[185] What Works Centre for Local Economic Growth, 'Innovation' (n 6) 12. See also Coglianese (n 30) 37; Cumming and Johan, 'Government Venture Capital Research' (n 146) 128.

[186] See What Works Centre for Local Economic Growth, 'Innovation' (n 6) 12; Coglianese (n 30) 38; OECD, 'Business Innovation Policies' (n 2) 119; Josselin and Le Maux (n 14) 10.

[187] 'Econometric analysis' uses statistical and economic theory techniques to 'attempt to isolate the effects of a … measure from other key influences on economic behaviour': Polackova Brixi et al (n 150) 24. It can provide valuable information (when done well), but requires understanding of econometric methods, access to reliable and complete data (including data that predate and postdate an incentive's introduction), and an appreciation of the broader context in which an incentive operates: see Cumming and Johan, 'Government Venture Capital Research' (n 146) 125–27; Murray et al, 'Government Co-Financed "Hybrid" Venture Capital Programmes' (n 8) 10; Alberto Abadie and Matias D Cattaneo, 'Econometric Methods for Program Evaluation' (2018) 10(1) *Annual Review of Economics* 465.

[188] Murray et al, 'An Independent Econometric Analysis' (n 19) 2.

[189] OECD, 'Business Innovation Policies' (n 2) 136.

[190] Cowling et al, 'Study of the Impact' (n 23) 8.

[191] See ibid 13–25.

compared the performance of companies that received funding through the schemes against the control group and also compared the performance of companies before and after receiving initial Enterprise Investment Scheme or Venture Capital Trusts-supported investment in order to quantify the effect of the schemes on business performance indicators (eg company age, size and sector).[192] The evaluators used data on the programmes collected by HM Revenue & Customs (rather than subjective data collected from recipients and non-recipients).[193]

Using a control group of non-participating entities helps to establish causality by allowing comparisons to be made between outcomes experienced and produced by the control group and by the incentive recipients.[194] When selecting the control group, however, evaluators need to be careful to account for selection bias, which may be observed or unobserved.[195] For example, when selecting a control group of venture capital fund managers, evaluators may find it difficult to know whether they are selecting fund managers that are more or less competitive than the fund managers who have participated in an incentive. It could be the case that the most competitive fund managers have participated in the incentive (because the eligibility criteria targeted them through a discretionary selection process),[196] but it could equally be the case that the least competitive fund managers have participated in the incentive (because the incentive was of the most value to these entities).[197] In either situation, the control group may have important differences to the recipient group that may go unrecognised and/or change over time.[198] Another factor that complicates the use of control groups is the difficulty of collecting data from these entities,[199] which are likely to have little incentive to share their private information for the purpose of evaluating incentives they did not participate in.

An alternative to creating a counterfactual scenario is to use an 'experimental' approach to determine causality, for instance by granting an incentive only to a random sample of eligible recipients, withholding it from another random sample of eligible recipients and then monitoring both groups over the long term.[200] This kind of approach to determining causality would be very robust, but would involve an expensive, large-scale and time-consuming process, and would be detrimental to the incentive's equity and accessibility. The European Commission notes that no experimental construct such as the one described here has actually been attempted in practice, and that it is unlikely to be attempted in future due to administrative and political difficulties.[201]

[192] ibid 7.
[193] OECD, 'Business Innovation Policies' (n 2) 136.
[194] What Works Centre for Local Economic Growth, 'Innovation' (n 6) 12.
[195] ibid; OECD, 'Business Innovation Policies' (n 2) 119.
[196] See OECD, 'Business Innovation Policies' (n 2) 120.
[197] See, eg What Works Centre for Local Economic Growth, 'Innovation' (n 6) 13 in relation to R&D incentives.
[198] ibid 19.
[199] See Hellmann and Schure (n 20) 28.
[200] European Commission, 'Effectiveness of Tax Incentives' (n 8) 27.
[201] ibid.

The reality is that many evaluations that assess outcomes 'do not use credible strategies to assess the causal impact of policy interventions'.[202] For instance, comparing the situation of incentive recipients before and after receipt of an incentive is insufficient to establish causality,[203] yet this method was reportedly used in relation to an evaluation of Canada's Labour-Sponsored Venture Capital Corporations tax incentive.[204] This evaluation, which utilised only data that post-dated the implementation of the programme, concluded that the programme did not result in the crowding out of private investors (a conclusion that Cumming and Johan described as 'completely erroneous' based on the data).[205] A lack of clear accounting for causality can raise questions about the impact of incentive effects. For instance, Israel's Yozma programme is often described as having achieved unparalleled success, having driven an increase in venture capital investment from USD 5 million to USD 3.3 billion from 1990 to 2000, the creation of more than 2000 startups over the same period and the raising of several larger independent follow-on funds.[206] Avnimelech and Teubal have stated that the Yozma programme 'triggered' the emergence of Israel's venture capital industry through stimulating critical mass.[207] They base the causality of this statement on the data showing a 'quantum jump' in venture capital activity after the Yozma programme's introduction, as well as on statements made and insights received primarily during two interviews they conducted with Ygal Erlich, the CEO of the Yozma programme and one of its principal architects.[208] However, it is unclear the extent to which outside factors occurring in Israel at the same time, such as a large increase in immigration and a steadily growing GDP, have been accounted for in this analysis. The authors themselves, in another paper, acknowledge that the 'fact of [venture capital] emergence that followed implementation of a targeted [venture capital] policy is no proof that such a policy caused [the] emergence'.[209] This is not to suggest that Yozma did not have a catalysing effect on the Israeli venture capital sector, but rather to highlight the fact that without clear evidence of causality, this outcome is difficult to substantiate. Employing a clear methodology for establishing causality, such as the use of a counterfactual, is therefore important and recommended.

[202] What Works Centre for Local Economic Growth, 'Innovation' (n 6) 12.

[203] OECD, 'Business Innovation Policies' (n 2) 118.

[204] See Arash Soleimani Dahaj, Brian P Cozzarin and Kambiz Talebi, 'Revisiting the Canadian Public Policy Towards Venture Capital: Crowding-out or Displacement' (2018) 45(5) *Science and Public Policy* 719.

[205] See Cumming and Johan, 'Government Venture Capital Research' (n 146) 126–27.

[206] Gil Avnimelech, Martin Kenney and Morris Teubal, 'Building Venture Capital Industries: Understanding the US and Israeli Experiences' (Berkeley Roundtable on the International Economy, March 2004) Working Paper No 160, 34.

[207] Gil Avnimelech and Morris Teubal, 'Venture Capital Start-up Co-evolution and the Emergence and Development of Israel's New High Tech Cluster' (2004) 13(1) *Economics of Innovation and New Technology* 33, 43–44.

[208] ibid 47–48.

[209] Gil Avnimelech and Morris Teubal, 'Targeting Venture Capital: Lessons from Israel's Yozma Program' in Anthony Bartzokas and Sunil Mani (eds), *Financial Systems, Corporate Investment in Innovation, and Venture Capital* (Edward Elgar, 2004) 85, 106–07.

6.3.4. Measuring Effectiveness

Once performance measures for evaluating an incentive have been selected, the relevant data has been collected and estimates have been made of additionality and causality, the process of measuring an incentive's effectiveness becomes quite simple. All that remains to be done is to compare the incentive's actual performance (using the data) with its intended policy outcomes.

An excellent example of how this process may be set up in practice can be seen in Canada's Venture Capital Catalyst Initiative (VCCI), which is a co-investment initiative through which the Canadian government, via the Business Development Bank of Canada (BDC), invests in venture capital funds and funds of funds. The initiative has one of the most comprehensive effectiveness evaluation strategies that is publicly available. Its 'Performance Measurement Framework' sets out the incentive's policy aims, standards indicating that these aims have been met (ie performance measures), the source of the data used to make this assessment, the baseline against which success is measured, the timeline of when assessment will occur and how causality will be established (by comparing recipients with baseline entities).[210] In doing this, it explicitly engages with steps one to four of the proposed methodology at [6.3] above. A slightly modified and condensed version of the Framework is set out in Table 9 as an illustration.

Table 9 A slightly modified version of the VCCI Performance Measurement Framework

Expected results	Indicators	Source	Baseline	Target	Frequency
Translate innovation into economic growth by helping high-potential companies grow	The long-term economic and financial performance of Canadian companies ... backed by VCCI in terms of employment growth and growth in revenue/sales, including exports	ISED, Statistics Canada	Similar non-recipients	Outperform baseline firms	2030, 2035, 2040

(continued)

[210] Innovation, Science and Economic Development Canada, 'Venture Capital Catalyst Initiative: Performance Measurement Framework' (2022) 10–12.

Table 9 ***(Continued)***

Expected results	**Indicators**	**Source**	**Baseline**	**Target**	**Frequency**
	The long-term innovation performance of Canadian companies … backed by VCCI in terms of the number of employees and R&D spending	ISED, Statistics Canada	Similar non-recipients	Outperform baseline firms	2030, 2035, 2040
	The proportion of Canadian companies supported by VCCI that achieve a merger or acquisition (M&A) or IPO exit event	BDC	50% of investments of liquidated venture capital funds have an exit by IPO or M&A	25% in 2035	2035, 2040
Increase the availability of venture capital	The number of funds-of-funds supported by VCCI	BDC	A previous initiative backed 4 funds-of-funds	4 or more	Annual until target met
	The proportion of Canadian companies supported by all VCCI streams that are life sciences companies	BDC	12%	Outperform baseline	Annual starting 2030
Improve the sustainability of the Canadian venture capital ecosystem and spur investment by generating market-aligned financial returns	Financial return of VCCI (pooled gross internal rate of return of the entire funds-of-funds)	BDC	n/a	7%	Annual starting 2030

(continued)

Table 9 ***(Continued)***

Expected results	Indicators	Source	Baseline	Target	Frequency
Deepen the pool of experienced venture capital fund managers by building Canadian talent and investment, and attract new expertise and capital to Canada's venture capital market	Proportion of venture capital fund managers supported under VCCI that have raised follow-on funds	BDC	n/a	40% in 2030, 50% in 2035	2030, 2035
Attract participation from private sector investors in venture capital funds	The total amount of investment in VCCI fund-of-funds	BDC	n/a	CAD 1.4 billion	Annual until target met
Improve diversity balance in Canadian venture capital fund managers	The percentage of women and non-binary senior investment professionals out of the total number of senior investment professionals of the fund managers supported	BDC	19% of venture capital partners were women	Outperform baseline	Annual until all funds invested
	The percentage of senior investment professionals identifying as member of a traditionally underserved group out of the total number of senior investment professionals of the fund managers supported	BDC	23% of venture capital partners identified as racialised Canadians; 10.3% of venture capital partners identified as LGBTQ2+	Outperform baseline	Annual until all funds invested

(continued)

Table 9 ***(Continued)***

Expected results	Indicators	Source	Baseline	Target	Frequency
Improve diversity balance in Canadian venture capital-backed entrepreneurs	The percentage of women and non-binary individuals on the management team	BDC	13%	Outperform baseline	Annual until all funds invested
	The percentage identifying as a member of a traditionally underserved group on the management team	N/A	N/A	N/A	Annual until all funds invested

This framework serves as an excellent blueprint for effectiveness evaluation of other incentives. Interestingly, the VCCI's aims have been adjusted slightly since the previous iteration of the programme in 2019 (see [2.5]). The initiative's policy aims are now slightly more achievable and focus more closely on diversity. The evaluation timelines have also been pushed out, perhaps indicating that the initial evaluation dates were too early (or that the initiative is taking longer than expected to achieve its aims).[211]

6.3.5. Measuring Efficiency

If it can be established that an incentive is effective at achieving its policy aims, it should then be considered whether the incentive achieves its aims in an efficient way. Evaluating an incentive's efficiency generally involves weighing the benefits it produces against the costs of providing it (financial, administrative, human and unintended) in a process known as a cost–benefit analysis (see [2.6]).[212] Where an incentive's costs outweigh the value of the benefits it produces, it will not be efficient (although it may or may not still be effective).[213] Incentives that are inefficient may need to be removed or replaced because they do not represent good value for money and therefore are difficult to justify (particularly if there is a more efficient alternative).[214] The termination of incentives as a result of evaluation is discussed

[211] See Innovation, Science and Economic Development Canada, 'Venture Capital Catalyst Initiative: Performance Measurement Framework' (April 2019).

[212] See Lester (n 2) 2; James (n 29) 3.

[213] See Easson (n 165) 74; Coglianese (n 30) 21.

[214] See Chen (n 165) 31.

further below at [6.4]. There may be some rare situations where an incentive is inefficient but still represents the best policy option available. In this instance the incentive may be retained, but its efficiency should be improved if possible.

Cost–benefit analyses are useful evaluation tools and have been described as the 'gold standard' of evaluation, but they can be difficult and costly to perform.[215] Most cost–benefit analyses involve major methodological challenges and may therefore not be entirely reliable.[216] In order for a cost–benefit analysis to be undertaken, costs and benefits must be identified, causally attributed to the incentive, measured and converted into a monetary value.[217] This can be a challenging and subjective exercise, with results differing depending on how important various measures are judged to be.[218] Costs and benefits also occur over time, making it difficult to calculate their true value.[219] As with other forms of evaluation, cost–benefit analyses are also made more challenging by a widespread lack of data. For example, the evaluators who undertook the government-requested evaluation of Australia's Innovation Investment Fund programme in 2010 were not able to take account of deadweight costs, displacement costs, the scale of additionality, revenue from the taxation of new employees, increased business taxation, reductions in welfare payments and local economic multipliers, as they generally would do in a full cost–benefit analysis, due to data constraints.[220] Instead, they were limited to estimating the costs associated with Innovation Investment Fund investees being liquidated, the potential benefits of investees undertaking IPOs and the returns that would have to be made on current investees (at the time) in order for losses under the programme to balance its returns.[221] This exercise, while still interesting, is obviously fairly limited when compared with a full cost–benefit analysis, so only presented an incomplete picture of the incentive's efficiency. In contrast, the 2021 evaluation of the UK's Enterprise Capital Funds programme undertook a full cost–benefit analysis (while acknowledging the assumptions and other uncertainties that could affect the results) and found that the programme is expected to deliver economic benefits that exceed its cost by around GBP 2.62 per GBP 1 of economic cost,[222] indicating that the programme is relatively efficient.

[215] Committee for Economic Development of the Conference Board, 'Regulation and the Economy: The Relationship and How to Improve It' (27 September 2017) www.ced.org/reports/regulation-and-the-economy. See also Stone (n 75) 53.

[216] ibid; Hans M van de Kar and Barbara L Wolfe (eds), *The Relevance of Public Finance for Policy-Making: Proceedings of the 41st Congress of the International Institute of Public Finance* (Wayne State University Press, 1987) 3.

[217] European Commission, 'Evaluating EU Activities' (n 40) 102–03; Chen (n 165) 8.

[218] See Stone (n 75) 51–53.

[219] See Lester (n 2) 18.

[220] Marc Cowling, Gordon Murray and Weixi Liu, 'IIF Equity Programme Assessment' (2010) 13–14.

[221] ibid 14.

[222] Ipsos MORI and George Barrett (n 25) 65.

The kinds of benefits that can be produced by an incentive where it is effective at addressing market failure are wide ranging and can include:

- additional investment that has been made as a result of the incentive;[223]
- increased investee survival and business creation rates;
- investment returns produced under the incentive, including returns to the private sector and any returns made to government that might help offset the cost of the incentive (see [5.2.3]);
- successful exits that create positive reputational benefits for the industry;
- creation of new jobs, including the added benefits of reduced unemployment and welfare payments;[224]
- increased tax revenue paid by new businesses and businesses that survive when they otherwise would have failed, as well as tax paid by their employees;[225]
- increased innovation, R&D spending, patenting and collaboration; and
- positive signalling effects and other spillovers.[226]

The costs of an incentive are similarly wide ranging, and may include:

- the actual cost of providing the incentive, including revenue forgone in the case of tax incentives (see [5.2.3]);[227]
- compliance costs for participants and investees;[228]
- administration costs, including the costs of paying regulators, creating incentive rules and guidance, publicising the incentive, monitoring the incentive and collecting data;[229]
- redundancy, deadweight and abuse costs where incentives provide windfalls and do not produce additionality (ie where an incentive is overly generous, or where recipients get away with making non-eligible investments);[230]
- failed investments that produce investment losses, liquidation costs and job losses;

[223] See James (n 29) v; Chen (n 165) 8, 28; Easson (n 165) 77.

[224] See Cowling et al, 'IIF Equity Programme Assessment' (n 220) 13–14; James (n 29) v, 32; Chen (n 165) 8, 23.

[225] See Cowling et al, 'IIF Equity Programme Assessment' (n 220) 14; Barkoczy et al (n 39) 228; Chen (n 165) 8; Bracewell-Milnes and Huiskamp (n 112) 121.

[226] See James (n 29) v, 32; Polackova Brixi et al (n 150) 22; Easson (n 165) 77; Barkoczy et al (n 39) 228; International Monetary Fund et al (n 104) 10.

[227] See OECD, 'Government Venture Capital for Technology-Based Firms' (n 6) 15; Barkoczy et al (n 39) 228.

[228] See Polackova Brixi et al (n 150) 22; Chen (n 165) 8.

[229] See James (n 29) v, 32; Chen (n 165) 8; Polackova Brixi et al (n 150) 22; Lester (n 2) 18.

[230] See Cowling et al, 'IIF Equity Programme Assessment' (n 220) 13; James (n 29) 26, 32; Easson (n 165) 75–76; Chen (n 165) 28.

- displacement of jobs from other industries (nullifies the value of jobs created);[231]
- the cost of distortion, such as crowding out, which damages the industry by driving away private investors;[232] and
- displacement of government support from other industries, which can lead to net efficiency losses.[233]

In some cases, it will be too difficult (or impossible) to quantify the benefits and costs produced by an incentive in monetary terms, and a cost–benefit analysis will not be feasible.[234] This may particularly be the case in relation to small incentives where the cost involved in undertaking a full cost–benefit analysis is not justified (see [6.2.4]).[235] In these situations, the next best approach is to undertake a cost-effectiveness analysis, which compares the outcomes produced by an incentive with its costs (although it does not place them into a common monetary unit or subtract costs from benefits).[236] Tax expenditure theory defines cost-effectiveness as 'the value of the change in economic behaviour that is directly attributable to the tax measure' (ie incremental investment) per dollar of tax revenue forgone.[237] It has been suggested that an incentive may be considered cost-effective (but not necessarily efficient) if one dollar of cost incurred in providing the incentive's benefits is matched by 'at least one dollar of incremental spending in the targeted activity'.[238] Hellmann and Schure, in their evaluation of British Columbia's Venture Capital Program, compared the tax generated by companies supported under the programme with the cost of the tax expenditures provided to participants. They noted that this comparison is transparent and easy to understand, although they acknowledged that, unlike a cost–benefit analysis, it does not take into account general equilibrium effects (ie economic multipliers), counterfactuals or externalities.[239] Furthermore, while the amount of tax credits provided under the incentive is easy to calculate and 'highly accurate', an estimation of taxes paid by investors and investees is much harder and may be subject to biases.[240]

James suggests that an initial approximation of an incentive's cost-effectiveness could be to compare the number of jobs created as a result of incremental

[231] See Cowling et al, 'IIF Equity Programme Assessment' (n 220) 13; International Monetary Fund et al (n 104) 10.
[232] See Chen (n 165) 29.
[233] See Lester (n 2) 2, 18; Cowling et al, 'IIF Equity Programme Assessment' (n 220) 13. For instance, government support may shift investment from activities 'where it earns a competitive private return to activities where it earns a lower rate of return', thereby putting 'downward pressure on the net economic benefit from providing assistance': Lester (n 2) 21.
[234] See Coglianese (n 30) 7.
[235] See broadly Lester (n 2) 19.
[236] Coglianese (n 30) 49; Lester (n 2) 18. See also European Commission, 'Evaluating EU Activities' (n 40) 103.
[237] Polackova Brixi et al (n 150) 21.
[238] ibid 22.
[239] Hellmann and Schure (n 20) 14.
[240] ibid 16.

investment with the incentive's redundancy costs (ie the cost incurred in subsidising investments that would have been made anyway).[241] This provides a ballpark cost per job created metric 'that can help policymakers decide if the incentive was worthwhile'.[242] Both of the cost-effectiveness measures discussed above fall short of calculating true efficiency because they do not take into account all the policy-induced economic and social costs and benefits associated with the incentive,[243] but they are certainly easier to estimate and may therefore be useful in many circumstances.

6.3.6. Drawing Conclusions on Incentive Performance

A final step in the evaluation of an incentive involves reaching conclusions about its success, value or worthiness based on its effectiveness and efficiency. For example, the 2010 Evaluation of British Columbia's Venture Capital Program, mentioned above, found that the programme 'is fundamentally valuable' to the province, primarily because 'companies in the program generate more taxes than they consume tax credits' and consistently create new jobs (among other things).[244] The evaluation reported that companies supported under the programme each added 2.43 new employees per year.[245] Where an incentive can be said to be effective and efficient at working towards achieving its policy aims, its existence will also be appropriate and necessary (see [6.4] below).

However, there are inherent difficulties that arise in interpreting and relying on the results of evaluations, and these should be considered when making conclusions. The first of these is that many evaluations, as discussed at various points above, may be unreliable themselves. This could be because reliable data is not available; because the evaluation methodology is not robust or credible (eg it may not account for causality) and may therefore provide misleading or incorrect results;[246] or because the results of the evaluation have been interpreted and/or reported in a biased way.[247] Even though external evaluators should have a 'certain degree of detachment' and may be less likely to be influenced by political factors and other biases than internal evaluators, the reliability of their results is still not guaranteed, and will be affected by the competency and integrity of the evaluation team, their access to data and ability to communicate with stakeholders, and their freedom to make conclusions based on their analysis.[248]

[241] James (n 29) 32.
[242] ibid.
[243] See Polackova Brixi et al (n 150) 22.
[244] Hellmann and Schure (n 20) 6.
[245] ibid 21.
[246] See Cumming and Johan, 'Government Venture Capital Research' (n 146) 124–25, 129.
[247] See Hussain (n 55) 630; ACT Government (n 1) 6.
[248] European Commission, 'Evaluating EU Activities' (n 40) 14. See also Lester (n 2) 22.

Even where evaluations produce reliable results, it can be difficult to know what lessons to take from them. For example, Brander et al undertook an analysis of government-supported capital in Canada, using data from 1996 to 2004, which found that companies funded by government-supported capital were less likely to have successful exits (and much less likely to have IPOs), produced lower exit values, produced fewer patents and did not seem to increase employment or competition.[249] While these results seem quite damning for the incentives in question, the authors noted that, despite these issues, the government support of venture capital in Canada may nevertheless play an important market development/expansion role if it fills a gap left by the private sector (eg by funding companies that were not promising enough to attract private funding).[250] This would only be the case, however, if the government support did not entirely crowd out the private sector (which has been an acknowledged problem in Canada, and was suggested to be the case based on the available data).[251] While the results of this analysis were therefore quite clear, it is not necessarily clear what the best way forward would be for the Canadian government in improving or concluding its incentives. The authors noted that a full cost–benefit analysis should be undertaken to properly determine whether the incentives should be considered successful.[252] In a similar vein, changes were made to the UK's Enterprise Investment Scheme and Venture Capital Trusts scheme in 2012, and while the changes made the incentives more generous, evaluation found that they did not result in a modification of investment behaviour for most recipients.[253] This may suggest that the changes were practically unnecessary, or perhaps that they were not well communicated to recipients. In either case, more information about the reasons behind the evaluation results may give the UK government a better idea of how to improve the incentive's effectiveness and ensure that future changes have their intended effect.

6.4. Impacts of Evaluation

Evaluations provide a natural point in time for governments to consider the provision of their incentives and assess whether these incentives are still necessary and appropriate.[254] If incentives remain necessary (ie if they have not yet met their policy aims, so there remains a market need for intervention) and are appropriate (ie effective and efficient enough to justify their continuation), then governments

[249] Brander et al, 'Government Sponsored versus Private Venture Capital' (n 102) 9.
[250] ibid.
[251] ibid 9, 36.
[252] ibid 43.
[253] Colahan et al (n 23) 21.
[254] See Coglianese (n 30) 47–48; Hendon et al (n 72) 58; Department of Prime Minister and Cabinet, *The Australian Government Guide to Regulation* (Australian Government, 2014) 51–52; Lester (n 2) 16, 21.

may consider retaining them and improving their operation and performance in response to evaluation results. In contrast, if incentives are not, or are no longer, necessary (ie because they have met their policy aims, or the market need that justified them has disappeared), or are ineffective or inefficient to the point that their continuation is not appropriate, then governments may decide to terminate them. Innovation-related policies are essentially 'experimental', and policymakers 'need to test and try out various approaches, with good systems in place to build on successful initiatives and shut down failures'.[255] Even incentives that are initially well designed 'can require subsequent amendment as costs and benefits change over time',[256] and evaluation is particularly important for policies such as venture capital incentives because it is generally not possible to predict their results until 'after the event'.[257] Where evaluations uncover problems in relation to an incentive, this should not provide 'automatic grounds for termination', but instead the information discovered should be used as a 'tool to provide a basis for improved policy'.[258]

The decision-making process in relation to retaining and improving incentives is represented in Figure 2.

Figure 2 Assessing whether an incentive should continue on the basis of evaluation results

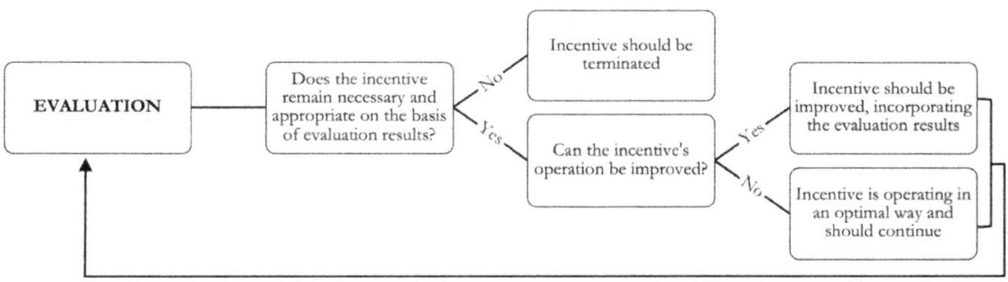

An example of an incentive that was responsively improved as a result of evaluation is the UK's Venture Capital Trusts scheme. The 2016 evaluation of the UK's Enterprise Investment Scheme and Venture Capital Trusts scheme indicated that Venture Capital Trusts served larger companies more than smaller ones, and that Venture Capital Trust investments were not perceived to be high risk.[259] As a result, the government was able to refocus the Venture Capital Trust investment rules on riskier businesses.[260] In comparison, Vermont's angel tax incentive, set

[255] What Works Centre for Local Economic Growth, 'Innovation' (n 6) 31.

[256] See Productivity Commission (n 6) 9.

[257] See Mark Dodgson, Alan Hughes, John Foster and Stan Metcalfe, 'Systems Thinking, Market Failure, and the Development of Innovation Policy: The Case of Australia' (2011) 40(9) *Research Policy* 1145, 1148.

[258] OECD, 'Business Innovation Policies' (n 2) 146.

[259] Colahan et al (n 23) 8–9.

[260] Emma Agyemang, 'Are VCTs Worth the Risk for Higher Earners?' *Financial Times* (11 October 2019) www.ft.com/content/28c30bea-e9bc-11e9-85f4-d00e5018f061; Kate Beioley, 'Tax-Efficient VCT

out at [6.3.2] above, and Australia's Innovation Investment Fund co-investment programme are examples of incentives that were terminated because they were perceived to be ineffective.[261]

Ideally, governments should look at prior evaluations and their results when designing – and before introducing – new incentives.[262] The knowledge gained from evaluation can provide policymakers with useful information for the design of future incentives, and using this knowledge can assist future decision-making and strengthen policymaking performance.[263] If it is done well, evaluation can 'provide a mechanism for learning from past programme performance' by identifying 'policy design elements that appear to be correlated with success'.[264] It has been noted that during venture capital growth cycles there often appears a 'proliferation of ill-advised policies that are usually reminiscent of the ones tried during the previous phase', and a 'distressingly large' number of these policies are seen to 'meet with minimal success or fail outright'.[265] Taking the results of prior evaluations into account before introducing new policies can hopefully help avoid this scenario.

Unfortunately, governments often either ignore the lessons of the past or draw on them in a 'selective' way.[266] For example, France has been criticised for failing to learn from poor evaluation results in regard to its government venture capital incentives. The country has an impressive range of generous incentives in place to support the venture capital sector; it was reported in 2014 that 95 per cent of venture capital-backed enterprises and 99 per cent of seed capital-backed enterprises were supported directly or indirectly by Bpifrance, France's public investment bank and innovation agency.[267] In fact, it has been suggested that France's venture capital strength may result 'entirely from highly elevated government intervention'.[268] Unfortunately, a 2016 review found that France's private and institutional investors have reduced their investment commitments in recent years (perhaps indicating a degree of crowding out due to over-generous government support).[269] By 2013, banks' share of venture capital funding in France had reportedly dropped to just 1 per cent.[270] Furthermore, the performance of government-supported venture capital in France is reportedly poor in comparison with other countries.[271] Milosevic and Fendt note that rather than trying to improve its incentives, France has instead

Market Suffers Drop in Demand After Rule Change' *Financial Times* (22 February 2019) www.ft.com/content/d25bfb48-3077-11e9-ba00-0251022932c8.

[261] See Hendon et al (n 72) 56; Barkoczy et al (n 39) 351–55.

[262] See, eg Department of Finance (n 9) 27.

[263] ACT Government (n 1) 5. See also Avnimelech et al (n 206) 47.

[264] What Works Centre for Local Economic Growth, 'Innovation' (n 6) 31.

[265] Avnimelech et al (n 206) 3.

[266] See OECD, 'Business Innovation Policies' (n 2) 146.

[267] Milosevic and Fendt (n 84) 663.

[268] ibid 660. See also Colombo et al, 'Venture Capital' (n 128) 22.

[269] Milosevic and Fendt (n 84) 660, 663.

[270] ibid.

[271] ibid 663–65.

perversely encouraged the repetition of 'vicious behaviors' and rewarded and cemented 'the present reality (of incentivized, facilitated fund-raising that neither leads to venture nor fund performance)'.[272] If this is the case, it represents a missed opportunity by the French government to improve the outcomes of its suite of venture capital incentives. However, given that France is also one of the leading venture capital industries in the world (based on venture capital investments as a proportion of GDP),[273] the French government may consider the money spent on its incentives to be justified, even if those incentives could potentially be made more effective or efficient.

In certain situations where governments are willing to cooperate, they can use the results of evaluations to proactively learn from each other. For example, the European Commission established the INNO-Partnering Forum between 2009 and 2012 specifically to 'identify, develop and exploit synergies between public innovation agencies in Europe and propose new approaches to innovation support for SMEs', as well as to accelerate the 'take-up of the most advanced innovation mechanisms with proven efficiency and impact'.[274] The Forum consisted of six partners, all European innovation agencies, being Vinnova (Sweden), Tekes (Finland), the Technology Strategy Board (the UK), Enterprise Ireland (Ireland), NL Agency (the Netherlands) and the Austrian Research Promotion Agency (Austria).[275] One of the tasks of the Forum was to undertake peer reviews of innovation support schemes (including venture capital incentives) that offer the 'best sources for the identification of good practices that seem to be of interest to other agencies and countries in Europe'.[276] This is a commendable approach to learning and improvement, but requires openness and a degree of mutual trust and confidence, as well as longevity.

The knowledge gained from evaluation, where it is made public, opens incentives up to discussion and scrutiny from the public.[277] Releasing reliable and timely evaluation data on incentives is therefore recommended as a matter of leading practice and should be encouraged.[278] Transparency can help increase confidence in incentives and trust in the governments implementing them,[279] as well as providing an impetus to improve incentive efficiency.[280] Releasing the results of evaluations can also help other countries work 'towards developing

[272] ibid 670.
[273] See OECD, 'Venture Capital Investments' (*OECD.Stat*, 19 October 2020) stats.oecd.org/Index.aspx?DataSetCode=VC_INVEST; OECD, *Entrepreneurship at a Glance 2017* (OECD, 2017) 125; OECD, 'Entrepreneurship at a Glance: 2018 Highlights' (10 October 2018) 15.
[274] Deuten (n 31) 5.
[275] ibid.
[276] ibid.
[277] See Burton and Sadiq (n 48) 78.
[278] See OECD Regulatory Policy Committee (n 2) 30; Department of Finance (n 9) 14; Murray et al, 'Government Co-Financed "Hybrid" Venture Capital Programmes' (n 8) 10; Cromwell Schmisseur (n 68) 6.
[279] ACT Government (n 1) 5. See also Brown et al (n 43) 36.
[280] See Lester (n 2) 26.

better evaluation processes'.[281] Furthermore, where evaluation data is released into the public domain, it will often be analysed by academics and other stakeholders, providing a free and beneficial form of 'evaluation quality control'.[282] Examples of incentives that have independently assessed and evaluated by academics include:

- Canada's Labour-Sponsored Venture Capital Corporations tax incentive (evaluated by Osborne and Sandler in 1998 and Cumming and MacIntosh in 2006);[283]
- the European Seed Capital Fund Scheme (evaluated by Murray in 1998);[284]
- Australia's Innovation Investment Fund programme (evaluated by Cumming in 2007);[285]
- Canada's Québec Business Investment Company tax incentive (which was evaluated by Carpentier and Suret in 2007);[286]
- Canada's suite of government incentives for venture capital (evaluated by Brander et al in 2008);[287]
- Australia's Pre-Seed Fund programme (evaluated by Cumming and Johan in 2009);[288]
- the UK's Regional Venture Capital Funds (evaluated by Webster in 2009);[289] and
- the UK's Enterprise Capital Funds (evaluated by Baldock in 2016);[290]

Other academic analyses have taken broader looks at the effects of government support for venture capital in particular jurisdictions without focusing on individual incentives.[291] To the extent that governments can facilitate the academic analysis of their incentives, they are likely to be able to use the results to improve their policies (even if these results are not always what they want to hear).

[281] See Wilson (n 26) 29.

[282] OECD, 'Business Innovation Policies' (n 2) 149. See also What Works Centre for Local Economic Growth, 'Innovation' (n 6) 37.

[283] Duncan Osborne and Daniel Sandler, 'A Tax Expenditure Analysis of Labour-Sponsored Venture Capital Corporations' (1998) 46(3) *Canadian Tax Journal* 499; Cumming and MacIntosh (n 139).

[284] Gordon C Murray, 'A Policy Response to Regional Disparities in the Supply of Risk Capital to New Technology-based Forms in the European Union: The European Seed Capital Fund Scheme' (1998) 32(5) *Regional Studies* 405.

[285] Cumming, 'Government Policy Towards Entrepreneurial Finance' (n 13).

[286] Cécile Carpentier and Jean-Marc Suret, 'On the Usefulness of Tax Incentives for Informal Investors' (2007) 9(1) *Venture Capital* 1.

[287] Brander et al, 'Government Sponsored versus Private Venture Capital' (n 102).

[288] Douglas Cumming and Sofia Johan, 'Pre-Seed Government Venture Capital Funds' (2009) 7(1) *Journal of International Entrepreneurship* 26.

[289] David C Webster, 'England's Regional Venture Capital Funds: A Review of Programme Outcomes and Stakeholder Perspectives' (Said Business School, 2009).

[290] Baldock (n 55).

[291] See, eg Colombo et al, 'Governmental Venture Capital' (n 103) 14–16; Munari and Toschi (n 112); Hendon et al (n 72); Benoît Leleux and Bernard Surelemont, 'Public versus Private Venture Capital: Seeding or Crowding Out? A Pan-European Analysis' (2003) 18(1) *Journal of Business Venturing* 81;

Despite these numerous benefits that can arise through the public dissemination of evaluation results, it should be recognised that 'there is often strong pressure from both regulators and government officials to make the evaluation "confidential," so that it will not be seen by the general public'.[292] Murray et al noted in 2012 that 'it is remarkable how few independent and formal programme evaluations are available in the public domain'.[293] Although this is understandable in some respects, it is suggested that the benefits from transparency (in terms of accountability and public confidence) are important enough to warrant a more open culture in regard to incentives and their evaluation.

6.5. Summary

Reliable, timely and consistent evaluation of government venture capital incentives helps governments identify and understand leading practices.[294] Furthermore, evaluation produces opportunities to learn about incentive design and implementation,[295] the details of which may make the difference between an incentive succeeding or failing.[296] Despite a lack of clear, robust evidence on the impact of venture capital incentives, it has been noted that policy interest in this area remains high, and while a number of lessons have been learned from past experiences, 'there is still much more to be shared, evaluated and analysed'.[297] Unfortunately, as has been seen in this chapter, the conditions for robust and rigorous evaluations are rarely met, and it has been observed that some 'government departments appear quite content that such limitations in the ability to conduct independent and robust evaluations continue'.[298]

The discussion in this chapter has highlighted the need for increased evaluation of government venture capital incentives, particularly in regard to their outcomes and impact (although process evaluations are also important). It is recommended that governments should always create a formal evaluation strategy at the time they design and introduce new incentives, and should also budget for evaluation

Douglas J Cumming, Luca Grilli and Samuele Murtinu, 'Government and Independent Venture Capital Investments in Europe: A Firm-Level Performance Analysis' (2017) 42 *Journal of Corporate Finance* 439; Milosevic and Fendt (n 84); Josh Lerner and Brian Watson, 'The Public Venture Capital Challenge: The Australian Case' (2008) 10(1) *Venture Capital* 1; Marco Da Rin, Giovanna Nicodano and Alessandro Sembenelli, 'Public Policy and the Creation of Active Venture Capital Markets' (2006) 90(8) *Journal of Public Economics* 1699; Gilles Duruflé, 'Government Involvement in the Venture Capital Industry: International Comparisons' (CVCA, May 2010).

292 Brown et al (n 43) 36.

293 Murray et al, 'Government Co-Financed "Hybrid" Venture Capital Programmes' (n 8) 6.

294 See broadly United Nations Economic Commission for Europe (n 129) 83; Coglianese (n 30) 7.

295 United Nations Economic Commission for Europe (n 129) 83.

296 Wilson (n 26) 31.

297 ibid 32.

298 Murray et al, 'Government Co-Financed "Hybrid" Venture Capital Programmes' (n 8) 10.

costs. They may want to engage an external evaluator to help them design their evaluation strategy and decide on things such as the frequency of evaluation, the performance measures that should be used and the kinds of data that need to be collected.

The suggested methodology for impact evaluation put forward in this chapter could form the basis for particular incentive evaluation strategies. Regardless of the strategy used, in order to ensure robust evaluations, governments should define clear and consistent performance measures, estimate the additionality and causality of outcomes, and measure the effectiveness and efficiency of their incentives in order to determine whether they remain appropriate and necessary, whether they should be improved or whether they should be terminated. Post-evaluation, governments should use the information produced to improve the design of future incentives, and they should release this information publicly in order to foster public confidence and an open and transparent culture of improvement.

The following chapter, which is the final chapter in this book, builds on the recommendations and principles set out in this chapter and the preceding ones to present a set of leading practice guidelines for venture capital incentives.

7

Leading Practice Guidelines for Government Venture Capital Incentives

7.1. Introduction

The primary question examined in this book is how governments can best design and implement incentives to promote increased venture capital investment in startups. Part of addressing this question has involved identifying leading practices across the policy development stages (introduction, form, targeting, implementation and evaluation). The preceding chapters have illustrated the amount of thought and care that goes into designing appropriate, effective and efficient incentives, and the number of important decisions that policymakers must consider through these processes. The examples highlighted throughout the chapters show that no two incentives are the same, even where they are similar in form and policy aims, and that there is no 'right' way to structure venture capital incentives, particularly given the vast differences that exist between jurisdictions in terms of legal structures, market characteristics and investment cultures.[1] Because of these differences, academics have found it challenging to make 'uniform policy recommendations' for governments in regard to venture capital incentives.[2] However, the emerging research in this area, and the growing experience of policymakers in designing and implementing incentives, gives us the opportunity to recognise practices that are likely to help incentives succeed and those that are not. This is a worthwhile task, as the impartial and objective guidance of practice and policy is one of the most important roles that academic study can play in this field.[3]

As foreshadowed in chapter one, this chapter delivers guidelines to policymakers, based on the research undertaken in this book, that will enhance their capacity to design appropriate, effective and efficient incentives, and will hopefully allow them to avoid making some of the mistakes that have impacted prior efforts in this space. The guidelines are framed as a set of fundamental principles that transcend any particular jurisdiction (meaning that they are inherently more open-ended

[1] See PricewaterhouseCoopers, 'Innovation: Government's Many Roles in Fostering Innovation' (January 2010) 4.

[2] Lisa Callagher, Peter Smith and Saskia Ruscoe, 'Government Roles in Venture Capital Development: A Review of Current Literature' (2015) 4(3) *Journal of Entrepreneurship and Public Policy* 367, 386.

[3] Douglas Cumming and Sofia Johan, 'Government Venture Capital Research: Fake Science and Bad Public Policy' (2019) 21(1) *Venture Capital* 121, 121.

than standards that apply at a granular level). The guidelines are set out below (see [7.2]), grouped with reference to the policy development stages mentioned above and used throughout the book. This chapter concludes by setting out some suggested directions for future research (see [7.3]) and some final thoughts on venture capital incentive policy design (see [7.4]).

7.2. Leading Practice Guidelines

7.2.1. Introducing New Incentives

Guideline 1(a): Governments Should Clearly Identify and Quantify the Market Need a Proposed Incentive is Intended to Address (see [2.3])

Before introducing a new incentive, governments should identify, collect evidence on and attempt to fully understand an existing market need by engaging with the private sector and undertaking empirical quantitative and qualitative research. In particular, governments should ensure that there is sufficient demand for venture capital to support the introduction of an incentive. While these recommendations may seem trite, many of the examples covered in this book demonstrate that governments do not always follow these steps. The process of identifying market need can help ensure that incentives are appropriate and are introduced for justifiable reasons. Even more importantly, it can help governments avoid introducing ill-considered, politically motivated or reactive policies that may (at best) waste resources or (at worst) actively harm the sector through an oversupply of capital.[4]

Guideline 1(b): Governments Should Implement Policies to Support the Emergence of Venture Capital in Order to Improve Chances of Incentive Success (see [2.4])

Governments should look holistically at their business, taxation and innovation systems to identify and rectify coordination failures. In particular, governments should support the demand side by making it easy for entrepreneurs to do business and introducing demand-side incentives where necessary,[5] and should facilitate venture capital investment by, if appropriate, relaxing corporate disclosure rules

[4] See Karen Wilson, 'Policy Lessons from Financing Young Innovative Firms' (OECD, June 2015) OECD Science, Technology and Industry Policy Papers No 24, 13–14; Gil Avnimelech, Martin Kenney and Morris Teubal, 'Building Venture Capital Industries: Understanding the US and Israeli Experiences' (Berkeley Roundtable on the International Economy, March 2004) Working Paper No 160, 13–14; Albert Bravo-Biosca, 'Access to Finance for Innovation: Rationales and Risks of Public Intervention' (The Innovation Policy Platform, 2014) 9.

[5] See Cromwell Schmisseur, 'Information and Observations on State Venture Capital Programs: Report for the US Department of the Treasury and Interested Parties in the State Small Business Credit Initiative (SSBCI)' (February 2013) 5; Gilles Duruflé, 'Government Involvement in the Venture Capital Industry: International Comparisons' (CVCA, May 2010) 19.

for startups, allowing the use of convertible and hybrid securities and limited partnership fund structures, allowing investment in venture capital funds by institutional investors, providing clarity on how venture capital investments will be taxed and reducing taxation barriers, creating a positive culture around venture capital investment and facilitating investment exits. These actions should help to create an environment 'that is conducive to entrepreneurship and venture capital investment', which, in turn, is a vital part of ensuring incentive success.[6]

Guideline 1(c): Governments Should Formulate Clear and Appropriate Policy Aims to Guide their Venture Capital Incentives (see [2.5])

An incentive's policy aims should be clearly articulated, should explicitly address the market need that the incentive is designed to meet and should point the incentive towards objective outcomes. The incentive's policy aims will form the evaluative basis for any evaluations of its success (see Guideline 5(e)), so should ideally be realistic and achievable.

Guideline 1(d): Governments Should Undertake a Preliminary Cost–Benefit Analysis to Assess a Proposed Incentive's Net Benefits (see [2.6])

Governments should assess the net benefit of their proposed incentive by considering whether the benefits it is intended to produce (eg addressing market failure and increasing venture capital investment) are likely to outweigh its projected costs (eg the cost of providing the incentive and any unintended negative distortions). If the costs of an incentive outweigh its benefits, the incentive is unlikely to be justified and should not be introduced. If the benefits outweigh the costs, on the other hand, the incentive may provide a valuable contribution to a country's innovation policy and should be pursued.

7.2.2. Incentive Form

Guideline 2(a): Governments Should Select Investment or Profit-Related Incentives According to their Need to Increase Investment Quantity (Investment-Related Preferred) or Quality (Profit-Related Preferred) (see [3.2] and [3.3])

Investment-related incentives are likely to be more effective than exit-related incentives at stimulating increased investment because they generally provide an

[6] Ann Leamon, Maria Susana Garcia-Robles and Josh Lerner, 'Best Practices in Creating a Venture Capital Ecosystem' (Multilateral Investment Fund of Inter-American Development Bank, December 2012) 35.

immediate benefit to investors that is not tied to investment success. Investment-related incentives may therefore be more appropriate in nascent venture capital markets where governments want to attract new entrants. However, investment-related incentives also tend to be expensive to provide, and carry risks of poor post-investment behaviour, compromised investment quality and market flooding.[7] Governments should temper these risks against the need to increase capital in the market. An appropriate approach may be to 'kick start' nascent markets using investment-related incentives, before phasing them out and replacing them with profit-related incentives, where necessary, as the market matures.

Profit-related incentives, on the other hand, are more likely to encourage high-quality investment and positive post-investment behaviour, because they only reward successful investments.[8] Profit-related incentives are also likely to be one of the cheapest incentive forms for governments to provide (particularly because they only subsidise profitable investments) and are not particularly vulnerable to abuse. However, they may provide less additionality than investment-related incentives to the extent that they reward investment that would have occurred anyway (making them redundant and increasing their deadweight costs).[9] It is recommended that profit-related incentives be used in more mature venture capital markets where governments want to help encourage investment quality (rather than quantity) while still incentivising venture capital investment.

Guideline 2(b): Governments Should Avoid the Use of Loss-Related Incentives and Should Instead Provide Symmetric Tax Treatment of Gains and Losses (see [3.4])

Loss-related incentives (tax-based loss relief and guarantees) are not recommended for use as venture capital incentives for a variety of reasons: they are likely to skew the risk–reward balance too far in favour of the private sector (which may encourage poor investment behaviour and low-quality investments); they tend to be expensive for governments to provide; and they may create a negative perception of the venture capital sector. Evidence from the UK's Enterprise Investment Scheme found that loss relief was not a key factor in most investors' decision to invest under the scheme (only 11 per cent of investors rated loss relief as essential to their investment decision).[10] This indicates that loss relief is unlikely to have a strong motivating effect on Enterprise Investment Scheme investors and may constitute a windfall where it is provided.

[7] See European Commission, 'Effectiveness of Tax Incentives for Venture Capital and Business Angels to Foster the Investment of SMEs and Start-ups: Final Report' (Taxation and Customs Union, 2017) Working Paper No 68, 202.

[8] See ibid 4.

[9] See ibid 70.

[10] Matt Colahan, John Higton, Lucy Royce, Rebecca Klahr, Jayesh Navin Shah and Marc Cowling, 'The Use and Impact of Venture Capital Schemes' (HM Revenue & Customs, February 2016) Research Report 355, 7.

Instead of offering loss-related incentives, it is recommended that governments provide investors with symmetric tax treatment in relation to their investments. Research indicates that symmetric tax treatment may stimulate the 'optimal' degree of risk-taking, unlike asymmetric loss relief, which has the capacity to trigger 'excessive' risk-taking.[11] Governments should therefore only provide tax-based loss relief where gains are taxed, and only to the extent necessary to bring the treatment of gains and losses into balance (eg if gains are fully taxable then losses should be fully deductable).[12]

Guideline 2(c): Governments Should Consider Implementing Direct Incentives Over Tax Incentives for Equity and Cost Reasons (see [3.2], [3.3])

Tax incentives and direct incentives such as grants and preferential returns can be similar in many respects. However, tax incentives may be less equitable than these kinds of direct incentives because they are generally only useful where entities have a tax liability. Direct incentives allow for easier tracking and prediction of incentive costs, but may be less politically attractive for governments for this reason. It is recommended that governments prioritise direct incentives over tax incentives in order to increase equity, encourage cross-border investment and help control incentive costs.

Nevertheless, the use of tax incentives is generally acceptable (particularly refundable tax credits, which avoid equity issues),[13] and this recommendation does not go so far as to say that direct incentives will always be preferable to tax incentives in every situation.

Guideline 2(d): Governments Should Consider the Following Recommendations and Cautions on Specific Incentive Forms (see [3.2] to [3.4])

While there is 'no single recipe for success' in selecting an incentive form[14] and most forms can work as venture capital incentives if designed well, some incentive forms are more appropriate (ie fit for purpose) than others. Table 10 sets out

[11] Pamela Palazzi, 'Taxation and Innovation' (OECD, 2011) OECD Taxation Working Papers No 9, 61–62.

[12] ibid. As noted in ch 3, the author previously held the opposite view (see Stephen Barkoczy and Tamara Wilkinson, *Incentivising Angels: A Comparative Framework of Tax Incentives for Start-Up Investors* (Springer, 2019) 102), but has since reconsidered on the basis of further consideration of Palazzi's theoretical research and Colahan et al's findings in relation to the UK's Enterprise Investment Scheme loss relief.

[13] See Philipp Ständer, 'Public Policies to Promote Venture Capital: How to Get National and EU Measures in Sync' (Jacques Delors Institut, 31 August 2017) 16; Stanley S Surrey and Paul R McDaniel, *Tax Expenditures* (Harvard University Press, 1985) 110.

[14] PricewaterhouseCoopers (n 1) 3.

recommendations and cautions for each incentive form. Implicit in the table is the understanding that all incentives provide some level of incentive for increased investment (whether large or small), and all incentives are provided at a cost (again, whether large or small). These considerations have not been factored into the table because they are difficult to compare on a purely theoretical basis and little relevant empirical research on this issue has yet been undertaken.

Table 10 Recommendations and cautions for each incentive form

Incentive form	Pros	Cons	Conclusion
Tax credits [3.2.1]	Stable as not based on tax rate; equitable when refundable	Inequitable when not refundable as only valuable to entities that pay tax; may be used for tax-minimisation purposes	**Recommend, but consider direct alternatives.** Tax credits in general have no major problems, but grants (or refundable tax credits) may provide more equitable alternatives[a]
Tax deductions [3.2.2]	None	Unstable; inequitable as only valuable to entities that pay tax; may be used for tax minimisation purposes	**Do not recommend.** Other forms are more appropriate (ie grants, tax credits)
Grants [3.2.3]	Stable; equitable; easy to calculate incentive costs	None	**Recommend.** Grants are an appropriate investment-related incentive form
Equity co-investment [3.2.4]	Help develop investor and fund-manager expertise	May be particularly likely to lead to oversupply/crowding out if too much capital is injected into the market	**Recommend with caution.** Equity co-investment incentives can help market development, but evidence of their impact is unclear
Loans [3.2.5]	Help develop investor and fund-manager expertise	The need for loan repayment can prejudice investment decisions and returns to the private sector;[b] may be particularly likely to lead to oversupply/crowding out if too much capital is injected into the market	**Do not recommend.** Equity co-investment incentives (with preferential returns if necessary) are more appropriate

(continued)

Table 10 *(Continued)*

Incentive form	Pros	Cons	Conclusion
Visa incentives [3.2.6]	Provide a cheap way for governments to bring more capital into the market	Investors may not be high-quality investors as they may invest only to receive a visa	**Neutral.** More information is required about the effects of visa incentives on the quality of investors and investments
Tax exemptions [3.3.1]	Stable as not tied to an entity's tax rate; may encourage high-quality investment by rewarding successes	Inequitable as only valuable to entities that pay tax and more valuable to entities with higher rates of tax; exemptions for fund managers may provide windfalls	**Recommend, but consider direct alternative.** Tax exemptions on exit taxes are appropriate, but exemptions on dividends and fund manager profits are unlikely to stimulate much increased investment
Reduced tax rates [3.3.2]	Stable as not tied to an entity's tax rate; may encourage high-quality investment by rewarding successes	Inequitable as only valuable to entities that pay tax and more valuable to entities with higher rates of tax; reduced tax rates for fund managers may provide windfalls	**Recommend, but consider direct alternative.** Reduced tax rates are appropriate but may provide less of an incentive effect than exemptions (but are also generally cheaper to provide)
Exit grants [3.3.3]	Stable; equitable; may encourage high-quality investment by rewarding successes; easy to calculate incentive costs	May be unfamiliar to many investors; may provide windfalls where investments would have occurred anyway	**Recommend.** Exit grants fulfil a similar function to exit tax exemptions or reductions, but their costs are likely to be easier to calculate
Reinvestment relief [3.3.4]	Stable as not based on tax rate	Inequitable as only valuable to entities that pay tax and more valuable to entities with higher rates of tax; can be complicated; may be used for tax-minimisation purposes; may provide windfalls where investments would have occurred anyway	**Neutral.** Reinvestment relief may be appropriate, depending on how it is designed, but more evidence of its effectiveness would be useful

(continued)

Table 10 ***(Continued)***

Incentive form	Pros	Cons	Conclusion
Preferential returns [3.3.5]	Stable; equitable; may encourage high-quality investment by rewarding successes	May encourage poor investment decisions and behaviour by removing too much risk from the private sector; may provide windfalls where investments would have occurred anyway	**Recommend with caution.** Preferential returns can sometimes be useful but should not remove too much private sector risk or they may exacerbate poor investment behaviour
Tax-based loss relief [3.4.1]	None	May encourage poor investment decisions; can be expensive to provide; may provide windfalls where investments would have occurred anyway	**Do not recommend.** Tax-based loss relief should only be provided if it is necessary for the purpose of providing symmetric tax treatment of gains and losses
Investment guarantees [3.4.2]	None	May encourage poor investment decisions; may provide windfalls where investments would have occurred anyway	**Do not recommend.** Guarantees are not recommended

[a] Stanley S Surrey, *Pathways to Tax Reform: The Concept of Tax Expenditures* (Harvard University Press, 1973) 99.

[b] United Nations Economic Commission for Europe, *Financing Innovative Development: Comparative Review of the Experiences of UNECE Countries in Early Stage Financing* (United Nations Publications, 2007) 84; See, eg Royal Norwegian Ministry of Trade and Industry, 'National Seed Capital Scheme' (December 2012) 5–6, investinor.no/wp-content/uploads/nhd-notifisering-nye-landsdekkende-sakornfond_jan-2013.pdf.

7.2.3. Targeting

Guideline 3(a): Governments Should Consider the Following Recommendations and Cautions in Targeting Direct Investors (see [4.2.1])

Some methods of targeting direct investors are more appropriate than others. Table 11 sets out recommendations and cautions for the various kinds of direct investor targeting criteria discussed in chapter four. Implicit in the table is the fact that all targeting criteria increase the cost and complexity of providing and administering incentives (some more than others), and the more criteria that are in place, the more the complexity of the incentive is increased (but the better targeted it may be).

Table 11 Recommendations and cautions for the various kinds of direct investor targeting criteria

Targeting criteria	Pros	Cons	Conclusion
Entity criteria [4.2.1.1]	Requiring investors to be individuals may help ensure that they are 'genuine' angels that will focus on early-stage investment	Excluding family offices, partnerships or syndicates may be overly restrictive as many genuine angels invest this way	**Neutral.** The appropriateness of these criteria depend on incentive policy aims
Wealth criteria [4.2.1.2]	Protect financially constrained investors from the risks of venture capital investment; wealthy investors have the resources to bear failed investments; excluding retail investors is unlikely to significantly reduce the pool of investors	May slightly reduce the pool of eligible investors	**Recommend.** Wealth criteria serve an appropriate investor protection purpose
Experience criteria [4.2.1.2]	Experienced investors may make better investment decisions, contribute more value-adding activities and produce more successful investments (higher investment quality); excluding retail investors is unlikely to significantly reduce the pool of investors	May exclude new entrants to the sector	**Recommend with caution.** Experience criteria should be imposed in conjunction with wealth criteria so that new entrants are not excluded
Domestic residence criteria [4.1.2.3]	Investment benefits accrue locally, investors are familiar with the local market and may be more motivated to provide value-adding activities	Excludes cross-border investments	**Neutral.** The appropriateness of these criteria depend on incentive policy aims
Arm's length/independence criteria [4.2.1.4]	Targets genuine third-party investors and helps avoid incentive misuse and deadweight costs	May exclude investors who take a formal role in their investee companies	**Recommend with caveat.** Arm's length/independence criteria should make provision for the participation of investors in investee

(continued)

Table 11 *(Continued)*

Targeting criteria	Pros	Cons	Conclusion
			businesses, because this helps support direct investment and the provision of value-adding activities by direct investors.[a] This may be done by only imposing arm's-length/independence criteria at the time an investment is made

[a] See European Commission (n 7) 77–78.

Guideline 3(b): Governments Should Consider the Following Recommendations and Cautions in Targeting Funds, Fund Managers and Passive Investors (see [4.2.2])

Some methods of targeting funds, fund managers and passive investors are more appropriate than others. Table 12 sets out recommendations and cautions for the various kinds of fund, fund manager and passive investor targeting criteria discussed in chapter four. As with Table 11, it is implicit that all targeting criteria increase the cost and complexity of providing and administering incentives (some more than others), and the more criteria that are in place, the more the complexity of the incentive is increased (but the better targeted it may be).

Table 12 Recommendations and cautions for the various kinds of fund, fund manager and passive investor targeting criteria

Targeting criteria	Pros	Cons	Conclusion
Minimum and maximum fund size criteria [4.2.2.1]	Ensure that funds have sufficient size to be commercially viable, to cover investment costs and to support investees through multiple funding rounds;[a] ensure that funds do not become too large, which could lead to inefficiency, reduced value-adding activities and investment drift	None, provided limits are appropriate to the market	**Recommend.** Minimum and maximum fund size criteria are generally appropriate provided limits are consistent with the market

(continued)

Table 12 *(Continued)*

Targeting criteria	Pros	Cons	Conclusion
Fund structure criteria [4.2.2.2]	Requiring funds to structure as limited partnerships means they are closed-end funds	May be unduly restrictive	**Neutral.** Fund structure criteria may be appropriate depending on an incentive's policy aims but should not unduly restrict funds from structuring in commercially preferred ways
Fund lifetime criteria [4.2.2.2]	Provide an end date for the provision of government incentives to a fund and a date for when investors (and the government, where relevant) can expect to receive returns	Economic conditions and other factors might make it impractical for funds to divest all their investments by a certain date[b]	**Recommend with flexibility.** Incentives should provide that funds have a lifetime in line with commercial norms, and may want to allow an optional extension for divestment that can be utilised as necessary
Fund manager experience criteria [4.2.2.3]	Fund managers with some experience in early-stage investing are more likely to make high-quality investments and contribute value-adding activities[c]	Requiring fund managers to be experienced may exclude some new entrants to the market	**Recommend with caution.** Experience criteria should not exclude new entrants with relevant experience in other kinds of investment if the incentive is intended to expand the venture capital sector
New fund manager criteria [4.2.2.3]	Encouraging new entrants can help deepen the market	New fund managers are less likely to produce high-quality investments and investment successes and may not provide the same level of value-adding services as experienced fund managers	**Neutral.** Targeting new fund managers may be appropriate in some situations depending on an incentive's policy aims

(continued)

Table 12 ***(Continued)***

Targeting criteria	Pros	Cons	Conclusion
Investment plan criteria [4.2.2.4]	Help ensure that fund managers have the intention and capacity to operate within the ambit of an incentive	Fund managers are almost certain to have an investment plan in place without an explicit requirement to do so; requiring an investment plan to be assessed by the regulator may add unnecessary administrative and compliance burdens	**Neutral.** These criteria may be redundant; more information on their effect would be useful
Value-adding activity criteria [4.2.2.4]	Send a positive message to incentive recipients about the kind of investment behaviour that is expected of them, may increase additionality and investment quality	Difficult to enforce	**Recommend.** Even if these criteria only provide a signalling effect to investors, they may be useful
Fund manager compensation criteria [4.2.2.4]	Where fund managers receive lower management fees and higher carried interest payments, they may be more likely to focus on producing successful investments and raising investment quality; this is also likely to help align the interests of fund managers, passive investors and the government	High-quality fund managers may be deterred from participating	**Recommend.** Fund manager compensation should be competitive and in line with commercial standards
Fund manager investment criteria [4.2.2.4]	Requiring fund managers to invest some of their own capital in the fund they manage may encourage the provision of value-adding activities	None	**Recommend.** Investment requirements are likely to be beneficial but should not require fund managers to invest

(continued)

Table 12 ***(Continued)***

Targeting criteria	Pros	Cons	Conclusion
			a burdensome amount of capital (as this could reduce accessibility and participation)
Sophisticated passive investor criteria [4.2.2.5]	Excluding retail investors from being passive investors protects them from losses	May slightly shrink the pool of investors	**Neutral.** Not many retail investors invest in venture capital funds, so these criteria may be redundant
Passive investor foreign residence criteria [4.2.2.6]	Foreign passive investors can increase the amount of capital in the market and may bring foreign expertise	Allowing only foreign investors to participate excludes domestic investors and may therefore shrink the pool of available capital (and may make tax incentives more likely to be deemed harmful tax practices under BEPS Action 5)	**Neutral.** These criteria may be appropriate depending on an incentive's policy aims. In general, incentives should encourage both foreign and domestic investors rather than excluding either group

[a] See Wilson (n 4) 11; Colin M Mason, 'Public Policy Support for the Informal Venture Capital Market in Europe: A Critical Review' (2009) 27(5) *International Small Business Journal* 536, 538–39; United Nations Economic Commission for Europe (Table 10b) 43.
[b] Robert Baldock, 'An Assessment of the Business Impacts of the UK's Enterprise Capital Funds' (2016) 34(8) *Environment and Planning C: Government and Policy* 1556, 1560–61.
[c] See OECD, 'Government Venture Capital for Technology-Based Firms' (1997) OCDE/GD(97)201, 20; Cromwell Schmisseur (n 5) 6; Ronald J Gilson, 'Engineering a Venture Capital Market: Lessons from the American Experience' (2003) 55 *Stanford Law Review* 1067, 1099–1100; Leamon et al (n 6) 45.

Guideline 3(c): Governments Should Consider the Following Recommendations and Cautions in Targeting Investments (see [4.3])

Some methods of targeting investments are more appropriate than others. Table 13 sets out recommendations and cautions for the various kinds of investment-targeting criteria discussed in chapter four. As with Tables 11 and 12 above, it is implicit that all targeting criteria increase the cost and complexity of providing and administering incentives (some more than others), and the more criteria that are in place, the more the complexity of the incentive is increased (but the better targeted it may be).

Table 13 Recommendations and cautions for the various kinds of investment targeting criteria

Targeting criteria	Pros	Cons	Conclusion
Equity criteria [4.3.1]	Equity investment is more likely to encourage active investment and may facilitate knowledge spillovers between investors and investees;[a] equity investment may therefore help produce high-quality investees	Commercial venture capital transactions often involve a range of debt and hybrid interests; requiring investments to only be made in the form of equity may discourage participation	**Recommend.** Equity criteria are appropriate, although some flexibility regarding convertible interests is unlikely to be detrimental and may help encourage participation[b]
New equity criteria [4.3.1]	Ensure that investment capital is channelled to the issuing startup; investment in second-hand equity does not channel new capital to investees and is likely to represent a deadweight cost	May prevent investors from increasing their ownership and control over an investee as they would do in commercial transactions	**Recommend.** New equity criteria are appropriate. Allowing some flexibility around the purchase of second-hand equity may be useful to facilitate investment (although it should not be incentivised)
Risk criteria [4.3.1]	Help target incentives at genuine venture capital investments, avoid incentive abuse and reduce deadweight costs	None	**Recommend.** Risk criteria are appropriate
Maximum investment/ interest criteria [4.3.2]	Encourage investors to diversify their investments; help prevent investment drift; may help control incentive costs[c]	May prevent follow-on investments; investments may be commercially unviable if the investment limit is too low; may be considered overly restrictive where they prevent investors from taking controlling stakes in investees	**Recommend.** Maximum investment or interest criteria perform important functions but should not be too low and should provide for follow-on investments (even if they are not expressly incentivised)

(continued)

Table 13 ***(Continued)***

Targeting criteria	**Pros**	**Cons**	**Conclusion**
Maximum investment limits per investor [4.3.2]	Help control incentive costs (particularly in regard to investment-related incentives)	May discourage investment over the annual limit	**Recommend.** Maximum annual investment criteria are particularly important for investment-related incentives such as tax credits as their costs can easily blow out
Investment timing criteria [4.3.3]	Ensure that investments are made within a certain time frame so that investors and governments have their capital returned in a timely way	Have the capacity to rush investment decisions, flood the market with capital and lead to suboptimal investments[d]	**Do not recommend.** Closed-end fund structures provide the same timing impetus while not putting the same artificial pressure on fund managers. Where timing criteria are used, they should allow investors a long enough time period to make careful investments
Minimum holding period criteria [4.3.3]	Help prevent abuse of incentives for tax purposes; combat short-termism and provide a signalling effect to investors; provide a measure of stability for investees; may facilitate knowledge transfer between investors and startups[e]	May be overly restrictive and deter investors where they are too long	**Recommend.** Minimum holding period criteria may increase both investor and investment quality, but should be of an appropriate duration (eg 1–3 years)
Maximum holding period criteria [4.3.3]	Limit the cost of incentives	Penalise investors for holding on to investments until they mature; may encourage premature divestment[f]	**Do not recommend.** Other methods for limiting incentive cost are more appropriate, such as curtailing incentives after a certain date (but not removing them completely); curtailing incentives after an

(continued)

Table 13 *(Continued)*

Targeting criteria	Pros	Cons	Conclusion
			investee reaches a certain size; and using a closed-end fund structure

[a] See European Commission (n 7) 78, 89, 179; Stephen Barkoczy, Tamara Wilkinson, Ann L Monotti and Mark Davison, *Innovation and Venture Capital Law and Policy* (Federation Press, 2016) 58–60.
[b] See European Commission (n 7) 14, 179.
[c] ibid 14, 202.
[d] See Duruflé (n 5) 16; OECD, 'Government Venture Capital' (Table 12c) 15; Leamon et al (n 6) 46, 54.
[e] European Commission (n 7) 14, 80, 202.
[f] ibid 14, 89.

Guideline 3(d): Governments Should Consider the Following Recommendations and Cautions in Targeting Investees (see [4.4])

Some methods of targeting investees are more appropriate than others. Table 14 sets out recommendations and cautions for the various kinds of investee targeting criteria discussed in chapter four. As with Tables 11–13 above, it is implicit that all targeting criteria increase the cost and complexity of providing and administering incentives (some more than others), and the more criteria that are in place, the more the complexity of the incentive is increased (but the better targeted it may be).

Table 14 Recommendations and cautions for the various kinds of investee targeting criteria

Targeting criteria	Pros	Cons	Conclusion
Maximum size criteria [4.4.1]	Make incentives more effective and efficient because small companies are likely to produce more additionality than larger companies	May exclude some deserving investees	**Recommend.** Targeting early-stage companies using a range of criteria (ie size, age and/or stage) can help counter investment drift while not being overly restrictive (and thereby excluding potentially worthy investees)[a]
Maximum age criteria [4.4.1]	Younger companies may be more likely to need government support and produce additionality than older companies	Age criteria may disqualify slow-growing startups from being supported under incentives (including those in regional areas)	**Recommend.** Targeting early-stage companies using a range of criteria (ie size, age and/or stage) can help counter investment drift while not being overly restrictive (and thereby

(continued)

Table 14 ***(Continued)***

Targeting criteria	**Pros**	**Cons**	**Conclusion**
			excluding potentially worthy investees). A maximum investee age (or time since the company began trading) of 5–10 years is likely to be appropriate in most jurisdictions, based on common practice
Stage criteria [4.4.1]	Provides a more flexible alternative to size and age criteria	Determined subjectively so can be unclear/difficult to assess	**Neutral.** Targeting early-stage companies using a range of criteria (ie size, age and/or stage) can help counter investment drift while not being overly restrictive (and thereby excluding potentially worthy investees)
Unlisted criteria [4.4.1]	Help reduce deadweight and redundancy costs, unlikely to exclude deserving startups	None	**Recommend.** Unlisted criteria are appropriate
Sector criteria [4.4.2]	May stimulate additionality by targeting innovative, high-growth or underserved sectors	Can result in favouritism and picking winners; may increase inefficiency and market distortion; may exclude worthy opportunities in other sectors[b]	**Do not recommend.** Past experience has indicated that sector criteria are not appropriate or beneficial. Sector exclusions should be used instead
Sector exclusions [4.4.2]	Excluding sectors such as finance and real estate from incentives may increase additionality and reduce redundancy and deadweight costs[c]	Sector exclusions may prevent genuinely innovative companies from participating in incentives	**Recommend with flexibility.** Sector exclusions are appropriate but should not be so restrictive that they prevent genuinely innovative companies from participating in incentives

(continued)

Table 14 *(Continued)*

Targeting criteria	Pros	Cons	Conclusion
Domestic residence criteria [4.4.3]	Ensure that the benefits of incentives (and any associated spillovers) accrue locally[d]	Can impose artificial barriers to migration, which may impact investee success and potentially depress investment returns	**Recommend with flexibility.** Residence criteria should only apply at the point of an initial investment (or for a limited time afterwards)
Regional location criteria [4.4.3]	Investing in regional investees may produce high levels of additionality	Regional areas often lack high-quality deal flow, the critical mass necessary to sustain venture capital markets and/or the components of a functioning innovation system.[e] Requiring investors to invest regionally may compromise investment success and returns, lead to investment drift and/or create oversupply[f]	**Do not recommend.** Past experience suggests that regional location criteria are not generally appropriate or beneficial
Diversity criteria [4.4.4]	May increase the number of diverse entrepreneurs receiving funding	Investors that are required to fund diverse investees only may struggle to find sufficient deal flow	**Do not recommend.** Incentives should include a preference for diverse investees, but should not explicitly require diverse investments to be made
High growth potential criteria [4.4.5]	May help target the incentive towards high-potential investees and therefore stimulate additionality	Subjective and difficult to measure	**Recommend.** High growth potential criteria may provide a useful targeting and signalling effect
Innovation criteria [4.4.5]	May help target the incentive towards innovative investees and therefore stimulate additionality	Subjective and difficult to measure	**Recommend.** Innovation criteria may provide a useful targeting and signalling effect

(continued)

Table 14 *(Continued)*

Targeting criteria	Pros	Cons	Conclusion
Need for funding criteria [4.4.5]	May increase additionality and reduce redundancy by not funding companies that could receive investment elsewhere	May encourage adverse selection by focusing incentives too closely on unviable startups	**Do not recommend.** Unlisted criteria provide a more appropriate alternative

[a] ibid 13, 176–77.
[b] See International Monetary Fund, Organisation for Economic Co-operation and Development, United Nations and World Bank, 'Options for Low Income Countries' Effective and Efficient Use of Tax Incentives for Investment' (Report to the G-20 Development Working Group, October 2015) 22; European Commission (n 7) 75.
[c] See Stephen Barkoczy and Peter Edmundson, 'Australasian and South East Asian Venture Capital Tax Expenditure Programs' (2009) 37(1) *Intertax* 56, 72; European Commission (n 7) 18, 76.
[d] European Commission (n 7) 76, 132.
[e] See Federico Munari and Laura Toschi, 'Assessing the Impact of Public Venture Capital Programmes in the United Kingdom: Do Regional Characteristics Matter?' (2015) 30(2) *Journal of Business Venturing* 205, 209, 219; Rebecca Harding, 'Venture Capital and the Regions: Not Always the Most Appropriate Funding Mechanism' (2000) 7(1) *New Economy* 49, 51–52; Jun Li, 'Government-Backed Venture Capital as a Science, Technology and Innovation (STI) Policy Instrument: A Chinese Perspective' (2016) 7(1) *STI Policy Review* 66, 82–83; Leamon et al (n 6) 47; BVCA and NESTA, 'From Funding Gaps to Thin Markets: UK Government Support for Early-Stage Venture Capital' (September 2009) 26.
[f] See Harding (ibid) 53; Munari and Toschi (ibid) 209; Avnimelech et al (n 4) 15.

7.2.4. Implementation, Administration and Monitoring

Guideline 4(a): Incentive Rules Should be Implemented Legislatively or Quasi-Legislatively (see [5.2.1])

Incentives that are implemented through legislation provide the highest levels of certainty and equity for recipients and transparency and accountability for governments because they are generally enacted in a more visible way and are more difficult to change on an ad hoc basis than incentives implemented in other ways.[15] Incentives that are implemented on a quasi-legislative basis (such as through programme guidelines) provide less certainty and transparency for recipients and potential recipients than legislatively based incentives because governments can change quasi-legislative rules more easily and with less oversight (although it might also be said on a positive note that this increases the extent to which the incentives can be responsively improved). Both legislatively and quasi-legislatively

[15] See Sebastian James, 'Tax and Non-Tax Incentives and Investments: Evidence and Policy Implications' (Investment Climate Advisory Services of the World Bank Group, September 2013) 38.

based incentives are preferable to incentives that are implemented informally or without specific, publicly available rules (ie completely at governmental discretion), as these kinds of incentives provide very low certainty and also increase the potential for incentive corruption, such as agency capture (see Guideline 4(i)).

Guideline 4(b): Incentive Rules Should be Clearly Drafted, Enforceable, Consistent and Accessible (see [5.2.1])

Incentives rules should be well drafted and written in plain language in order to make them easy for recipients (and regulators) to understand and apply. They should be made publicly available online and kept up to date. Changes to incentive rules should be communicated clearly and ideally in advance.[16] Governments should assist recipients to navigate and access incentives by providing detailed guidance on their application (eg the UK's Venture Capital Schemes Manual).[17] Following these suggestions will help promote incentive equity, certainty, accessibility, effectiveness and efficiency.

Guideline 4(c): Incentives Should have Clear Time Frames (Whether they are Time-Limited or Open-Ended) that are Consistent with their Budgets (see [5.2.2])

Governments should plan for incentives to be in place over the long term as they often take many years to produce results. Incentives that are started and stopped within a short time frame are likely to struggle to reach their intended policy aims,[18] and the resources put into providing an incentive can therefore be wasted if it is terminated too early. Incentives that have a clear end date may provide certainty to recipients, facilitate financial forward planning and encourage investors to change their investment behaviour more effectively than open-ended incentives.[19] Governments should therefore consider implementing end dates (sunset provisions) when they introduce their incentives. Time-limited incentives may include an explicit possibility of renewal if they perform well and remain necessary,[20] although this may decrease certainty. When incentives are terminated, advance notice of this termination should be provided so that participants can account for windfall losses. Incentives may sometimes need to be rolled out on a gradual basis to avoid flooding the market with capital.

[16] See European Commission (n 7) 182, 198.

[17] HM Revenue & Customs, 'Venture Capital Schemes Manual' (22 March 2021) www.gov.uk/hmrc-internal-manuals/venture-capital-schemes-manual.

[18] Wilson (n 4) 30.

[19] See International Monetary Fund et al (Table 14b) 23; US Department of the Treasury, *The Case for Temporary 100 Percent Expensing: Encouraging Business to Expand Now by Lowering the Cost of Investment* (Report, 29 October 2010) 6.

[20] See Mark Burton and Kerrie Sadiq, *Tax Expenditure Management: A Critical Assessment* (Cambridge University Press, 2013) 222.

Guideline 4(d): Governments Should Implement Measures to Control Incentive Costs (see [5.2.3])

Incentives that operate according to budgets with clear funding limits are less likely to experience cost blowouts; budgets can therefore help avoid premature termination or curtailment of incentives. Even with a budget in place, governments should be aware of controlling incentive costs. Some ways they can do this are:

- minimising administrative and compliance costs by ensuring that incentive rules are clear and easy to follow (see Guideline 4(b)), streamlining application processes and providing for online applications (see Guideline 4(f)), and making sure that reporting requirements are consistent and concise (see Guideline 4(h));
- setting a clear time frame for incentives (and budgeting accordingly) (see Guideline 4(c));
- targeting investors, investments and investees tightly to control uptake and limit the provision of incentives (for instance, through fund lifetime criteria or maximum annual investment criteria) (see Guidelines 3(a) to (d));[21]
- considering whether incentives are overly generous (and reducing their value if they are) to increase efficiency and reduce deadweight;[22] and
- limiting opportunities for incentive abuse and misuse (see Guideline 4(i)).

Guideline 4(e): Governments Should Provide Regulators with Sufficient Training and Resources (see [5.3.1])

In order to administer an incentive effectively, regulators need to have appropriately trained and experienced staff (ideally with private sector experience and a thorough understanding of early-stage investment, startups and the venture capital industry).[23] This experience is particularly important for decision-making processes. Governments may need to arrange for regulatory staff to be trained,[24] and should also ensure that regulators have sufficient financial and administrative resources to perform their functions effectively.[25]

[21] See Stephen Barkoczy and Daniel Sandler, *Government Venture Capital Incentives: A Multi-Jurisdiction Comparative Analysis* (Australian Tax Research Foundation, 2007) 37–38.

[22] ibid 36.

[23] See Josh Lerner, 'When Bureaucrats Meet Entrepreneurs: The Design of Effective "Public Venture Capital" Programmes' (2002) 112(477) *Economic Journal* F73, F80. See also Gordon Murray, Marc Cowling, Weixi Liu and Olga Kalinowska-Beszczynska, 'Government Co-Financed "Hybrid" Venture Capital Programmes: Generalizing Developed Economy Experience and its Relevance to Emerging Nations' (Kauffman International Research and Policy Roundtable, 11–12 March 2012) 9–11, 22.

[24] See Cromwell Schmisseur (n 5) 6.

[25] See Alex Easson, *Tax Incentives for Foreign Direct Investment* (Kluwer Law International, 2004) 159; Ashley C Brown, Jon Stern, Bernard Tenenbaum and Defne Gencer, *Handbook for Evaluating Infrastructure Regulatory Systems* (World Bank, 2006) 217.

Guideline 4(f): Incentives Should Implement Efficient Application and Approval Processes (see [5.3.2])

Application and approval processes help protect the integrity and efficiency of incentives by only allowing eligible recipients to benefit from incentives in relation to their eligible investments,[26] and can also help regulators collect information about incentives and their recipients. Approval processes should be available online and should be streamlined and easy to navigate, with clear eligibility and/or merit criteria (see Guideline 4(a)), so that they do not unnecessarily increase administration and compliance costs.[27] Regulators should communicate clearly and promptly with incentive recipients[28] and attempt to process decisions as quickly as possible.

Guideline 4(g): Regulatory Decision-Making Should be Transparent, Consistent and Defensible (see [5.3.3])

Decisions made on a transparent, consistent and defensible basis increase incentive equity, create certainty and confidence for investors, and help reduce the scope for incentive corruption. Incentive rules should explain how applicants are assessed against the relevant criteria and how each criterion is weighted.[29] Decisions-makers and the roles that they play should also be clearly articulated.[30] These measures help govern regulatory decision-making and limit the arbitrary exercise of discretion.[31] Making regulatory and administrative decisions publicly available builds a body of precedent that may help recipients predict the likely outcomes of decisions and increase regulatory consistency.[32]

Regulators should have final decision-making authority, and should fully enforce their decisions, standards and rules in order to increase incentive effectiveness, efficiency and integrity.[33]

Guideline 4(h): Incentives Should Include Mandatory Reporting Requirements (see [5.4.1])

Incentives should require regulators, recipients and investees to comply with reporting requirements that provide for the collection of data on the activities of

[26] See OECD, 'Tax Incentives for R&D and Innovation' (2016) 5.

[27] See European Commission (n 7) 153.

[28] Productivity Commission, 'Identifying and Evaluating Regulation Reforms' (December 2011) xv.

[29] See Department of Finance, *Commonwealth Grants Rules and Guidelines 2017* (2017) 21; Deborah A Stone, *Policy Paradox and Political Reason* (HarperCollins, 1988) 235.

[30] Department of Finance (n 29) 17.

[31] International Monetary Fund et al (Table 14b) 24.

[32] World Bank, *World Development Report 2005: A Better Investment Climate for Everyone* (Oxford University Press, 2004) 102.

[33] See Brown et al (n 25) 187, 192.

recipients and investees. Collecting data in this way facilitates the monitoring of incentive operation, costs, targeting and performance,[34] and is likely to be subsequently useful for incentive evaluation.[35] Reporting requirements should be clear and streamlined in order to encourage compliance and limit administrative costs. Governments should maintain consistency in reporting requirements and definitions to avoid generating confusion and extra work for recipients.[36] Data that may be useful to collect includes the number of applicants, the number of incentive recipients, the investee sector or industry, the investee stage of development, the investment staging and syndication, the number of investments made per investor/fund manager, the location of the investments/investees, how investments are exited, the cost of providing and administering incentives, and records of decisions made.[37]

Guideline 4(i): Incentives Should be Designed to Minimise the Risks of Abuse, Misuse and Corruption (see [5.4.2])

Incentive design can minimise risks of abuse and misuse in several ways (note that these will not be relevant in relation to every incentive):

- by using approval processes to ensure the eligibility of recipients and activities (ie not using a completely self-assessed as-of-right process) (see Guideline 4(f));[38]
- by using reporting requirements to maintain oversight of investor and investee activities (see Guideline 4(h));
- by excluding related-party investments to ensure that investments are genuine third-party investments (see Guideline 3(a));
- by requiring fund managers to invest a certain amount of their own capital in a fund to align their interests with those of the government (see Guideline 3(b));
- by requiring investments to be made in the form of new equity in order to avoid redundancy (see Guideline 3(c));
- by requiring investments to be held at risk to avoid redundancy (see Guideline 3(c));
- by imposing minimum holding periods on investments (particularly in relation investment-related incentives) to avoid misuse for tax purposes (see Guideline 3(c));

[34] See ibid 193, 197; James (n 15) 35.
[35] See Cumming and Johan, 'Government Venture Capital Research' (n 3) 125.
[36] See Productivity Commission, 'Identifying and Evaluating Regulation Reforms' (n 28) xiv–xv.
[37] See broadly Douglas Cumming and Sofia Johan, 'Pre-Seed Government Venture Capital Funds' (2009) 7(1) *Journal of International Entrepreneurship* 26, 32–33.
[38] See OECD, 'Tax Incentives' (n 26) 5.

- by excluding investees in certain non-innovative sectors from receiving investment under incentives to minimise redundancy (see Guideline 3(d));
- by using specific anti-avoidance mechanisms such as clawback provisions to remove recipients' access to incentive benefits if they do not meet targeting or other incentive criteria;[39] and
- by avoiding the use of incentive forms that reward poor investor behaviour (such as loss relief or guarantees (see Guideline 2(b)).

Governments can help guard against incentive corruption by requiring regulatory transparency, particularly with regard to recipient approval processes, and by requiring regulators to make decisions based on publicly available rules (see Guidelines 4(a) and 4(g)).[40] Incentives should limit the opportunities for lobbying and rent-seeking behaviour by recipients and interest groups and should prevent incentive recipients from influencing approval and other decision-making processes.[41] These processes should be impartial and should not favour incumbent recipients.[42]

7.2.5. Evaluation and Measuring Success

Guideline 5(a): Governments Should Evaluate their Incentives in Accordance with a Planned Evaluation Strategy (see [6.2])

It is important for governments to evaluate their incentives to gauge how well they operate and how effective and efficient they are at achieving their policy aims.[43] Both process and impact evaluations are important for identifying how and why incentives works,[44] and both kinds of evaluation should be provided for in an incentive's evaluation strategy.

Governments should create evaluation strategies for their incentives when they are implemented, in order to facilitate data collection and to make sure that evaluation costs are included in incentive budgets. Evaluation should be undertaken regularly according to a timeline.[45]

[39] See Barkoczy and Wilkinson (n 12) 87.

[40] See International Monetary Fund et al (Table 14b) 23; Leamon et al (n 6) 31; Department of Finance (n 29) 35; James (n 15) 29, 34, 40.

[41] See OECD, 'Business Innovation Policies: Selected Country Comparisons' (2011) 17.

[42] ibid.

[43] See ibid 15; John Lester, 'Managing Tax Expenditures and Government Program Spending: Proposals for Reform' (2012) 35(5) *The School of Public Policy Publications* 1, 16; OECD Regulatory Policy Committee, 'Recommendation of the Council on Regulatory Policy and Governance' (2012) 26; ACT Government, 'Evaluation Policy and Guidelines' (December 2010) 3; United Nations Economic Commission for Europe (Table 10b) 83.

[44] See Cary Coglianese, 'Measuring Regulatory Performance: Evaluating the Impact of Regulation and Regulatory Policy' (OECD, August 2012) Expert Paper No 1, 7, 34–35; OECD, 'Business Innovation Policies' (n 41) 118.

[45] See OECD, 'Government Venture Capital' (Table 12c) 20; Leonard E Burman, 'Is the Tax Expenditure Concept Still Relevant?' (2003) 56(3) *National Tax Journal* 613, 621.

Guideline 5(b): Governments Should Consider Evaluating Incentives in Accordance with the Proposed Six-Step Methodology (see [6.3])

The methodology for evaluating incentives proposed in chapter six is as follows:

1. Identify relevant measures of success (which should be tied to incentive policy aims) (see [6.3.1]). An incentive's effectiveness is judged with reference to how well it achieves its policy aims, meaning that the performance measures against which an incentive is evaluated should be tied to these aims.[46] This will depend on incentive aims being appropriate and clearly defined (see Guideline 1(c)).[47] The performance measures used to evaluate incentives should be logical, defensible and measured systematically and consistently from the time an incentive is implemented.[48]
2. Collect the necessary quantitative and qualitative data on incentive operation, outcomes and costs (see [6.3.2]). Wider data on the state of the market should also be collected pre- and post-incentive introduction.[49] Data collection on any necessary counterfactual scenario or control group should form part of the data collection strategy.
3. Establish or estimate the extent to which outcomes represent an increase over what would have occurred in the absence of the incentive (additionality) and the extent to which outcomes can be attributed to the incentive (causality) (see [6.3.3]). Evaluators can estimate additionality and causality through subjective surveys of and interviews with recipients and investees and through comparing these entities with a control group. Whether evaluators use a counterfactual scenario, subjective questions or some other method to estimate causality, they should be careful to account for selection and response biases.[50]
4. Evaluate the extent to which the incentive has been effective and efficient in meeting its policy aims through an impact evaluation (see [6.3.4]).[51]
5. Evaluate the incentive's efficiency by comparing its costs and benefits through a cost–benefit analysis or a cost-effectiveness analysis (see [6.3.5]).[52]
6. Come to a conclusion on whether the incentive remains appropriate, based on its effectiveness and efficiency (see [6.3.6]). Incentives that are ineffective or inefficient (ie their costs outweigh their benefits) may need to be improved

[46] See Wilson (n 4) 31.

[47] See, eg Department of Prime Minister and Cabinet, *The Australian Government Guide to Regulation* (Australian Government, 2014) 51; OECD Regulatory Policy Committee (n 43) 4.

[48] See Cromwell Schmisseur (n 5) 6; European Commission (n 7) 5; Department of Prime Minister and Cabinet (n 65) 51–52.

[49] See Cumming and Johan, 'Government Venture Capital Research' (n 3) 125.

[50] What Works Centre for Local Economic Growth, *Innovation: Grants, Loans and Subsidies* (October 2015) Evidence Review No 9, 12–13; OECD, 'Business Innovation Policies' (n 41) 119.

[51] See Lester (n 43) 16.

[52] See ibid 2; Hana Polackova Brixi, Christian MA Valenduc and Zhicheng Li Swift (eds), *Tax Expenditures – Shedding Light on Government Spending Through the Tax System: Lessons from Developed and Transition Economies* (World Bank, 2004) 21–22.

or removed as they are unlikely to remain appropriate.[53] Likewise, incentives that have achieved their policy aims and are no longer necessary should also be terminated. Policymakers should engage in a process of continued dynamic learning in relation to their incentives,[54] and should feed the results of evaluation into future decision-making and design processes in order to learn from past experience and improve incentives.[55]

Guideline 5(c): Governments Should Make the Results of Evaluations Publicly Available (see [6.4])

Governments should publicise the results of evaluation as transparently as possible (while maintaining participant confidentiality where necessary).[56] This opens incentives up to discussion and scrutiny from the public and academia,[57] helps increase confidence in incentives and trust in the governments implementing them,[58] and helps other governments work 'towards developing better evaluation processes'.[59] Ideally, governments should look at the prior results of evaluations when designing – and before introducing – new incentives. Learning from previous successful and unsuccessful incentives can assist future decision-making and policy development, and strengthen policymaking performance, in relation to both future and current incentives.[60] The more evaluations are released into the public domain, the easier this task is.

7.3. Directions for Future Research

Despite the large amount of research undertaken on venture capital as an asset class and the impressive number of venture capital incentives implemented by governments around the world, there are still more questions than answers about how government venture capital incentives impact the venture capital market and how governments can best stimulate the venture capital sector. This lack of knowledge is exacerbated by a lack of evaluation of current and former incentives (as discussed

[53] See Duanjie Chen, 'The Framework for Assessing Tax Incentives: A Cost–Benefit Analysis Approach' (Workshop on Tax Incentives and Base Protection, United Nations, 23–24 April 2015) 13; Coglianese (n 44) 48.

[54] See United Nations Economic Commission for Europe (Table 10b) 43.

[55] See OECD Regulatory Policy Committee (n 43) 22.

[56] See ibid 26; OECD, 'Business Innovation Policies' (n 41) 149; Department of Finance (n 29) 14.

[57] See Burton and Sadiq (n 20) 78; OECD, 'Business Innovation Policies' (n 41) 24; What Works Centre for Local Economic Growth (n 50) 37.

[58] See ACT Government (n 43) 5; Department of the Attorney-General and Justice, 'Grants Management Framework: Principles and Policies for Best Practice in the Administration of Grants' (July 2017) 6; Brown et al (n 25) 36.

[59] Wilson (n 4) 29.

[60] See ACT Government (n 43) 5; Avnimelech et al (n 4) 47.

in chapter six) and a lack of transparency around policy formation. Research on the actual real-world outcomes and effects of government venture capital incentives is lacking, as discussed in the previous chapter, and little is known about the impact of particular design features of incentives.[61] As an example, consider Australia's Innovation Investment Fund co-investment programme, which ran from 1998 to 2014. Although the programme was formally evaluated twice, much is still unknown about its design and impact. For instance, while the programme was reportedly based on Israel's successful Yozma programme, it differed quite significantly from Yozma in its structure and operation (Yozma offered buyout options for private investors, while the Innovation Investment Fund programme split returns between the government and the private sector on a 10:90 basis, among other things). Why did the Australian government make these changes, departing from the positive blueprint provided by Yozma? Understanding the reasons for these policy decisions may help to provide some insight into what the Australian government was specifically hoping to achieve with the programme. Furthermore, although evaluation of the programme demonstrated that, during its tenure, it introduced a number of new fund managers to the sector and supported a range of startups that went on to have varying levels of success, the long-term outcomes and impacts of the programme have not been studied.[62] From a vantage point of eight years after the Innovation Investment Fund programme's termination, it remains unclear whether this termination (which seems to have been politically motivated) came at the appropriate time or not. Following the termination of the programme in 2014, Australia's venture capital industry has continued to grow.[63] Does this indicate that the Innovation Investment Fund programme was, or had become, redundant? Does it indicate that the programme was cancelled at the perfect time? Or, on the other hand, does it indicate that the programme supported the growth of Australia's venture capital industry and could have helped it reach even greater heights had it continued? The reality is that without data (especially qualitative data that helps establish causality) we may never know. The extent to which the public is able to access this kind of data in relation to current and future incentives rests in the hands of the government.

In a similar vein, further data, information and research would also be useful in relation to understanding the incentive effects provided by different kinds of incentive forms. For example, the 2016 evaluation of the UK's Enterprise Investment Scheme asked recipients to rank the importance of each kind of tax benefit provided under the incentive in regard to the decision to invest.[64]

[61] See European Commission (n 7) 202.

[62] See Gordon Murray, Marc Cowling and Weixi Lui, 'An Independent Econometric Analysis of the "Innovation Investment Fund" Programme (IIF) of the Australian Commonwealth Government: Findings and Implications' (Department of Innovation, Industry, Science and Research, 2010); Douglas Cumming and Sofia Johan, 'Venture's Economic Impact in Australia' (2016) 41(1) *Journal of Technology Transfer* 25; Barkoczy et al (Table 10a) 354–55.

[63] Australian Government, *Venture Capital Tax Concessions Review* (2022) 18.

[64] Colahan et al (n 10) 6–7.

This provided empirical evidence of the motivational effects of different incentive forms on investors. This kind of data could have a great deal of influence on incentive design, but can only really be obtained through subjective reports from programme recipients and investees. While this data may be subject to bias, it is suggested that the more governments, regulators and/or evaluators put processes in place to collect this kind of subjective information, the more understanding can be gained about how particular design features affect incentive operation. This, in turn, can help us understand why certain incentives do or do not work.

In addition to further research on policy design and operation, further research on incentive performance and impact would also be useful, as there remains disagreement over whether government venture capital incentives, as a whole, are broadly effective.[65] In short, it is hard to know whether incentives do actually result in net improvements to the venture capital sector. A range of robust studies has found some evidence of success from various government venture capital incentives, as well as a not-inconsiderable number of problems. A prime example is the broad analysis by Brander et al, which examines the impact of government venture capital incentives on markets and concludes that government intervention has an overall favourable impact on levels of venture capital investment.[66] Cumming and Johan likewise note that, in sum, most studies show a positive role for government intervention in the early-stage venture capital market, provided that incentives are efficient and designed in partnership with private investors (rather than in competition with them).[67] In particular, this positive role is evident in relation to signalling the investment quality of startups to other investors, the development of prototypes and patents, and improved exits.[68] In contrast, some of the concerns that have been raised about incentives include that they may unintentionally result in the elimination of competitive advantage, particularly where they are adopted widely across jurisdictions,[69] and that they may lower investment quality due to the addition of marginal projects being funded.[70] More robust economic information about the impacts and outcomes of venture capital incentives on venture capital markets and the effect (if any) of these concerns would, therefore, be useful. As with the points above, the production of this information depends to a large extent on the approaches taken by governments towards evaluation of their incentives.

[65] See Productivity Commission, *Business Set-up, Transfer and Closure* (Productivity Commission, 30 September 2015) Productivity Commission Inquiry Report No 75, 9; European Commission (n 7) 64–65; Wilson (n 4) 31; Carolin Bock and Martin Watzinger, 'The Capital Gains Tax: A Curse but also a Blessing for Venture Capital Investment' (2019) 57(4) *Journal of Small Business Management* 1200, 1229.

[66] James A Brander, Qianqian Du and Thomas Hellmann, 'The Effects of Government-Sponsored Venture Capital: International Evidence' (2015) 19 *Review of Finance* 571, 611.

[67] Cumming and Johan, 'Government Venture Capital Research' (n 3) 124.

[68] ibid.

[69] See OECD, 'Tax Incentives' (n 26) 1.

[70] Barry Bracewell-Milnes and JCL Huiskamp, *Investment Incentives: A Comparative Analysis of the Systems in the EEC, the USA and Sweden* (Kluwer, 1977) 117–18.

7.4. Final Thoughts

It has been noted that there is a 'fine art' to designing venture capital incentives and ensuring that they achieve their desired effect,[71] and that the 'problems of achieving a well-structured incentive are in themselves formidable'.[72] These problems are exacerbated by the 'uncertain and unpredictable nature of innovation'.[73] Despite ongoing attempts by policymakers to design robust and logical incentives, some incentives undoubtedly 'succeed as much by accident as design'.[74] That being said, it is not impossible to create venture capital policies that set the stage for a flourishing venture capital ecosystem.[75] Good policy creates incentives for investment, and ensures that 'rules are defined, explained, and followed'.[76] Governments ideally facilitate these outcomes by engaging in a process of continuous improvement for their incentives whereby they undertake evaluation, reflect on the results and manage their incentives accordingly.[77]

Of course, it should be assumed that the current state of 'leading practice' as recommended in the guidelines in this book will evolve with changing economic conditions, better understanding of investment processes and driving market forces, and more research into the operation and outcomes of incentives. Many future lessons remain to be learnt, some of which will undoubtedly arise from incentives that exist now, as well as those which have just been and are yet to be conceived. However, while there are still uncertainties and challenges to be overcome in designing effective and efficient venture capital incentives, we can attempt, as Surrey exhorts us, to 'at least attempt not to repeat past mistakes in future solutions'.[78] This is particularly important because government venture capital incentives are likely here to stay; in fact, without sustained government support, it is unlikely that early-stage venture capital activity would have existed 'in other than a vestigial form outside the informal Business Angel sector',[79] and if such support were to cease, many venture capital sectors would likely collapse.[80] In light of this, it is hoped that the leading practice guidelines presented in this book will prove useful for policymakers in designing government venture capital incentives that are appropriate, effective and efficient at supporting this important sector of the market into the future.

[71] Barkoczy et al (Table 10a) 32.
[72] Surrey (n 15) 149.
[73] Mark Dodgson, Alan Hughes, John Foster and Stan Metcalfe, 'Systems Thinking, Market Failure, and the Development of Innovation Policy: The Case of Australia' (2011) 40(9) *Research Policy* 1145, 1148.
[74] ibid 1148.
[75] Leamon et al (n 6) 60.
[76] ibid.
[77] See ibid.
[78] Stanley Surrey, 'Tax Incentives as a Device for Implementing Government Policy: A Comparison with Direct Government Expenditures' (1970) 83(4) *Harvard Law Review* 705, 738.
[79] Murray et al (n 41) 11.
[80] See Josh Lerner, *Boulevard of Broken Dreams: Why Public Efforts to Boost Entrepreneurship and Venture Capital Have Failed – and What to Do About It* (Princeton University Press, 2009) 5; Leamon et al (n 6) 13, 16; United Nations Economic Commission for Europe (Table 10b) 41, 51.

BIBLIOGRAPHY

Books and Book Chapters

Abraham, Lars, *Venture Capital in Germany and the US: Differences and the Influence of Culture* (Freiberg TU Bergakademie, 2009)

Avnimelech, Gil and Morris Teubal, 'Targeting Venture Capital: Lessons from Israel's Yozma Program' in Anthony Bartzokas and Sunil Mani (eds), *Financial Systems, Corporate Investment in Innovation, and Venture Capital* (Edward Elgar, 2004) 85

Barkoczy, Stephen and Daniel Sandler, *Government Venture Capital Incentives: A Multi-Jurisdiction Comparative Analysis* (Australian Tax Research Foundation, 2007)

Barkoczy, Stephen and Tamara Wilkinson, *Incentivising Angels: A Comparative Framework of Tax Incentives for Start-Up Investors* (Springer, 2019)

Barkoczy, Stephen, Don Maloney and Wayne Ngo, *Pooled Development Funds Handbook* (Australian Tax Practice, 2001)

Barkoczy, Stephen, Tamara Wilkinson, Ann L Monotti and Mark Davison, *Innovation and Venture Capital Law and Policy* (Federation Press, 2016)

Bean, Jonathan J, *Big Government and Affirmative Action: The Scandalous History of the Small Business Administration* (University Press of Kentucky, 2001)

Black, John, Nigar Hashimzade and Gareth Myles, *A Dictionary of Economics*, 4th edn (Oxford University Press, 2012)

Black, Julia, Martin Lodge and Mark Thatcher (eds), *Regulatory Innovation: A Comparative Analysis* (Edward Elgar, 2006)

Block, Joern, Geertjan De Vries and Philipp Sandner, 'Venture Capital and the Financial Crisis: An Empirical Study Across Industries and Countries' in Douglas Cumming (ed), *The Oxford Handbook of Venture Capital* (Oxford University Press, 2012) 37

Bracewell-Milnes, Barry and JCL Huiskamp, *Investment Incentives: A Comparative Analysis of the Systems in the EEC, the USA and Sweden* (Kluwer, 1977)

Braithwaite, John, 'Regulation' in Kenneth Wiltshire (ed), *Governance and Economic Efficiency* (Committee for Economic Development of Australia, 1994) 163

Brooks, Neil, 'The Logic, Policy and Politics of Tax Law' in Tim Edgar, Daniel Sandler and Arthur Cockfield (eds), *Materials on Canadian Income Tax*, 14th edn (Carswell, 2010) 1

Brown, Ashley C, Jon Stern, Bernard Tenenbaum and Defne Gencer, *Handbook for Evaluating Infrastructure Regulatory Systems* (World Bank, 2006)

Burton, Mark and Kerrie Sadiq, *Tax Expenditure Management: A Critical Assessment* (Cambridge University Press, 2013)

Cumming, Douglas, 'Introduction' in Douglas Cumming (ed), *The Oxford Handbook of Venture Capital* (Oxford University Press, 2012) 1

Cumming, Douglas and Sofia A Johan, *Venture Capital and Private Equity Contracting: An International Perspective*, 2nd edn (Elsevier, 2014)

Cumming, Douglas and Sofia Johan, 'Government Intervention in the Venture Capital Market' in Stefano Caselli, Guido Corbetta and Veronica Vecchi (eds), *Public Private Partnerships for Infrastructure and Business Development* (Palgrave MacMillan, 2015) 237

Darcy, John W, *Japan Master Tax Guide 2016/17*, 14th edn (Wolters Kluwer, 2016)

De Clercq, Dirk and Sophie Manigart, 'The Venture Capital Post-Investment Phase: Opening the Black Box of Involvement' in Hans Landström (ed), *Handbook of Research on Venture Capital* (Edward Elgar, 2007) 193

Department of Prime Minister and Cabinet, *The Australian Government Guide to Regulation* (Australian Government, 2014)
Easson, Alex, *Tax Incentives for Foreign Direct Investment* (Kluwer Law International, 2004)
European Commission, *Evaluating EU Activities: A Practical Guide for the Commission Service* (European Communities, 2004)
Ferris, Bill, *Inside Private Equity*, 2nd edn (Allen & Unwin, 2013)
Global Intellectual Property Center, United States Chamber of Commerce, *The Roots of Innovation: US Chamber International IP Index*, 5th edn (February 2017)
Hashimzade, Nigar, Gareth Myles and John Black, *A Dictionary of Economics*, 5th edn (Oxford University Press, 2017)
Josselin, Jean-Michel and Benoît Le Maux, *Statistical Tools for Program Evaluation: Methods and Applications to Economic Policy, Public Health, and Education* (Springer, 2017)
Just, Richard E, Darrell L Hueth and Andrew Schmitz, *The Welfare Economics of Public Policy: A Practical Approach to Project and Policy Evaluation* (Edward Elgar, 2004)
Khemani, RS and DM Shapiro, *Glossary of Industrial Organisation Economics and Competition Law* (OECD, 1993)
Krever, Richard, 'Tax Deductions for Charitable Donations: A Tax Expenditure Analysis' in Richard Krever and Gretchen Kewley (eds), *Charities and Philanthropic Institutions: Reforming the Tax Subsidy and Regulatory Regimes* (Australian Tax Research Foundation, 1991)
Landström, Hans and Colin Mason, 'Venture Capital Research: The Road Ahead' in Hans Landström and Colin Mason (eds), *Handbook of Research on Venture Capital, vol 2: A Globalizing Industry* (Edward Elgar, 2012) 283
Lerner, Josh, *Boulevard of Broken Dreams: Why Public Efforts to Boost Entrepreneurship and Venture Capital Have Failed – and What to Do About It* (Princeton University Press, 2009)
Metrick, Andrew and Ayako Yasuda, *Venture Capital and the Finance of Innovation*, 2nd edn (Wiley, 2001)
Murray, Gordon, Ari Hyytinen and Markku Maula, 'Growth Entrepreneurship and Finance' in Reinhilde Veugelers et al, *The Evaluation of the Finnish National Innovation System* (ETLA, 2009) 147
OECD, *Entrepreneurship at a Glance 2017* (OECD, 2017)
OECD, *Financing SMEs and Entrepreneurs 2015: An OECD Scoreboard* (OECD, 2015)
OECD, *Financing SMEs and Entrepreneurs 2016: An OECD Scoreboard* (OECD, 2016)
OECD, *Financing SMEs and Entrepreneurs 2019: An OECD Scoreboard* (OECD, 2019)
OECD, *OECD Reviews of Innovation Policy: Norway* (OECD, 2008)
OECD, *OECD Science, Technology and Industry Scoreboard 2013: Innovation for Growth* (OECD, 2013)
OECD, *OECD Territorial Reviews: Norway* (OECD, 2007)
OECD, *OSLO Manual 2018: Guidelines for Collecting, Reporting and Using Data on Innovation*, 4rd edn (OECD, 2018)
OECD, *Regulatory Policy and Governance: Supporting Economic Growth and Serving the Public Interest* (OECD, 2011)
OECD, *Science, Technology and Industry Outlook 2012* (OECD, 2012)
OECD, *Science, Technology and Industry Scoreboard 2009* (OECD, 2009)
OECD, *SMEs in Libya's Reconstruction: Preparing for a Post-Conflict Economy* (OECD, 2016)
OECD, *Supporting Investment in Knowledge Capital, Growth and Innovation* (OECD, 2013)
OECD, *Tax Expenditures in OECD Countries* (OECD, 2010)
OECD, *Technology, Productivity and Job Creation: Best Policy Practices* (OECD, 1998)
Ogus, Anthony I, *Regulation: Legal Form and Economic Theory* (Hart Publishing, 1994)
Oranburg, SC, 'Start-up Financing' in Fernando Pacheco-Torgal et al (eds), *Start-Up Creation: The Smart Eco-Efficient Built Environment* (Woodhead Publishing, 2016) 57
Oxford English Dictionary (online), 'Incentive' (def A3)
Patton, Michael Quinn, *Utilization-Focused Evaluation*, 4th edn (Sage Publications, 2008)
Plagge, Arnd, *Public Policy for Venture Capital: A Comparison of the United States and Germany* (Deutscher Universitätsverlag, 2006)

Polackova Brixi, Hana, Christian MA Valenduc and Zhicheng Li Swift (eds), *Tax Expenditures – Shedding Light on Government Spending Through the Tax System: Lessons from Developed and Transition Economies* (World Bank, 2004)
Rossi, Peter H, Mark W Lipsey and Howard E Freeman, *Evaluation: A Systematic Approach*, 7th edn (Sage Publications, 2004)
Siow Song Teng, Harold, *Government Policy and Critical Success Factors of Small Businesses in Singapore* (Cambridge Scholars Publishing, 2011)
Stone, Deborah A, *Policy Paradox and Political Reason* (HarperCollins, 1988)
Surrey, Stanley S and Paul R McDaniel, *Tax Expenditures* (Harvard University Press, 1985)
Surrey, Stanley S, *Pathways to Tax Reform: The Concept of Tax Expenditures* (Harvard University Press, 1973)
Taleb, Nassim Nicholas, *The Black Swan: The Impact of the Highly Improbable*, 2nd edn (Random House, 2010)
Van de Kar, Hans M and Barbara L Wolfe (eds), *The Relevance of Public Finance for Policy-Making: Proceedings of the 41st Congress of the International Institute of Public Finance* (Wayne State University Press, 1987)
Victorian Innovation Economy Advisory Board (IEAB), Submission No 89 to Productivity Commission, *Public Support for Science and Innovation* (Productivity Commission, 9 March 2007)
Windholz, Eric L, *Governing Through Regulation: Public Policy, Regulation and the Law* (Routledge, 2018)
World Bank, *World Development Report 2005: A Better Investment Climate for Everyone* (Oxford University Press, 2004)

Journal Articles and Other Periodicals

Abadie, Alberto and Matias D Cattaneo, 'Econometric Methods for Program Evaluation' (2018) 10(1) *Annual Review of Economics* 465
Alperovych, Yan, Alexander Groh and Anita Quas, 'Bridging the Equity Gap for Young Innovative Companies: The Design of Effective Government Venture Capital Fund Programs' (2020) 49(10) *Research Policy* 104051
Alperovych, Yan, Georges Hübner and Fabrice Lobet, 'How Does Governmental Versus Private Venture Capital Backing Affect a Firm's Efficiency? Evidence from Belgium' (2015) 30(4) *Journal of Business Venturing* 508
Amit, Raphael, James Brander and Christoph Zott, 'Why Do Venture Capital Firms Exist? Theory and Canadian Evidence' (1998) 13(6) *Journal of Business Venturing* 441
Arcot, Sridhar, 'Participating Convertible Preferred Stock in Venture Capital Exits' (2014) 29(1) *Journal of Business Venturing* 72
Armour, John and Douglas Cumming, 'The Legislative Road to Silicon Valley' (2006) 58(4) *Oxford Economic Papers* 596
Arner, Douglas, Jànos Barberis and Ross Buckley, 'The Evolution of Fintech: A New Post-Crisis Paradigm?' [2016] *UNSWLRS* 62
Avnimelech, Gil and Morris Teubal, 'Venture Capital Start-up Co-evolution and the Emergence and Development of Israel's New High Tech Cluster' (2004) 13(1) *Economics of Innovation and New Technology* 33
Avnimelech, Gil and Morris Teubal, 'Creating Venture Capital Industries that Co-Evolve with High Tech: Insights from an Extended Industry Life Cycle Perspective on the Israeli Experience' (2006) 35(10) *Research Policy* 1477
Avnimelech, Gil, Alessandro Rosiello and Morris Teubal, 'Evolutionary Interpretation of Venture Capital Policy in Israel, Germany, UK and Scotland' (2010) 37(2) *Science and Public Policy* 101

Baldock, Robert, 'An Assessment of the Business Impacts of the UK's Enterprise Capital Funds' (2016) 34(8) *Environment and Planning C: Government and Policy* 1556
Banal-Estañol, Albert, Inés Macho-Stadler, Jonás Nieto-Postigo and David Pérez-Castrillo, 'Early Individual Stakeholders, First Venture Capital Investment, and Exit in the UK Startup Ecosystem' (2023) 80 *Journal of Corporate Finance* 102420
Barkoczy, Stephen and Peter Edmundson, 'Australasian and South East Asian Venture Capital Tax Expenditure Programs' (2009) 37(1) *Intertax* 56
Bates, Timothy, 'Government as Venture Capital Catalyst: Pitfalls and Promising Approaches' (2002) 16(1) *Economic Development Quarterly* 49
Becsky-Nagy, Patrícia, 'The Special Aspects of Venture Capital's Value Creating Mechanisms in Hungary' (2016) 12(3) *Journal of Entrepreneurship, Management and Innovation* 31
Bertoni, Fabio and Tereza Tykvová, 'Does Governmental Venture Capital Spur Invention and Innovation? Evidence from Young European Biotech Companies' (2015) 44(4) *Research Policy* 925
Black, Bernard S and Ronald J Gilson, 'Venture Capital and the Structure of Capital Markets: Banks Versus Stock Markets' (1998) 47(3) *Journal of Financial Economics* 243
Bock, Carolin and Martin Watzinger, 'The Capital Gains Tax: A Curse but also a Blessing for Venture Capital Investment' (2019) 57(4) *Journal of Small Business Management* 1200
Bonini, Stefano and Senem Alkan, 'The Political and Legal Determinants of Venture Capital Investments Around the World' (2012) 39(4) *Small Business Economics* 997
Bottazzi, Laura and Marco Da Rin, 'Venture Capital in Europe and the Financing of Innovative Companies' (2002) 17(34) *Economic Policy* 229
Botazzi, Laura, Marco Da Rin and Thomas Hellmann, 'Who Are the Active Investors? Evidence from Venture Capital' (2008) 89(3) *Journal of Financial Economics* 488
Braithwaite, John, 'Rewards and Regulation' (2002) 29(1) *Journal of Law and Society* 12
Brander, James A, Qianqian Du and Thomas Hellmann, 'The Effects of Government-Sponsored Venture Capital: International Evidence' (2015) 19 *Review of Finance* 571
Burman, Leonard E, 'Is the Tax Expenditure Concept Still Relevant?' (2003) 56(3) *National Tax Journal* 613
Byrne, Donna M, 'Progressive Taxation Revisited' (1995) 37(3) *Arizona Law Review* 739
Callagher, Lisa, Peter Smith and Saskia Ruscoe, 'Government Roles in Venture Capital Development: A Review of Current Literature' (2015) 4(3) *Journal of Entrepreneurship and Public Policy* 367
Carpentier, Cécile and Jean-Marc Suret, 'On the Usefulness of Tax Incentives for Informal Investors' (2007) 9(1) *Venture Capital* 1
Chemmanur, Thomas J, Karthik Krishnan and Debarshi K Nandy, 'How Does Venture Capital Financing Improve Efficiency in Private Firms? A Look Beneath the Surface' (2011) 24(12) *The Review of Financial Studies* 4037
Cincera, Michele and Julien Ravet, 'Financing Constraints and R&D Investments of Large Corporations in Europe and the US' (2010) 37(6) *Science and Public Policy* 455
Colombo, Massimo G, Douglas J Cumming and Silvio Vismara, 'Governmental Venture Capital for Innovative Young Firms' (2016) 41(1) *Journal of Technology Transfer* 10
Coyle, John F and Joseph M Green, 'The SAFE, the KISS, and the Note: A Survey of Startup Seed Financing Contracts' (2018) 103 *Minnesota Law Review* 42
Cumming, Douglas, 'Government Policy Towards Entrepreneurial Finance: Innovation Investment Funds' (2007) 22(2) *Journal of Business Venturing* 193
Cumming, Douglas, 'Misinforming the Public about Public Policy Towards Venture Capital' (2011) 13(1) *Venture Capital* 99
Cumming, Douglas, 'Public Policy and the Creation of Active Venture Capital Markets' (2011) 13(1) *Venture Capital* 75
Cumming, Douglas, 'Public Economics Gone Wild: Lessons from Venture Capital' (2014) 36 *International Review of Financial Analysis* 251
Cumming, Douglas and Sofia Johan, 'Pre-Seed Government Venture Capital Funds' (2009) 7(1) *Journal of International Entrepreneurship* 26

Cumming, Douglas and Sofia Johan, 'Phasing Out an Inefficient Venture Capital Tax Credit' (2010) 10(3) *Journal of Industry, Competition and Trade* 227
Cumming, Douglas and Sofia Johan, 'Venture's Economic Impact in Australia' (2016) 41(1) *Journal of Technology Transfer* 25
Cumming, Douglas and Sofia Johan, 'Government Venture Capital Research: Fake Science and Bad Public Policy' (2019) 21(1) *Venture Capital* 121
Cumming, Douglas and Dan Li, 'Public Policy, Entrepreneurship, and Venture Capital in the United States' (2013) 23 *Journal of Corporate Finance* 345
Cumming, Douglas J and Jeffrey G MacIntosh, 'Crowding Out Private Equity: Canadian Evidence' (2006) 21(5) *Journal of Business Venturing* 569
Cumming, Douglas J, Luca Grilli and Samuele Murtinu, 'Government and Independent Venture Capital Investments in Europe: A Firm-Level Performance Analysis' (2017) 42 *Journal of Corporate Finance* 439
Dahaj, Arash Soleimani, Brian P Cozzarin and Kambiz Talebi, 'Revisiting the Canadian Public Policy Towards Venture Capital: Crowding-out or Displacement' (2018) 45(5) *Science and Public Policy* 719
Da Rin, Marco, Giovanna Nicodano and Alessandro Sembenelli, 'Public Policy and the Creation of Active Venture Capital Markets' (2006) 90(8) *Journal of Public Economics* 1699
Decker, Ryan, John Haltiwanger, Ron Jarmin, and Javier Miranda, 'The Role of Entrepreneurship in US Job Creation and Economic Dynamism' (2014) 28(3) *Journal of Economic Perspectives* 3
Dimitrova, Lora and Sapnoti K Eswar, 'Capital Gains Tax, Venture Capital, and Innovation in Start-Ups' (2023) 27(4) *Review of Finance* 1471
Dodgson, Mark, Alan Hughes, John Foster and Stan Metcalfe, 'Systems Thinking, Market Failure, and the Development of Innovation Policy: The Case of Australia' (2011) 40(9) *Research Policy* 1145
Eisenhardt, Kathleen M, 'Agency Theory: An Assessment and Review' (1989) 14(1) *Academy of Management Review* 57
Enrich, Peter D, 'Saving the States from Themselves: Commerce Clause Constraints on State Tax Incentives for Business' (1996) 110(2) *Harvard Law Review* 337
Fałat-Kilijańska, Ilona, 'How to Strengthen the Polish Venture Capital Market? An Analysis of the Solutions in Selected Countries' (2015) 4(25) *Financial Sciences* 9
Fletcher, Keith, 'Incorporated Limited Partnerships: Venture Capital's Contribution to Legal Development' (2004) 17(2) *Australian Journal of Corporate Law* 157
Finances Québec, 'Adjustments to Certain Measures Announced in the Budget Speech of June 12, 2003' (18 July 2003) 2003-3 *Bulletin d'Information* 2
Forsaith, David, 'Venture Capital in Australia: The MIC Program and Subsequent Developments' (1993) 2(1–2) *Small Enterprise Research* 36
Gilson, Ronald J, 'Engineering a Venture Capital Market: Lessons from the American Experience' (2003) 55 *Stanford Law Review* 1067
Gilson, Ronald J and David M Schizer, 'Understanding Venture Capital Structure: A Tax Explanation for Convertible Preferred Stock' (2003) 116 *Harvard Law Review* 874
Giudici, Paolo and Peter Agstner, 'Startups and Company Law: The Competitive Pressure of Delaware on Italy (and Europe?)' (2019) 20 *European Business Organization Law Review* 597
Golis, Christopher, 'How to Make Risk Irresistible: Incentives for Venture Capital' (1991) 3 *JASSA: Finsia Journal of Applied Finance* 5
Gompers, Paul A and Josh Lerner, 'Venture Capital and the Creation of Public Companies: Do Venture Capitalists Really Bring More Than Money?' (1997) 1(1) *The Journal of Private Equity* 15
Grilli, Luca and Samuele Murtinu, 'Government, Venture Capital and the Growth of European High-Tech Entrepreneurial Firms' (2014) 43(9) *Research Policy* 1523
Hall, Bronwyn H, 'The Financing of Research and Development' (2002) 18(1) *Oxford Review of Economic Policy* 35
Harding, Rebecca, 'Venture Capital and the Regions: Not Always the Most Appropriate Funding Mechanism' (2000) 7(1) *New Economy* 49

Harding, Rebecca, 'Plugging the Knowledge Gap: An International Comparison of the Role for Policy in the Venture Capital Market' (2002) 4(1) *Venture Capital* 59

Hellmann, Thomas, 'The Allocation of Control Rights in Venture Capital Contracts' (1998) 29(1) *RAND Journal of Economics* 57

Hendon, John R, Joseph R Bell, Brittany Blair and Don K Martin, 'State-Funded Angel Investor Tax Credits: Implementation and Perceived Effectiveness in a Sample of States Within the United States' (2012) 1(1) *Journal of Entrepreneurship and Public Policy* 50

Hisrich, Robert D, Saŝa Petković, Veland Ramadani and Léo-Paul Dana, 'Venture Capital Funds in Transition Countries: Insights from Bosnia and Herzegovina and Macedonia' (2016) 23(2) *Journal of Small Business and Enterprise Development* 296

Howard, Christopher, 'Testing the Tools Approach: Tax Expenditures Versus Direct Expenditures' (1995) 55(5) *Public Administration Review* 439

Howland, Marie, 'Measuring Capital Subsidy Costs and Job Creation: The Case of Rural UDAG Grants' (1990) 56(1) *Journal of the American Planning Association* 54

Hussain, Syed Adil, 'Growing the Malaysian Venture Capital and Private Equity Industry' (2010) 1(4) *Islam and Civilisational Renewal* 629

Jeng, Leslie A and Philippe C Wells, 'The Determinants of Venture Capital Funding: Evidence Across Countries' (2000) 6(3) *Journal of Corporate Finance* 241

Johan, Sofia, Denis Schweizer and Feng Zhan, 'The Changing Latitude: Labor-Sponsored Venture Capital Corporations in Canada' (2014) 22(2) *Corporate Governance: An International Review* 145

Kállay, László and Erika Jáki, 'The Impact of State Intervention on the Hungarian Venture Capital Market' (2020) 33(1) *Economic Research-Ekonomska Istrazivanja* 1130

Kenney, Martin, 'How Venture Capital Became a Component of the US National System of Innovation' (2011) 20(6) *Industrial and Corporate Change* 1677

Keuschnigg, Christian, 'Taxation of a Venture Capitalist with a Portfolio of Firms' (2004) 56 *Oxford Economic Papers* 285

Keuschnigg, Christian and Søren Bo Nielsen, 'Public Policy for Venture Capital' (2001) 8(4) *International Tax and Public Finance* 557

Keuschnigg, Christian and Søren Bo Nielsen, 'Tax Policy, Venture Capital, and Entrepreneurship' (2002) 87(1) *Journal of Public Economics* 175

Keuschnigg Christian and Søren Bo Nielsen, 'Taxes and Venture Capital Support' (2003) 7(3) *European Finance Review* 515

Keuschnigg, Christian and Søren Bo Nielsen, 'Taxation and Venture Capital Backed Entrepreneurship' (2004) 11(4) *International Tax and Public Finance* 369

Kirihata, Tetsuya, 'Japanese Government Venture Capital: What Should We Know?' (2018) 12(1) *Asia Pacific Journal of Innovation and Entrepreneurship* 14

Koh, Francis CC and Winston TH Koh, 'Venture Capital and Economic Growth: An Industry Overview and Singapore's Experience' (2002) 47(2) *The Singapore Economic Review* 243

Kortum, Samuel and Josh Lerner, 'Assessing the Contribution of Venture Capital to Innovation' (2000) 31(4) *The RAND Journal of Economics* 674

Krever, Richard, 'Taming Complexity in Australian Income Tax' (2003) 25(4) *Sydney Law Review* 467

Krever, Richard, 'Analysing Implicit Tax Expenditures' (2011) 35(2) *Melbourne University Law Review* 426

Laine, Markus and Sami Torstila, 'The Exit Rates of Liquidated Venture Capital Funds' (2005) 10(1) *The Journal of Entrepreneurial Finance* 53

Leitner, Yaron, 'Convertible Securities and Venture Capital Finance' (2009) Q3 *Business Review (Federal Reserve Bank of Philadelphia)* 18

Leleux, Benoît and Bernard Surelemont, 'Public Versus Private Venture Capital: Seeding or Crowding Out? A Pan-European Analysis' (2003) 18(1) *Journal of Business Venturing* 81

Lerner, Josh, 'When Bureaucrats Meet Entrepreneurs: The Design of Effective "Public Venture Capital" Programmes' (2002) 112(477) *Economic Journal* F73

Lerner, Josh and Brian Watson, 'The Public Venture Capital Challenge: The Australian Case' (2008) 10(1) *Venture Capital* 1

Lester, John, 'Managing Tax Expenditures and Government Program Spending: Proposals for Reform' (2012) 35(5) *The School of Public Policy Publications* 1

Li, Jun, 'Government-Backed Venture Capital as a Science, Technology and Innovation (STI) Policy Instrument: A Chinese Perspective' (2016) 7(1) *STI Policy Review* 66

Li, Wenli, 'Government Loan, Guarantee, and Grant Programs: An Evaluation' (1998) 84(4) *Economic Quarterly* 25

Lim, Sojin and Yeonbae Kim, 'How to Design Public Venture Capital Funds: Empirical Evidence from South Korea' (2015) 53(4) *Journal of Small Business Management* 843

Luukkonen, Terttu, Matthias Deschryvere and Fabio Bertoni, 'The Value Added by Government Venture Capital Funds Compared with Independent Venture Capital Funds' (2013) 33 *Technovation* 154

Manigart, Sophie, Koen De Waele, Mike Wright, Ken Robbie, Philippe Desbrières, Harry J Sapienza and Amy Beekman, 'Determinants of Required Return in Venture Capital Investments: A Five-Country Study' (2002) 17 *Journal of Business Venturing* 291

Mason, Colin M, 'Public Policy Support for the Informal Venture Capital Market in Europe: A Critical Review' (2009) 27(5) *International Small Business Journal* 536

Mason, Colin M and Richard T Harrison, 'Improving Access to Early Stage Venture Capital in Regional Economies: A New Approach to Investment Readiness' (2004) 19(2) *Local Economy* 159

Megginson, William L, 'Toward a Global Model of Venture Capital?' (2004) 16(1) *Journal of Applied Corporate Finance* 89

Mellos, Kon and Nick Wormald, 'Australia: Private Equity Trends and Developments' [2002] *International Financial Law Review* 51

Milosevic, Miona and Jacqueline Fendt, 'Venture Capital and Its French Exception: Explaining Performance through Human Capital, Policy and Institutional Failures' (2016) 43(5) *Science and Public Policy* 660

Mohr, Lawrence B, 'Determinants of Innovation in Organizations' (1969) 63(1) *American Political Science Review* 111

Munari, Federico and Laura Toschi, 'Assessing the Impact of Public Venture Capital Programmes in the United Kingdom: Do Regional Characteristics Matter?' (2015) 30(2) *Journal of Business Venturing* 205

Murray, Gordon C, 'A Policy Response to Regional Disparities in the Supply of Risk Capital to New Technology-based Forms in the European Union: The European Seed Capital Fund Scheme' (1998) 32(5) *Regional Studies* 405

Murray, Gordon, 'Early-stage Venture Capital Funds, Scale Economies and Public Support' (1999) 1(4) *Venture Capital* 351

Nanda, Ramana and Matthew Rhodes-Kropf, 'Investment Cycles and Startup Innovation' (2013) 110(2) *Journal of Financial Economics* 403

O'Shea, Margaret and Candice Stevens, 'Governments as Venture Capitalists' (1998) 213 *OECD Observer* 26

Ollivierre, Scott, 'The Influence of Taxation on Capital Structure in Venture Capital Investments in Canada and the United States' (2010) 68(1) *University of Toronto Faculty of Law Review* 9

Osborne, Duncan and Daniel Sandler, 'A Tax Expenditure Analysis of Labour-Sponsored Venture Capital Corporations' (1998) 46(3) *Canadian Tax Journal* 499

Owen (Baldock), Robyn and Colin Mason, 'The Role of Government Co-investment Funds in the Supply of Entrepreneurial Finance: An Assessment of the Early Operation of the UK Angel Co-investment Fund' (2016) 35(3) *Environment and Planning C: Politics and Space* 434

Owen (Baldock), Robyn, David North and Ciarán Mac an Bhaird, 'The Role of Government Venture Capital Funds: Recent Lessons from the UK Experience' (2019) 28(1) *Strategic Change* 69

Payne, Jennifer, 'Private Equity and Its Regulation in Europe' (2011) 12(4) *European Business Organization Law Review* 559

Pereira, Alvaro, 'Designing Startup Corporate Law: A Minimum Viable Product' (2022) 42 *Review of Banking and Finance Law* 367

Peroni, Robert J, 'Tax Reform Interrupted: The Chaotic State of Tax Policy in 2003' (2004) 35(3) *McGeorge Law Review* 277

Phalippou, Ludovic, 'An Inconvenient Fact: Private Equity Returns & The Billionaire Factory' (2023) 30(1) *The Journal of Investing* 11

Popov, Alexander and Peter Roosenboom, 'Venture Capital and Patented Innovation: Evidence from Europe' (2012) 27(71) *Economic Policy* 447

Poterba, James M, 'Venture Capital and Capital Gains Taxation' (1989) 3 *Tax Policy and the Economy* 47

Ramadani, Veland, 'Venture Capital Financing in the Republic of Macedonia: What Is Done and What Should Be Done?' (2014) 3(2) *ACRN Journal of Finance and Risk Perspectives* 27

Reid, Gavin C, 'The Application of Principal-Agent Methods to Investor–Investee Relations in the UK Venture Capital Industry' (1999) 1(4) *Venture Capital* 285

Repullo, Rafael and Javier Suarez, 'Venture Capital Finance: A Security Design Approach' (2004) 8(1) *Review of Finance* 75

Sadiq, Kerrie, 'Powering Innovation Through Tax Concessions: The Changing Research & Development Tax Incentives' (2014) 16(1) *Journal of Australian Taxation* 1

Sapienza, Harry J and Anil K Gupta, 'Impact of Agency Risks and Task Uncertainty on Venture Capitalist–CEO Interaction' (1994) 37(6) *Academy of Management Journal* 1618

Sapienza, Harry J, Allen C Amason and Sophie Manigart, 'The Level and Nature of Venture Capitalist Involvement in Their Portfolio Companies: A Study of Three European Countries' (1994) 20(1) *Managerial Finance* 3

Seoudi, Imam and Salma Mahmoud, 'Public Policy for Venture Capital: A Comparative Study of Emirates, Saudi Arabia and Egypt' (2016) 7(1) *Review of Business and Finance Studies* 19

Skrobiszewski, Francis J, 'Market Making: How Enterprise Funds Can Jump-Start Stagnant Economies (Innovations Case Narrative: Enterprise Funds)' (2012) 7(2) *Innovations: Technology, Governance, Globalization* 33

Surrey, Stanley, 'Tax Incentives as a Device for Implementing Government Policy: A Comparison with Direct Government Expenditures' (1970) 83(4) *Harvard Law Review* 705

Surrey, Stanley S, 'Federal Income Tax Reform: The Varied Approaches Necessary to Replace Tax Expenditures with Direct Governmental Assistance' (1970) 84(2) *Harvard Law Review* 352

Thuronyi, Victor, 'Tax Expenditures: A Reassessment' (1988) 1988 *Duke Law Journal* 1155

Tuomi, Krista and Lopo De Castro Neto, 'Innovation and Venture Capital Policy in Brazil and South Africa' (2013) 8(2) *Journal of Technology Management and Innovation* 35

Urban, Rebecca, 'Venture Capitalists Call for Guarantee on Funds' *The Australian* (5 January 2013)

Van Hoecke, Mark, 'Methodology of Comparative Legal Research' (2015) 12 *Law and Method*

Walker, Graham, 'Can DCFs Succeed where MICs Fail? $2bn of Development Funds: Here's How' (1991) 4 *JASSA: Finsia Journal of Applied Finance* 24

Wan, Victor, 'Financing High Technology: The Australian Venture Capital Market' (1989) 9 *Technovation* 337

Weisbach, David A and Jacob Nussim, 'The Integration of Tax and Spending Programs' (2004) 113(5) *Yale Law Journal* 955

Zhang, Jing and Poh-Kam Wong, 'Networks vs Market Methods in High-Tech Venture Fundraising: The Impact of Institutional Environment' (2008) 20(5) *Entrepreneurship and Regional Development* 409

Reports and Similar Documents

ACT Government, 'Evaluation Policy and Guidelines' (December 2010)

Alperovych, Yan, Alexander Peter Groh and Anita Quas, 'When Can Government Venture Capital Funds Bridge the Equity Gap?' (European Financial Management Association Conference, 2017)

Australian Government, 'International Comparison of Australia's Taxes' (3 April 2006)

Australian Government, Innovation and Science Australia, 'Annual Report 2018–19' (2019)
Australian Government, *Venture Capital Tax Concessions Review* (2022)
Australian Government, Department of Industry, Science and Resources, 'Venture Capital Dashboard FY 2022/3' (2023) www.industry.gov.au/sites/default/files/2020-02/venture-capital-dashboard.pdf
Australian Government, The Board of Taxation, 'Review of Taxation Arrangements Under the Venture Capital Limited Partnership Regime' (June 2011)
Avnimelech, Gil, Martin Kenney and Morris Teubal, 'Building Venture Capital Industries: Understanding the US and Israeli Experiences' (Berkeley Roundtable on the International Economy, March 2004) Working Paper No 160
Bannock Consulting, 'Innovative Instruments for Raising Equity For SMEs in Europe' (June 2001) Study ContractETD/00/503116
Baygan, Günseli, 'Venture Capital Policy Review: Israel' (OECD, 28 January 2003) STI Working Paper 2003/3
Becker, Ralf and Thomas Hellmann, 'The Genesis of Venture Capital – Lessons from the German Experience' (CESifo Conference on Venture Capital, Entrepreneurship, and Public Policy, November 2002) CESifo Working Paper No 883
Bird, Richard M, 'Tax Challenges Facing Developing Countries' (Institute for International Business, March 2008) Working Paper No 9
Bpifrance, 'Garantie de Fonds Propres Relance: Dispositif Doté par l'État et Géré par Bpifrance 2021–2024' (June 2022)
Brander, James A, Edward J Egan and Thomas F Hellmann, 'Government Sponsored Versus Private Venture Capital: Canadian Evidence' (National Bureau of Economic Research, May 2008) Working Paper No 14029
Bravo-Biosca, Albert, 'Access to Finance for Innovation: Rationales and Risks of Public Intervention' (The Innovation Policy Platform, 2014)
British Business Bank, 'Enterprise Capital Funds: Guidance for Prospective Managers' (November 2014)
British Business Bank, 'The Enterprise Capital Fund Programme' (September 2019) www.british-business-bank.co.uk/wp-content/uploads/2019/09/ECF_Brochure_Version2_Sep2019_FINAL.pdf
Bundesministerium für Wirtschaft und Energie, 'Richtlinie zur Bezuschussung von Wagniskapital privater Investoren für junge innovative Unternehmen INVEST – Zuschuss für Wagniskapital' (Federal Gazette Notice, 21 December 2020)
BVCA and NESTA, 'From Funding Gaps to Thin Markets: UK Government Support for Early-Stage Venture Capital' (September 2009)
Center for Regional Economic Competitiveness and Cromwell Schmisseur, 'Program Evaluation of the US Department of Treasury State Small Business Credit Initiative' (October 2016)
Chen, Duanjie, 'The Framework for Assessing Tax Incentives: A Cost–Benefit Analysis Approach' (Workshop on Tax Incentives and Base Protection, United Nations, 23–24 April 2015)
Cherry, Elyse, et al, 'No Exit: The Challenge of Realizing Return on Community Development Venture Capital Investments' (The Ford Foundation, 5 October 2000)
Chief Minister's Department (ACT), 'Evaluation Policy and Guidelines' (ACT Government, December 2010)
Christofidis, Constantin and Olivier Debande, 'Financing Innovative Firms Through Venture Capital' (European Investment Bank, February 2001)
Coglianese, Cary, 'Measuring Regulatory Performance: Evaluating the Impact of Regulation and Regulatory Policy' (OECD, August 2012) Expert Paper No 1
Colahan, Matt, John Higton, Lucy Royce, Rebecca Klahr, Jayesh Navin Shah and Marc Cowling, 'The Use and Impact of Venture Capital Schemes' (HM Revenue & Customs, February 2016) Research Report 355
Colombo, Massimo, Fabio Bertoni and Terttu Luukkonen, 'Venture Capital: Policy Lessons from the VICO Project' (2011)
Congressional Research Service, 'SBA Small Business Investment Company Program' (3 September 2021) Report R41456

Cowling, Marc, Peter Bates, Nick Jagger and Gordon Murray, 'Study of the Impact of the Enterprise Investment Scheme (EIS) and Venture Capital Trusts (VCTs) on Company Performance' (HM Revenue & Customs, 2008) Research Report 44

Cowling, Marc, Gordon Murray and Weixi Liu, 'IIF Equity Programme Assessment' (2010)

Cowling, Marc, Weixi Liu, Gordon Murray, Josh Sieple and Paul Nightingale, 'BIS Equity Schemes Evaluation' (Department of Business Innovation and Skills, 2011)

Cromwell Schmisseur, 'Information and Observations on State Venture Capital Programs: Report for the US Department of the Treasury and Interested Parties in the State Small Business Credit Initiative (SSBCI)' (February 2013)

De Angelis, Luca, 'Italy and Startups: Harnessing a Country of Innovators' (Master of Public Policy, Harvard University, 2017)

Deloitte, 'International Tax: Slovenia Highlights 2020' (January 2020)

Deloitte, 'Fund Management in Singapore: A Summary of the Regulatory and Tax Framework' (2021)

Denes, Matthew, Xinxin Wang and Ting Xu, 'Financing Entrepreneurship: Tax Incentives for Early-Stage Investors' (December 2019)

Department of Finance Canada, 'Growing the Middle Class: Budget 2016' (22 March 2016)

Department of Finance, *Commonwealth Grants Rules and Guidelines 2017* (2017)

Department of Industry (Australia), *Australian Innovation System Report 2013* (2013)

Department of Industry, *Innovation Australia: Annual Report 2013–14* (2014)

Department of Industry, Innovation, Science, Research and Tertiary Education (Australia), 'A Plan for Australian Jobs – The Australian Government's Industry and Innovation Statement' (2013)

Department of Industry, Science, Energy and Resources, 'Venture Capital Limited Partnerships (VCLPs) Customer Information Guide' (February 2020)

Department of Industry, Tourism and Resources and AusIndustry, *Pooled Development Funds Registration Board: Annual Report 2004–2005* (2005)

Department of Innovation, Industry, Science and Research, *Innovation Investment Fund Program Progress Report* (2011)

Department of the Attorney-General and Justice, 'Grants Management Framework: Principles and Policies for Best Practice in the Administration of Grants' (July 2017)

Deuten, Jasper, 'Venture Capital Investment Guarantee Programme by OSEO' (INNO Partnering Forum, 2011)

Duffner, Stefan, 'Principal-Agent Problems in Venture Capital Finance' (Department of Finance, University of Basel, November 2003) Working Paper No 11/03

Duruflé, Gilles, 'Government Involvement in the Venture Capital Industry: International Comparisons' (CVCA, May 2010)

EBAN and BOFIDI, 'Compendium of Fiscal Incentives: Tax Outlook in Europe – Business Angels Perspective' (2017)

Economics Division, Queensland Treasury and Trade, 'Queensland Government Program Evaluation Guidelines' (Queensland Government, November 2014)

European Commission, 'Effectiveness of Tax Incentives for Venture Capital and Business Angels to Foster the Investment of SMEs and Start-ups: Final Report' (Taxation and Customs Union, 2017) Working Paper No 68

European Commission, 'Appendix 2: Good Practice Fiches' (June 2017) Final Report TAXUD/2015/DE/330

European Court of Auditors, 'Centrally Managed EU Interventions for Venture Capital: In Need of More Direction' (2019) Special Report No 17

European Investment Fund, 'European Angels Fund' (December 2016) www.eif.org/news_centre/publications/eaf/eaf_en.pdf

European Investment Fund, *Annual Report 2016; Supporting Smart, Sustainable and Inclusive Growth for SMEs* (April 2017)

Federal Ministry for Economic Affairs and Climate Action, 'INVEST – Venture Capital Grant' (April 2023)

Federal Ministry for Economic Affairs and Energy, 'INVEST – Venture Capital Grant' (December 2016)

Federal Ministry of Economic Affairs and Energy, 'Financing Start-ups and Growth: Overview of Funding Instruments' (November 2020) www.bmwk.de/Redaktion/EN/Downloads/financing-start-ups-and-growth-overview-of-funding-instruments.pdf?__blob=publicationFile&v=1

Federal Research Division, Library of Congress, 'Measuring the Role of the SBIC Program in Financing Small Businesses' (July 2017)

Gornall, Will and Ilya A Strebulaev, 'The Economic Impact of Venture Capital: Evidence from Public Companies' (Stanford University Graduate School of Business, 2015) Research Paper 3362

Gottschalk, Sandra, Jürgen Egeln, Frank Herrmann, Silke Hupperts, Bettina Müller, Karsten Reuss, Mila Köhler, Johannes Bersch and Simona Wagner, 'Evaluation of the Public Funding Program "INVEST – Grant for Venture Capital": English Short Version' (BMWi, July 2016)

Government of Canada, 'Budget 2013 – Labour Sponsored Venture Capital Corporations (LSVCC) Tax Credit' (15 July 2015) www.canada.ca/en/revenue-agency/programs/about-canada-revenue-agency-cra/federal-government-budgets/budget-2013/budget-2013-labour-sponsored-venture-capital-corporations-lsvcc-tax-credit.html

Gvetadze, Salome, Kristian Pal and Wouter Torfs, 'The Business Angel Portfolio Under the European Angels Fund: An Empirical Analysis' (European Investment Fund, January 2020) Research and Market Analysis Working Paper 2020/62, www.eif.org/news_centre/publications/eif_working_paper_2020_62.pdf

Hellmann, Thomas and Paul Schure, 'An Evaluation of the Venture Capital Program in British Columbia' (Ministry of Small Business, Technology and Economic Development, June 2010)

Hindle, Kevin and Christopher Golis, 'Australia's Venture Capital Industry: Past Performance, Present Structure and Future Prospects' (Frontiers of Entrepreneurship Research, 2001)

HM Revenue & Customs, 'Income Tax: Venture Capital Schemes – Risk to Capital Condition' (22 November 2017) www.gov.uk/government/publications/income-tax-venture-capital-schemes-risk-to-capital-condition/income-tax-venture-capital-schemes-risk-to-capital-condition

HM Revenue & Customs, 'HS393 Seed Enterprise Investment Scheme – Income Tax and Capital Gains Tax Reliefs (2018)' (6 April 2021)

HM Revenue & Customs, 'Venture Capital Trusts Statistics Commentary' (10 December 2019) assets.publishing.service.gov.uk/government/uploads/system/uploads/attachment_data/file/850830/VCT_National_Statistics_2019_Commentary.pdf

Holmes, Anne and Hannah Gobbett, 'Tax Expenditures: Costs to Government that are not in the Budget' in Parliamentary Library, *Briefing Book: Key Issues for the 44th Parliament* (2013)

Inland Revenue Board of Malaysia, *Venture Capital Tax Incentives* (9 May 2016) Public Ruling No 2/2016

Innovasjon Norge, 'Annual Accounts Innovasjon Norge 2018' (29 March 2019)

Innovation, Science and Economic Development Canada, 'Venture Capital Catalyst Initiative: Call for Expressions of Interest' (2017)

Innovation, Science and Economic Development Canada, 'Venture Capital Catalyst Initiative: Performance Measurement Framework' (April 2019)

Innovation, Science and Economic Development Canada, 'Venture Capital Catalyst Initiative: Performance Measurement Framework' (2022)

International Monetary Fund, Organisation for Economic Co-operation and Development, United Nations and World Bank, 'Options for Low Income Countries' Effective and Efficient Use of Tax Incentives for Investment' (Report to the G-20 Development Working Group, October 2015)

Ipsos MORI and George Barrett, 'Enterprise Capital Funds: Interim Evaluation' (November 2021)

Irish Tax and Customs, 'Relief for Investment in Corporate Trades' in *Tax and Duty Manual* (April 2023) Part 16-00-02, www.revenue.ie/en/tax-professionals/tdm/income-tax-capital-gains-tax-corporation-tax/part-16/16-00-02.pdf

Italian Ministry of Economic Development, Directorate General for Industrial Policy, Competitiveness and SMEs, 'The Italian Startup Act: Italy's Policy Framework to Support Innovative Startups' (8 July 2019) www.mise.gov.it/images/stories/documenti/Executive%20summary%20ISA%2007_2019.pdf

James, Sebastian, 'Tax and Non-Tax Incentives and Investments: Evidence and Policy Implications' (Investment Climate Advisory Services of the World Bank Group, September 2013)

Kato, Andrew, Sumner LaCroix and James Mak, 'Small State, Giant Tax Credit: Hawaii's Leap into High Technology Development' (University of Hawai'i Economic Research Organisation, 27 October 2009) Working Paper No 2009-3

Khemani, RS and DM Shapiro (eds), *Glossary of Industrial Organisation Economics and Competition Law* (OECD)

KPMG, *China Tax Alert* (Issue 15, May 2017) 2 assets.kpmg.com/content/dam/kpmg/cn/pdf/en/2017/05/china-tax-alert-15.pdf

KPMG, 'Reserved Alternative Investment Fund' (2017)

Kraemer-Eis, Helmut, Antonia Botsari, Julien Brault and Frank Lang, 'EIF Business Angels Survey 2019: Market Sentiment, Public Intervention and EIF's Value Added' (EIF, 2019) EIF Working Paper No 2019/60

Leamon, Ann and Josh Lerner, 'Creating a Venture Ecosystem in Brazil: FINEP's INOVAR Project' (Harvard Business School, 8 May 2012) Working Paper 12-099

Leamon, Ann, Maria Susana Garcia-Robles and Josh Lerner, 'Best Practices in Creating a Venture Capital Ecosystem' (Multilateral Investment Fund of Inter-American Development Bank, December 2012)

Lerner, Josh, 'Innovation, Entrepreneurship and Financial Market Cycles' (OECD, March 2010) OECD Science, Technology and Industry Working Paper No 2010/3

Lerner, Josh, David Moore and Stuart Shepherd, 'A Study of New Zealand's Venture Capital Market and Implications for Public Policy' (LECG, 2005)

Lilischkis, Stefan, 'Policies in Support of High-Growth Innovative SMEs' (European Commission, June 2011) INNO-Grips Policy Brief No 2

Loyens & Loeff, 'The Luxembourg Investment Company in Risk Capital (SICAR)'

Management and Investment Companies Licensing Board, Annual Reports (1983–84 to 1990–91)

Maula, Markku and Gordon Murray, *Finnish Industry Investment Ltd: An International Evaluation* (Ministry of Trade and Industry, January 2003)

Microsoft, 'Best Practices for Innovation: Microsoft's Innovation Management Framework' (June 2013)

Ministry of Business, Innovation and Employment, 'Update on the Venture Capital Fund's Progress and the Wider Capital Markets' (17 August 2020)

Ministry of Economic Development, 'Evaluation of the Venture Investment Fund' (November 2009)

Ministry of Trade and Industry Singapore, 'Section 13H and Fund Management Incentive' (2020) www.mti.gov.sg/-/media/MTI/COS-2020/Microsite/Factsheets/ESG-Media-Fact-Sheet-on-Section-13H-and-Fund-Management-Incentive-at-MTI-COS.pdf#:~:text=What%20is%20it%3F,Singapore%2Dbased%20businesses%20and%20startups.&text=Further%20boost%20the%20vibrancy%20of%20the%20startup%20ecosystem%20in%20Singapore

Monetary Authority of Singapore, 'Securities and Futures Act (cap 289): Frequently Asked Questions (FAQs) on the Licensing and Registration of Fund Management Companies' (1 June 2023)

Murray, Gordon, Marc Cowling and Weixi Liu, 'An Independent Econometric Analysis of the "Innovation Investment Fund" Programme (IIF) of the Australian Commonwealth Government: Findings and Implications' (Department of Innovation, Industry, Science and Research, 2010)

Murray, Gordon, Marc Cowling, Weixi Liu and Olga Kalinowska-Beszczynska, 'Government Co-Financed "Hybrid" Venture Capital Programmes: Generalizing Developed Economy Experience and its Relevance to Emerging Nations' (Kauffman International Research and Policy Roundtable, 11–12 March 2012)

National Australia Bank, 'NAB Special Report: A Survey of Business Innovation in Australia: Key Findings' (September 2015) business.nab.com.au/wp-content/uploads/2015/09/Innovation-Report-Summary.pdf

National Venture Capital Association, *2023 Yearbook* (National Venture Capital Association, 2023)

NZ Growth Capital Partners, 'Aspire NZ Seed Fund – FAQs' (November 2022) www.nzgcp.co.nz/assets/Uploads/NZGCP-Aspire-FAQ_Nov22.pdf

OECD Regulatory Policy Committee, 'Recommendation of the Council on Regulatory Policy and Governance' (2012)
OECD, 'Business Innovation Policies: Selected Country Comparisons' (2011)
OECD, 'Entrepreneurship at a Glance: 2018 Highlights' (10 October 2018)
OECD, 'Government Venture Capital for Technology-Based Firms' (1997) OCDE/GD(97)201
OECD, 'Harmful Tax Practices – 2018 Progress Report on Preferential Regimes: Inclusive Framework On BEPS: Action 5' (OECD/G20 Base Erosion and Profit Shifting Project, 2019)
OECD, 'Innovation and Growth: Rationale for an Innovation Strategy' (2007)
OECD, 'Recommendation of the Council on Regulatory Policy and Governance' (2012)
OECD, 'Tax Incentives for R&D and Innovation' (2016)
OECD, 'Venture Capital and Innovation' (1996)
Palazzi, Pamela, 'Taxation and Innovation' (OECD, 2011) OECD Taxation Working Papers No 9
Pinelli, Maria and Uschi Schreiber, 'Funding the Future: Access to Finance for Entrepreneurs in the G20' (Ernst & Young, 2013)
PricewaterhouseCoopers, 'Innovation: Government's Many Roles in Fostering Innovation' (January 2010)
Productivity Commission, 'Identifying and Evaluating Regulation Reforms' (December 2011)
Productivity Commission, *Business Set-up, Transfer and Closure* (Productivity Commission, 30 September 2015) Productivity Commission Inquiry Report No 75
Public and Corporate Economic Consultants, 'Scottish Enterprise: Economic Impact of the Scottish Venture Fund' (December 2012)
Queensland Treasury, 'Queensland Government Program Evaluation Guidelines' (2020)
Republic of Turkey, Ministry of Treasury and Finance, *Regulation on Business Angels* (2018)
Saarikoski, Matti, Pekka Roine, Juha Ruohonen, Antti Halonen, John Sulin and Herve Lebret, *Evaluation of Finnish Industry Investment Ltd* (Ministry of Employment and the Economy, January 2014)
Sadiq, Kerrie, 'An Analysis of Tax Expenditures Versus Direct Expenditures' (Australasian Tax Teachers Association Conference, 2008)
Science and Technology Committee (UK), *Bridging the Valley of Death: Improving the Commercialisation of Research* (Report No 8 of Session 2012–13, 4 March 2013)
Securities Commission Malaysia, 'Venture Capital Tax Incentives Guidelines' (18 April 2014)
Securities Commission Malaysia, 'Guidelines on Registration of Venture Capital and Private Equity Corporations and Management Corporations' (2020) SC-GL/1-2015 (R1-2020)
Silicon Valley Bank, 'Trends in Healthcare Investments and Exits 2019: Mid-Year Report' (2019)
Small Business Service (UK) and Almeida Capital, 'A Mapping Study of Venture Capital Provision to SMEs in England' (October 2005)
Ständer, Philipp, 'Public Policies to Promote Venture Capital: How to Get National and EU Measures in Sync' (Jacques Delors Institut, 31 August 2017)
StartupAUS, *Crossroads 2015: An Action Plan to Develop a Vibrant Tech Startup Ecosystem in Australia* (StartupAUS, 2015)
Startup Investor SG and Enterprise Singapore, 'Startup Investor SG: Section 13H and the Fund Management Incentive', ssn-core-prod-files.s3.ap-southeast-1.amazonaws.com/2020-05/Factsheet_S13H_FMI_11%20May.pdf
StartupSG and Enterprise Singapore, 'Angel Investor Tax Deduction (AITD) Frequently Asked Questions (FAQs)' (February 2020) ssn-core-prod-files.s3.ap-southeast-1.amazonaws.com/2020-02/AITD%20FAQs_site%20%28002%29.pdf
The Association of Investment Companies, 'Transforming Small Business: VCT Investment Review' (August 2017)
The Auditor General, 'Management of the Innovation Investment Fund Program' (2003) Audit Report No 12
Treasury and Department of Industry, Innovation, Science, Research and Tertiary Education, 'Review of Venture Capital and Entrepreneurial Skills' (2012)
Treasury Committee, *Venture Capital* (2022–23, HC 134)

United Nations Economic Commission for Europe, *Financing Innovative Development: Comparative Review of the Experiences of UNECE Countries in Early Stage Financing* (United Nations Publications, 2007)

United States Department of the Treasury, 'The Case for Temporary 100 Percent Expensing: Encouraging Business to Expand Now by Lowering the Cost of Investment' (29 October 2010)

United States Department of the Treasury, 'SSBCI Program Profile: Venture Capital Program' (May 2011)

Vaekstfonden, 'Investor Framework Agreement' (22 September 2022)

Webster, David C, 'England's Regional Venture Capital Funds: A Review of Programme Outcomes and Stakeholder Perspectives' (Said Business School, 2009)

What Works Centre for Local Economic Growth, 'Access to Finance' (November 2014) Evidence Review No 4

What Works Centre for Local Economic Growth, 'Innovation: Grants, Loans and Subsidies' (October 2015) Evidence Review No 9

Wilson, Karen E and Filipe Silva, 'Policies for Seed and Early Stage Finance: Findings from the 2012 OECD Financing Questionnaire' (OECD, October 2013) OECD Science, Technology and Industry Policy Papers No 9

Wilson, Karen, 'Policy Lessons from Financing Young Innovative Firms' (OECD, June 2015) OECD Science, Technology and Industry Policy Papers No 24

Internet Materials

Accounting and Corporate Regulatory Authority, 'Variable Capital Companies' (24 March 2021) www.acra.gov.sg/business-entities/variable-capital-companies

Agyemang, Emma, 'Are VCTs Worth the Risk for Higher Earners?' *Financial Times* (11 October 2019) www.ft.com/content/28c30bea-e9bc-11e9-85f4-d00e5018f061

Armstrong-Cerfontaine, Alexandrine, Larry Jordan Rowe, Daniel S Kim, James Bowden, 'Private Equity and Venture Capital Global Guide' (*Thomson Reuters Practical Law*, 2021) uk.practicallaw.thomsonreuters.com/Browse/Home/International/PrivateEquityandVentureCapitalGlobalGuide?transitionType=Default&contextData=(sc.Default)&firstPage=true

'Aspire NZ Seed Fund' (Web Page) sg.dynamosoftware.com/new/WebForm?id=59b99920-5194-4b47-88bd-1127a65a18c3&tn=new_zealand_growth_capital_partners

Aspire NZ Seed Fund, 'Aspire NZ Seed Fund is Set to Increase Support for Tech Start-Ups' (25 June 2020) www.nzgcp.co.nz/assets/Media/Aspire-release_250620.pdf

Association of the Luxembourg Fund Industry, 'RAIF (Luxembourg Reserved Alternative Investment Fund)' (2021) www.alfi.lu/en-GB/Pages/Setting-up-in-Luxembourg/Alternative-investment-funds-legal-vehicles/RAIF-(Luxembourg-Reserved-Alternative-Investment-F

Association of the Luxembourg Fund Industry, 'SICAR (Investment Company in Risk Capital)' (2021) www.alfi.lu/en-GB/Pages/Setting-up-in-Luxembourg/Alternative-investment-funds-legal-vehicles/SICAR-(Investment-Company-in-Risk-Capital)

Atkins, Jason, 'SAFE Notes: A Simple Way to Raise Funds For Startups' (*Cake Equity*, August 2023) www.cakeequity.com/guides/safe-notes#:~:text=SAFE%20note%2C%20also%20known%20as,into%20equity%20in%20the%20future

Australian Government, Department of Home Affairs, 'Business Innovation and Investment (Provisional) Visa (subclass 188) Significant Investor Stream' (1 October 2021) immi.homeaffairs.gov.au/visas/getting-a-visa/visa-listing/business-innovation-and-investment-188/significant-investor-stream#

Australian Investment Council, 'Investment', www.aic.co/AIC/Investment/How-does-venture-capital-work.aspx

Australian Taxation Office, 'Tax Incentives for Early Stage Investors: Qualifying for the Tax Incentives' (7 April 2021) www.ato.gov.au/Business/Tax-incentives-for-innovation/In-detail/Tax-incentives-for-early-stage-investors/?anchor=Thesophisticatedinvestortest#Thesophisticatedinvestortest

Bailey, Michael, 'Early Stage Innovation Company Investor Tax Breaks Misunderstood' *Australian Financial Review* (4 May 2017) www.afr.com/leadership/entrepreneur/early-stage-innovation-company-investor-tax-breaks-misunderstood-by-founders-investors-20170504-gvyr4x#ixzz4idVp A5H7.

Beioley, Kate, 'Tax-Efficient VCT Market Suffers Drop in Demand After Rule Change' *Financial Times* (22 February 2019) www.ft.com/content/d25bfb48-3077-11e9-ba00-0251022932c8

British Columbia, 'Tax Credits', www2.gov.bc.ca/gov/content/employment-business/investment-capital/venture-capital-programs/eligible-business-corporation/tax-credits#:~:text=Individual%20investors%20are%20entitled%20to,previous%20calendar%20year's%20tax%20return

Bundesministerium für Wirstchaft und Klimaschutz, 'INVEST – Zuschuss für Wagniskapital', www.bmwk.de/Redaktion/DE/Dossier/invest.html

Chapman Tripp, 'Chapman Tripp Supports Consolidation of NZX Boards' (4 July 2017) www.mondaq.com/pressrelease/24878/chapman-tripp-supports-consolidation-of-nzx-boards

'Circulaire 2020/C/75 sur la Réduction Tax Shelter pour des Entreprises (Sociétés) qui Débutent' (*MinFin*, 2020) eservices.minfin.fgov.be/myminfin-web/pages/public/fisconet/document/d28beac8-7b60-4a2d-9fed-bb026e269306?_ga=2.196813610.748963670.1591597718-924005305.1588834086

Clune, Bronwen, 'The Innovation Investment Fund Branded a Failure' (*SmartCompany*, 28 April 2014) www.smartcompany.com.au/startupsmart/advice/startupsmart-funding/the-industry-innovation-fund-branded-a-failure/

Committee for Economic Development of the Conference Board, 'Regulation and the Economy: The Relationship and How to Improve It' (27 September 2017) www.ced.org/reports/regulation-and-the-economy

Controller and Auditor-General, 'New Zealand Venture Investment Fund' (2012) oag.parliament.nz/2012/efficiency-stories/corporate/new-zealand-venture-investment-fund

CORFO, 'Fondo Etapas Tempranas Perfil Empresa Perfil Administradoras: Inversión y Financiamiento', https://www.corfo.cl/sites/cpp/convocatorias/fondo_etapas_tempranas_tecnologicas_perfil_administradoras

CORFO, 'What Is the Early Stage Tech Fund', wapp4.corfo.cl/fondoetapastempranas/investors.html

Eddy, Kester, 'EU-funded Venture Capital Model Proves to be Double-edged Sword' *Financial Times* (2 October 2014) www.ft.com/content/bb6aeea6-374a-11e4-b45c-00144feabdc0

EFTA Surveillance Authority, 'Two New Norwegian Seed Capital Schemes Approved by the EFTA Surveillance Authority' (15 July 2005) www.eftasurv.int/newsroom/updates/two-new-norwegian-seed-capital-schemes-approved-efta-surveillance-authority

European Investment Fund, 'JEREMIE – Joint European Resources for Micro to Medium Enterprises' (2024) www.eif.org/what_we_do/resources/jeremie/index.htm?lang=-en

Federal Ministry of Economic Affairs and Energy, 'Financing for Start-ups, Company Growth, and Innovations', www.bmwi.de/Redaktion/EN/Dossier/financing-for-start-ups-company-growth-and-innovations.html

Gage, Deborah, 'The Venture Capital Secret: 3 Out of 4 Start-Ups Fail' *Wall Street Journal* (20 September 2012) www.wsj.com/articles/SB10000872396390443720204578004980476429190

Government of Canada, 'Venture Capital Catalyst Initiative', ised-isde.canada.ca/site/sme-research-statistics/en/venture-capital-catalyst-initiative

HM Revenue & Customs, 'Enterprise Investment Scheme: Overview of EIS Reliefs' (14 September 2020) www.gov.uk/hmrc-internal-manuals/venture-capital-schemes-manual/vcm10010

HM Revenue & Customs, 'Tax Relief for Investors Using Venture Capital Schemes' (7 July 2021) www.gov.uk/guidance/venture-capital-schemes-tax-relief-for-investors

HM Revenue & Customs, 'VCT: Investor Income Tax Reliefs: "Front-end" Income Tax Relief: Who Can Claim Relief' (9 March 2016) www.gov.uk/hmrc-internal-manuals/venture-capital-schemes-manual/vcm51020

HM Revenue & Customs, 'Venture Capital Schemes Manual' (22 March 2021) www.gov.uk/hmrc-internal-manuals/venture-capital-schemes-manual

IF, 'European Angels Fund (EAF)' (2021) www.eif.org/what_we_do/equity/eaf/index.htm

'Immigrant Investor Venture Capital (IIVC) Program' (*Immigration.ca*, 26 October 2018) www.immigration.ca/immigrant-investor-venture-capital-iivc-program

Inland Revenue Authority of Singapore, 'Angel Investors Tax Deduction Scheme (AITD)' (7 January 2022) www.iras.gov.sg/taxes/individual-income-tax/basics-of-individual-income-tax/special-tax-schemes/angel-investors-tax-deduction-scheme-(aitd)

Innovation and Technology Commission, 'Innovation and Technology Venture Fund (ITVF)' (1 November 2021) www.itf.gov.hk/l-eng/ITVF.asp

Irish Tax and Customs, 'Capital Gains Tax (CGT) on the Sale, Gift or Exchange of an Asset' (24 June 2021) www.revenue.ie/en/gains-gifts-and-inheritance/transfering-an-asset/how-to-calculate-cgt.aspx

'Is the Polish Government Drowning Its Innovators in Money?' (*StartupYard*) startupyard.com/is-the-polish-government-drowning-its-innovators-in-money/

'Labour-sponsored Venture Capital Corporation Funds' (*Saskatchewan*) www.saskatchewan.ca/residents/taxes-and-investments/tax-credits/labour-sponsored-funds#:~:text=The%20tax%20credit%20is%2032.5,Savings%20Plan%20(RRSP)%20eligible

LAVCA, 'FINEP Celebrates 10 Years of INOVAR, Nearly R$5b Committed to VC in Brazil' (11 November 2010) lavca.org/2010/11/11/finep-celebrates-10-years-of-inovar-nearly-r5b-committed-to-vc-in-brazil/

'List of Pooled Development Funds' (*Business.gov.au*, 18 January 2024) business.gov.au/grants-and-programs/pooled-development-funds/list-of-pooled-development-funds

Litan, Robert, 'Regulation', *The Library of Economics and Liberty*, www.econlib.org/library/Enc/Regulation.html

McKinley, John W and Craig J Wright, 'Rollover of Gains on Certain Property Dispositions' [1 July 2014] *Journal of Accountancy*, www.journalofaccountancy.com/issues/2014/jul/201410000.html

'Migrating to the Main Board and NZX Listing Rules from 1 January 2019' (*NZX*, 2019) www.nzx.com/regulation/nzx-rules-guidance/nzx-listing-rules-review/nxt-and-ax-issuer-migration

Ministry of Trade and Industry, 'Section 13H and the Fund Management Incentive', www.mti.gov.sg/-/media/MTI/COS-2020/Microsite/Factsheets/ESG-Media-Fact-Sheet-on-Section-13H-and-Fund-Management-Incentive-at-MTI-COS.pdf?la=en&hash=EF5F623133EA06A08AC6BC8204CEAEA2CA376B09#:~:text=S13H%20provides%20tax%20exemption%20for,concessionary%20tax%20rate%20of%205%25

Mintz, Jack M, 'Equity-Based Incentives are not the Way to Encourage Innovation' *Financial Post* (26 February 2020) financialpost.com/opinion/jack-m-mintz-equity-based-incentives-are-not-the-way-to-encourage-innovation

NZ Growth Capital Partners, 'About NZGCP' (2020) www.nzgcp.co.nz/about-us/

NZ Growth Capital Partners, 'Aspire NZ Seed Fund' (2020) www.nzgcp.co.nz/funding/aspire-seed-fund/

NZ Growth Capital Partners, 'Elevate NZ Venture Fund' (2020) www.nzgcp.co.nz/funding/elevate-venture-fund/

'NZX's Alternative Market Trading Dwindles' *New Zealand Herald* (5 October 2010) www.nzherald.co.nz/business/news/article.cfm?c_id=3&objectid=10678299

OECD, 'Venture Capital Investments' (*OECD.Stat*, 19 October 2020) stats.oecd.org/Index.aspx?DataSetCode=VC_INVEST

PFR Ventures, 'National Capital Fund', pfrventures.pl/en/kfk.html

PFR Ventures, 'PFR Ventures Portfolio', pfrventures.pl/en/portfolio.html?Tab=database

'Portugal Golden Visa – Invest in Portugal and Get the Residence Permit' (*Schengen Visa Info*, 2021) www.schengenvisainfo.com/eu-golden-visas/portugal-golden-visa/

PwC, 'Ghana: Corporate – Tax Credits and Incentives' (*Worldwide Tax Summaries*, 29 July 2021) taxsummaries.pwc.com/ghana/corporate/tax-credits-and-incentives#:~:text=Interest%20and%20dividends%20from%20investment,after%20the%20year%20of%20disposal

PwC, 'People's Republic of China' (*Worldwide Tax Summaries*, 15 January 2024) taxsummaries.pwc.com/peoples-republic-of-china/corporate/tax-credits-and-incentives

PwC, 'Worldwide Tax Summaries' (2021) taxsummaries.pwc.com/

Read, Ellen, 'Celebrating the Alternative Stock Exchange' *New Zealand Herald* (17 November 2004) www.nzherald.co.nz/business/news/article.cfm?c_id=3&objectid=3610916

Reuters, 'NZX Plans to Scrap Junior Markets NXT and NZAX' (27 June 2017) www.reuters.com/article/us-nzx-exchange/nzx-plans-to-scrap-junior-markets-nxt-and-nzax-idUSKBN19H2MR

Royal Norwegian Ministry of Trade and Industry, 'National Seed Capital Scheme' (December 2012) investinor.no/wp-content/uploads/nhd-notifisering-nye-landsdekkende-sakornfond_jan-2013.pdf

Sciabica, Sophia, 'Brazil's INOVAR: Building an Entrepreneurship Ecosystem' (*Americas Quarterly*, 5 August 2014) www.americasquarterly.org/content/brazils-inovar-building-entrepreneurship-ecosystem

Securities Commission Malaysia, 'Venture Capital Incentives', www.sc.com.my/development/vcpe/venture-capital-tax-incentives

Service Public Fédéral Finances, 'Investir dans une Petite Entreprise (Tax Shelter Start-Up/Scale-Up)' (*Finances.belgium.be*) finances.belgium.be/fr/particuliers/avantages_fiscaux/tax-shelter-%E2%80%93-investir-dans-une-entreprise-qui-d%C3%A9bute

Shah, Sohin, 'How Disruptive Startups Spread the Wealth by Encouraging Derivative Businesses' (*Entrepreneur Asia Pacific*, 3 June 2015) www.entrepreneur.com/article/246783

Spreds, 'Frequently Asked Questions: What is the Tax Shelter and Who Benefits from It?', www.spreds.com/en/faq/tax-shelter/200

Spreds, 'Lower your Taxes by Investing in Startups and Scaleups', www.spreds.com/en/tax-shelter

'Startup America' (*The White House: President Barack Obama*, 2011) obamawhitehouse.archives.gov/economy/business/startup-america/commitments

Strebulaev, Ilya A and Will Gornall, 'How Much Does Venture Capital Drive the US Economy? Two Scholars Measure the Economic Impact of VC-funded Companies' (Stanford Graduate School of Business, 21 October 2015) www.gsb.stanford.edu/insights/how-much-does-venture-capital-drive-us-economy

Thrasher, Michael, 'Another Sign That Venture Capital Is Slowly Improving' *Institutional Investor* (24 January 2024) www.institutionalinvestor.com/article/2crbj8sww9uo9fypyrpj4/portfolio/another-sign-that-venture-capital-is-slowly-improving

Vicerrectoría de Investigación y Estudios Avanzados, 'Fondo Etapas Tempranas Tecnológicas Perfil Empresas' (Pontificia Universidad Católica de Valparaíso) www.pucv.cl/uuaa/vriea/fondo-etapas-tempranas-tecnologicas-perfil-empresas

'What Tax Incentive Schemes Exist to Encourage PE/VC Investment?' (*Thomson Reuters Practical Law*, 1 January 2019) uk.practicallaw.thomsonreuters.com/3-525-3665?originationContext=knowHow&transitionType=KnowHowItem&contextData=(sc.Search)&navId=FAD4BFB474734069D01A698A3AD69597&comp=pluk&firstPage=true&bhcp=1

Zhang, Hannah, 'VC Exit Value Sags to Lowest Level Since the GFC' *Institutional Investor* (6 July 2023) www.institutionalinvestor.com/article/2bvxcyfqesuymrafaja4g/portfolio/vc-exit-value-sags-to-lowest-level-since-the-gfc

INDEX

www.ingramcontent.com/pod-product-compliance
Ingram Content Group UK Ltd.
Pitfield, Milton Keynes, MK11 3LW, UK
UKHW020135290926
15471UKWH00003B/505

9 781509 976355